Islam, Science Fiction and Extraterrestrial Life

'This original and much-needed book fills a huge gap in the subject of astrobiology and society. Never before have the relations between astrobiology and Muslim science, culture, and politics been rendered in such vivid detail and with such solid scholarship. A must read for historians, theologians, and the general public interested in both Muslim culture and alien life.'

Steven J. Dick, Former NASA Chief Historian, Former Baruch S. Blumberg NASA/Library of Congress Chair in Astrobiology

'*Islam, Science Fiction and Extraterrestrial Life* provides a kaleidoscopic view of the rich variety of ways in which Muslims have imagined, sought, and encountered life beyond our planet.'

Alireza Doostdar, Assistant Professor, Divinity School and the College, The University of Chicago

'Determann presents readers with an engaging, in-depth and scholarly investigation into the ways in which Islamic writers, over the centuries, have written, thought about and engaged with the concept of extraterrestrial life. Determann breaks much new ground and makes a valuable contribution to our understanding of the history of the relationship between out-of-this-world ideas and religion, in particular Islam.'

David Weintraub, Professor of Astronomy and Director of Program in Communication of Science & Technology, Vanderbilt University

Islam, Science Fiction and Extraterrestrial Life

The Culture of Astrobiology in the Muslim World

Jörg Matthias Determann

I.B. TAURIS
LONDON • NEW YORK • OXFORD • NEW DELHI • SYDNEY

I.B. TAURIS
Bloomsbury Publishing Plc
50 Bedford Square, London, WC1B 3DP, UK
1385 Broadway, New York, NY 10018, USA
29 Earlsfort Terrace, Dublin 2, Ireland

BLOOMSBURY, I.B. TAURIS and the I.B. Tauris logo are trademarks of Bloomsbury Publishing Plc

First published in Great Britain 2021
This paperback edition published 2023

Cover design: Adriana Brioso
Cover image © Ayham Jabr

A catalogue record for this book is available from the British Library.

A catalog record for this book is available from the Library of Congress.

ISBN: HB: 978-0-7556-0127-1
PB: 978-0-7556-5036-1
ePDF: 978-0-7556-0129-5
eBook: 978-0-7556-0130-1

Typeset by Integra Software Services Pvt. Ltd.

To find out more about our authors and books visit www.bloomsbury.com and sign up for our newsletters.

To my daughter, Maria, and her imagination

Contents

List of Figures ix

Preface x

1 Lord of the Worlds 1

Islam and science fiction 5

Islamic world building 15

Scientific imagination 26

Chapters in Muslim world building 36

2 Missions and Mars 39

First contacts 42

God knows best 48

Plants on planets 58

3 Trips to the Moon 71

Pharaohs and fairies 78

Turksploitation 91

Cinematic circulations 96

4 Islamic UFO Religions 105

Black uplifts 111

Muslim ufology 117

Flying saucers as jinn 128

5 Building Nations and Worlds 141

National space 143

Galactic Mamluks 149

Eliza in wonderland 168

Figures

1 *Damascus under Siege-7* (2016) 2
2 *Damascus under Siege-3* (2016) 3
3 Hosam Elzembely speaking at the Asia-Pacific Science Fiction Convention in Beijing in 2018 21
4 'The Last Jedi' (2013) 76
5 The astronomers in the Selenite palace in Georges Méliès's *A Trip to the Moon* (1902) 79
6 All Eyes on Egipt Bookstore in Brooklyn, 2019 117
7 Cover of *All Tomorrows* (2004) 197
8 'Qu triumphant in the fall of Man', incorporating Leonardo da Vinci's *Vitruvian Man* 198
9 'SpaceMosque' 206
10 'SpaceMosque' 207
11 *Desi Star Trek* (2018) 209

Preface

While growing up in Germany and Austria during the 1980s and 1990s, popular adaptations of the *One Thousand and One Nights* such as Disney's *Aladdin* made a big impression on me as they did on many other children around the world. I loved fantastic creatures like the Genie. In the 2010s, I made further connections between speculative fiction and the Muslim world. In 2013, when I first came to Doha, I was mesmerized by its skyline. Having been used to the older architecture of Vienna, the Qatari capital looked to me like a city of the future. Over the years of living in the Gulf state, my friends and I jokingly compared different buildings to structures in outer space or on alien planets. John Laprise likened the Education City Mosque to a 'starport', and Jimmy Roach and I called the Qatar Foundation Headquarters a 'Borg cube'.

Despite such futuristic architecture and a tradition of fantastical tales, the Muslim world is still not commonly associated with science fiction. Religion, repression and rote learning have often been blamed for a perceived lack of creativity, imagination and future-oriented thought.[1] Nevertheless, even authoritarian countries have produced highly imaginative accounts on one of the frontiers of knowledge: astrobiology, or the study of life in the universe. Despite the influence of conservatives, I argue that the Islamic tradition has been generally supportive of conceptions of extraterrestrial life. For example, the Qur'an repeatedly refers to God as 'lord of the worlds', and Muslims have combined such notions with global astrobiological research and science fiction. The universe's strangest beings can thus be seen as creations, and evidence for the existence, of an all-powerful God. Governments too have played a positive role through their support of scientific research and writing. In any case, repression probably helped science fiction more than hurt it. Censorship arguably encouraged authors to disguise criticism of contemporary politics by setting plots in future times and on distant planets. If you are looking to explore connections between science, culture and politics in the Muslim world further, I hope this book will be insightful for you. It might also be stimulating, if you

[1] Khammas, 'The Almost Complete Lack'.

ever wonder about some of humanity's biggest questions. Are we alone in the universe? And what would it mean for one of our greatest faiths, if we are not?

I hope you will enjoy our cosmic journey. This book will take you to little-known dimensions of Muslim culture and religion, such as wildly popular adaptations of *Star Wars* and mysterious movements centred on UFOs. You will enter strange new worlds of the imagination created in Arabic, Malay, Persian, Turkish and Urdu texts and films. You will also discover how scientists in and from Muslim-majority countries have been at the forefront of the exciting search for extraterrestrial life, the ultimate Other.

This book could not have been written without the contributions of many people. Foremost are my research assistants who helped me understand sources in different languages. İrfan Batur and Haldun Faruk Gümüş reviewed many Turkish films and books for me. Shima Aeinehdar and Linda binti Ridzuan Chun examined Persian and Indonesian works respectively. Maphuza Akter and Mosammat Samiha Sadeka read Bengali fiction. Anusheh Zaman, Fajr Aamir and Walli Ullah analysed Urdu material. As part of their work, all of my assistants shared with me their deep cultural insights. Anusheh, Fajr, İrfan, Linda, Maphuza, Samiha and Shima were part of the Student Employment Program at Virginia Commonwealth University in Qatar. I thank Noor AlOraidi and Zeyad Bateiha for enabling their dedicated work. I am further indebted to my supervisors, especially Patty Paine and Byrad Yyelland, for their never-ending support and mentorship. At I.B. Tauris, an imprint of Bloomsbury, my editor Sophie Rudland, has been extremely helpful and enthusiastic. In addition, I acknowledge assistance by Sorcha Thomson and Yasmin Garcha. Matt Sparrow was an outstanding copy-editor, Ruth Ellis a meticulous indexer and Damian Penfold a stellar project manager.

I was fortunate to discuss the research for this book with various audiences in Africa, Asia, Europe and North America. In 2018, Alena Kulinich invited me to lecture about Arabic science fiction at Seoul National University in Korea. During the same year, I spoke at the conference of the British Society for Middle Eastern Studies at King's College London. I also had the honour of presenting at the World Congress for Middle Eastern Studies in Seville, Spain. Furthermore, I displayed a poster at the thirtieth General Assembly of the International Astronomical Union in Vienna, Austria. The Middle East Working Group at Virginia Tech sponsored another appearance of mine, which Carmen Gitre and William Ochsenwald kindly organized. In 2019, I was privileged to speak at Al Akhawayn University in Ifrane, Morocco. This was followed by a talk as part of the Council on Middle East Studies Colloquium at Yale University in New

Haven, Connecticut. In July of the same year, I presented at a symposium on 'Science Fiction Beyond the West: Futurity in African and Asian Contexts'. July Blalack and Tasnim Qutait led this event at SOAS University of London. I am indebted to Junita Patrick and Mary Amat for their help with the logistics of many of my trips.

At home in Qatar too, I was fortunate to present at different venues. In 2018, I spoke at the Qatar Faculty Forum moderated by Sara Hillman at Texas A&M University. The following year, Clyde Wilcox allowed me to discuss Muslim science fiction with the students of his course on Interstellar Politics at Georgetown University. In 2019, I had the opportunity to address the Department of Humanities and the Gulf Studies Center at Qatar University. I am very grateful to Peter-Polak Springer, Mohammed Khalifa Al-Kuwari, Mahjoob Zweiri and Paul Christians for making this possible. Later during the same year, Ali Fathollah-Nejad invited me to lecture at the Brookings Doha Center. Finally, from the comfort of my beautiful Doha home, I participated in the first Twitter conference of the British Society for the History of Science in 2020.

This book benefited from numerous other exchanges outside of conferences and seminars as well. I will be forever indebted to the anonymous reviewers commissioned by I.B. Tauris for their excellent comments. Informally, the following colleagues at Virginia Commonwealth University gave me feedback on parts of my manuscript: Holiday Powers, Jesse Ulmer, Maysaa Al-Mumin, Radha Dalal, Robert Bianchi, Ryan Browning and Sadia Mir. Several friends from other institutions in Education City were readers as well: Anto Mohsin, Ayman Shabana, Clyde Wilcox and Danielle Jones. A long list of peers based outside of Qatar provided me with additional observations and much other help. This list comprises the following experts in the history and social studies of science: Alireza Doostdar, Daniel Stolz, Hala Auji, Parviz Tarikhi, Robert Morrison, Stefano Bigliardi and Steven Dick. The list also includes a number of scholars of the arts: Anwesha Maity, Bodhisattva Chattopadhyay, Emad El-Din Aysha, Joan Grandjean, Max Kramer, Nat Muller, Nora Parr and Peter Hill. Several protagonists of the book shared their views with me as well. They include Azrul Jaini, Cevdet Mehmet Kösemen, Nozair Khawaja, Sohrab Rahvar and Syed Muneeb Ali.

Moreover, I would like to acknowledge a number of people who helped me access the different materials that are cited in this book. My interviewees shared with me many items from their personal libraries and archives. Special thanks go to Hosam Elzembely, Iraj Fazel Bakhsheshi, Reza Mansouri and Saks Afridi for being extraordinarily generous. Rama Firmansyah introduced me to various creators of science fiction in Indonesia. Numerous other people alerted me to interesting material as well. They include Alaa Laabar, Fred Nesta, Hüseyin Sen, Maureen Buja, Rhys Himsworth, Trinidad Rico and Pius Vögele. At Virginia Commonwealth University in Qatar, Amy Andres, Beena Noorudeen and Iman Mazhar promptly ordered many books in different languages. The Qatar National Library, the British Library and Yale University Library granted me access to a vast range of materials. Zotero made it easy for me to keep track of all the items cited in my bibliography.

I owe my greatest debt to my family, however. My parents, Michael and Sibylle, allowed me as a child and teenager to spend countless hours watching television series. Besides *Aladdin*, they include *Star Trek: The Next Generation*, *The X-Files* and *Futurama*. I also fondly remember playing numerous video games with my brothers, Christian and Claudius, including *StarCraft*, *Freelancer* and *Halo*. These activities nurtured my interest in science fiction from an early age. More recently, I was able to benefit from wonderful conversations about Middle Eastern and South Asian history and politics with my parents-in-law, Peter and Sophia Vaz. They have been extremely interested in, and encouraging of, my work since 2015. That year, I met my wife, Jeanne Vaz. She has been not just an enormous help and a fantastic partner in life, but also an inspiration. In 2019, she gave me the gift of our daughter, Maria, to whom this book is dedicated. Here, I must also thank our nanny and housekeeper, Marilou Magsayo Semetara, who has been incredible in her work for our family.

1

Lord of the Worlds

'it is time we realized there is only "one world" even in history. If there is to be an "Islamic world," this can be only in the future'

– Marshall Hodgson, *The Venture of Islam*[1]

During the war that had begun in 2011, various forces fought over Syria. In the surrealist art of Ayham Jabr, one of them was Martian. Unlike the woman whom he loved, Jabr did not flee his country as a refugee. Instead, the young graphic designer stayed in Damascus. With little more than a laptop, an internet connection and a pirated copy of Adobe Photoshop, he created digital collages and distributed them via social media. One of his series made in 2016 was entitled *Damascus under Siege* (Figures 1 and 2). Combining scanned photographs and images found on the web, the collages show Martian spaceships hovering over his home city. 'They say they came for peace', Jabr commented. 'But who is really coming for peace? What they really brought is total annihilation.' The artist remained defiant. Those who were trying to destroy Syria would not succeed. 'After all the wars' in the past, his country had 'stood up again'.[2]

With his surrealism, Ayham Jabr was unusual among the artists who lived through the Syrian Civil War. Although he continued to work in the capital, he did not produce simple propaganda for the government. President Bashar al-Assad and his family hardly appeared. Nor was Jabr among the many artists who engaged in acts of creative resistance against the regime.[3] His work was mainly critical of foreign interventions. 'The terror the West is sending us is worse than hell itself', complained Jabr. His response was largely pacifist. The

1 Hodgson, *The Venture*, 58.
2 Köhler, 'No One Bombs'.
3 cooke, *Dancing*.

Figure 1 *Damascus under Siege-7* (2016). Courtesy of Ayham Jabr.

actual attacks on Damascus, and the ones of his imagination, were 'about greed, the illusion of power and striving for eternal reputation'. In the end, the violence did not produce any winners. 'Everyone has lost relatives', Jabr lamented. 'That is what is so hideous about the war: destruction and sorrow will cover all of us.'[4]

While Ayham Jabr was unusual among visual artists, he was not the only creator of science fiction in wartime Syria. Various amateurs created videos and memes inspired by Japanese anime series like *UFO Robot Grendizer* with their simple plots of good versus evil. Even if they were critical of the government, social media activists thus reused Arabic-dubbed material that had been broadcast by state television stations since the 1980s.[5] The Ministry

[4] Köhler, 'No One Bombs'.
[5] Al-Ghazzi, 'Grendizer'.

Figure 2 *Damascus under Siege-3* (2016). Courtesy of Ayham Jabr.

of Culture itself also published an entire magazine entitled *Science Fiction*. The editor-in-chief was the scientist, broadcaster and writer Taleb Omran. He was supported by an advisory board consisting of authors from Egypt, France, Kuwait, Lebanon and Morocco. The periodical included stories, reviews and literary studies. Other parts of the magazine were dedicated to science, both mainstream and fringe. An issue from 2013, for instance, featured articles on black holes, pollution and 'visitors from space in historical documents'.[6] The Arabic text of the various issues was interspersed with colourful images from popular global productions, such as *StarCraft*, *Star Trek* and *Star Wars*. Probably reproduced without permission, these images added appeal to the stories in a cost-effective way.

[6] Ḥūsh, 'Zuwwār'.

Science Fiction was one of the outcomes of the Lucian the Syrian Symposium, which had been held with sponsorship by the Ministry of Culture in Damascus in 2007. It was named after Lucian of Samosata, who wrote *A True Story* about a trip to the Moon in the second century. After discussing the history and philosophy of science fiction, the participants passed several recommendations. Besides the establishment of the magazine, they asked for support for the translation of literature into and from Arabic. Another suggestion was the teaching of their genre in secondary schools and at universities. The top recommendation, however, was the creation of an Association of Arab Science Fiction Writers, which was realized two years later.[7]

Although sponsored by a national institution, the Lucian the Syrian Symposium had an impact beyond the country's borders. Prominent authors, including Nehad Sherif from Egypt and Taibah Al-Ibrahim from Kuwait, were among the speakers. 'Overall the event was impressive', reported Kawthar Ayed, then a graduate student in Aix-en-Provence and Sousse. 'I have in the past attended SF events in Tunisia, France, Spain and so forth, but nowhere with such a reception, nor such broadmindedness.' Riad Agha, the minister of culture gave the opening speech, defending science fiction as a worthy genre and acknowledging his personal interest. Newspapers covered the symposium, and talks were recorded for a weekly television programme presented by Taleb Omran.[8]

The state's support for science fiction was remarkable for surviving long into the Syrian Civil War. By the time of its outbreak in March 2011, thirty-three issues of *Science Fiction* had appeared. Subsequently, the magazine's frequency was reduced from monthly to quarterly. Still, by January 2019, sixty-eight issues plus accompanying books had been produced. In addition, Omran established a new monthly called *Scientific Literature* in 2013. This periodical was issued by Damascus University and used a similar style and layout. Authors from elsewhere in the Arab world continued to advise the Syrian editor-in-chief. Amid shortages of all kinds, sixty-three issues of the magazine had appeared by November 2018. In the meantime, Omran had founded yet another literary journal called *Circles of Creativity*, which included Arabic science fiction as well. The Syrian Arab News Agency regularly publicized new issues of all three periodicals alongside updates from the front line.

7 Al-Shammās, 'Al-nadwah al-ūlá'.
8 Ayed, 'Lucien de Samosate le Syrien'.

Islam and science fiction

Taleb Omran had thus convinced his government to invest scarce resources in a highly speculative endeavour. 'Why science fiction?' asked Riad Agha in his opening article of the first issue of *Science Fiction*. This form of literature was the 'legitimate son of the age of science in which we live'. Science fiction was also 'a smart education tool that gives children a more comprehensive view and understanding of science, its achievements and its offerings'. Agha then quoted the American writer Isaac Asimov, whose name he Arabized as 'Isḥāq ʿAẓīmūf'. Out of 100 children reading science fiction, at least one would later become a scientist, Asimov had predicted.[9] In a subsequent opening article to the second issue of *Science Fiction*, Agha again stressed the importance of the genre. This form of fiction is 'the literature of the future'.[10]

In emphasizing the educational value of the genre, Riad Agha meant its fictional as much as its scientific aspects. 'Man is an imaginative being', the official stressed. 'The more he excels in imagining, the more he excels in innovation and invention.' 'Imagination is the evocation of images' before they are fully understood. Children create images, in which they 'drive a spacecraft' or 'meet intelligent beings from other planets'.[11] Agha further mentioned dreams of defeating old age and sickness, landing on 'distant planets' and meeting with 'the beings of other worlds'. Such creatures could be portrayed as 'aggressive' and 'authoritarian', striving for control and influence. Alternatively, they may be 'peaceful' and 'seeking friendship, love, and cooperation'.[12]

Many observers of Arab politics would have been surprised by the minister's commitment to nurturing the imagination. In 2009, the British journalist Brian Whitaker published a book titled *What's Really Wrong with the Middle East.* He wrote, 'Education in the Arab countries is where the paternalism of the traditional family structure, the authoritarianism of the state and the dogmatism of religion all meet, discouraging critical thought and analysis, stifling creativity and instilling submissiveness.'[13] Whitaker based his criticism on the United Nations' *Arab Human Development Report 2003.* This document had claimed that 'curricula taught in Arab countries seem to encourage submission,

9 Riyāḍ Aghā, 'Al-khayāl al-ʿīlmī'.
10 Riyāḍ Aghā, 'Adab al-khayāl al-ʿilmī'.
11 Riyāḍ Aghā, 'Al-khayāl al-ʿīlmī', 5.
12 Riyāḍ Aghā, 'Adab al-khayāl al-ʿilmī'.
13 Whitaker, *What's Really Wrong*, 19.

obedience, subordination and compliance, rather than free critical thinking'.[14] It is puzzling then that an authoritarian regime would support science fiction as a very liberated genre, especially as it was struggling to control its population.

Did the Syrian state sponsor science fiction as a kind of 'commissioned' or 'licensed criticism'?[15] In other words, did speculative art serve as a safety valve for grievances or at least as a breathing space amid repression? The titles of some of Omran's novels, such as *The Search for Other Worlds*, might suggest escapism.[16] The magazine *Science Fiction* also offered some criticism of Arab politics, while avoiding mentions of the Syrian president Bashar al-Assad. The first issue included an article by the Syrian writer Zuhair Ghanem under the title 'The Fiction of Arabic Science Fiction Literature'. 'We have science fiction writers, but don't say that we have a science fiction literature', he cautioned. This genre in the Arab world was still in its infancy, he claimed, 'because of the dire conditions, backwardness, illiteracy, and the absence of mental structures and scientific research'. He further explained, 'we consume the products of science and do not contribute to it'. Reasons for the underdevelopment of Arabic science fiction also included 'the lack of reform, democracy and freedom of opinion'.[17]

In addition to being a means of releasing pressure and distracting from urgent realities, could science fiction have served as a sophisticated form of propaganda? By including critical voices, such as Ghanem's, were the magazines intended to support a facade of free speech and thought? Some of Omran's books displayed the logos of the Frankfurt Book Fair and the Arab Capital of Culture,[18] indicating that they were meant at least in part for foreign consumption. While interacting with many outsiders, the editor could be trusted as a loyal servant of the Syrian state. From Tartus, a stronghold of the Alawite-dominated regime, he had long worked as a professor at Damascus University and presented science programmes on radio and television.

Like Jabr, Omran was critical of the role of Western powers in the Middle East. In 2003, after the United States had started its War on Terror, he had published the novel *Dark Times*. On the title page, the book offers 'a depiction of a century whose horrific features had appeared on September 11'.[19] The novel is set in the near future, after a great power has waged a 'war of justice' and

14 United Nations Development Programme, *Arab Human Development Report*.
15 cooke, *Dissident Syria*, 72.
16 ʿUmrān, *Al-baḥth*.
17 Ghānim, 'Khayāl adab al-khayāl al-ʿilmī al-ʿArabī', 39, 42.
18 ʿUmrān, *Fī kawkab*; *Dawwāmāt al-khawf*.
19 ʿUmrān, *Al-azmān al-muẓlimah*.

colonized lands from the Mediterranean to Central Asia. It controls them through absolute monarchies that have the veneer of democracy. The appointment of client kings is legitimized through fake elections and empty concepts, such as 'popular sovereignty'.[20] Acts of resistance are denounced as terrorism. One good American doctor, however, puts himself in danger by saving a Syrian scientist who is detained as a terrorist.[21]

The regime type described in *Dark Times* was reminiscent of the Arab 'monarchic republic' or *jumlakah*. In such a hybrid system, presidents like Hafez al-Assad sought to perpetuate their families' hold on power through quasi-dynastic succession.[22] Nevertheless, Arab politics alone would be an insufficient frame for explaining Syrian science fiction. Taleb Omran's biography extended beyond his home country to other parts of the Muslim world. With a scholarship from the Indo-Syrian cultural exchange programme, Omran had completed a doctorate in mathematics at Aligarh Muslim University in 1984.[23] His encounter with a diversity of 'civilizations', 'races' and 'languages' in India had contributed to his writing, as he later explained.[24] Omran maintained his connection with Aligarh after his return to Syria. He acknowledged his former professors' help in a scientific article in the *Journal of the University of Kuwait* in 1989, for instance.[25] As for his literary work, it attracted the attention of critics not just in Arab countries, but also in Iran, a staunch ally of the Syrian government.[26]

It is useful to look at the Muslim world as a whole in order to understand another important factor shaping Syrian science fiction besides politics, namely religion. Brian Whitaker diagnosed 'religious sensitivities' as an obstacle for the development of the genre in the Arab world. The journalist quoted Muhammad al-Munajjid,[27] a Syrian-born Salafi scholar who had studied in Saudi Arabia. Back in 1999, al-Munajjid had issued a fatwa about the permissibility of reading science fiction on his website *Islam Question and Answer*. 'If these stories include lies, such as Darwin's theory (evolution), and other things that are contrary to the facts stated by Islam and the facts of natural science', the mufti wrote, 'then the Muslim should avoid them'. Ideas that amount to 'unbelief' include 'putting life and death in the hands of some created being' or 'saying that scientists in

20 ʿAyyād, 'Al-khayāl al-istishrāfī al-siyāsī al-ʿArabī', 42–43; Ayed, 'La fiction', 52–53.
21 Ayed, 'L'Image', 107.
22 Billingsley, *Political Succession*, 145.
23 Omran, 'Structures'.
24 Naṣīr, 'Liqāʾ'.
25 Omran, 'Almost Product Structures', 219.
26 Khānlarī, 'Pazhūhishī pīrāmūn-i utūpiyā-yi mudirn'.
27 Whitaker, 'Star Trekking'.

laboratories can create something from nothing'. Other intolerable imaginations were 'making inanimate things come alive, creating life from a fossil that has been dead for many millenia, or travelling to the future then coming back to the present'. 'Some people claim that this is just entertainment', the scholar acknowledged. However, even if it was not religiously forbidden, it could still be a waste of Muslims' time.[28]

Al-Munajjid's hostility towards the genre was shared by other conservatives in Saudi Arabia. Ibraheem Abbas and Yasser Bahjatt experienced such opposition, when they published their novel *HWJN*. Its plot centres on a romance between Sawsan, a medical student, and Hawjan, a ninety-year-old jinni from another dimension. Also part of the story are Sawsan's father and a sorcerer who seek to fight the 'devils' haunting her. Following rejections by publishers, the co-authors launched their own press. They named it Yatakhayaloon (They Imagine) or the League of Arabic SciFiers.[29] *HWJN* became a bestseller in Saudi Arabia after its publication in 2013. However, members of the religious police, the Committee for the Promotion of Virtue and the Prevention of Vice, entered bookshops and demanded that *HWJN* be taken off the shelves. According to Abbas, the work was seen as promoting sorcery, devil-worship and idolatry.[30] Although sales in the kingdom were subsequently allowed to proceed, Kuwait and Qatar imposed their own bans on the book.[31]

Elsewhere in the Muslim world, promoters of science fiction struggled against religious conservatives as well. In 2016, the Pakistani author Tehseen Baweja asked, 'How do you help somebody break free from the shackles of orthodoxy and conformity?' He acknowledged that 'This is a very real and deep-rooted problem in today's Pakistani society.' He lamented, 'we have taught ourselves to curb our imagination rather than let it run wild'. The author's contribution to a solution was to set up the Salam Award for Imaginative Fiction. Worth 500 dollars, it was named after the Pakistani physicist and Nobel laureate Abdus Salam.[32] While science fiction authors served as judges, two scientists were advisers. The first was Pervez Hoodbhoy, a nuclear scientist with a doctorate from the Massachusetts Institute of Technology. The second was Salman Hameed, an associate professor at Hampshire College, also in Massachusetts.[33]

28 Al-Munajjid, '3324'.
29 Al-Jeffery, 'Bridging'.
30 Ian Campbell, 'Still a Better Love Story'; Morayef, 'Arab Science Fiction'.
31 Fossett, 'Can Science Fiction'.
32 Baweja, 'New Prize'.
33 Baweja, 'Advisors'.

Tehseen Baweja saw science fiction as being in competition with religious literature and therefore attempted to exclude much of the latter from his own contest. 'I don't know if science fiction as a genre even exist for Pakistani readers', he wrote. 'When you go to book stores, you don't find any books other than religious ones or text books needed for school.' As a result, 'our Pakistani readers are deprived of a great source of intellectual stimulation that can definitely counter the ill effects of extremist doctrinations'.[34] Within the genre, the scope of the Salam Award for Imaginative Fiction was broad. According to the rules, 'anything from alien invasions to fantasy universes, and comic science fiction to dark fantasies is valid'. 'What's not acceptable though is religiously-oriented stories of good versus evil, stories that target a particular group/community, or stories that contain hate speech.'[35]

Baweja blamed not just religious conservatism, but also pointed to wider social and economic factors. 'We still don't encourage ourselves to think outside-the-box and don't sufficiently appreciate those around us that do so', he complained. 'We'd encourage a child who wants to become an engineer or doctor, more than a kid who wants to be, let's say, a video game designer.' Such a mindset might boost economic growth in the short term, but 'will impair our ability to innovate and lead', he warned. The writer thus called upon his society to 'start rewarding those who can let their imagination run wild'. It should 'embrace diversity rather than conformity'.[36]

While being aware of other pressures, Baweja and his advisers were still most concerned about religious intolerance and close-mindedness. The writer named his award after Abdus Salam not just in celebration of Pakistani scientific achievement; it was also a sign of protest against the persecution of the Ahmadiyya community, to which Abdus Salam had belonged.[37] Baweja further commended Pervez Hoodbhoy for 'highlighting the sad state of our education system that promotes orthodoxy and disincentivises unconventional thinking'.[38] Hoodbhoy himself argued that 'the insistence that religion must be brought into everything – including science – puts certain critical faculties to sleep'. He observed that children in Pakistan were often asked to reproduce facts without reasoning, thus learning science 'as though they were memorising a holy text'.[39]

34 Baweja, 'Science Fiction'.
35 Baweja, 'Rules'.
36 Baweja, 'I Set up'.
37 Baweja, 'New Prize'.
38 Baweja, 'I Set up'.
39 Hoodbhoy and Bigliardi, 'Science', 73–74.

Both opponents, like al-Munajjid, and proponents, such as Baweja, might give the impression that Islam was at odds with science fiction. However, the relationship was more complex. Although Saudi conservatives sought to ban the novel *HWJN*, the encounter of humans and jinn had been part of Islamic literature starting with the Qur'an itself. The Syrian artist Ayham Jabr also claimed to have been inspired by the tradition of his faith. 'We live in a religious world. And religion is the source of all fiction', he claimed. 'I was raised by surreal religious stories. And now they are stuck in my head.' He gave the examples of Muhammad's splitting of the Moon and his ascension to heaven, the staff of Moses transforming into a snake, and Jesus walking on water. 'Those used to be funny stories when I was a child', Jabr added.[40] He even went so far as to call the Qur'an 'the first work of SF'.[41]

The Qur'an does not just contain miraculous stories similar to fantasy novels. Beyond this, even strictly literal readings of the scripture seem to support the idea of the plurality of worlds, which has been the basis of much science fiction. Qur'an 1:2 translates as 'praise to God, lord of the worlds'. In total, the expression 'lord of the worlds' (*rabb al-ʿālamīn*) occurs forty-two times in the scripture. The word 'worlds' by itself appears seventy-three times altogether, but never in the singular. The specific form of the plural is intriguing too. The common plural of 'worlds' in Arabic is *ʿawālim*. The plural ending *–īn* in *ʿālamīn* is normally reserved for male humans. Examples include *muʾminīn* (believers), *banīn* (sons) or *nabīyīn* (prophets).[42] Therefore, *ʿālamīn* not only means 'worlds', but also suggests 'men'.

Of course, before the Copernican Revolution, most Muslims would not have understood the Qur'anic 'worlds' as planets. The combined influence of Aristotle and Ptolemy would have precluded a view of Earth as a sibling of Venus or Mars, all orbiting the same star. Instead, many Muslim scholars differentiated between an inferior, terrestrial and a superior, celestial world. They also distinguished a sphere of sensory perception from one of ideas. The intelligent inhabitants of these realms include jinn and angels in addition to humans.[43] Despite much exegetical effort, however, the word 'world' remained vague enough to allow for almost infinite interpretations. The philosophers al-Biruni and Ibn Sina and the poet Nizami Ganjavi were among many medieval

40 Köhler, 'No One Bombs'.
41 Grandjean, 'Les collages'.
42 Calderini, '*Tafsīr*', 52.
43 El-Zein, *Islam*.

figures who discussed the plurality of worlds.[44] Yet, they hardly exhausted the concept. Later writers thus found it easy to apply *ʿālam* to modern cosmology. In Taleb Omran's *The Search for Other Worlds*, for instance, an Arab spaceship passes by various planets and moons on its way to Alpha Centauri. This novel was part of a series of books that promised to 'take the reader to worlds in which reality is mixed with fiction, science with the hidden powers of man, and the reasonable with the unfamiliar'.[45]

As the Qur'an's opening chapter forms part of prayers,[46] the expression 'lord of the worlds' has been on the lips of many Muslims on a daily basis. However, other parts of the scripture allow for the imagination of extraterrestrial life too. Qur'an 42:29 means: 'And among His Signs is the creation of the heavens and the earth, and the living creatures that He has scattered through them.' This particular translation was the work of the Indian Abdullah Yusuf Ali and first published in the 1930s. His rendering formed the basis of an official Saudi edition printed in Medina five decades later. The editors had chosen Ali's translation for its 'choice of words close to the meaning of the original text, accompanied by scholarly notes and commentaries'. One of these footnotes by Ali reads: 'Life is not confined to our one little Planet. It is a very old speculation to imagine some life like human life on the planet Mars.' He continued, 'Though no scientific demonstration is possible, it is reasonable to suppose that Life in some form or other is scattered through some of the millions of heavenly bodies scattered through space. What a wonderful Sign of Allah! The Almighty Who created such countless beings has surely the power to bring them together.'[47]

Egyptian scientific and religious authorities agreed with such readings of the Qur'an. One expert in both areas was Muhammad Ghamrawy. His older brother Mahmud was a senior scholar at Cairo's al-Azhar Mosque,[48] one of the oldest centres of Islamic learning. Muhammad was very knowledgeable about scripture too. In the late 1920s, he contributed to *The Meaning of the Glorious Koran*. This English translation was authored by the British convert Marmaduke Pickthall and sponsored by the Nizam of Hyderabad in India. Following studies in England, Ghamrawy taught at Cairo's College of Medicine.[49] He combined his interests in science and religion by searching for natural knowledge within the sacred text.

44 Hullmeine, 'Al-Bīrūnī'; Bausani, 'Niẓāmī di Gangia'.
45 'Umrān, *Al-baḥth*.
46 Muzaffar Iqbal, 'Islamic Theology', 217.
47 Presidency of Islamic Researches, Ifta, Call and Guidance, *The Holy Qur-ān*, vi, 1484.
48 Al-Baṭāwī, 'Muḥammad Aḥmad al-Ghamrāwī'.
49 Pickthall, *The Meaning*, vii.

Verses about the plurality of worlds were part of what made Islamic scripture divine, according to Ghamrawy. In 1947, he published an article on 'Scientific Aspects of the Miracle of the Qur'an' in the magazine *Arrissalah* (The Message). He rejected the notion that the Qur'anic 'worlds' are the realms of the humans, jinn and angels or the kingdoms of plants and animals. When the text mentions 'seven heavens' and an equal number of earths, it does not mean different layers of our planet. Instead, Ghamrawy preferred the modern astronomical understanding that situates our planet within the solar system, and such systems within galaxies. The Egyptian referred his readers to *Worlds without End*, a book by the English Astronomer Royal, Harold Spencer Jones.[50] Ghamrawy's arguments were repeated in a book titled *Islam in the Age of Science*, which was published posthumously in 1973. Abd-el-Halim Mahmoud, the Grand Imam of al-Azhar, endorsed this book, praising the author in the foreword.[51]

Islamic authorities distant from Cairo and Medina similarly read the existence of extraterrestrial beings in the Qur'an. One of them was Mirza Tahir Ahmad, the fourth caliph and head of the Ahmadiyya. Following legislation against his community in Pakistan, he migrated to London in 1984. Three years later, he was invited to give a lecture on Islam at the University of Zurich. It resulted in a book on *Revelation, Rationality, Knowledge and Truth*, which included a chapter about 'The Quran and Extraterrestrial Life'. Ahmad's interpretation was less literal, but equally affirmative of the plurality of worlds. He translated parts of 65:12 as follows: 'Allah is He Who created seven heavens, and of the earth the like thereof.' This means that 'the universe comprises many units of heavens, each divided into groups of seven (a perfect number), each having at least one earth to it which will be supported by the entire system of that heaven (galaxy)'. As for 42:29, it 'speaks not only of the possibility of extraterrestrial life, but it categorically declares that it does exist'.[52]

Islamic scripture itself thus hardly constrained science fiction. Qur'anic verses were vague enough to allow for diverse visions of the universe. One example are the 'living creatures' (*dābbah*), which God has scattered through the heavens. To Abdullah Yusuf Ali, *dābbah* meant 'beasts, living crawling creatures of all kinds'. According to other commentators, the word denotes 'any sentient, corporeal being capable of spontaneous movement'.[53] Mirza Tahir Ahmad for

50 Al-Ghamrāwī, 'Al-nāḥiyah al-ʿilmīyah'.
51 Al-Ghamrāwī, *Al-Islām*.
52 Mirza Tahir Ahmad, *Revelation*, 330–31.
53 Mimouni and Guessoum, 'Islam'.

his part denied that the word could refer to swimming and flying animals, ghosts and spiritual life.[54] Overall, however, most scholars conceded the possibility that extraterrestrial life was intelligent. Perhaps the same was true for Muslims with little expertise in exegesis. In an interview for *Time* magazine in 1986, Hafez al-Assad spoke of his long-standing interest in unidentified flying objects. He was even able to imagine an 'extraterrestrial power' trying to solve Arab conflicts with Israel. The Syrian president expected such a power to be 'unbiased', in contrast to the United States. 'It should offer advice to both sides, not deal with guns, planes or billions of dollars.' And if it does, it should do so 'evenhandedly'.[55]

At various times, Muslims wondered not just whether aliens were fair, but also whether they shared their faith. 'Abd Allah ibn 'Abbas, one of the earliest exegetes, understood that the 'seven earths' each had their own prophets, including Adam, Abraham, Noah, Jesus and Muhammad.[56] In the twentieth century, this tradition was endorsed by the Pakistani scholar Abul A'la Maududi in his *Understanding the Qur'an.* Yet, he simultaneously promoted a more modern view of the universe. Commenting on 65:12, he wrote that 'the countless stars and planets seen in the sky are not all lying desolate, but like the earth there are many among them which are inhabited'.[57] However, unless other worlds are largely identical to ours, imagining Islam on them is not straightforward. Important practices seem to have been designed specifically for humans on Earth. A pilgrimage to Mecca from a distant planetary system could be challenging, as would be determining the location of the Kaaba and thus the direction of daily prayers. How would Muslims light years away be able to observe the phases of the Moon and thus the beginning and end of the month of Ramadan? Long rotation periods of some planets might also make fasting from sunrise to sunset seem impossible.[58]

Nevertheless, such challenges perhaps inspired Muslim imaginations more than constrained them. Solutions to problems of Islamic living in outer space already emerged in the context of humans venturing into low Earth orbit. When Malaysia sent its first astronaut to the International Space Station in 2007, its Department of Islamic Development issued guidelines on praying, fasting and disposing dead bodies in the new environment.[59] The space programme of the

54 Mirza Tahir Ahmad, *Revelation*, 331.
55 Time, 'An Interview'.
56 Mimouni and Guessoum, 'Islam'.
57 Maududi, '65. Surah At Talaq'.
58 Weintraub, *Religions*, 161–68.
59 Zook, 'Making Space'.

United Arab Emirates in the 2010s generated similar thought. In preparation for the Hope Mars Mission, the Mohammed bin Rashid Space Centre in Dubai began publishing the children's magazine *Red Planet* in 2016. It featured a comic about an 'alien encounter' between the Emirati astronaut Aisha and purple, one-eyed creatures named Areen and Lameeka. More for adults was an article by the British writer Shelina Janmohamed in the Abu Dhabi newspaper *The National* in 2018. It bore the title 'From Mosques on Mars to Meeting Martians: The Dilemmas awaiting Muslims in Space'. Janmohamed envisaged that human colonists on the red planet use 3D printing to build 'mosques with rotating prayer spaces that constantly adjust themselves to remain pointed at Makkah'.[60]

Although some questions about extraterrestrial life seem distant and abstract, they were on the minds of not just writers, but also of senior officials. The Malaysian astrophysicist Mazlan Othman was one of them. In 1999, she was appointed director of the United Nations Office for Outer Space Affairs (UNOOSA) in Vienna. Three years later, she became director general of Malaysia's National Space Agency. After the successful mission of her country's first astronaut, she returned to UNOOSA. In 2010, various media described her as a possible contact person for aliens who arrive on Earth and ask, 'take me to your leader'. Othman was quick to deny that she had been chosen for such a role.[61] However, she did state that 'the United Nations forums are a ready-made mechanism' for a coordinated response to alien signals.[62]

Despite not being known as a science fiction writer herself, Othman was similarly imaginative of extraterrestrial life as Taleb Omran. 'On our own Earth, bacteria, single-cell life has been found in the vents of volcanoes, under the ice in Antarctica', she said in 2011. 'Even if the other planets have harsh environments, there could still be life.' She cautioned against the idea that such life forms necessarily have hands, legs or eyes. 'Can you imagine a situation where life has evolved so much that life exists only in an energy form?' she asked. Such organisms would not need to understand 'any particular language' in order to communicate with earthlings. Instead, they could 'read your brain waves'.[63]

The Malaysian astrophysicist recognized religious implications of contact with extraterrestrial life, even if she preferred to talk in more general rather than specifically Islamic terms. Othman explained, 'philosophically, scientifically,

60 Janmohamed, 'From Mosques'.
61 Weaver, 'UN Plan'.
62 Othman, 'Supra-Earth Affairs', 699.
63 UN News Centre, 'Interview'.

religiously, whatever way you look at it, the possibilities are there' for alien life to exist in any form between single cells and 'pure energy'.[64] In an interview for the *Scientific Malaysian* magazine in 2013, she raised contested questions about the ethics of travelling to other planets and encountering alien life: 'What do we bring with us? Do we bring our religion? Do we bring our culture?' Othman predicted that travelling to a planet as close as Mars would already 'change how we see ourselves and our civilization'.[65]

Islamic world building

Islam not only allowed for science fiction. The two could also be combined. There was not just science fiction by Muslims, but also 'Islamic science fiction'. These three words formed the title of a book review on *Islam Online*, a Qatar-based competitor to Muhammad al-Munajjid's website.[66] It was associated with Yusuf al-Qaradawi, an intellectual leader of the Muslim Brotherhood. The subject of the review was *The Ultimate Revelations*, a novel published by the Indian engineer Jamshed Akhtar in 1996. In the plot, the cooling of the sun threatens Earth with a new ice age. A scientist named Hamza tries to avert the apocalypse by decoding an extraterrestrial message in the Qur'an. This fictional character continues the actual work of the Egyptian-American biochemist Rashad Khalifa, who claimed to have discovered a secret mathematical structure within the scripture.[67]

The numerology of *The Ultimate Revelations* was controversial. Rashad Khalifa himself had been accused of heresy and stabbed to death in 1990, with a member of Al-Qaeda implicated.[68] Jamshed Akhtar escaped this fate or anything like the violent reaction to Salman Rushdie's magical realist novel *The Satanic Verses*. However, one reviewer in the *Journal of Islamic Science* described Akhtar as 'desperately seeking logic'.[69] In contrast, Yusuf al-Qaradawi's website was very sympathetic. 'Few Muslims have thought about using science fiction as a Da'wah tool', *Islam Online* stated, *da'wah* being an Arabic word for proselytizing. 'In what can be termed as "religious science fiction," the author has creatively used

64 Ibid.
65 Chong and Soo, 'Meet the Scientist'.
66 Islam Online, 'Book Review'.
67 Akhtar, *The Ultimate Revelation*.
68 Pipes, 'How Dare You', 42.
69 Akhtar, 'Press Reviews'.

his God-given abilities to present Islam.' The review concluded that Akhtar's book was a 'good read for anyone and contains tons of information on subjects as varied as the formation of the solar system, atmospheric impacts, cosmology, comparative religion, mathematical structure of Quranic stories, the lives of the prophets, evolution of Islamic Sciences and the uniqueness of the Arabic language'.[70]

Combining scripture and the fantastic, Islamic science fiction has roots that can be traced back to medieval writings. They include stories of Muhammad's ascension to heaven and al-Maʿarri's *Epistle of Forgiveness*, which resembles Dante's *Divine Comedy*.[71] Riad Agha himself justified his support for science fiction with reference to the Arab literary heritage. Besides al-Maʿarri, the minister mentioned philosophical texts by Ibn Tufayl and al-Farabi as well as the *One Thousand and One Nights*.[72] Nevertheless, works such as *The Ultimate Revelations* were still profoundly modern, especially in their focus on science and technology. In contrast to medieval utopias, they were also more clearly situated on a timeline marked by historical progress. Such visions of the future that were both high-tech and Islamic appeared in the late Ottoman Empire and partly responded to threats from European powers. A novel by Mustafa Nazım from 1915 was entitled *Envisioning Progress and Islamic Civilization in a Dream*. After the Ottoman defeats in the Balkan Wars, the author imagined a union of African and Asian states. The setting is a futuristic Istanbul during the twenty-third century, complete with skyscrapers and electric tramways.[73]

After the collapse of the Ottoman Empire, its Turkish successor state sought to replace a pan-Islamic utopia with a national one. The adoption of a Latin-based alphabet for the Turkish language further cut off young people from much of Ottoman literature. Nonetheless, Kemal Atatürk's government sponsored some highly speculative writing. Seeking to give the nation a new history, the founder of the Turkish Republic himself read widely about ancient civilizations, both real and fictional. He ordered the translation of books on the legendary lost continent Mu by the British occult writer James Churchward. Atatürk also requested his ambassador in Mexico to study similarities between Turkish and Mayan. For discovering that the words for 'hill' in both languages were almost the same (*tepe* and *tepek*), he even gave the diplomat the surname Mayatepek.[74]

70 Islam Online, 'Book Review'.
71 Cooperson, 'Remembering', 172.
72 Riyāḍ Aghā, 'Al-khayāl al-ʿīlmī', 4.
73 Mignon, 'Entre quête scientifique'.
74 Foss, 'Kemal Atatürk', 829. Toprak, *Darwin'den Dersim'e Cumhuriyet*, 484–529.

Kemalist interests in civilizations distant from Mecca and Medina contributed to a setback for Islamic science fiction in Turkey. However, by the 1980s, the subgenre had re-emerged together with Islamism. A prominent representative was Ali Nar, who was ironically the product of a religious education system controlled by the secular state. Born in 1941, he had studied at an İmam Hatip school in Erzurum. After completing his exams at another Islamic institution in Istanbul, he worked as a teacher in religious schools himself. In 1988, he published a novel titled *Space Farmers*, which was set fifty years into the future. The hero of the story is the astronaut Hasan II who has been chosen by the Space Commission of the Islamic Union in Aleppo for a mission. The union's space programme was itself created by Müsebbih, an ideal-type modern Islamic scholar and scientist. The aim is to explore other planets for their agricultural potential. However, for Hasan II, the mission has a mystical dimension as well. The protagonist compares his task to an ascension to heaven, mirroring Muhammad's.[75]

Like Mustafa Nazım at the beginning of the century, Ali Nar dreamed of Muslim dominance. His Islamic Union reigns supreme, and Islamic republics stretch from Azerbaijan to the Philippines and South Africa. The Western world is weakened by internal disorder, and only a few Jews are left in the desert. In his mission, Hasan II is joined by twenty-four other Muslim space farmers from Afghanistan, Malaysia, Nigeria, Turkey and other countries. They use Arabic as their official language, with simultaneous translations into others. They also carry watches that show prayer times and perform ablutions with purified sand. Their main spaceship has ninety-nine sections, corresponding to the number of God's names. Further Islamic references are scattered throughout the novel, and Qur'anic verses appear at the beginning of almost every chapter.[76]

In imagining an Islamic future, Ali Nar also drew on the Ottoman past. After exploring Venus, Mars and Jupiter, Hasan II discovers the fortieth planetary system. He names its star Sun II and its middle planet World II. He finds it to be Earthlike and begins his agricultural research programme, exposing plants and animals to the new environment. By accident, he encounters Tursin, an elderly man wearing Ottoman dress and speaking old Turkish. It turns out that Tursin is a former companion of the Ottoman admiral and geographer Piri Reis who had disappeared from Earth and ended up on World II. Tursin, however, believes himself to be on the mythological mount Qaf, searching for the benevolent bird

75 Szyska, 'On Utopian Writing', 115–18.
76 Nar, *Uzay Çiftçileri*.

Simurgh. Because of the relativity of time and space, Tursin is ageing slower than people on Earth. At the end of the novel, Hassan II returns to Earth, where he is celebrated. Yet, he is almost killed by a Western soccer player, which results in an international dispute.[77]

Despite their incorporation of religious heritage, authors like Ali Nar struggled to be taken seriously by their literary establishments. The Egyptian realist author Naguib Mahfouz once dismissed the entire genre of science fiction as 'empty talk' that 'lacked depth' and was 'useless'.[78] Jamshed Akhtar explained that his novel was 'self-published as no major publisher accepted it'. 'It was a stupid move' he regretted. 'Though the book received good reviews in numerous newspapers of India and UAE, my inept handling of its distribution, ruined the book's chances of creating large scale exposure of the research.'[79] The Turkish postmodern writer Orhan Pamuk paid attention to the subgenre of Islamic science fiction, but was also aware of its difficulties. In his novel *Snow*, the protagonist Necip is himself writing science fiction. Set in the year 3579, Necip's novel within a novel describes a red planet named Gazzali. Its people live a rich and easy life, but materialism does not bring them spiritual satisfaction. Anxious about God and existence, a number of Gazzalians set up the Islamic Lycée for the Study of Science and Oration.[80] A later conversation includes the acknowledgement that 'if you said I was writing an Islamist science-fiction novel', Western readers would 'just laugh'.[81]

Lacking recognition by many peers and publishers, authors of Islamic science fiction were slow to establish themselves. It took Jamshed Akhtar fourteen years to publish a second book, and this time it was non-fiction. It explores similar themes, as the title suggests: *In Search of Our Origins: How the Quran Can Help in Scientific Research*.[82] In the meantime, Akhtar's peers persisted in their writing and their quest for acceptance. They did so also in other countries with a long history of repressing Islamist voices, such as Egypt. One of the most important representatives of the subgenre was the ophthalmologist Hosam Elzembely. His father Abdelhamid was a prominent literary critic who had promoted what he called 'moderation'. This word, in Arabic *wasaṭīyah*, was taken from a medieval Qur'anic commentary by al-Tabari. According to Elzembely, his father's project

77 Szyska, 'On Utopian Writing', 119–20.
78 'Ayyād, 'Adab al-khayāl al-'ilmī', 65.
79 Akhtar, 'The Background'.
80 Pamuk, *Snow*, 106.
81 Ibid., 419.
82 Akhtar, *In Search*.

was thus rooted in the 'Arab-Islamic civilization'. As a form of 'authentic Arab thought', he claimed, moderation was opposed by the 'leftist' proponents of 'Westernization' and secularism who were dominating the Egyptian cultural bureaucracy. Elzembely continued his father's legacy through science fiction. In 2001, he published three novels with the support of the ageing and ailing Abdelhamid: *The Half-Humans*, *The Wondrous Planet* and *America 2030*.[83]

Elzembely was highly ambitious in his vision for the Muslim world. *The Wondrous Planet* was dedicated to 'every Arab-Islamic leader', urging them 'to realize their peoples' dream of Arab-Islamic unity'. The text was equally dedicated to 'every young man and woman in our Arab-Islamic world'. The author called upon them 'to realize the dream of the renaissance of the Arab-Islamic civilization'. His books offered a blueprint. *The Half-Humans* and *The Wondrous Planet* centred on a 'United Islamic State'. Its territory, subdivided into regions like the Arabian Peninsula and North Africa, stretches from Nouakchott to Baku, Tehran and Islamabad. Scientists communicate across these expanses via the United Islamic Computerized Network (UICN).[84]

In his imagination of an Islamic future, Elzembely also drew heavily on his region's history and heritage. The author envisioned the United Islamic State as a republic headed by a president rather than as a caliphate. Yet, in *The Wondrous Planet*, the state's most advanced spaceship is called *al-Qadisiyah*. This name refers to the location of a Muslim victory against the Sassanians in the year 636. One of the protagonists is called Salah al-Din, perhaps after the twelfth-century sultan Saladin.[85] In *The Half-Humans*, another spacecraft is called *al-Buraq*, after the creature that brought Muhammad to Jerusalem and into heaven.[86] His other novel, *America 2030*, was dedicated to the 'people of the past Arab-Islamic civilization with sincere love and respect and appreciation'. The volume was equally devoted to the 'people of the next Arab-Islamic civilization, which I see on the horizon, with sincere pride'.[87]

Publishing his books in the same year as the September 11 attacks, Elzembely hoped to avoid the trope of the 'clash of civilizations'. Instead, in his dedication to *The Wondrous Planet*, he called upon the peoples of 'Earth, the Moon, and Mars' to look at the 'Arab-Islamic civilization from the perspective of the

83 Al-Miṣrīyūn, 'Najl rāʾid al-wasaṭīyah al-ʿArabīyah'. On Elzembely's work, see also Aysha, 'Better Late'.

84 Al-Zambīlī, *Al-kawkab al-ʿajīb*, 3, 12, 91.

85 Ibid., 11, 126–27.

86 Al-Zambīlī, *Anṣāf al-bashar*, 45.

87 Al-Zambīlī, *Amrīkā 2030*, 3.

dialogue of civilizations'.[88] He thus echoed a call for civilizational exchange made by the Iranian president Mohammad Khatami. Nevertheless, in *America 2030*, Elzembely put the Muslim world in opposition to the Anglophone West. Subtitled *The Story of the World's Collapse*, the novel describes a devastating nuclear war. On the one side is the dictatorial American Empire, which is joined by Australia and Britain. On the other side is the Arab-Islamic Union, which allies itself with other parts of the globe in an attempt to resist American domination. As nuclear winter threatens all life on Earth, the spaceship *Yarmouk* sets out on a 'voyage of hope', to 'establish a virtuous society somewhere in the universe'. The name *Yarmouk* refers to the site of another caliphal victory in the year 636, this time against the Byzantines.[89]

While Islamic history and politics inspired Elzembely, they do not appear to have limited his imagination. Earthly empires were not the only ingredients of his science fiction. Especially strange, and partly based on his medical knowledge, was his depiction of extraterrestrial life. As the title suggests, *The Half-Humans* features a hybrid species between people from Earth and from an extrasolar planet. These creatures, which Muslim astronauts discover on Saturn's moon Titan, depend on an immunosuppressive drug against 'genetic rejection'.[90] *The Wondrous Planet* bears the subtitle *First Dialogue with an Intelligent Virus*. This novel was inspired by Elzembely's doctoral research on the herpes virus, which he considered 'so cunning'.[91] In his imagination, good herpes viruses from the planet S 60 arrive as refugees on Earth. After establishing contact with the scientist Salah al-Din, they convince the United Islamic State to send the starship *al-Qadisiyah* to their planet and 'liberate' it from their evil counterparts. The good viruses are thus able to return home and send greetings 'to Islam, to the religion of peace, love, safety, and civilization'.[92]

Although not a full-time writer, Elzembely became an important figure in the promotion of Arabic science fiction in general. Already as a high school student in London during the 1980s, he had experienced *Star Wars*, the video game *Space Invaders*[93] and British fascination with the genre in general. 'That planted the first seed of love in me', he said. Back in Egypt, his father introduced him to the older authors Nehad Sherif and Mustafa Mahmoud. In 2001, just before

88 Al-Zambīlī, *Al-kawkab al-ʿajīb*, 3.
89 Al-Zambīlī, *Amrīkā 2030*, 154.
90 Al-Zambīlī, *Anṣāf al-bashar*, 36–37.
91 Bhatia, 'An Interview'.
92 Al-Zambīlī, *Al-kawkab al-ʿajīb*, 126, 137.
93 Bhatia, 'An Interview'.

completing his medical education, Elzembely became a member of the Writers' Union of Egypt. Eleven years later, after the revolution against President Hosni Mubarak, Elzembely founded the Egyptian Society for Science Fiction. His ophthalmological clinic in Cairo served as headquarters. The group organized cultural salons with various writers. In addition, it held short story competitions and published anthologies under the title *Sun of Tomorrow*.[94]

Unlike Taleb Omran in Syria, Hosam Elzembely enjoyed hardly any government support for his promotion of science fiction. In an interview in 2018, he claimed that his country had 'only about ten' active writers like himself and an equal number of critics. One of the reasons was that few authors combined the three necessary characteristics: 'strong scientific foundation, literary talent, and love for this genre'. He added that 'our society, media, and governments do not pay much attention to this kind of literature'. He thus urged that there were 'national' reasons to embrace the genre. It 'accelerates the process of enlightenment' and 'inspires scientists with more ideas'. Seeking like-minded people, he participated in the Asia-Pacific Science Fiction Convention in Beijing in 2018 (Figure 3). There, he also led Egypt to become a founding member of the Asia Science Fiction Association.[95]

The only other Muslim-majority founding member of this association was Malaysia. Despite being less populous than Egypt and Turkey, the country has also been a major producer of Islamic literature. The constitution of the

Figure 3 Hosam Elzembely speaking at the Asia-Pacific Science Fiction Convention in Beijing in 2018. Courtesy of APSFcon, picture taken by Wu Ying and Wang Zhitao.

[94] Qualey, 'The Director'.
[95] Al-Jammāl, 'Ḥusām al-Zambīlī'.

federation made Islam the official religion, even as it sought to preserve Malaysia as a secular state. After race riots in 1969, Prime Minister Abdul Razak Hussein launched the New Economic Policy in an attempt to increase the wealth of Malay Muslims. In the context of rising Islamic movements globally, the government and civil society also promoted the Malay language and Muslim culture. In 1975, the Islamic affairs section of the prime minister's office organized a competition for short stories that incorporated Islamic values. In the following years, the Federation of Malaysian Islamic Writers was established, and a conference on 'Islam as a Source of Arts' took place in Kuala Terengganu. Furthermore, the Institute of Language and Literature headquartered in Kuala Lumpur as well as student associations organized Islamic poetry nights.[96]

Promotion of Malay literature also encompassed speculative fiction. A prominent representative of the umbrella genre was Mohd Faizal Musa, who used the pen name Faisal Tehrani. Born in Kuala Lumpur in 1974, he had begun taking lessons organized by the Institute of Language and Literature at the age of sixteen. He also studied at Klang Islamic College in Selangor and earned a bachelor's degree in Islamic studies at the University of Malaya. At the beginning of his career, he was more interested in sex, money and fame than religion, however. 'When I was young, I wanted to be a writer for the wrong reasons', he later confessed. 'I wanted to show off to my friends.' In his early years, he wrote erotic short stories. His income allowed him to be the first among his classmates to possess a mobile phone.[97]

During the late 1990s, Tehrani moved from sexual to social and political topics. 'I wanted to become a responsible writer', he explained. He met the author and activist A. Samad Said who gave him many books by 'writers from countries that are oppressed'. Tehrani was also inspired by the 'fire and courage' of Shahnon Ahmad, another prominent writer and a member of the Malaysian Islamic Party. Both figures advised Tehrani to analyse 'people' and 'issues'. He found the latter in the state of Kedah, where the government took over land for a prawn breeding project. 'The villagers told me stories different from what was reported in the media', explained Tehrani. 'They were oppressed.' This experience inspired him to write a novel about the confiscation of farmers' land by a rich person. His next novel focused on the student movement, demonstrations, human rights and oppression. Many readers felt that his work

96 Tahir, *Modern Malay Literary Culture*, 65; Musa, 'Exploration'.
97 S., 'Writing'.

reminded them of Anwar Ibrahim, whose dismissal as deputy prime minister and arrest had provoked mass protests at the time.[98]

After the attacks of September 11, Tehrani turned from intra-Malaysian oppression to Western colonization. In 2002, he published the novel *1515*. As the title suggests, it is set in the early sixteenth century. However, in Tehrani's alternative vision of history, forces led by Nyemah Mulya drive away the Portuguese who seek to capture Malacca. After liberating Goa, the female warrior marries a Chinese Muslim in Jeddah. With the help of Turkey and Spain, the Malays conquer Lisbon in 1515. They rule Portugal until 1580 and leave traces there that last until the present. In an article in 2010, Salleh Yaapar, a scholar at Universiti Sains Malaysia, considered the novel as 'a unique text within contemporary Malay literature'. 'Among recent novels in Malaysia it is one of the most difficult readings, but probably the most refreshing and rewarding one.'[99] Using an expression from *Star Wars*, which has also been appropriated by other scholars of postcolonial literatures,[100] Yaapar entitled his article 'The Empire Strikes Back'.

From alternate history, Tehrani moved seamlessly to science fiction. Two years after the publication of *1515*, he published a novel with a similar title: *1511 Hijri (Combat)*. It is set in the early sixteenth century of the Islamic lunar calendar, that is, in the late twenty-first century. Tehrani tells the story of a high-tech war between young Muslims on the one side and America and Israel on the other. An evil American president tries to invade Mecca and Medina in order to destroy the Kaaba and seize Muhammad's body. Muslims under the pious general Syarifah Nusaybah fight back with cyborgs, biobots, robots and other advanced technologies named *Mikraj* and *Ababil*. These names refer to Muhammad's ascension to heaven and miraculous birds in the Qur'an respectively.[101] Fulfilling 'the fantasy of many young readers', as the author claimed, the novel has Muslim soldiers take over the White House.[102]

Tehrani's visions of the Muslim past and future earned him not just fans. He also faced accusations of being an extremist and ultra-nationalist. He rejected such allegations, while defending the importance of Islam and the Malay language in this work. He found it hard to avoid writing about his faith. 'It is just inside me.' He claimed to focus on human rights, which he considered 'part of religion', and on 'oppression'. With reference to *1511 Hijri (Combat)*, he explained, 'A certain

98 Ibid.
99 Yaapar, 'The Empire Strikes Back'.
100 Ashcroft et al., *The Empire*.
101 Tehrani, *1511H*.
102 S., 'Writing'.

Western power is oppressing many countries, so I speak against it.' He mentioned the American wars in Iraq and earlier in Vietnam and Korea. Tehrani did not want to be seen as anti-Western per se, however. 'One day, when China becomes a super power and starts oppressing other countries, I will write about it.' As for Malay, he stressed its status as his country's official language. Therefore, it should be used in the instruction of science and mathematics.[103]

Given that Tehrani's views were considered extreme, it comes as no surprise that he was met with intolerance. His pen name identified him as 'Faisal of Tehran'. The author insisted that this name did not reflect any leaning towards Shia Islam, which was banned in Malaysia. Instead, at the beginning of his career, a foreign-sounding name promised attention from publishers. However, he did develop interests in the oppressed Shia community of his home country. In 2008, he published a passion play about the murder of Muhammad's grandson Husayn under the title *Karbala*. Perceived sympathies for the Shia led to the banning of this and other works as well as to threats of arrest and death.[104]

Tehrani's controversial status did not deter other Malaysian authors from following in his footsteps, at least when it came to producing Islamic science fiction. A similar but more ambitious effort in Islamic world-building was undertaken by Azrul Jaini from Sarawak. Like Tehrani, he was interested in the politics of the wider Muslim world. As a teenager, 'Palestinian issues' caught his attention. His first manuscript, which a local publisher rejected, was a novel about the Arab–Israeli war in 1973. In addition to conflicts on Earth, Jaini liked delving into battles on imaginary worlds. A *Star Wars* fan since the age of nine, he also enjoyed playing the video games *Warcraft II* and *III*, *StarCraft* and *MechCommander*. Together with a fellow student on a university foundation programme in 2003, he developed the idea of a game focused on a Muslim colony in space. His friend, who was planning to study software engineering in Japan, told him: 'You write the story, I'll make the game.'[105]

Azrul Jaini's friend did move to Japan, but abandoned the idea of an Islamic science fiction game. This left Jaini pursuing his dream in the form of a novel. He drafted it during his second year of study at the International Islamic University Malaysia. Coincidentally, in 2007, the publisher PTS was looking for works of science fiction that were 'Muslim in nature'.[106] Immediately convinced,

[103] Ibid.
[104] Wieringa, 'A *Ta'ziya*'.
[105] Azrul Jaini, via Facebook Messenger, 2018.
[106] Lent, *Asian Comics*, 165.

PTS issued Jaini's book under the title *Galaxy of the Virtuous*. Like Tehrani's military fiction, the novel involves an epic conflict between good and evil, but one encompassing numerous planets. Galactic Muslims led by the young caliph Zulqarnain struggle against forces of the tyrannical Cybernetic Cyborg Empire commanded by General Furious. Also part of his universe are Zionists, pirates and descendants of Greeks and Germans who together form the Athens Colony. Accompanying the novel are numerous entries in Azrul Jaini's blog *Islamic Sci-fi*, which provide details about his imaginary worlds.[107]

Azrul Jaini also drew heavily on the Qur'an in his world-building. Zulqarnain, literarily 'he of the two horns', is named after a figure commonly identified with Alexander the Great. Planets in his universe carry the names and numbers of different chapters. They include Anfal An-8, Furqan Fr-25 and Hadid Hd-57. Aadiyat Ad-100 also refers to a surah and means 'The Chargers'. However, in Jaini's universe, it is the name of a class of spacecraft that carries up to twenty mujahidin into battle.[108] The name Ababil appears in *Galaxy of the Virtuous* too, this time referring to a type of fighter used in fleet defence. It can operate from a Saifullah carrier, Asadullah cruiser, space platform or base.[109] Saifullah means 'God's sword' and Asadullah 'God's lion'. TAQWA, that is, 'piety', appears as an algorithm.[110]

Not just scripture, but also history served as a source of Azrul Jaini's imagination. In the *Galaxy of the Virtuous*, the reader encounters a Reconquista Confederation, named after the medieval Christian expansion on the Iberian Peninsula. The Umayyad caliph ʿUmar ibn ʿAbd al-ʿAziz and Saladin are also referred to.[111] Mujahidin are divided into 'conventional', 'elite' and 'anti-terror units'. They are armed with ion swords and Nur rifles, meaning 'light'.[112] The Zion militia, in contrast, carry Uzi-92 guns, and the pirates AK-470 rifles.[113] These weapons appear as futuristic versions of submachine guns and assault rifles developed in Israel and the Soviet Union respectively. The Athens Colony is defended by a Phalanx Infantry Regiment and a Volkssturm battalion, which was named after a militia set up during the last months of World War II.

Finally, *Galaxy of the Virtuous* was not just part of wider Islamic and global science fiction. The novel also stood in the tradition of Malay literature

107 Jaini, *Galaksi Muhsinin*; 'Saifaiislami'.
108 Jaini, '[GM] Aadiyat Ad-100'.
109 Jaini, 'Pejuang Angkasa Galaksi Muhsinin: Ababil'.
110 Jaini, '[ESC] Algoritma TAQWA (3)'.
111 Jaini, '[GM] Hologram Hijrah'.
112 Jaini, '[GM] Mujahidin Galaksi Muhsinin'.
113 Jaini, 'Cerpen Latar'; Jaini, 'Siapakah Liga Lanun?'

specifically. Jaini's novel includes examples of the centuries-old poetic form of pantun, quatrains with rhymes and a fixed rhythm. A dialogue in chapter twenty, entitled 'The Caliph and the Emperor', contained the following stanza: *Kutawarkan Islam engkau bertingkah,/ Angkuhmu melangit hatimu lengah,/ Khabarmu berkuasa semesta dijamah,/ Pendekar Nusantara tampil menggugah!*[114] The lines translate as: 'I offered you Islam, but haughty you are/ Your pride sky-high, yet your heart is heedless/ seeming powerful, you are swallowing the universe/ The pendekar of the archipelago stands in your way!' Pendekar is a Malay word for a master of martial arts, and Jaini's caliph carries a *kris*. This advanced lightsabre was named after a traditional curved blade from Southeast Asia.

Depictions of mujahidin as heroes in a cosmic battle between good and evil were not far from the ideologies of violent extremists. Some science fiction writers, like Faisal Tehrani, shared with many jihadists a commitment to struggling against colonialism and oppression. However, creators of Islamic science fiction were not necessarily narrow-minded. Anti-American or anti-Zionist works might be uncomfortable, if not alarming, to those worrying about the violence associated with such thought. Yet, like jihadi culture,[115] they are worth studying. More than that, any novelists drawing on sacred texts, even if they had learned them by rote, also demonstrate how much Islamic traditions were able to support creativity and the imagination in modern times.

Scientific imagination

Scripture and history were not the only sources of Islamic science fiction, let alone of all science fiction by Muslims. Especially when it comes to works about extraterrestrial life, research in the physical and biological sciences was perhaps as important as religion. Some Muslim-majority countries and their diasporas were heavily involved in the advancement of such studies. Kazakhstan, for instance, played not just a leading role in astronautics through its Baikonur Cosmodrome, but was also a pioneer in the study of life in the universe. The Almaty-based astronomer Gavriil Tikhov coined the term 'astrobotany' in 1945. In addition, he was among the earliest promoters of the word 'astrobiology'.[116]

[114] Jaini, *Galaksi Muhsinin*, 268.
[115] Hegghammer, 'Introduction'.
[116] Briot, 'The Creator'.

Many space researchers in Kazakhstan, including Tikhov, came from elsewhere in the Soviet Union and did not identify as Muslims. Nevertheless, the Baikonur Cosmodrome nurtured dreams of life in space for many Muslims and fulfilled them for some. In the late 1980s, Mohammed Fares from Syria, Musa Manarov from Azerbaijan and Abdul Ahad Mohmand from Afghanistan all left Earth on Soviet rockets. During the next decade, the Kazakhs Toktar Aubakirov and Talgat Musabayev followed. In 2006, the Iranian-American engineer Anousheh Ansari too departed from Baikonur, becoming the first female space tourist and the first Muslim woman in space. 'Our Universe is a place of infinite wonders', she wrote. 'As a young girl in Iran, I marveled at the stars in the beautiful night skies and dreamed of flying into space one day, and I know that many share this dream with me.'[117]

Space research in Kazakhstan relied on the vast human and material resources of the Soviet state, which was secular, but accommodating of Islam.[118] However, even in the Islamic Republic of Pakistan, some people were able to overcome educational and economic challenges and pursue a career in astrobiology. One of them was Nozair Khawaja from Wazirabad, a town known mainly for the production of cutlery. After graduating from a public high school, he studied at Punjab University in Lahore. His parents struggled to pay for his education, and after completing his degree in space sciences, he returned to Wazirabad to support them. He taught mathematics and physics in local schools for eight years before earning a master's degree in astronomy at the University of Turku in Finland in 2011. He wrote his thesis on the calibration of COSIMA, the Cometary Secondary Ion Mass Analyser onboard the *Rosetta* spacecraft. This instrument studied dust particles emitted by the comet 67P/Churyumov–Gerasimenko.[119] The body itself had been discovered in 1969 on a photographic plate exposed at an observatory in Kazakhstan.[120]

From Finland, Khawaja moved to Germany, while keeping his connections to Pakistan alive. In 2016, he completed a doctoral dissertation at Heidelberg University on organic compounds in the rings of Saturn.[121] This time, he used data collected by the Cosmic Dust Analyzer onboard the *Cassini* orbiter. He remained in Germany as a postdoctoral researcher on the project Habitat-OASIS (Habitability of Oceans and Aqueous Systems on Icy Satellites). On

117 Anousheh Ansari, 'Space', 103.
118 Tasar, *Soviet*.
119 Khan, 'Pakistan's Man'.
120 Kronk and Meyer, *Cometography*, 241.
121 Khawaja, 'Organic Compounds'.

the side, he founded the Astrobiology Network of Pakistan in 2017. This group sought to spread awareness about the discipline by organizing lectures and outreach events. Khawaja was especially quick in reaching people in his home province, where the network established a Lahore chapter and collaborated with the Khwarizmi Science Society. One of the network's advisers was Mansoor Ahmed, a Pakistani-American astrophysicist who had worked on the Hubble and James Web space telescopes.[122]

Despite his great ambitions, Nozair Khawaja was cautious in his imagination of extraterrestrial life. 'So far, we don't have any clear evidence of any form of alien life', he told the Pakistani magazine *Eos* in 2018. The possible discovery that he considered most 'realistic' and of most concern to scientists was one of microbial life. Though potentially not as dangerous as the encounter with an 'alien civilisation', contact with microbes was challenging. 'As far as the current space exploration is concerned, the scientific community is very sensitive and taking necessary steps for planetary protection to avoid any type of contamination from Earth to other planets and vice versa', he explained.[123] In order to prevent the transfer of microorganisms to Saturn's potentially habitable moons, the *Cassini* spacecraft itself had been destroyed through a controlled fall into the planet's atmosphere in 2017.[124]

Khawaja's investigations, though at the cutting edge, were widely recognized as part of mainstream science. Funding for his research in Germany came from both the Deutsche Forschungsgemeinschaft and the European Research Council. Between 2016 and 2019, he published three articles in *Science*, the peer-reviewed journal of the American Association for the Advancement of Science.[125] The National Aeronautics and Space Administration bestowed a Group Achievement Award upon him and other members of the Cassini Cosmic Dust Analyzer Team. Signing the certificate in 2018, NASA Administrator Jim Bridenstine recognized 'exceptional team performance and ground breaking discoveries in characterizing sources, sinks, and dynamics of Saturn's dust environment'. During the same year, the Pakistani researcher also received a Horneck-Brack Award from the European Astrobiology Network Association.

In contrast to Khawaja's studies, other inquiries were often considered fringe. However, these kinds of research were sometimes hard to distinguish and their

[122] Khan, 'Pakistan's Man'.
[123] Ibid.
[124] Blaber and Verrecchia, 'Cassini-Huygens'.
[125] Altobelli et al., 'Flux'; Hsu et al., 'In situ Collection'; Buratti et al., 'Close Cassini Flybys'.

categorization contested. In the twenty-first century, Fawaz Alshammari from Saudi Arabia, for instance, published in both the *International Journal of Astrobiology* and the more controversial *Journal of Cosmology*. In the former, he concluded that bacteria ejected from Earth inside rocks could be transferred to other planets.[126] In the latter publication, he suggested that microbes were 'currently' arriving on Earth from space.[127] Sidra Ramzan, a member of the Astrobiology Network of Pakistan, found that some people made fun of her field and dismissed it as 'pseudoscience'. She attributed this behaviour to their lack of knowledge about astronomy in general.[128] Yet, the historian Michael Gordin writes that 'No one in the history of the world has ever self-identified as a pseudoscientist.'[129] The more speculative the research is, the closer it is also to science fiction. Research about extraterrestrial life was among the most speculative endeavours.

It is thus not surprising that even some professional astrobiologists were interested in the supernatural as much as the natural. One of them was Fariha Hasan, an associate professor at Quaid-i-Azam University in Islamabad and an adviser to the Astrobiology Network of Pakistan. 'Being a Muslim we know life won't be possible with just chemical combinations only until a Superior source adds the soul into it', she explained. 'We can try to initiate a chemical reaction in a flask, take the required elements of life like Carbon, Hydrogen, Nitrogen, Oxygen, Phosphorus, Sulphur that we call CHNOPS in Astrobiology.' However, 'even after mixing all these elements, we can't make a life'. She asserted, 'We need a force and that force is a supernatural being (Allah).'[130]

To avoid excluding influential contributors to the debate about extraterrestrial life, I employ a broad view of science and its culture. I am thus using the term 'scientific imagination' to refer to products as different as science fiction films, journal articles in astrobiology and books about UFOs. The 'scientific imagination' was not confined to people who would have self-identified as 'scientists'.[131] Medieval philosophers possessed a 'scientific imagination' too, especially when it came to the idea of the plurality of worlds.[132] The same goes for writers, such as H. G. Wells, the author of *The War of the Worlds*.[133] The word 'scientific

[126] Wainwright et al., 'Bacteria'.
[127] Wainwright et al., 'Are Microbes'.
[128] Sidra Ramzan, via Facebook Messenger, 2019.
[129] Gordin, *The Pseudoscience Wars*, 1.
[130] Maqsood, 'A Talk'.
[131] Holton, *The Scientific Imagination*.
[132] Grant, 'Scientific Imagination'.
[133] Wagar, 'H. G. Wells'.

imagination' is also a literal translation of the Arabic term for science fiction, *khayāl ʿilmī*. Drawing on the Arabic language, Persian speakers called the genre *ʿilmī takhayyulī* or 'scientific-imaginative'. (In Turkish, a similar expression, *hayal-bilim*, was discussed, but abandoned in favour of *bilim kurgu.*)[134]

By investigating the scientific imagination in various forms, my book is distinct from other histories of science fiction in Muslim-majority countries. Scholarship on Arabic or Urdu science fiction, for instance, has mostly focused on short stories, novels, plays and films.[135] I have greatly benefited from this work. At the same time, I am studying not just literary and film history, but also the history of science, and thus intellectual history in a broader sense. I am equally interested in products of scientific and journalistic research, whether mainstream or fringe, as I am in depictions that are explicitly fictional. The protagonists of this book therefore comprise professional scientists and journalists alongside writers and visual artists. I do not seek to judge the plausibility of their different imaginations. Instead, I am trying to understand the production of different theories and images within their historical contexts.

Rather than stressing distance between different kinds of writing and visualization, I am especially interested in cross-fertilizations between different creators and genres. Muslim-majority countries were the sites of artistic astrobiology and astrobiological art, for instance. The Astrobiology Network of Pakistan organized competitions of sketches and paintings about any aspect of life in the universe. One of its members, Rabeea Rasheed, also asked her pupils at the Lahore Grammar School to design their own rover for a mission to Mars.[136] Elsewhere in the Muslim world, extreme environments inspired artists too. In 2010, Mount Merapi in Java erupted, covering more than a thousand hectares of land with ash, rock and mud. 'It looked very much like a desolate extraterrestrial world', said the Belgian researcher Angelo Vermeulen, who was invited by an Indonesian art collective. Plants would only grow on top of the volcanic ash years afterwards, as fertilizing nitrogen slowly returns. Vermeulen sought to accelerate this process through what was reminiscent of terraforming, the making of a world hospitable for Earthlike life. Together with Indonesian artists and scientists from Gadjah Mada University in Yogyakarta, he designed a seven-metre tower on which to grow legumes with the help of nitrogen-fixing bacteria. The pyramidal

[134] Işiklar Koçak and Aydın, 'Science Fiction', 33.

[135] Ian Campbell, *Arabic Science Fiction*; Barbaro, *La fantascienza*; Boutz, 'Generic Cues'; Aḥmad ʿAlī, ʿAbʿād al-zamān'; Eqbal, 'Urdu Mein Science Fiction Ki Riwayat'.

[136] Rasheed, 'Astrobiology'.

structure was intended to be not just a field laboratory, but also an 'artistic monument' and a 'symbol of hope for villagers keen to see a vegetative rebirth'.[137]

Like terraforming itself, the Mount Merapi project was controversial. The hypothetical process was 'a touchy subject in the astrobiology community', Vermeulen acknowledged. 'It's pretty much the opposite of the notion of investigating precious life in other places – you're basically rejecting a location's nature to change it to what you know.' While careful not to promote such 'Earth-shaping', the Belgian researcher sought to discuss it. He described the process as 'a mirror on human society'. 'It's essentially an extreme form of colonization, and so this can reflect on errors made in the past with colonialism', he explained.[138] One of his own mistakes, he admitted, was that he had not involved local villagers in the planning and design stages from the start. As a result, he had raised suspicions that he was working with the Indonesian government to remove farmers from their lands and to introduce new plants.[139]

Colonization was a shared experience for many people across the Muslim world. This raises the question to what extent science fiction, with its strong connections to the colonial encounter, was similar from Morocco to Indonesia and among Muslim diasporas elsewhere. Many authors seem to share views of a conflict between the global South and North. A work comparable to Taleb Omran's *Dark Times* was *Mirrors of Dead Hours* by the Tunisian Mustapha Kilani. Set in the year 2725, it imagines a totalitarian state that has imprisoned the people of the South. Because of the nuclear waste deposited by the countries of the North, the air in the Third World-like space is too polluted to breathe. This makes the people of the South dependent on oxygen bottles provided by the state and on gas masks that silence them.[140]

Not only the exaggeration, but also the inversion, of relations between the global South and North was a frequent fantasy. The novel *The Blue Flood* by the Moroccan author Abdessalam Bakkali, for instance, features an 'ideal city' deep in the Sahara, in which scientists and a powerful artificial intelligence pursue research. To give another example, Abdelaziz Belkhodja, also from Tunisia, imagined a future Republic of Carthage in his novel *The Return of the Elephant*. As Western powers suffer from economic crises and collapse, North Africa is witnessing a 'unique technological development' based on renewable energy.

137 Dance, 'Terraforming'.
138 Choi, 'Artistic Astrobiology'.
139 Dance, 'Terraforming', 4235.
140 Ayed, 'La science-fiction arabe', 32, 36.

Westerners thus come to Carthage in search of jobs, and a young American protagonist gains the 'golden opportunity' to study there.[141]

Several authors explicitly conceived of their writing as a form of resistance. In 1990, Taleb Omran met Naguib Mahfouz, who had recently won the Nobel Prize in Literature. Although the Egyptian had been dismissive of science fiction earlier, he encouraged the Syrian. Omran despaired over the difficulty of achieving 'true peace' as 'as a single superpower is on its way to swallow everything'. 'But we will resist the might with creativity and dream', Mahfouz responded. 'Follow your dreams of peaceful worlds among the planets.'[142] In 2019, Emad El-Din Aysha, an active member of the Egyptian Society for Science Fiction, recorded 'the sci-fi contribution to Arabic resistance literature'. In the socialist *Monthly Review*, he emphasized that 'science fiction has become a *refuge* from the concerns of realist literature and the debilitating problems of everyday Arab life'. The genre 'is the one way you can talk about Palestine quite directly, especially in a country like Egypt. It is the one place in which you can fight back'.[143]

Whether they used the term 'resistance' or not, what many authors from across the Muslim world shared was a reaction to domination by Western powers. Working in the spheres of science and culture, they complemented the efforts of politicians to achieve independence for their countries. However, their struggle was not simply one of the formerly colonized against formations of empire. Compared to indigenous people from Australia or Canada, natives of Egypt or Syria could easily see themselves not just as victims of, but also as heirs to, vast empires. By naming spaceships *al-Qadisiyah* and *Yarmouk*, Hosam Elzembely celebrated early Islamic expansion at the same time as he was critical of American imperialism. The Abbasid and Ottoman empires also provided plenty of material for world-building, just as ancient Rome served as the model for *Star Trek*'s Romulans.

Because science fiction has become such a massive genre, it would be hard to grasp all its postcolonial elements. Between 1967 and 2016 alone, the librarian Hal Hall indexed around 80,000 book reviews and 110,000 book-length studies, articles and news notes about science fiction and fantasy across the world. He also advised the website *Islam and Science Fiction*, which was run by the Pakistani data scientist Muhammad Aurangzeb Ahmad.[144] Still, even

141 ʿAyyād, 'Adab al-khayāl al-ʿilmī', 18, 21. See also Ian Campbell, 'False Gods'.
142 ʿUmrān, 'Maʿa Najīb Maḥfūẓ', 7.
143 Aysha, 'In Protest'.
144 Muhammad Aurangzeb Ahmad, 'Islam Sci-Fi Interview with Hal. W. Hall'.

with powerful search and data analytics tools, a comprehensive account of all science fiction related to Islam and Muslim-majority countries would be challenging. The best I can aim for seems to be an examination of major trends with examples from different countries.

Reflecting the diversity of Muslim-majority countries, products of the scientific imagination among their inhabitants were far from uniform. Climatic differences alone were enough for the building of vastly different worlds. In *Star Wars* and other films, the deserts of Egypt, Tunisia and United Arab Emirates were made to represent surfaces of the Moon and other planets. In tropical Indonesia, on the other hand, it was perhaps easier to imagine a world with abundant water. Norman Erikson Pasaribu from Jakarta, for instance, composed a poem entitled 'A History-to-Come of Helmbrellas: Their Features and Fates'. The poem begins with alien spaceships striking Earth. Three-quarters of the human population are killed, but the Ulxian invasion is repelled. As the Ulxians consist mostly of water, their remains turn into massive rainclouds. The sky turns pitch black, and it rains non-stop. Humans struggle to keep away all water with a series of new technologies combining helmets and umbrellas. Plasma shields, anti-gravity fields and lasers all prove futile against the onslaught of raindrops.[145]

Not just the diversity of natural environments, but also long-standing human variations contributed to different science fiction across Muslim-majority countries. To give another example from Indonesia, Riawani Elyta and Syila Fatar set out to combine a futuristic fantasy with local history and culture. The result was the 2014 novel *Trinil Gate*. It features not just mystic rituals, but also fossils discovered at the Javanese site of Trinil during the late nineteenth century. These fossils were first identified as belonging to a new species named *Anthropopithecus erectus* and later categorized as *Homo erectus*. In the authors' imagination, mankind had driven the Pithes into outer space by destroying their environment. Under the dome of an advanced spaceship, they have regrown a forest that supplies them with fruits and unpolluted water and air. Yet, their numbers were further diminished as a result of exploitation by another extraterrestrial species. Their only surviving female is their dying queen. They thus abduct young women by means of a teletransporter for cross-breeding.[146]

Not just prehistory, but also ancient history provided diverse inspirations. Abdelaziz Belkhodja's future Republic of Carthage is based on the Phoenician state. For Iranians too, pre-Islamic heritage was an important resource and

[145] Pasaribu, 'A History-to-Come of Helmbrellas'.
[146] Elyta and Fatar, *Gerbang Trinil*.

reference. Inspired by Jules Verne, Abdolhosain Sanatizadeh from Kerman wrote a novel entitled *Rostam in the Twenty-second Century*. After first appearing in a newspaper, it was published in book form in 1934. Sanatizadeh envisions an inventor bringing Rostam, the hero of the *Shahnameh* (Book of Kings), back to life. In the future environment, Rostam mistakes technology for magic. Moreover, he believes an aeroplane to be the mythological bird Simurgh.[147] Time travel is also a theme of *Guardian Angel*, a novel by Iraj Fazel Bakhsheshi published in 2008. Bakhsheshi, a Tehran-based mining engineer, has a detective move back to the sixth century BC. His mission is to protect Cyrus the Great, the founder of the Achaemenid Empire, from another time traveller. The detective kills the assassin and becomes memorialized as a 'guardian angel' in a golden portrait. More importantly, he saves the Cyrus Cylinder. This artefact becomes key to the advancement of humanity and its defence against an alien fleet thousands of years later.[148]

Despite the enormous variations in nature and culture, I use the term 'Muslim world' as an umbrella term and a convenient shorthand for the global Islamic community and its lands. This expression itself has a global intellectual history and is problematic.[149] It has grouped Muslims worldwide and often emphasized unity over, or amid, diversity. An Islamic 'nation' (in Arabic *ummah*) is an 'imagined community'[150] similar to others. Used by promoters and critics of Islam alike, the idea may often appear distorted and hardly representative of many Muslims and their actual lives. However, perhaps because of its distortions, it has also been very influential since the late nineteenth century. It is therefore hard to ignore, especially in a book on imaginations. Indeed, much science fiction from Egypt, Malaysia, Turkey and other countries reflected and promoted dreams of a united Islamic world.

Recognizing the importance of a global Islamic community as an idea, I explore conceptions of extraterrestrials among people in and from Muslim-majority countries. I am especially interested in references to Islam and its civilization in ideas about the ultimate Other. 'Islamic civilization' is, of course, another intellectual construct. It was perhaps partly invented by orientalists,[151] but has gained importance beyond scholarly circles. Public institutions like Qatar's Museum of Islamic Art have used the idea to connect creative products

147 Ghaeni, 'The History', 468.
148 Bakhshishī, *Firishtah-yi nigahbān.*
149 Aydin, *The Idea.*
150 Anderson, *Imagined Communities.*
151 Haridi, *Das Paradigma.*

from various places across Africa, Asia and Europe. I am asking whether extraterrestrial civilizations have been imagined as Islamic too. Are there other Muslim worlds in the universe? To what extent have utopian and dystopian societies been framed in religious terms?

Because the Qur'an allows for various interpretations, it is not sufficient for understanding specific Islamic imaginations of extraterrestrial life. While recognizing the scriptural basis for many texts and visual artworks, I am interested in the full breadth of sources for ideas about other worlds. I am asking what inspired people from the Muslim world to conceive of space aliens in a particular way. Did the most imaginative writers and artists study the natural sciences, the humanities or both? To what extent did they derive images from older traditions, such as the *Arabian Nights*, turning flying carpets into flying saucers? If so, it is worth investigating how such traditions combined with modern products of astrobiological research and the 'mass cultural genre system'.[152]

In addition to the creators' biographies, my book investigates the institutional settings that facilitated the production and circulation of texts and images about extraterrestrial life. Of special significance is the role of states. Throughout modern history, Muslims have been subjected to the rise of a variety of regimes: imperial, colonial, and independent, republican and monarchical, Islamic and secular. As a result, the politics of religion differed significantly between Syria and Saudi Arabia, for instance. Yet, many of these governments were similarly authoritarian and controlling on the one hand and committed to educational and technological development on the other. I am asking to what extent state institutions enabled people to think creatively, especially about life on the final frontier. Was censorship an obstacle to creative expression? Or did it rather channel political and social criticism away from realism towards science fiction? In other words, to what extent did repression encourage writers to discuss sensitive issues by setting their stories on distant planets? In such cases, science fiction authors engaged in significant 'estrangement'.[153] They rendered familiar politics even more alien than those working in other genres.

While certain dynamics were similar in different parts of the Muslim world, they also had their specificities. Individuals and institutions need to be understood within national and regional contexts and the larger historical processes that shaped them. In the nineteenth and early twentieth centuries,

[152] Rieder, *Science Fiction.*
[153] Ian Campbell, *Arabic Science Fiction*, 9.

Christian missionaries and their Muslim competitors established modern periodicals that served as platforms for debates about different views of the universe. The growth of space research, including the emergence of astrobotany, in such cities as far from Moscow as Almaty was in part due to the evacuation of Soviet scientists from Europe during World War II. In the twenty-first century, wars in the Middle East provided inspiration for the imagination of alien invasions in Iraq and Syria, including Ayham Jabr's surrealist art.

Chapters in Muslim world building

Each chapter of this book focuses on different media, but my narrative is still broadly chronological. Chapter 2 focuses on scientific journals and popular magazines, two types of periodicals that only slowly became distinct from one another over the course of the nineteenth and early twentieth centuries. These publications do not just spread the heliocentric model across different empires. They also covered claims of the discovery of canals and plants on Mars. Combined with scripture, modern scientific knowledge, whether established or speculative, was repeatedly used by competing Christian and Muslim religious entrepreneurs to bolster their authority.

Chapter 3 moves from paper to film. It analyses the imagination of extraterrestrial life in the cinemas of Turkey, Egypt and Pakistan, mainly during the Cold War. Filmmakers from these countries borrowed liberally from global productions. However, even those who copied entire scenes and scores from the likes of *Star Wars* still adapted their productions for local consumption. References to local customs and Islam made the strange familiar and funny. The circulation and adaptation of global science fiction was also shaped by national politics. Despite similar sizes of their populations, economies and film industries, Turkey produced vastly more science fiction movies than Iran did. This raises the question whether secularism was more permissive of the scientific imagination than Islamism.

While film industries were concentrated in major cities, such as Cairo and Istanbul, observations of unidentified flying objects were widely dispersed across urban and rural areas. Chapter 4 discusses the various ufological texts that appeared in Arabic, Turkish, Urdu and other languages especially from the 1960s onwards. Their authors were influenced not just by movies, but also by writings on religious and paranormal phenomena. Aliens were thus associated with the jinn and Satan. Although ufological works appeared on the fringes of both science and religion, their popularity exceeded those of many mainstream publications. Some books even gave rise to entire movements that combined Islam with the belief in UFOs.

Equally popular as ufological literature were novels and short stories that were explicitly designated as science fiction. Chapter 5 follows the careers of several prominent authors in Pakistan, Bangladesh, Egypt and Indonesia. They include Ibne Safi, Muhammed Zafar Iqbal, Nehad Sherif and Eliza Handayani. Many of these writers were not as Islamic in their world-building as Azrul Jaini in Malaysia. However, they still created Muslim heroes that entire nations could identify with and cheer for. As such, their work was also part of the postcolonial nation-building. Such genre fiction emerged after formal independence in the decades after World War II and grew with liberalizations especially after 1980.

Like this first chapter, the final one again touches on imaginations in a variety of forms. I will pay special attention to research on extrasolar planets and visual arts, including games. From recent creations, the chapter extrapolates what future science fiction in the Muslim world could look like. Challenges and opportunities for creative productions not only come from scientific advances, but also from social and political developments. They include wars, sanctions, and bans on the theory of evolution.

While this book largely focuses on modern media, aliens have even invaded traditional arts and craft. Creatures from *Flash Gordon*'s planet Mongo appeared on a batik cloth from Java that was probably made in the late 1930s or early 1940s. The artist adapted bird men, lizard men and horned villains that challenge the hero in the comic strip.[154] One of many space-age poets was the Iraqi Fadhil Al-Azzawi. He published 'poems from a UFO window', in which he lands on Mars and travels to more distant planets.[155] In the 2010s, Malaysian puppetmasters used *Star Wars*, which itself drew on older myths, to attract new audiences to shadow plays. They thus cut out figures of Darth Vader, Luke Skywalker and other characters from a 'a galaxy, far, far away'.[156]

As 'E. T. culture'[157] was pervasive, it can hardly be captured in a single volume. Besides poetry and film, science fiction in Turkey appeared in advertising and even crossword puzzles.[158] Looking across the Muslim world, futuristic

[154] Gittinger, 'Extraterrestrial Inspiration'.
[155] Al-Azzawi, 'Poems'.
[156] Krich, '"Star Wars"'.
[157] Battaglia, 'Insiders' Voices'.
[158] Atılgan, *Einführung*.

architecture alone has almost become too abundant to cover. Already during the mid-1980s, American mosques had 'flying saucer domes' and 'rocket minarets'. In Miami, a marine pressure vessel taken from a junkyard was subsequently removed from the roof by police order.[159] However, this was only a minor setback, as elites employed star architects to build cities of the future across Asia. Abu Dhabi's Masdar, designed by Foster and Partners, was referred to as a 'spaceship in the desert'.[160] Adrian Smith and Gordon Gill won the competition for the Masdar Headquarters as well as the grounds of the Expo 2017 in Astana. Kazakhstan's pavilion was named Nur Alem (Light of the World). However, the giant glass globe was informally called the 'Death Star'.[161]

Whereas much futuristic architecture is a recent phenomenon, the wider extraterrestrial culture is the product of a millennia-old debate. Leading historians have mostly focused on Western figures arguing for and against life on other worlds.[162] They include astronomers like Johannes Kepler, philosophers, such as Immanuel Kant, and novelists like H. G. Wells. However, Muslim thinkers too have long engaged in what became a global discussion. If the plurality of inhabited planets has been 'the myth of the modern age',[163] Muslims fully participated in its creation.

[159] Inquiry, 'Flying Saucer Domes'.
[160] Günel, *Spaceship*.
[161] James Palmer, 'Kazakhstan'.
[162] Dick, *Plurality*; *Life*. Crowe, *The Extraterrestrial Life Debate*.
[163] Guthke, *The Last Frontier*, xi.

2

Missions and Mars

Benoît de Maillet never saw the appearance of *Telliamed* in print. By the time of its publication in 1748, he had already been dead for ten years. That he refrained from bringing the book out during his lifetime was not due to a lack of means, however. A nobleman trusted by King Louis XIV, de Maillet had served in different diplomatic roles, including as French consul in Cairo between 1692 and 1708. Based on his stay, he had also prepared a *Description of Egypt*, which preceded Napoleon's monumental project of the same name.[1] Both of de Maillet's works were edited by the abbot Jean-Baptiste Le Mascrier. In the meantime, *Telliamed* drew enough interest for its manuscripts to circulate secretly, even as the author remained semi-anonymous. (*Telliamed* is de Maillet spelled in reverse.) Readers were lured to wide-ranging wisdoms from an ostensibly oriental source, as promised by a long subtitle: *Conversations between an Indian Philosopher and a French Missionary on the Diminution of the Sea, the Formation of the Earth, the Origin of Man, etc.*

Although the author belonged to a Catholic family and had served the crown for decades, *Telliamed* was published in the Dutch Republic rather than in France. This was similar to *The Adventures of Telemachus*, another controversial work of the early Enlightenment. It was authored by François Fénelon, an archbishop and royal tutor.[2] What made *Telliamed* contentious was that even after years of editing by a clergyman, it was still seen as in conflict with Catholic dogmas. In particular, it seemed to contradict biblical accounts of creation by offering a theory of the plurality of worlds and panspermia. De Maillet speculated that miniscule seeds exist on all celestial bodies and in the space between them.

1 Ouasti, 'La description', 73–74.
2 Hill, 'The Arabic Adventures', 175.

These seeds give rise to life in oceans across the universe. As water subsides on planets and their moons, life appears on land as well.[3] This theory derived in part from the consul's observation of the impact of floods on Egyptian agriculture as measured by the Nilometer.[4]

Telliamed was one of the first books to offer an elaborate theory of panspermia, the idea that life exists throughout the cosmos.[5] However, when it came to the plurality of worlds, de Maillet acknowledged the influence of his friend Bernard de Fontenelle[6] and earlier European thinkers. The book was dedicated to 'the illustrious Cyrano de Bergerac, author of the imaginary journeys in the sun and the Moon'. The author describes himself as a 'very faithful imitator' of the seventeenth-century writer.[7] Later in the book, the protagonist refers to a treatise by the Dutch astronomer Christiaan Huygens. In the words of Telliamed, Huygens 'pretends to prove, not only that there are men and animals in our planets and their satellites, but also, that these men have the same knowledge as we in astronomy and geometry'.[8]

Like other Enlightenment writers, de Maillet built not just on the works of Europeans. Spreading controversial new ideas by putting them into the mouths of fictional orientals was popular in absolutist France. Other examples include Montesquieu's *Persian Letters* and Voltaire's 'Dialogue between a Brahmin and a Jesuit'. De Maillet invented not just the philosopher Telliamed, but also another figure named Omar the Learned (perhaps after Omar Khayyam). Other Muslim sources were real, however. One of the most important was the book *Marvels of Creatures and Strange Things Existing* by Zakariya al-Qazwini from the thirteenth century. Further authors include the fifteenth-century al-Maqrizi and perhaps the tenth-century al-Masʿudi.[9]

It is possible that de Maillet received at least some inspiration from Muslim contemporaries of his as well. His *Conversations between an Indian Philosopher and a French Missionary* are set in Cairo, and the character Telliamed refuses to declare his religion. The French novelist Gustave Flaubert later called *Telliamed* an 'Arabic book'. Nevertheless, the work's direct influence on astrobiological debates in the Muslim world remained limited. In the port of Damietta, works

3 Maillet, *Telliamed* (1748).
4 Claudine Cohen, *Science*, 41.
5 Gargaud and Tirard, 'Exobiology', 340.
6 Claudine Cohen, *Science*, 29.
7 Maillet, *Telliamed* (1748).
8 Maillet, *Telliamed* (1797), 224.
9 Ducène, 'Les sources arabes'.

by Enlightenment authors, including Fénelon and Voltaire, had already been translated into Arabic in the early nineteenth century. Despite de Maillet's connections to Egypt, *Telliamed* was not among them.[10]

Serious engagement by natives of North Africa perhaps only began in the late twentieth century. Tunisian-born Claudine Cohen started studying de Maillet in Paris during the 1980s and later published a book about *Telliamed* in French.[11] The Libyan Amar Abdusalam Laswd began a thesis at the University of Sheffield with several pages dedicated to the work. The dissertation, which was completed in 2008, investigates possible extraterrestrial origins of bacteria. According to Laswd, de Maillet 'was one of the first moderns to see the Earth, not as the centre of creation, but merely one part of a vast cosmic sea of life'. The Libyan continued, 'By being one of the first to express what might be called a post-Copernican view of biology, De Maillet's contribution deserves to be better known.'[12] In 2010, this statement was repeated in an article co-authored by Laswd's Saudi colleague Fawaz Alshammari and entitled 'The Forgotten History of Panspermia and Theories of Life from Space'.[13]

Even if knowledge of *Telliamed* in Muslim-majority countries remained rare, the book represented a form of astrobiological exchange encompassing multiple regions of the world. Although the *Conversations between an Indian Philosopher and a French Missionary* were fictional, they still seemed plausible at the time. As consul to Egypt, de Maillet protected not just French commercial interests, but also missionaries.[14] More than that, in 1702, Louis XIV appointed him as his ambassador to Abyssinia with a special commission to convert its people. The diplomat resigned from this particular position, perhaps for political reasons or for lack of religious conviction.[15] However, this setback for French religious expansionists was small and temporary.

European missionary activities across Africa and Asia only intensified during the colonial era. By the nineteenth century, many Christians engaged Muslims in real debates about extraterrestrial life. In these exchanges, religious entrepreneurs also competed in claiming modern science for their respective traditions. Harmonizing their scriptures with new knowledge confirmed by the telescope and modern mathematics required unprecedented readings. Instead

10 Hill, 'The First Arabic Translations'.
11 Claudine Cohen, 'L'« Anthropologie »', 45; *Science*.
12 Laswd, 'Studies', 7.
13 Wainwright and Alshammari, 'The Forgotten History'.
14 Read, 'De Maillet', 54.
15 Claudine Cohen, *Science*, 19.

of being strict and dogmatic, many promoters and defenders of faith had to be creative. The new periodicals emerging out of missionary and colonial encounters stimulated the scientific as much as the religious imagination.

The missionaries' influence on astrobiology even outlived the French and other colonial empires that supported them. Part of their legacy was Forman Christian College in Lahore, which had been established as Mission College by the American Presbyterian Charles Forman in 1864. Despite its name, the institution taught many Muslim leaders, such as the later president Pervez Musharraf. In 2013, three years before becoming an adviser to the Salam Award for Imaginative Fiction, the physicist Pervez Hoodbhoy accepted a chair at the college. The rector praised Hoodbhoy as an 'outstanding educationist dedicated to reinvigorating critical thinking and novel research methods'.[16] Forman Christian College was also a centre for the Astrobiology Network of Pakistan and educated Syed Muneeb Ali, one of its founding members.[17]

First contacts

Astronomical exchanges involving evangelists in South Asia went back much further than the establishment of Forman Christian College or even de Maillet's work. By the time of *Telliamed*'s first printing, European missionaries had already been present in India for over two centuries. They had first arrived as part of colonial projects, but soon found local patrons as well. In 1510, Portuguese forces captured Goa, and in 1542, were followed by the newly established Society of Jesus under Francis Xavier. The Jesuits impressed Indian leaders with their learning and were asked by the Mughal emperor Akbar to join his court. Subsequently, missionaries brought telescopes to South Asia, directed observatories, and created maps in the service of various rulers.[18] They thus introduced much European knowledge, while learning about Indian astronomical traditions.[19] Even though the Jesuits largely failed at converting local elites, they served as conduits of scientific exchange.

This dialogue often encompassed practical astronomical knowledge related to geography rather than cosmology, however. Outside of *Telliamed*, there is

16 Pakistan Today, 'Pervez Hoodbhoy'.
17 Astrobiology Network of Pakistan, 'Core Team'.
18 Udías, *Searching*, 55; Razaullah Ansari, 'Introduction', 371.
19 Raina, 'The French Jesuit Manuscripts'.

little evidence for sixteenth- and seventeenth-century missionaries in India having lengthy discussions about either the plurality of worlds or the heliocentric model. Even the eighteenth-century ruler Jai Singh, who built observatories and was in close contact with Jesuit astronomers, seemed hardly aware of these ideas.[20] Perhaps the main reason for the absence of post-Copernican cosmology was that Catholics made up the overwhelming majority of missionaries in India between the sixteenth and eighteenth centuries. On the whole, they also seemed to have been much more committed to dogmas than either de Maillet or Le Mascrier. At the time, leaders of the church considered both Copernicanism and the plurality of worlds as heresies. Robert Bellarmine, an Italian Jesuit and cardinal, was influential in the Roman Inquisition's proceedings against Giordano Bruno and Galileo Galilei.[21] In Portugal, which was the main source of European astronomical knowledge for Jai Singh, Jesuits controlled higher education and only gradually came to support heliocentrism.[22]

By the late eighteenth century, however, Copernicanism had gained widespread acceptance across Europe. With the heliocentric view came the idea that the other planets were physical objects subject to the same laws as Earth. They could thus be imagined as worlds too. Indian Muslim travellers encountered and wrote about these ideas. One of them was Mir Muhammad Husayn, a physician and poet based in Murshidabad in Bengal. He had the epithet 'Isfahani', signifying either a family connection or a visit to Iran. By spending time in the British capital in the 1770s, he gained the additional appellation 'Landani'. On his return, he wrote an Arabic tract that was known by different titles. One of them was 'The Description of Europe and the Modern World, with some Problems of Modern Mathematical Sciences according to European Scholars'. Another version was 'The Theories of European Scholars concerning Planets and Heavens'.[23]

Mir Muhammad Husayn not only recounted European discoveries, but also sought to harmonize them with his faith. He explained that the invention of the telescope had produced new knowledge of the sun, the planets and their satellites. His tract also discussed Saturn's rings and moons, parallel lines on the surface of Jupiter, the changing phases of Venus and sunspots. The scholar further mentioned observations of thousands of stars, including seventy in the constellation Pleiades. 'Each of the fixed stars along with its planets and

20 Sharma, 'Jai Singh'.
21 Martinez, 'Giordano Bruno', 362.
22 Hanson, 'Portuguese Cosmology', 84.
23 Razaullah Ansari, 'European Astronomy', 133–34.

satellites is a universe by itself', he argued. The sun with Earth and the other planets similarly formed a 'universe' or 'world' (*'ālam*). The author further deduced that the number of such 'universes' (*'awālim*) is 'infinite'. God's signs are thus not confined to Earth. On the contrary, the existence of an infinite number of worlds demonstrates God's omnipotence.[24]

While Mir Muhammad Husayn's tract was in Arabic, a contemporary of his produced major accounts of European astronomy in Persian. This was Mirza Abu Taleb, an administrator from Lucknow in northern India whose father had migrated there from Isfahan. In 1799, Abu Taleb travelled to Europe in the company of an officer of the East India Company. In London, seeing an orrery left a deep impression on him. He wrote that this mechanical model exhibited 'all the revolutions of the Solar system, with such perspicuity as must convince the most prejudiced person of the superiority, nay, infallibility, of the Copernican System'. He added, 'I was so much delighted by the novelty of this exhibition, and the information I received from it, that I went to see it several times.' Yet, his religious conviction was hardly shaken by the experience. His travel memoir conceded glory to God as 'the Lord of all worlds'. He further praised Muhammad as the 'Chosen of Mankind' and 'the traveller over the whole expanse of the heavens'.[25] Upon his return to India, Abu Taleb wrote tracts on the 'new astronomy', arguing that geocentrism was 'impossible'. He explained the terminology of the new system, such as aphelion and perihelion. In addition, he introduced Uranus and the asteroids Ceres and Pallas to his readers.[26]

As Copernicanism gained increasing acceptance among scholars, it entered the curricula of Indian colleges and schools. Colonial and missionary institutions taught modern astronomy in order to convince the native population of the superiority of European knowledge over local traditions. Charles Grant, a chairman of the East India Company, hoped that Christian understandings of the universe would challenge the 'absurdity' of Hindu mythology in particular. Modern explanations of eclipses would shatter the Vedic astrological lore of 'Rahu and Ketu', for instance. By gradually introducing the different branches of natural philosophy, Grant believed that Indian minds could be changed and 'error' dispelled.[27] James Thomason, a subsequent servant of the East India Company, was one of the main benefactors of Agra College, which was

[24] Ibid., 134.
[25] Abu Taleb Khan, *Travels*, 1–2, 283.
[26] Razaullah Ansari, 'European Astronomy', 135–37.
[27] Tiwari, 'A Transnarrative', 1270.

established in the 1820s. Books such as John Herschel's *Outlines of Astronomy* and William Paley's *Natural Theology* were translated into Urdu and taught at the college.[28]

Despite the power of their technology, the attempt by colonial administrators and missionaries to equate European astronomy with Christianity largely failed Many Indians were attracted by modern science, but not willing to give up their own scriptures. A Hindu scholar teaching at Agra College even thanked James Thomason for his donations by dedicating a book to him on the harmony of Western science and Hindu philosophy.[29] Many Muslims pursued a similar path.[30] Instead of abandoning the Qur'an, they sought to reform contemporary Muslim attitudes and practices. Such was the interest of Obaidullah Ubedi, a professor at the New Hooghly College near Calcutta. In 1877, he published an essay with a long title: 'Reciprocal Influence of Mahomedan and European Learning and Inference therefrom as to the Possible Influence of European Learning on the Mahomedan Mind in India'. Ubedi complained that the Muslim intellect had 'remained less susceptible than that of their Hindoo brethren to the influence of European learning. Their conceit that they are already possessed of learning and civilisation has hindered them from making progress in European science'.[31]

While Ubedi urged his fellow Muslims to embrace new scientific knowledge, he defended Islam. 'There is no doubt that our scripture may be easily reconciled with modem scientific truth', he argued. He also asserted the superiority of the Qur'an over the Bible. 'If any of our co-religionists hold the doctrine of the plurality of worlds, he is not liable to be burnt like Bruno, according to our holy precepts', Ubedi explained. In this sentence, the Muslim scholar referred to the execution of the Dominican friar and cosmologist by the Roman authorities in 1600. Ubedi then cited the first chapter of the Qur'an with its Arabic expression *rabb al-ʿālamīn*: 'I can indeed discover some hints in the first verse of the beginning of our scripture about the plurality of the worlds; as when it says: "Praise be to God the Governor or Supporter of the Worlds".'[32]

Much more prominent as a Muslim reformer than Obaidullah Ubedi was Syed Ahmad Khan from Delhi, who had strong family ties to the Mughal court. After receiving a traditional religious education, he worked as a clerk in the law courts

28 Livingston, *In the Shadows*, 194–95.
29 Ibid., 195.
30 S. Irfan Habib, 'Reconciling Science'.
31 S. Irfan Habib, 'Viability', 2354.
32 Ibid.

of Agra. Associating with British servants of the East India Company, he first learned there that Earth revolved and rotated. Initially, he was not convinced. However, especially after the unsuccessful Indian Rebellion of 1857, he became impressed by the power that modern science and technology gave the British.[33] As Agra College primarily targeted Hindus, he led the establishment of a new institution for Muslims in Aligarh. It was called the Muhammadan Anglo-Oriental College or in Arabic *Madrasat al-ʿUlūm* (School of Sciences).[34] This institution, which would become Aligarh Muslim University, not only taught new knowledge as it was published in European languages. Its librarians also preserved the manuscripts of earlier Indian travellers to Europe, such as Mir Muhammad Husayn and Mirza Abu Taleb.[35] Syed Ahmad Khan himself did not consider the Qur'an as a text of science. He argued that the scripture could not be used to prove either heliocentrism or geocentrism, as it was 'not concerned with these problems of astronomy'. The reformer insisted on the possibility of reconciling the Qur'an with new discoveries through reinterpretation, however. He emphasized that 'the Work of God and the Word of God can never be antagonistic to each other'. He conceded that 'we may, through the fault of our knowledge, sometimes make mistakes in understanding the meaning of the Word'.[36]

Confident in the superiority of their own faith and its harmony with modern science, some Indian Muslims became missionaries themselves. Especially active were members of the Ahmadiyya movement, which emerged in the Punjab in the late nineteenth century. Prominent among them was Khwaja Kamal-ud-Din, a lawyer trained at Forman Christian College. He did not convert to Christianity, but entertained friendly relations with missionaries, including his alma mater's principal James Ewing. Nevertheless, in reaction to the Christians' activities, Kamal-ud-Din, like other Ahmadis, sought to expand his own community. In 1912, he established a Muslim mission in Woking, England. He also began editing a monthly journal entitled *Muslim India and Islamic Review*. Published in London, it was marketed in Britain as well as its colony.[37]

Although provincial in some respects, Kamal-ud-Din's base at Woking had already been a meeting place between Islam and science fiction for a few decades. The Hungarian-born scholar Gottlieb Leitner, a former principal of Lahore's Government College, established an Oriental Institute there in 1884.

[33] Livingston, *In the Shadows*, 196–97.
[34] Lelyveld, 'Disenchantment', 89.
[35] Razaullah Ansari, 'European Astronomy', 134–35.
[36] Gosling, *Science*, 25.
[37] Weitbrecht, 'A Moslem Mission'.

For the Muslim students that Leitner hoped to attract, the Begum of Bhopal funded the construction of a mosque in an Anglo-Indian design.[38] H. G. Wells, who lived in Woking during the mid-1890s, imagined both buildings being destroyed by Martians in his novel *The War of the Worlds*. 'I saw the tops of the trees about the Oriental College burst into smoky red flame', he wrote. 'The pinnacle of the mosque had vanished, and the roof-line of the college itself looked as if a hundred-ton gun had been at work upon it.'[39]

It is unclear how Woking's Islamic community felt about the imagined destruction in *The War of the Worlds*, which was first serialized in 1897. However, Muslims in Mombasa, Nairobi, Kampala and London protested against a later book of his: *A Short History of the World*, first published in 1922. In this work, Wells described the prophet Muhammad as a man of 'shifty character', 'very considerable vanity, greed, cunning, self-deception and quite sincere religious passion'.[40] Nevertheless, it took until 1938 – and perhaps German agitation – for this passage to gain notoriety among Muslims. The police commissioner in Kampala noted that only one of the city's bookshops had stocked the work and sold not more than six copies. In Woking, protestors were intent on marching from the mosque to Wells's doorstep, but appeared to have been dissuaded by the police.[41]

Muslims demonstrated against the English writer as a historian rather than as a science fiction writer. Well's representation of Martian life seemed to have been less controversial. Broadly, Khwaja Kamal-ud-Din, like the Christian missionaries before him, used the authority of modern science to promote his faith. The first volume of *Muslim India and Islamic Review*, published in 1913, contains an article on 'The Quran and the Science of Astronomy'. The author was Mohamad Abul Hasan Siddiqi, a late registrar at the High Court of Hyderabad. He noted that the Qur'an, 'as a word of God', 'should not say anything against the established principles of material sciences'. The court official thus emphasized his scripture's superiority over the Bible for the understanding of the cosmos. 'The first chapter of the Book of Genesis has always been a puzzle to the church commentators, who have spared no pains to reconcile the holy writs to the searches in the realm of science', Siddiqi claimed. 'But the Last Book of God, the Quran, has saved its believers from such a labour-lost task.'[42]

38 Naylor and Ryan, 'The Mosque', 43–44.
39 Wakeford, 'Wells', 24–25.
40 Wells, *A Short History*, 251–52.
41 Piscatori, 'The Rushdie Affair', 767–68.
42 Siddiqi, 'The Quran', 170.

Unlike Syed Ahmad Khan, Siddiqi thus interpreted the Qur'an as supporting the heliocentric model. 'And the sun revolves in her place of rest', he translated the beginning of 36:38. He dismissed the notion of the sun's motion around Earth as 'an unwarranted conjecture'. 'In these days, when the science of astronomy has been based on modern principles, it has been established that the sun, like other fixed stars, occupies a fixed place in space', the official explained. 'It has no orbital motion, but it rotates round its axis within a certain time.' That the Qur'an contains such facts was evidence for its divinity. 'At the time of the revelation of the Holy Quran no one had even an idea or suspicion of this rotation of the sun round its axis', Siddiqi emphasized. 'This is a miracle of the Holy Book, which no learned man can deny.'[43]

Similar to the efforts of their Christian competitors in India, the success of the Ahmadi missionaries in England was limited. Nonetheless, by 1914, the number of converts was sufficient for Kamal-ud-Din to establish a British Muslim Society.[44] Reaching beyond this circle, publications like *Muslim India and Islamic Review* propagated the idea of the plurality of worlds and the relevance of scripture for understanding nature. In 1916, the periodical, by then renamed *Islamic Review & Muslim India*, published an article on 'The Problem of Life'. It was authored by Nathan or Nur-ud-Din Stephen, an early convert and researcher on spiritism. Stephen argued that neither science nor human power had so far been able to produce a life form, not even an amoeba or a jellyfish. 'It is the gift of God, Who alone can produce or create it', Stephen stressed. The convert then quoted chapter 30 of the Qur'an: 'God bringeth forth the Living out of the Dead, and He bringeth forth the Dead out of the Living.' Life itself was therefore 'one of the greatest answers we have both to the atheist and agnostic'. It was a 'daily, hourly, living testimony to the existence of an All-powerful, Beneficent, and Eternal God and Creator'.[45]

God knows best

While India was integrated into the intellectual and religious networks of the British Empire, the Ottomans withstood Western imperialism for longer. This was in part due to alliances that mitigated threats and sustained a balance of power

43 Ibid., 170–71.

44 Gilham, 'Marmaduke Pickthall', 55.

45 Stephen, 'Nature's Problems', 36. On the author, see Gilham, *Loyal Enemies*, 119, 163–65.

in Europe. Especially strong in the early modern period was the relationship between the Ottoman and the French monarchs, who saw the Habsburgs as a common enemy. Their friendship was expressed through an exchange of gifts, including scientific books. Through them, Ottoman elites came into contact with post-Copernican astronomy. Around 1640, the court in Istanbul received the *New Richelian Ephemerides of the Celestial Movement*. Its author was Noël Duret, a cosmographer to King Louis XIII and Cardinal Richelieu. In 1660, Ibrahim of Szigetvár, a Hungarian convert to Islam, translated this book from Latin into Arabic. Although Duret was anti-Copernican, the *New Richelian Ephemerides* provided the Ottomans with one of the earliest references to the heliocentric system.[46]

Over the following two centuries, Copernicanism slowly made further inroads into the Ottoman lands. This process was pushed along by increasing military pressure. In 1770, the Ottoman navy suffered a devastating defeat at the hands of a Russian fleet that had sailed from the Baltic to the Mediterranean. In order to improve navigation in its aftermath, Sultan Mustafa III requested 'the best books of European astronomy' from the Royal Academy of Sciences in Paris. One of them was the *Treatise of Astronomy* by Jérôme de Lalande, who held a chair at the Collège de France. In the late eighteenth and the nineteenth century, de Lalande's work was translated in Istanbul, Aleppo and Cairo. Ottoman scholars valued this text primarily as a tool to predict the positions of celestial bodies. The translators paid little attention to de Lalande's heliocentric cosmology. An Arabic translation completed in Aleppo during the 1860s even transformed the text into a geocentric one. In this version of the text, Uranus and the asteroids Juno, Ceres, Pallas and Vesta all rotate around Earth.[47]

If the introduction of Copernicanism to the Near East ever took the form of a revolution, it was by means of the printing press in the second half of the nineteenth century. Christian missionaries were key to this process. After their arrival in the Levant, they soon engaged locals in scientific debates, including about life in the universe. Protestants and Catholics competed with one another in seeking to convert Eastern Christians and, ultimately, Muslims. Similar to the colonial and missionary efforts in India, American evangelists promoted the natural sciences in order to fight perceived 'superstitions' and demonstrate the 'power of truth'.[48] However, many Protestants were split over whether to embrace or reject the theory of evolution. Catholic missionaries were quick to

46 Ben-Zaken, 'The Heavens'.
47 Stolz, *The Lighthouse*, 148–55.
48 Elshakry, 'The Gospel', 178.

exploit such a perceived gulf between faith and reason in their competitors' writings. The Roman church on the whole did not oppose evolution, and its Jesuit order emphasized that faith was rational.[49]

The competition between Protestants and Catholics was perhaps most intense in Syria. Missionaries were attracted by the area's biblical significance and the presence of many native Christians. Between the middle of the nineteenth century and the early twentieth, Europeans and Americans established new institutions for the propagation of theological and scientific ideas. In 1866, the Syrian Protestant College (SPC) was founded in the growing port city of Beirut. In response, French Jesuits moved their seminary there from the more isolated town of Ghazir and turned it into the Université Saint-Joseph (USJ). While American and British businessmen patronized the SPC, France supported the USJ as part of its economic and cultural penetration of the Levant. Both institutions built not just libraries with the latest scientific publications in English and French, but also modern observatories with telescopes. Drawing on these resources, converts teaching at the two rival universities founded some of the first Arabic periodicals that covered modern science, including astronomy. In 1876, Yakub Sarruf and Faris Nimr, instructors at the SPC, began editing *Al-Muktataf* (The Selection). In 1898, Louis Cheikho, a Jesuit priest and faculty member at the USJ, started publishing *Al-Machriq* (The Orient).

Missionary and imperial competition in the Near East promoted not only science, but also fiction. Butrus al-Bustani, a Protestant convert from Mount Lebanon, published a modern *Arabic Encyclopedia*, in which Earth appears as the third planet of the solar system.[50] In addition, he translated John Bunyan's *The Pilgrim's Progress* and Daniel Defoe's *Robinson Crusoe* into Arabic. Both novels contained lessons that were considered useful by missionaries and the Syrian bourgeoisie alike. The Arabic *Robinson Crusoe* was printed several times by the American Mission Press in Beirut.[51] Similar, but original, works soon appeared as well. In 1865, Francis Marrash, the son of an Aleppine merchant with consular connections, published a utopia entitled *The Forest of Justice*. The protagonists, King Freedom, Minister Love-Peace, and the Captain of the Army of Civilization, discuss their battle against the Kingdom of Slavery. At the time, Marrash was an apprentice of

49 Robert Bell Campbell, 'The Arabic Journal', 160.
50 Al-Bustānī, *Dā'irat al-ma'ārif*, 117.
51 Hill, 'Early Translations'.

John Wortabet, a physician and later SPC faculty member.[52] In 1892, the American Mission Press also printed a book by the Syrian scholar entitled *Nature's Testimony to the Existence of God and Divine Law*. Following the format of William Paley's *Natural Theology*, Marrash postulated a deity based on the perfection of the universe.[53] The 'greatest evidence' for him was the existence of innumerable 'astronomical worlds'.[54]

While Protestant missionaries tended to promote English novels, Jesuits were instrumental in introducing Jules Verne to Arab audiences. In the 1870s and 1880s, the order's press in Beirut published two Arabic editions of his novel *Five Weeks in a Balloon*. The translator was Joseph Sarkis, an Ottoman administrator from Damascus and former student of the Jesuits.[55] His family had survived Mount Lebanon's civil war in 1860 and subsequently enjoyed, like other Christians, French protection in Beirut.[56] A similar bureaucrat who had benefited from French education in the Levant was the jurist Iskender Ammoun. As a child, he had escaped the destruction of his hometown Deir al-Qamar (Monastery of the Moon). After completing his legal education, Ammoun worked at an Egyptian court, while also pursuing his literary interests.[57] In 1885, he published a translation of Verne's *Journey to the Centre of the Earth* in Alexandria.[58]

Catholics and Protestants sought to convince Near Eastern populations to accept their respective truths by publishing new scientific knowledge and, on occasion, denouncing their competitors' writings as pseudoscientific.[59] In 1898, for instance, *Al-Muktataf* reported on the discovery of harmful microbes in holy water that is 'placed in some churches for blessing'.[60] Louis Cheikho responded with 'laughter'. The priest explained that holy water consisted of normal water with 'a little bit of salt'. If it contained microbes, then it had nothing to do with its holiness, but with the well it was taken from. Cheikho went on to mock *Al-Muktataf*'s editors, comparing them to an astronomer who is so focused on the observation of the planets that he stumbles and falls into a well.[61] In 1904,

52 Hill, 'Utopia', 215–17.
53 Livingston, *In the Shadows*, 71.
54 Marrāsh, *Shahādat al-ṭabīʿah*, 13.
55 Holt, 'Narrative', 66–70; Warn, *Al-riḥlah al-jawwīyah*.
56 Sarkīs, *Muʿjam al-maṭbūʿāt*, 1022–23.
57 Al-Ziriklī, *Al-aʿlām*, 302–3.
58 Fīrn, *Al-riḥlah al-ʿilmīyah*.
59 Robert Bell Campbell, 'The Arabic Journal', 166.
60 Al-Muqtaṭaf, 'Ḍarar al-māʾ al-muqaddas'.
61 Shaykhū, 'Ḍarar al-māʾ al-muqaddas'.

Cheikho further criticized a claim in *Al-Muktataf* that men's breasts had once been identical to those of women, but dried up, as men had stopped feeding their children to focus on war and strenuous work.[62]

Western missionaries in the Ottoman Empire targeted primarily Eastern Christians, and their publications avoided direct attacks on Islam. Nevertheless, Muslim 'religious entrepreneurs' soon emulated the evangelists' techniques in their quest to become 'opinion leaders'.[63] One of the most successful was Rashid Rida, who came from a family of landowners near Tripoli in Syria. Born in 1865, he studied under Husayn al-Jisr, a 'Muslim natural theologian' and apologist for the sharia.[64] In addition to his instruction at al-Jisr's National School, which emphasized the reconciliation of religion and science, Rida had read *Al-Muktataf*.[65] In 1898, the same year as the founding of *Al-Machriq*, he created his own journal, *al-Manār* (The Lighthouse). Published in Cairo, his periodical primarily sought to reform Islam, but also entered into a dialogue with Christians about scientific and religious topics. In 1913, *al-Manār* published a long account by Muhammad Tawfiq Sidqi, an Egyptian physician, on 'The Books of the New Testament and the Beliefs of Christianity'. This provoked a reply from Louis Cheikho in *Al-Machriq*. The priest challenged claims by Sidqi that the doctrine of the divinity of Christ was inconsistent and that the New Testament was referring to Muhammad rather than Jesus.[66]

Not just the plurality of worlds, but also the idea of extraterrestrial life formed part of the Arabic periodicals emerging out of the missionary milieu. The first issue of *Al-Muktataf*, published in 1876, included an article about the 'terrains, nature and inhabitants of the Moon'. According to the anonymous author, 'some philosophers' argue that because of the Moon's lower gravity, the bodies of its 'people are bigger than those of Earth's'. If this was the case, the writer reasoned, their houses and cities would be larger too and thus visible from Earth. The text mentioned other claims that the Moon represents a 'ruined world' whose water, air and people had disappeared. If the Moon had plants, its surface would change with the seasons. The account concluded that the natural satellite did not have 'inhabitants' like Earth's.[67]

62 Al-Mashriq, 'Fākihah', 1128.
63 Green, *Terrains*, 2.
64 Elshakry, 'Darwin's Legacy', 201.
65 Cole, 'Rashid Rida', 281.
66 Robert Bell Campbell, 'The Arabic Journal', 174–75.
67 Al-Muqtaṭaf, 'Al-Qamar', 11–12.

Al-Muktataf continued to publish accounts that were sceptical, but also imaginative, of life existing on other bodies in the solar system. The journal's second volume contained an article on Jupiter. 'Most likely', the anonymous author argued, its inhabitants were not like those of Earth either 'because of their different conditions'. As the planet receives less sunlight, humans 'would find Jupiter a dark and cold place'. Jupiter's 'soil' could be hotter and its atmosphere brighter, in order to compensate for lack of solar radiation. 'This does not prevent habitation by creatures like us', conceded the author. However, gravity precludes the growth of larger ones like 'trees, elephants, and camels'. The writer was conscious that he was merely offering 'suppositions' without 'definitive prove'. Employing a phrase used by Christian and Muslims alike, the article ended with 'God knows best'.[68]

Al-Muktataf largely relied on European publications in the library of the Syrian Protestant College for its scientific articles. Yet, Faris Nimr had some practical experience in observation as well. He assisted Cornelius Van Dyck, an American missionary and faculty member, in the college's observatory. The latter was well-acquainted with the Jesuit astronomer Angelo Secchi in Rome, who used the word 'canals' to describe dark, elongated structures on Mars.[69] One night, while observing the planet through his telescope, Van Dyck showed Nimr what appeared to be lines. 'Do you think that these are made by nature?' the professor asked. 'How can they be made by living things?' Nimr was not sure about what he saw. 'If only I had been born five-hundred years from today', Van Dyck wished, 'so that I know what time has in store for us'. His assistant quietly said to himself, 'Even if you were born after a thousand years, you would still be grieved' by what remains 'hidden'.[70]

Both Van Dyck and Nimr had left the Syrian Protestant College by the mid-1880s following a controversy over Charles Darwin's work.[71] Nimr, however, continued to publish *Al-Muktataf* from Cairo and retained an interest in life on Mars. In 1891, he travelled to Europe and visited the Brera Observatory in Milan. There, he met Giovanni Schiaparelli, an Italian astronomer who continued Angelo Secchi's practice of speaking about 'canals' on Mars. In a century that saw the opening of the Suez Canal, such waterways denoted feats of engineering and sparked much excitement. In France and America, the astronomers Camille

68 Al-Muqtaṭaf, 'Al-Mushtarī', 83–84.
69 Al-Muqtaṭaf, 'Al-ab Anjilū Sikkī'.
70 Nimr, 'Baʿda ʿahdī', 486–87.
71 On this dispute, see Elshakry, *Reading Darwin*.

Flammarion and Percival Lowell popularized the idea of intelligent life on Mars further, while many others were sceptical.[72] Schiaparelli told Nimr, 'some follow me and others contradict me'. From his own observations, the Syrian claimed that the lines on Mars had vanished for ten years and then reappeared.[73]

Faris Nimr was rare among Ottoman subjects to have had direct experience of working in an astronomical observatory. However, an increasing number of readers followed the debates about life on other planets via the new Arabic periodicals. Another one of these publications was *al-Ṭabīb* (The Physician). It had been established by Cornelius Van Dyck and his colleague George Post at the SPC in 1874.[74] After Van Dyck had left the college, Arabs from the same mixed Catholic and Protestant milieu took over the editorship. One of them, Ibrahim al-Yaziji, was the son of a contributor to a Protestant-led translation of the Bible. He himself, however, was employed by the Jesuit press in Beirut and affiliated with the Université Saint-Joseph. Al-Yaziji had also worked as the chief assistant to the Jesuit scholar Augustin Rodet, a competing biblical translator.[75] Another editor of *al-Ṭabīb* was Khalil Saadeh, a physician trained at the Syrian Protestant College.[76]

Although primarily a medical journal, *al-Ṭabīb* followed *Al-Muktataf* in publishing articles on a wide range of scientific topics. One contribution from 1884 was entitled 'The Living Creatures on the Planets'. The anonymous author wondered about the abundance of celestial bodies and the possibility of their inhabitation. The article then discussed Mercury, which it presumed to be the hottest planet due to its proximity to the sun. The writer argued that this body could exhibit moderate temperatures only at the poles. Therefore, any Mercurians were living there rather than around the equator. However, it was conceivable for thick clouds to lower temperatures in other areas too. The other extreme in terms of temperature was represented by Uranus and Neptune. Uranus's extended orbital period produced long summers, which could allow for life. On the other hand, equally lengthy winters would be challenging. As for Neptune, as the most distant planet it would receive even less sunlight.[77]

Between the two extremes of Mercury and Neptune, *al-Ṭabīb* focused mostly on Venus and Mars as the closest planets to Earth. As for Venus, the author again

72 Crossley, 'Percival Lowell'.
73 Nimr, 'Baʿda ʿahdī', 487.
74 Auji, 'Printed Images'.
75 Auji, *Printing Arab Modernity*, 33; Somekh, 'Biblical Echoes', 191.
76 Marten, *Attempting*, 82.
77 Al-Ṭabīb, 'Al-khalāʾiq al-ḥayyah' (1884).

suspected that any inhabitants were living near the poles. In the case of Mars, it possessed the most indications for life. Dark lines seen through a telescope could be evidence of water vapour. The article further speculated about the existence of clouds, rainfall and rivers. Red spots appearing in the summer and vanishing in winter could represent plant coverage – supposing that Martian plants were red. The journal also reported claims that red was the colour of the soil. Nevertheless, the author concluded that it was possible for Mars to exhibit similar forms of life as Earth.[78]

Life on other planets remained a popular topic in the Arabic periodicals coming out of the missionary milieu for decades. In 1902, Louis Cheikho published an article entitled 'The Inhabitants of Mars' in *Al-Machriq*. He excitedly compared the early twentieth century to the late fifteenth. Newspapers and magazines were speaking of a 'great discovery' similar to America's. The news was: 'Rejoice, oh human, you are not alone in space. You have companions like you who live in the stars that your eyes can see in the blackness of the night.' The American astronomers Andrew Ellicott Douglass and William Pickering had observed light coming from Mars, which could have been electrical in origin. This led Cheikho to ask whether the stars and planets have inhabitants, and whether 'humans like us' live on Mars.[79]

Cheikho sought answers to both questions in scripture. The priest quoted Psalm 19:1: 'The heavens declare the glory of God; the skies proclaim the work of His hands.' The Jesuit thus found it conceivable that God created 'speaking organisms to praise Him in these skies as His servants do on Earth'. The inhabitants of other planets could be 'offspring of Adam'. God is, after all, 'free, as He is wise, to do what He wants and as He wants it'. Mars has air, water and probably plants too, Cheikho speculated. However, in the end, research on Martian life consisted of 'assumptions and imaginations'. 'God knows best' and is 'the guide of His servants', the priest concluded.[80]

Missionary institutions found it convenient to support natural theology by the likes of Cheikho or Marrash. However, on occasion, they also gave rise to more materialist explanations of life in the universe. Shibli Shumayyil, a classmate of Yakub Sarruf's at the Syrian Protestant College, supported the idea of spontaneous generation.[81] He further translated Ludwig Büchner's

[78] Al-Ṭabīb, 'Al-khalāʾiq al-ḥayyah' (1885).
[79] Shaykhū, 'Sukkān al-Mirrīkh', 173–75.
[80] Ibid., 175–76, 179.
[81] Elshakry, 'Darwin's Legacy', 136–38.

commentaries on Charles Darwin's work into Arabic. Mansur Jurdak, a later mathematician and astronomer at the SPC, also applied the theory of evolution. In 1908, he published an article in *Al-Muktataf* titled 'Canals on Mars and Life on It'. The scientist drew heavily on Percival Lowell's publications. He stated that canals were 'evidence of urbanization and a symbol of progress'. 'Every time man progresses in civilization', Jurdak explained, he builds roads, railways and factories 'according to the laws of evolution which require the preservation and proliferation of the species'. Because water on the planet was scarce, molten ice was transported via canals from the poles to 'oases' for irrigation purposes.[82]

Rather than having a grim view of evolution in terms of competition and struggle for survival, Jurdak's imagination of Martian society was utopian. The scientist argued that 'if it is true that the canals are the works of industry, there are without doubt creatures of more sophisticated rationality and more complete understanding than human beings'. The digging of canals from the poles to the equator was an indication that Martians were 'united for the common good and cooperating'. This enables them to 'resist nature, which had almost killed them'. Life on the planet had possibly begun in the seas, as it did on Earth, Jurdak reasoned. When the water was depleted, Martians 'adapted to their circumstances' according to the 'laws of evolution'. He concluded that the inhabitants of Mars were 'closer to perfection' than their counterparts on Earth.[83]

Most articles in *Al-Muktataf* and *Al-Machriq*, whether religious or materialist, avoided attacking Islam directly. However, the wider missionary efforts soon led the Egyptian physician Muhammad Tawfiq Sidqi to emulate the Christian natural theologians and to defend his faith. In 1908, he published a multipart article in *al-Manār* entitled 'The Qur'an and Science: An Interpretation of Language, History, Geography, and Medicine'. He argued that the scripture contained many scientific facts that were unknown during the time of the prophet Muhammad. They include Earth's rotation and the common origin of all planets in 'smoke'. These facts were evidence that the Qur'an was 'not made by a human being, but came down from God'.[84]

A few years later, Sidqi continued this line of argument in another article in *al-Manār* entitled 'Astronomy and the Qur'an: A View on the Heavens and Earth'. This text was an expanded version of content that had previously appeared in an Egyptian student magazine. Natural science could not contradict

82 Jurdāq, 'Tura' al-Mirrīkh', 111.
83 Ibid., 111–12.
84 Ṣidqī, 'Al-Qur'ān', 452, 454.

the Qur'an, Sidqi postulated, because it is 'truly God's revelation. The truth does not contradict the truth'. The physician added that the scripture contained 'precise scientific propositions' that were not known in Muhammad's time. One of them was the plurality expressed in the praise of God as 'lord of the worlds'. Another idea was that fixed stars were moving independently from one another rather than being embedded in the same rotating sphere, as 'the ancients had believed'. Such propositions were 'among the eternal scientific miracles of the Qur'an'. As such, they were evidence for the 'truth of the prophet and the veracity of the Qur'an'.[85]

The scientific propositions that Sidqi read in scripture also comprised ideas about life on other planets. A verse about God's creation of animals in the heavens and on Earth agreed with scientists' opinions according to the physician. He further argued that other planets had good and evil spirits, like the angels and demons on Earth. To sceptics, he pointed out that such invisible beings were as real as microbes and electricity. The physician considered the life forms on different spheres as entirely separate from one another, however. If animals were trying to leave Earth, they would not find any air to breath and 'die instantly'. If an evil spirit was trying to escape the atmosphere in order to mix with the spirits of other planets, it would be swallowed and burnt by a meteor. The Egyptian further contended that God favoured the 'children of Adam' over many, but not all of His creations. Nor were all worlds created for humans, just as the oceans were created specifically for marine life. Such insights, Sidqi stressed, confirmed the Qur'an's agreement with modern science, in contrast to other scriptures. Therefore, each new discovery was also supporting Islam and upsetting other religions.[86]

It is doubtful how effective the attempt to propagate either Islam or Christianity through scientific publications ultimately was. The overall Protestant effort to convert the Middle East failed,[87] as did the Catholic. Nevertheless, through the periodicals printed in Cairo and Beirut, a considerable number of Arabic speakers learned about speculations about life in the universe. *Al-Muktataf* had around 3,000 subscribers in 1892, with each copy possibly being accessed by multiple people. *Al-Manār*'s subscriptions numbered about 500 in 1901, but reportedly doubled in the following year.[88] Copies were sent far beyond the Ottoman Empire, including to British India and the Dutch East Indies.[89]

85 Ṣidqī, ''Ilm al-falak', 593–94, 597–98.
86 Ibid., 591–94, 597.
87 Makdisi, *Artillery*.
88 Sheehi, 'Arabic Literary-Scientific Journals', 443, 448.
89 Bluhm, 'A Preliminary Statement'.

By connecting people across the Indian Ocean and the Mediterranean, *al-Manār* thus contributed to the imagination of a global Muslim community as well.

Despite having possibly thousands of readers, *al-Manār*'s influence in claiming modern science for Islam was limited too. As the idea of the Muslim world spread, so did the notion of the West as its counterpart. In the eyes of many Muslims, even those who did not directly experience colonialism, much of modern science and technology became associated with European powers. In his book, *Seven Pillars of Wisdom*, T. E. Lawrence wrote about a conversation with his Arabian companions about telescopes and distant stars during World War I. 'What will now happen with this knowledge?' inquired Mohammed. 'Many learned and some clever men together will make glasses as more powerful than ours, as ours than Galileo's', Lawrence responded, 'and yet more hundreds of astronomers will distinguish and reckon yet more thousands of now unseen stars, mapping them, and giving each one its name. When we see them all, there will be no night in heaven'. Auda provokingly asked, 'Why are the Westerners always wanting all?' He added, 'Behind our few stars we can see God, who is not behind your millions.' Lawrence responded, 'We want the world's end, Auda.' 'But that is God's', protested Zaal.[90]

It is unknown whether Lawrence's fellow fighters were familiar with the contents of *Al-Muktataf* or *al-Manār*. Copies of both were circulating in the Arabian Peninsula.[91] In any case, the Arab warriors certainly shared the curiosity of the journal's contributors in extraterrestrial life. 'Are there men on these greater worlds?' Mohammed asked. 'God knows', responded Lawrence. 'And has each the Prophet and heaven and hell?' Auda interrupted him. 'Lads, we know our districts, our camels, our women. The excess and the glory are to God. If the end of wisdom is to add star to star our foolishness is pleasing.' Auda then turned the conversation onto money and focused on the quest to capture Aqaba from the Ottomans.[92]

Plants on planets

Figures like *Al-Muktataf*'s co-editor Faris Nimr were both interested in, and sceptical of, the idea of Martian canals. However, another man from the Ottoman Empire named Eugène Antoniadi became one of the most dedicated

90 Lawrence, *Lawrence of Arabia*, 282.
91 Sheehi, 'Arabic Literary-Scientific Journals', 443; Āl Bassām, *Khizānat al-tawārīkh*, 17.
92 Lawrence, *Lawrence of Arabia*, 282.

to disproving it. He was born in Istanbul in 1870 into a wealthy Greek family with strong connections to Europe. His brother Dorotheos married the daughter of a British baronet. Eugène received a good education in English and French as well as the sciences.[93] Further trained as an architect, Antoniadi soon applied his artistic skills to astronomy. In 1888, he observed Jupiter with his three-inch refractor in Istanbul and submitted a drawing to the French magazine *L'Astronomie*.[94] This periodical, which Camille Flammarion had founded, had readers and contributors around the world. Between 1889 and 1893, Antoniadi also published sketches of Saturn and the sun.[95]

European astronomers, including Flammarion, quickly recognized Antoniadi's talents. In addition to *L'Astronomie*, the Istanbulite published in the *Journal of the Liverpool Astronomical Society*. In 1890, he became a founding member of the British Astronomical Association. The following year, he entered the Société astronomique de France, which Flammarion had recently established. Antoniadi even joined Flammarion's private observatory in Juvisy near Paris as an assistant. In 1896, he also became director of the British Astronomical Association's Mars Section, which provided him with even more contacts. Among his correspondents were Giovanni Schiaparelli and Percival Lowell.[96]

While Antoniadi spent most of his adult life in France, he retained his connections to the Ottoman lands. In 1902, he married Katherine Sevastupulo, a fellow Greek born in the empire. She too became a member of the British Astronomical Association and supported her husband's research. In 1904, he obtained a permission from Sultan Abdul Hamid II to document the interior of the Hagia Sophia. Over four months, the astronomer created around a thousand photographs and as many sketches of the mosque and former cathedral. These images made it into a three-volume book about the monument, which was printed in 1907.[97] Six years later, Antoniadi published an article titled 'The Wonder of the Basilicas' in the French magazine *Je sais tout* (I Know Everything). At the time of the Balkan Wars, he asked whether the cross would soon replace the crescent on top of the dome again.[98] Only in 1928, however, after the dissolution of the Ottoman Empire, did Antoniadi and his wife become French citizens.[99]

93 McKim, 'The Life and Times of E.M. Antoniadi, 1870–1944. Part 1', 169.
94 Antoniadi, 'La planète Jupiter'.
95 Antoniadi, 'Observation de Saturne'; 'Curieuses déformations'.
96 McKim, 'The Life and Times of E.M. Antoniadi, 1870–1944. Part 1', 164–67.
97 Ibid., 168–69.
98 Antoniadi, 'La merveille de basiliques', 107.
99 McKim, 'The Life and Times of E.M. Antoniadi, 1870–1944. Part 1', 169.

The astronomer retained an interest in the Near East and published a book on ancient Egyptian astronomy in 1934.[100]

Although Antoniadi benefited from his relationship with Camille Flammarion, he turned against his patron's views on Mars. Already during the late 1890s, he questioned the form and nature of the canals.[101] In 1909, he was able to use the great refractor of the Meudon Observatory near Paris for detailed observations of the red planet. His artistic skills, which were enhanced during his work on the Hagia Sophia, enabled him to draw the Martian surface meticulously. His images only showed natural features, dispelling the idea of canals. He thus challenged the authority of both Flammarion and Lowell.[102] In 1930, Antoniadi published a book on *The Planet Mars*, in which he contended that the canals were an 'illusion'. He also claimed that 'advanced life must have been confined to the past, when there was more water on Mars than there is now'. He added, 'today we can expect nothing more than vegetation around the vast red wildernesses of the planet'.[103]

While Antoniadi convinced many of his peers, he did not end discussions about life in the solar system. Even as the missionary effort subsided, the periodicals that had emerged out of it continued to publish articles on the topic. Another one of these platforms was the Egyptian magazine *Al-Hilal* (The Crescent). It had been founded in 1892 by Georgie Zaidan, yet another former student at the Syrian Protestant College. He had followed his teachers Faris Nimr and Yakub Sarruf to Cairo in the mid-1880s and subsequently assisted them in publishing *Al-Muktataf*.[104] Zaidan's own magazine rapidly surpassed *Al-Muktataf* in circulation, reaching 5,000 subscribers in its first year.[105] In 1922, *Al-Hilal*, then edited by Zaidan's son Emile, published an anonymous article entitled 'Life on the Planets and Earth'.[106]

According to *Al-Hilal*, there was increasing evidence of extraterrestrial life forms. Unlike Muhammad Tawfiq Sidqi, the anonymous author considered it possible for organisms to move between planets. The magazine gave the example of the German geologist Otto Hahn who had claimed to have discovered fossils of sponges and corals in a meteorite from Hungary. *Al-Hilal* added that 'carbon,

[100] McKim, 'The life and times of E.M. Antoniadi, 1870–1944. Part 2', 224.
[101] McKim, 'The life and times of E.M. Antoniadi, 1870–1944. Part 1', 167.
[102] McKim, 'The life and times of E. M. Antoniadi, 1870–1944. Part 2', 219–20.
[103] Antoniadi, *The Planet Mars*, 33, 67.
[104] Holt, 'Narrating'.
[105] Sheehi, 'Arabic Literary-Scientific Journals', 448.
[106] Al-Hilāl, 'Al-ḥayāt'.

water, and oxygen' were present in such rocks, suggesting that the planets from which they had originated bore life. The article also referred to a thesis by William Thomson, Lord Kelvin, that the first life had come to Earth from another world. This would explain why no new life was being spontaneously generated. *Al-Hilal*'s writer speculated that perhaps on another planet the 'climatic conditions' were different so as to allow for the development of life from inanimate matter.[107]

Besides meteorites, *Al-Hilal* considered another means by which organisms could travel between planets. The magazine referred to an article by an American astronomer about sunlight carrying germs from Mercury and Venus to Earth. *Al-Hilal*'s anonymous author expressed doubts over whether the 'cold' on Mercury allowed for any life. In contrast, Venus's atmosphere was helpful for generating bacteria. Such germs could spread into space, and while some die, others could be carried in 'cells of sunlight'. The material nature of light was confirmed by Albert Einstein, the author noted. Therefore, 'we are hit from time to time by diseases' of unknown origin. If the theory was correct, germs from Earth would likewise be taken by sunlight further into space. Because of constant contact between celestial bodies, life forms on them would not be 'entirely different' from one another. Appearing a few years after the pandemic nicknamed the Spanish Flu, the article likely resonated with readers. *Al-Hilal*'s editor noted that its contents were both 'frightening and reassuring'.[108]

Al-Machriq propagated similar ideas about space-travelling germs at least until the 1930s. A frequent contributor was 'Abd al-Masih Zahr. His writings drew heavily on French texts, including a *Scientific Apologia of the Christian Faith* by Jean-Baptiste Senderens, and indirectly on Camille Flammarion's work. In an article on 'Life on the Celestial Bodies' from 1930, Zahr explained that microbes are able to survive extreme temperatures and radiation in outer space. As the sperm of new life are crossing the solar system, he expected creatures on the different planets to be similar. However, he was left wondering where the first cell had come from. 'This is the secret of life', he concluded, which cannot be explained 'without God'.[109] In 1931, Zahr expanded his natural theology in an article entitled 'True Science Proves the Existence of God'. According to him, numerous famous scientists had recognized God as the 'Lord' and 'Creator' of the universe.[110] They include William Herschel, Pierre-Simon Laplace and

[107] Al-Hilāl, 'Al-ḥayāt', 298–99.
[108] Ibid., 297–99.
[109] Zahr, 'Al-ḥayāt', 249.
[110] Zahr, 'Al-ʻilm al-ḥaqīqī yuthbit wujūd Allāh 1', 210.

Urbain Le Verrier. Zahr concluded with Psalm 14:1, which had also appeared on the title page of Marrash's *Nature's Testimony to the Existence of God and Divine Law*: only 'the fool says in his heart, "There is no god"'.[111]

As ideas about extraterrestrial life kept appearing in Arabic periodicals, even traditionally educated scholars could hardly escape them. The scientific imagination then shaped important books on Qur'anic exegesis. One of them was *The Jewels* by the Egyptian Tantawi Jawhari, a multi-volume work first published in the 1920s and 1930s. The author was a prominent scholar trained at al-Azhar in Cairo.[112] He still maintained a separation of a superior, celestial world from an inferior, terrestrial world. Yet, other parts of his cosmology were more modern. He described the upper world as consisting of galaxies with innumerable suns of vastly different sizes.[113] He gives the example of a star in Orion that is 25 million times larger than our sun. This view of the universe fed into a utopia entitled *Dreams of Politics and How Universal Peace Can Be Realized.* In this work published in 1935, the sheikh imagines visiting a planet in Orion that is more than a million times bigger than Earth. Accompanied by spirits and greeted by beautiful men and women, he felt as if he was in paradise. He is then tested on his ability to use various sciences for the greater good.[114]

As reading modern science in the Qur'an became widespread, professional astronomers engaged in it too. In 1937, Abdel Hamid Samaha of the Helwan Observatory near Cairo gave a lecture on cosmological ideas in the Qur'an at the Lund Observatory in Sweden. He quoted several verses stating that 'those who are in the heavens or on Earth pray' for God. The astronomer took these statements as 'indication to the existence of life either identical, similar or probably different to ours in the outer space'. He added, 'Not merely because I am a Mohamedan but also as a scientist I am inclined to believe that such is at least very probable.' The Egyptian criticized a claim by the English scientist James Hopwood Jeans that 'life on the earth was a mere accident and that it does not exist anywhere else'. Even if life on Earth had developed by chance, Samaha argued, the 'immense number of stars' suggests that this 'happy accident has occurred more than once in the past'.[115]

[111] Zahr, 'Al-ʿilm al-ḥaqīqī yuthbit wujūd Allāh 2', 250, 257.
[112] Daneshgar, *Ṭanṭāwī Jawharī*, 19.
[113] Calderini, '*Tafsīr*', 57; Jawharī, *Al-jawāhir*, 13–14.
[114] Jawharī, *Al-aḥlām*, 7–9.
[115] Samaha, 'Notes', 4–5.

Samaha also propagated similar views among Arab audiences for the rest of his life. In addition to scientific papers in English, he wrote a popular Arabic book entitled *In the Depths of Space*, which asked 'Are there other worlds?' He wrote that 'people often wonder whether there are earths like our Earth and whether there is life' on them. The astronomer affirmed that the planets and their moons are 'earths' too. However, life is 'impossible' on all of them, except Mars and Venus, in whose cases its existence is still doubtful. The Egyptian further stated that many scientists held life on Earth to be an 'accident'. He confessed ignorance of how life had appeared – except as an expression of 'the Creator's will' by him saying 'Be!' However, if life was an accident, he found it 'likely' to be repeated among the millions of stars and galaxies.[116]

Samaha's religious beliefs did not prevent him from collaborating with scientists from the Soviet Union, a secular state ruled by an atheist party. As part of the International Geophysical Year in the late 1950s, he supported an expedition by the Soviet Academy of Sciences to Aswan.[117] It was led by the astronomer Vasiliy Fesenkov, who was based in Kazakhstan. There and in the neighbouring Soviet republics, people of Muslim backgrounds were still able to hold leading positions, including in scientific administration. The mathematician Tashmukhamed Kary-Niyazov, for instance, had become the first president of the Academy of Sciences of Uzbekistan in 1943. Three years later, the geologist Kanysh Satbayev had become his counterpart in Kazakhstan.[118] Muslim traditions were not entirely excluded from these academies. Kary-Niyazov, for instance, studied the astronomy of the fifteenth-century ruler Ulugh Beg.[119]

Although based in Kazakhstan, neither Vasiliy Fesenkov nor his colleague and promoter of astrobotany Gavriil Tikhov were Muslims. They did not even come from Muslim-majority parts of the Russian Empire. Tikhov, the son of a railway employee, was born in a village near Minsk. Fesenkov, offspring of a teacher, hailed from Novocherkassk, a town close to the Black Sea. After initial training in Russia, Tikhov and Fesenkov continued their education at the University of Paris. Tikhov subsequently worked at the Pulkovo Observatory near Saint Petersburg, and Fesenkov at Kharkiv and later in Moscow. Both survived the Russian revolution and became prominent scientists in the Soviet Union. Fesenkov founded the *Astronomicheskiĭ Zhurnal*, a periodical that was known

[116] Samāḥah, *Fī aʿmāq al-faḍā'*, 78–83.
[117] Fesenkov, 'Expedition'.
[118] Sievers, 'Academy Science'.
[119] Demidov, 'Russia', 190.

in English as *Soviet Astronomy*. He also became a full member of the Soviet Academy of Sciences, while Tikhov was elected a corresponding member.[120]

Tikhov and Fesenkov did not end up in Kazakhstan out of any particular interest in the region's Muslim heritage. Instead, their move happened for scientific and military reasons. In 1941, the astronomers travelled to Almaty to observe a solar eclipse. In the meantime, German forces invaded the western parts of the Soviet Union. They destroyed the Pulkovo Observatory, captured Kharkiv and attacked Moscow. In response to the German advances, the Soviet leadership moved military industries and scientific personnel eastwards. Unable to return, and finding the observing conditions in Kazakhstan to be excellent, Fesenkov thus proposed the establishment of an Institute of Astronomy and Physics in Almaty. He promised that this institute would carry out research relevant to the war effort. This included observations in conditions of limited visibility, such as fog and darkness, and secret signalling using polarized light. The Soviet Academy of Sciences approved the new institute in October 1941, at the beginning of the Battle of Moscow.[121]

With senior scientists from elsewhere in the Soviet Union taking up residency, Kazakhstan quickly became a centre for global space research. Unlike other academies in Central Asia, the Kazakh and Uzbek ones pulled their own weight within the Soviet scientific community.[122] In 1949, the Kazakh academy already had more than a thousand scientific workers.[123] The following year, Fesenkov's Institute of Astronomy and Physics was divided into an Astrophysical Institute and a Physical-Technical Institute.[124] In the mid-1950s, the Soviets established their launch facility in Baikonur. At this location closer to the equator, rockets received additional speed from the Earth's rotation. Thinly populated, the area also promised less risk to urban centres and greater secrecy. Between 1957 and 1963, the first satellite, dog, man, and woman were all launched from Baikonur into space.[125]

While many Soviet engineers dedicated themselves to putting living beings into outer space, Gavriil Tikhov was more concerned with existing life on other planets. Already during the first two decades of the twentieth century, he had photographed Mars from Pulkovo and written about its canals.[126] He later

[120] Tejfel, 'Gavriil Adrianovich Tikhov'; Kharitonov and Vilkoviskij, 'Life'.
[121] Kharitonov and Vilkoviskij, 'Life', 263–64.
[122] Sievers, 'Academy Science', 260.
[123] Korol, *Academy of Sciences*, 4.
[124] Kharitonov and Vilkoviskij, 'Life', 264.
[125] Villain, 'A Brief History', 133.
[126] Tikhoff, 'Note préliminaire'; 'L'application'.

changed his mind and, like other leading astronomers, followed Antoniadi in discarding the idea of artificial structures on the surface. However, the Russian astronomer remained convinced that plants exist on the red planet. In 1947, with the support of Kanysh Satbayev, he established the astrobotanical section of the Kazakhstan Academy of Sciences. Because spectral analyses of Mars did not reveal any chlorophyll, he was looking for plants on Earth that might similarly remain hidden. He focused on vegetation in cold and dry climates, such as the Pamir Mountains of Tajikistan and the Arctic.[127]

Tikhov mainly worked with Muslims from Central Asia rather than the Near East. However, having been educated in Paris, he read some of the same literature as people in Egypt or Lebanon. Of particular inspiration to his group of astrobotanists was, again, the work of Camille Flammarion. In a paper from 1960, A. K. Suslov, one of Tikhov's associates, celebrated the French astronomer as the 'forefather of astrobiology'. Suslov acknowledged that Flammarion had not been an atheist, but an 'advocate of mysticism and spiritualism'. The Frenchman had 'worshipped astronomy as the science of the living universe'. Although an opponent of materialism himself, Flammarion deserved credit as a popularizer of science. He had turned an 'aristocratic' into a popular science and ultimately contributed to the development of people's observatories in the Soviet Union. According to Suslov, the Frenchman had believed that on 'any planet, mankind in time will reach such a perfect state that freedom of action will only lead to good', that is, to 'Communism'.[128]

As the astrobotanists appeared ideologically in line, the Soviet government supported their work as part of the wider space programme. In 1961, on the occasion of Yuri Gagarin's flight, Vasily Parin, a pioneer in space medicine, published an article in the Russian magazine *Ogoniok* (Spark). He argued that spacefaring had catalyzed a new science called 'cosmic biology'. This discipline was studying how organisms fare on space flights as well as on other planets. One of its branches was astrobotany as developed by Tikhov. Parin called it 'poetical and fantastic'. At the same time, he argued, it was of practical relevance for future space explorers. Man should know 'to what he will be exposed on other planets'. In addition, studying the effects of space flights on humans, seeds and microorganisms promised advances in medicine and agriculture on Earth.[129]

127 Briot, 'The Creator', 179; Omarov and Tashenov, 'Tikhov's Astrobotany', 86.
128 Suslov, 'C. Flammarion'.
129 Parin, *Cosmos*.

Generous state support came with ideological constraints. Tikhov's patron Satbayev was dismissed as president of the Kazakhstan Academy of Sciences as part of a purge in 1952.[130] He was only reinstated after Joseph Stalin's death.[131] Tikhov himself expressed his commitments to foreign audiences as well. In 1955, he published an article in the *Journal of the British Astronomical Association* under the title 'Is Life Possible on Other Planets?' He clarified that astrobotany was 'based on the principles of Michurinist biology first of all, on the dialectical unity of the organism and its environment'. He explained that 'Dialectical materialism teaches that life is a law-governed phenomenon which appears as an iron necessity resulting from the development of matter.' One of these laws was the 'general rule that the individual development of a living being recapitulates the history of the species'. The reddish colour of young Martian plants in spring thus represented an earlier stage of their evolution. The same process was confirmed by the study of plants on Earth.[132]

The question of extraterrestrial life was thus for Tikhov also one of materialism versus idealism. The academician emphasized this in a book titled *Reaching for the Stars*, which was published in English translation in 1960. Part of an idealist world view was the notion that Earth is at the centre of the universe. Modern astronomy had blasted geocentrism 'to bits', he stressed. 'Even the portion of the Universe accessible to observation has no centre.' He argued that biological geocentrism was similarly untenable. By this he meant 'the claim that the Earth is the model habitat most suitable for life, one that is central in this respect to some degree, and that any deviation from its physical properties makes the genesis and evolution of life impossible'. To the astrobotanist, such a claim 'contradicts all we know about the evolution and forms of matter'. It was as absurd as Martian academicians denying the presence of life on Earth.[133]

Tikhov's ideological conformity probably made it harder for Western botanists to take his work seriously. Especially critical of Soviet biology in general was Conway Zirkle of the University of Pennsylvania. In 1951, he offered an appraisal of the work of his peers behind the Iron Curtain at a meeting of the American Association for the Advancement of Science. He argued that the forced change from genetics to Michurinism, as advocated by Stalin's protégé

[130] Zenkovsky, 'Ideological Deviation', 433.
[131] Sievers, 'Academy Science', 261.
[132] Tikhov, 'Is Life Possible', 194, 199, 201.
[133] Tikhov, *Reaching*, 143–46.

Trofim Lysenko, had resulted in 'the catastrophic decline in the quality of the personnel engaged in biological and agricultural research'. While 'Russian astronomers seem to be doing excellent work', Zirkle considered astrobotany 'an odd development'. 'The astrobotanists claim to have discovered life on Mars', he wrote sceptically. 'They also claim that the climate of Mars resembles that found in parts of Siberia, hence the flora of these regions are being studied so that the astrobotanists can learn what plant life is like on Mars.' He mocked, 'We really cannot exaggerate or parody this stuff.'[134] In 1953, Zirkle published an article on 'The Involuntary Destruction of Science in the USSR'. In it he denounced astrobotany as an 'amusing quackery'.[135]

While Tikhov failed to impress many botanists outside the Soviet Union, he was more successful among space scientists. Albert George Wilson, a former director of the Lowell Observatory who was working for the RAND Corporation, visited Almaty in 1958. He acknowledged that Americans had recognized the achievements of the Russian rocket scientist Konstantin Tsiolkovsky too late. 'We correct this mistake by a recognition of Tikhov's works.'[136] During the following two years, articles on astrobotany were published in the *South African Journal of Science* and *Spaceflight*, a magazine of the British Interplanetary Society.[137] The Russian's work also made it into an American textbook on *Basic Astronautics* and a volume on *Intelligent Life in the Universe*, which was co-authored by Carl Sagan.[138] NASA, too, translated transactions of the Kazakh academy's astrobotanical section.[139] The research by Tikhov and his collaborators thus contributed to the growing field of astrobiology.

While astrobiology developed elsewhere, the astrobotanical work in Kazakhstan came to an end. After Tikhov's death in 1960, the Kazakh academy closed his section. Municipal authorities wanted to preserve his house, observatory and 'astrobotanical garden'. They even supported the creation of a museum and planetarium. However, these plans were cancelled, despite protests in the press.[140] The decline of astrobotany was perhaps related to increasing criticism of Michurinism after Stalin's death in 1953. Trofim Lysenko slowly lost influence and was removed as director of the Institute of Genetics of the

[134] Zirkle, 'An Appraisal of Science', 101, 106.
[135] Zirkle, 'The Involuntary Destruction', 281.
[136] Tejfel, 'Gavriil Adrianovich Tikhov', 721.
[137] Bazykine, 'The New Science'; Tikhov, 'What Is Astrobotany?'
[138] Ordway, III et al., *Basic Astronautics*, 254, 273; Shklovski and Sagan, *Intelligent Life*, 254, 275.
[139] Tikhov, *Observations*.
[140] Tejfel, 'Gavriil Adrianovich Tikhov', 721.

Soviet Academy of Sciences in 1965.[141] Around this time, a wider generational shift took place in the Kazakh academy. Tikhov's early supporter Kanysh Satbayev passed away in 1964. During the same year, Vasiliy Fesenkov, the director of the Astrophysical Institute in Almaty, returned to Moscow, where he chaired the Soviet academy's meteorite committee.[142] Tikhov's Kazakh collaborators may have stayed on. However, their names, such as that of senior laboratory technician B. B. Intykbayeva, faded from records and memories.[143]

Although Tikhov's house and garden did not become objects of official preservation, his astrobotanical work left another form of popular legacy: in science fiction. Through his books, articles and public lectures, he inspired many people, such as the writer Alexander Kazantsev. The latter hailed from Akmolinsk, a town that would become – under the name Astana – the capital of Kazakhstan. He studied in Tomsk in Siberia and became an engineer and colonel in the Red Army. In this position, World War II caused him to move west rather than east. In 1945, he was charged with capturing technology from occupied Austria. While driving through Hungary, he learned about the atomic bombing of Hiroshima. Further investigations led him to revisit the Tunguska event, the flattening of 2,000 square kilometres of forest in Siberia in 1908. He interpreted the catastrophe as the result of a nuclear reaction.[144]

Kazantsev first published his idea in 1946 in 'Explosion: The Story of a Hypothesis'. In this text, various actual scientists, including Vasiliy Fesenkov, appear. They are joined by a mysterious, black-skinned, red-haired woman whose heart is located on the right side of her body. In the author's imagination, she had suddenly appeared in Siberia at the time of the Tunguska event. With the ability to 'heal with just her eyes', she becomes a shaman for people from the region. Kazantsev suggests that she is the survivor of alien visitors to Earth. In the end, one character says: 'There is also the possibility that the explosion took place not in a uranium meteorite, but in an interplanetary spaceship that ran on atomic energy.'[145]

While Kazantsev's hypothesis encountered resistance from meteorite researchers like Fesenkov, it was popular. In 1950, the writer Boris Liapunov confirmed the thesis in a sketch titled 'From the Depth of the Universe'.[146]

141 Barry Cohen, 'The Descent', 229.
142 Kharitonov and Vilkoviskij, 'Life', 264.
143 Kutyreva et al., 'Characteristics', 74; Victor Tejfel, email, 30 June 2018.
144 Rubtsov, *The Tunguska Mystery*, 65–68.
145 Kazantsev, 'Explosion'.
146 Schwartz, 'Guests', 227–28.

Kazantsev himself developed the idea in another story titled 'A Visitor from Outer Space', which was first published in 1951. The hero of the story is an astrobotanist and student of Gavriil Tikhov. In a commentary accompanying the main text, Kazantsev stressed that the 'materialist conception of the universe is in accord with the origin and development of life on other planets wherever conditions are favourable'. Astrobotany is praised as 'a new Soviet science created by one of our most outstanding astronomers'. Kazantsev further lauded Tikhov as 'the first scientist in the world to photograph the canals on Mars'. The author acknowledged that 'so far not all scientists share G. A. Tikhov's views'.[147] However, one reviewer in the journal *Soviet Astronomy* still accused Kazantsev of misrepresenting Soviet science.[148]

Despite attempts at repression by some scientists, Kazantsev's ideas spread beyond the borders of the Soviet Union. The young Polish author Stanisław Lem included the thesis of the Tunguska spaceship in his first novel *The Astronauts* in 1951. This novel was then adapted as a film that appeared in English as *First Spaceship on Venus*.[149] In Egypt, the writer Abdul Razzak Naufal picked up the idea from Boris Liapunov, but interpreted it religiously. He mentioned Liapunov in two books entitled *God and Modern Science* and *Heaven and the People of Heaven*. Naufal added to the Tunguska event a 'mysterious explosion' on Mars, which the Japanese amateur astronomer Tsuneo Saheki had observed in 1949. In *God and Modern Science*, the Egyptian asked: 'Is this not evidence of the miraculousness of the Qur'an, which mentions the existence of life in the heavens and on Earth fourteen centuries ago? Is there any doubt about who revealed the Qur'an?'[150]

Whether promoted by religious missionaries or materialists, modern astronomy and astrobiology thus also served as resources for religious entrepreneurs from across the Muslim world. Rather than embracing either Christianity or communism, scholars like Naufal sought to reconcile new natural knowledge with the Qur'an. Heliocentrism was firmly established among scientists, whereas the existence of extraterrestrial life remained in doubt. Yet, as both ideas entered Arabic periodicals, they were even used by traditionally educated scholars to strengthen their authority. At the same time as

147 Kazantsev, 'A Visitor', 111, 116, 119, 122.
148 Perel', 'Visitor'.
149 Schwartz, 'Guests', 228.
150 Nawfal, *Al-samā'*, 92; *Allāh*, 213–16.

industrial communications connected the faithful and contributed to the notion of the Muslim world,[151] writers employed the science as well as the mysteries of the universe to emphasize the truth of Islam.

Although astronomers led by Eugène Antoniadi had disproven the existence of canals on Mars, astrobotany in Kazakhstan and related science fiction continued to feed the imagination. In the middle of the twentieth century, portrayals of life elsewhere in the solar system appeared not just on paper but increasingly on the silver screen. Taking artistic liberties, filmmakers around the world depicted not just Mars, but even the Moon as inhabited by beautiful women and other intelligent beings. Such visions were as wide-reaching as the research by migrant scientists like Antoniadi and Tikhov. Just as these two astronomers frequently published in English and French, directors employed a visual language that was global, including recognizable images of robots and flying saucers. However, in order to reach broad audiences, they had to adapt the contents to local tastes. In Muslim-majority countries, this often meant cultures shaped by Islamic traditions.

[151] Green, 'Spacetime'.

3

Trips to the Moon

A Pakistani woman can marry an alien, as long as he is Muslim.[1] This was one of the possible messages of the film *Shanee*, released in 1989. Starring veteran actors, it had many classical elements, such as a complicated romance and a struggle against a villain. Unusual for South Asian cinema, however, the movie begins with the landing of a flying saucer. An alien appears and assumes the form of Shanee, a recent murder victim. In this guise, he is warmly welcomed by surprised villagers and especially by the victim's fiancée Hina, who is played by Babra Sharif. The impostor initially refuses to marry Hina, but over the course of the movie, he falls in love with her. In addition to relationship challenges, the alien faces the threat of Shanee's murderer. Yet, in action-packed scenes, the locals help the alien and Hina defeat the villain and his thugs.[2]

Shanee was pioneering among Pakistani movies not just through the extraterrestrial elements of its plot, but also in its visual effects. The alien has spectacular superpowers in addition to being handsome. He walks through a closed door, rips off a man's arm and prevents a train from running over Hina. Later in the film, the impostor survives electrocution in the villain's lair. The child he has with Hina has the ability to shoot lasers out of his eyes. In the final scene, these lasers drive away criminals, allowing for an escape aboard a flying saucer.[3] The sound effects used in these battles were purchased from Los Angeles.[4] Indicating further influence by Hollywood, the saucer is reminiscent of the mothership in *Close Encounters of the Third Kind*. The

1 Kazi, 'Pakistani Sci-Fi'.
2 Rizvi, *Shanee*.
3 Ibid.
4 Suhayb Alavi, 'Super Hero's "Homecoming"'.

director Saeed Rizvi later described himself as a big fan of Steven Spielberg as well as of John Carpenter and James Cameron.[5]

Unlike American science fiction blockbusters by Spielberg and others, the main characters in Rizvi's film are all Muslims. The villagers generally appear pious and frequently refer to God in their conversations. After discovering that Shanee's lookalike is an impostor, they initially refuse to support him. Hina and her grandfather feel betrayed and doubt whether the alien even believes in God. The extraterrestrial responds that God and His prophet's message are not restricted to 'your world'. Alien hearts, the film suggests, contain the same faith. The impersonator then opens his shirt in a Superman-like manner. Revealed is not the letter 'S', but the first *kalimah* (word) in South Asian Islam: 'There is no god but God. Muhammad is the messenger of God.' To the astonishment of the villagers, the bright Arabic letters float into the room and then into the sky.[6]

Even without the claim that extraterrestrials are Muslims, the production of a science fiction movie like *Shanee* was remarkable in Pakistan. After the partition of British India, the country's filmmakers faced many political challenges. In 1949, a minister of industry declared, 'In principle Muslims should not get involved in film-making. Being the work of lust and lure, it should be left to infidels.' Filmmaking could be tolerated and taxed, but should neither be supported nor celebrated.[7] Adaptations of speculative fiction from abroad often involved some form of Islamization. Such was the case with *Zinda Laash* from 1967, which was also marketed as *Dracula in Pakistan* and *The Living Corpse*. The film's prologue contains a verse from the Qur'an and a warning not to attempt to cheat death.[8]

After the 1960s, further restrictions appeared. The Pakistan Censor Board, a corrupt bureaucratic body, plagued directors. As part of a coup d'état, General Muhammad Zia-ul-Haq declared martial law in 1977 and cancelled all previous censor certificates. During his tenure as president, the government sought to ban all movies that 'impair accepted moral standards' or 'hurt national sentiments'.[9] After his death in 1988, groups outside the Pakistani state enforced their own restrictions. When the Taliban assumed control over the Swat district in 2007,

[5] Omair Alavi, 'The Return'.
[6] Rizvi, *Shanee*.
[7] Khan and Ahmad, 'From *Zinda Laash*', 150.
[8] Kazi, 'Pakistani Sci-Fi'.
[9] Khan and Ahmad, 'From *Zinda Laash*', 150.

they closed cinemas and set fire to DVD shops. As cinemas often spliced films with pornography,[10] this violence probably enjoyed some support from local conservatives.

Despite political challenges, Pakistan produced around eighty films per year by the late 1990s.[11] Nevertheless, the making of *Shanee* was still exceptional, and its director had to rely mostly on family resources. Fortunately, Saeed Rizvi's father Rafiq had been involved in productions since before the partition of India. The inspiration for *Shanee* came from a commercial for a cement company, in which a laser was energizing a factory. After seeing the clip in 1985, Rafiq advised Saeed to make a film using the same effects. 'There was no help from the government in those days and not a single penny was invested from the private sector as well, as they thought I was crazy', Saeed later recalled. With the help of an experienced writer from his father's team, he completed a script and started shooting in 1987. Rafiq died the following year, but was still credited as the producer.[12]

Shanee achieved some critical, but limited commercial success. The film received several Nigar Awards, but presumably did not generate enough revenue for Rizvi to produce a sequel.[13] Instead, his next project was a low-budget horror movie titled *Beheaded Man*. For much of his career, Rizvi concentrated on producing television commercials. It took almost three decades for him to attempt a return to science fiction. In 2015, he spent several months in New York and Los Angeles in order to catch up with the latest technology, including advanced digital cameras and computer-generated imagery. He planned to use these tools for another 'film in the vein of Hollywood blockbusters' that would 'revolve around an alien invasion'.[14] However, he still complained that the Pakistani state was failing to 'play its role in supporting the film industry'. 'It didn't even accept the fact that we were the ones who paid huge amounts of money in taxes', Rizvi grumbled. 'Sadly, the government has never realised the actual potential of the film industry in our country.'[15]

The scarcity of films about extraterrestrial life from Pakistan stands in contrast to India. In 1967, more than twenty years before *Shanee*, Pakistan's neighbour had already released two major science fiction films. The first, *Wahan Ke Log*

[10] Ibid., 157–58.
[11] Ali Nobil Ahmad, 'Film', 84.
[12] Suhayb Alavi, 'Super Hero's "Homecoming"'.
[13] Walker, 'Urdu Science Fiction'.
[14] Express Tribune, 'SOS'.
[15] Mazhar and Qamar, 'Saeed Rizvi'.

(The Aliens), features an evil scientist, ray guns and flying saucers.[16] In the second film, *Trip to Moon*, an astronaut fights robots, missiles and an alien rhinoceros in order to save a princess. As was common for Bollywood, these battle sequences are interspersed with beautiful women singing and dancing – lunar ones in this case.[17] During the 1970s, the Indian production of science fiction films dropped. This perhaps had to do with disappointment over government development plans and disillusionment with science as a means to fight poverty and other social ills. Positive imaginings of technological futures were arguably harder to sell in this context.[18] Nevertheless, India may have contributed indirectly to the boom in American science fiction films during the same period. *The Alien*, written by Satyajit Ray in 1967, was supposed to be produced by Columbia Pictures. This film, which was about a Bengali boy and a visitor from outer space, was never realized. However, Ray's script circulated in Hollywood and could have influenced Spielberg's film *E.T. the Extra-Terrestrial*.[19]

By the twenty-first century, space aliens were again a popular theme in Indian cinema. The year 2003 saw the release of *Koi ... Mil Gaya* (I Found Someone). In this Hindi film, a scientist contacts extraterrestrials via the syllable *Om*. In 2014, *PK* starring Aamir Khan became one of the highest-grossing Indian films,[20] reaching many viewers in Pakistan too. In this film, an alien lands naked on a research mission to Rajasthan, but is stranded when the remote control for his spaceship is stolen. Saeed Rizvi remarked that 'many people have told me that the first scene of the film in which the spaceship descends to Earth reminds them of *Shanee*'. The director added, 'If the first scene of the biggest hit in Indian cinema reminds them of my film – a Pakistani film – I would take that as a compliment, any day.'[21]

Islam in any general sense can hardly be blamed for the relative scarcity of Pakistani science fiction films, as Bollywood has had important Muslim contributors too. *Wahan Ke Log* was directed and produced by Nisar Ahmad Ansari, who was also one of the actors. Sultan Ahmed from Lucknow assisted Ansari in producing the film at K. Asif Studios in Bombay. Shakeel Badayuni, an Urdu poet, wrote the lyrics, and S. M. Qureshi was responsible for make-up. Muslim contributors also included the art director, the set designer and

[16] N. A. Ansari, *Wahan*; Kaur, 'The Fictions', 290.
[17] Sundaram, *Trip*.
[18] Lakkad, 'Cultural Imaginaries', 109–10.
[19] Kaur, 'The Fictions', 283.
[20] Lakkad, 'Cultural Imaginaries', 113–17.
[21] Omair Alavi, 'The Return'.

supporting actors.[22] In *Trip to Moon*, Anwar Hussain from Calcutta played the king of Mars. The lyrics were partly written by Shamsul Huda Bihari, an experienced songwriter from northern India. Other Muslims included a playback singer, a supporting actor and a sound assistant.[23]

As Muslim filmmakers were active in both countries, did the politics of religion make a difference? Did Indian secularism enable science fiction more than Pakistani Islamism? The emergence of films like *Koi ... Mil Gaya* in the context of rising Hindu nationalism seems to contradict this.[24] On the whole, however, secular states were among the most prominent producers of the genre globally. They included countries with otherwise very different political and economic systems, such as the United States and the Soviet Union. 'Astroculture'[25] seems to have entered the visions of progress of secular governments especially quickly. Although Alexander Kazantsev's imaginations met opposition from some Soviet scientists, they were popular on screen as well as in writing. The author from Kazakhstan inspired not just *First Spaceship on Venus*, he also wrote the underlying novel and script for *Planet of Storms* from 1962. The Syrian Taleb Omran considered the latter movie of similar importance to two major Western productions from the end of that decade: Stanley Kubrick's *2001: A Space Odyssey* and Franklin Schaffner's *Planet of the Apes*.[26]

Looking at Middle Eastern countries seems to confirm a broadly negative effect of Islamism on the production of science fiction films. Although comparable in its authoritarianism to the socialist states, Saudi Arabia started banning cinemas during the decade in which the hits by Kubrick and others appeared and the Cold War space race was in full swing. While supporting the introduction of television, King Faisal sided with conservatives who objected to public theatres as bringing unrelated men and women together. In the twenty-first century, repression of cinema slowly faded.[27] However, as late as 2017, the grand mufti Abd al-Aziz Al al-Shaykh denounced cinemas alongside singing concerts as a 'depravity'. These venues, he remarked, 'might show movies that are libertine, lewd, immoral and atheist, because they rely on films imported to change our culture'.[28]

22 Gupta, 'India', 284.
23 Sundaram, *Trip*.
24 Alessio and Langer, 'Science Fiction'.
25 Geppert, 'European Astrofuturism', 8.
26 'Umrān, *Al-'ālam*.
27 Sakr, 'Placing Political Economy', 221–22.
28 Agence France-Presse, 'Saudi Mufti'.

The long ban on cinemas did not mean that Saudi Arabia was entirely closed to global science fiction. Shaweesh, a Riyadh-based artist, inserted icons of popular culture into historical photographs, for instance. His particular inspiration came from an image of the Egyptian president Anwar El-Sadat visiting Disneyland and meeting Mickey Mouse and Pluto. Shaweesh created similar encounters with characters from *Star Wars*, such as Yoda. Using a photograph from 1945, the artist ironically juxtaposed the alien with Faisal, who was then a prince and foreign minister (Figure 4). Shaweesh chose the Jedi master not just for his wisdom, but also because he and his lightsabre were green like the Saudi flag. In 2017, the photomontage somehow ended up in social studies textbooks published by the Saudi Ministry of Education. The minister himself apologized for the 'unintended mistake'. His agency withdrew the copies and 'formed a legal committee to determine the source of the error and to take the proper measures'.[29]

Figure 4 'The Last Jedi' (2013). Courtesy of Shaweesh.

[29] Hubbard, 'Saudi Textbook'.

The opposition of Wahhabi clerics to cinemas arguably influenced the Taliban, who tried to suppress movies not just in Pakistan, but also in Afghanistan. Such hostility was not restricted to Sunnis, however. Movie theatres drew the ire of Shia conservatives in Iran before and during the revolution of 1979. Nevertheless, within a few years of gaining power, the revolutionaries did sponsor a vibrant film industry.[30] Many productions dealt with problems within contemporary Iranian society. Their number became large enough to form their own genre called *ijtimāʿī* (social). Curiously though, science fiction was rare.[31] One example is *I Love Earth* by Abolhassan Davoodi from 1994, in which an alien befriends a Tehran taxi driver.[32] As in *Shanee*, a complicated romance is also part of the plot, but with more comedic elements. However, with such movies remaining one-offs, were Islamic regimes hostile to wild cinematic imaginations?

The politics of religion perhaps contributed to a dearth of science fiction films in Iran, Pakistan and Saudi Arabia. However, could costs have been another factor? Science fiction films were generally more expensive to make than those within the genre of social realism. This had to do with more elaborate, fantastic-looking sets, costumes and props. Countries like the United States, the Soviet Union and India had more resources and larger markets to support science fiction than even populous Muslim-majority countries. Nevertheless, a huge budget was not a necessity for much science fiction. Despite sanctions, the Iranian movie industry had the expertise and equipment to contribute to the genre at least in modest ways. Artists were able to produce impressive, albeit not cutting-edge, visual effects. A flying saucer with colourful lights in *I Love Earth* looks similarly convincing to the one in *Shanee*. In subsequent decades, the use of computer-generated imagery spread. One master of this art was Ali Pourahmad, a graduate of Azad University, who set up Hundred Studio Productions in Bandar Abbas in 2004. Largely self-funded through daytime work for Iran Air, he produced clips of alien organisms, planets and spacecraft.[33]

The case of Iran thus invites us to investigate the relationship between Islam and science fiction cinema further. Davoodi's *I Love Earth* did appear during a period of liberalization following the war with Iraq. However, a major production was at least conceivable in Iran even at the height of the country's Islamic revolution. Amid the hostage crisis in 1980, the Central Intelligence

30 Ali Nobil Ahmad, 'Film', 84.
31 Aysha, 'SF in Iran'.
32 Dāwudī, *Man Zamīn rā dūst dāram*.
33 Pourahmad, 'About HSP'.

Agency used a fake film called *Argo* as a cover for the rescue of six American diplomats from Tehran. The trapped officials were disguised as Canadian filmmakers who had been scouting locations. Iran's rugged landscapes and an underground bazaar were seen as fitting for a movie set on an alien planet. In an elaborate scheme, the CIA acquired the movie rights for Roger Zelazny's novel *Lord of Light*, which drew on Hindu and Buddhist traditions. The agency further conspired with the make-up artist John Chambers, who had worked on *Planet of the Apes* and *Star Trek*. A fake company paid for advertisements, and *Hollywood Reporter* and *Variety* published news articles.[34] In the end, the cover of science fiction enabled the Americans to escape the new Islamic regime.

In order to fully understand the whole range of factors affecting science fiction cinema in Muslim-majority countries, it is insufficient to look at Iran, Pakistan and Saudi Arabia alone. Egypt and Turkey, two of the largest film producers in the Muslim world, deserve close attention as well. The Turkish Republic in particular seems to confirm a connection between secularism and production of science fiction films during the twentieth century. However, the development of the movie industries in different national contexts also had specificities beyond the relationship between religion and the state. What cinematic products the scientific imagination gave rise to depended on wider political and economic changes, including fluctuating levels of subsidies and bureaucratic control.

Furthermore, despite the importance of national politics and economics, no cinema of a Muslim-majority country developed in isolation. Many productions by Muslims were influenced by a tradition of European and North American films that reached back to the early twentieth century. Western artists themselves frequently created fantastic extraterrestrial landscapes by drawing on exotic ones on Earth. They thus in turn drew on images from and of the Muslim world, including orientalist ones. A number of major science fiction films, whether from Turkey or the United States, were then the products of exchange and circulation between East and West. As such, they were global and local at the same time.

Pharaohs and fairies

At the beginning of the world's movie production about alien life stood *A Trip to the Moon*, released in 1902. It was directed by Georges Méliès, a prolific French artist and innovator in special effects. The plot was simple enough to be

[34] Bearman, 'How the CIA'.

understood by audiences worldwide. The setting is a Moon teeming with life. In fact, the entire celestial body displays the face of the Man in the Moon. In an image that would become iconic, a giant cannon on Earth shoots a capsule in the shape of a bullet straight into his eye. Astronomers exit the vehicle and explore the lunar surface, walking through forests of giant mushrooms. Subsequently, they defend themselves against Selenites, green insectoids that carry spears, but explode when hit with force. The Selenites capture the explorers and march them to their king's palace (Figure 5). However, one astronomer lifts him off his throne and throws him to the ground, causing him to explode. Chased by the other Selenites, the men run back to the capsule and return to Earth.

Although religious references are largely absent from *A Trip to the Moon*, Méliès was influenced by Middle Eastern lands. As a young man, he had experienced stage magic in London's Egyptian Hall, which exhibited the cultures of the Nile. Besides *A Trip to the Moon*, Méliès made numerous orientalist short films. In 1897, for instance, he created *The Funny Muslim*, *Sale of Slaves for the Harem* and *Dance in the Palace*. In *A Trip to the Moon*, Méliès borrowed more directly from Jules Verne and H. G. Wells than from any Muslim author.[35] However, Verne himself had also produced orientalist works, such as the novels *Around the World in Eighty Days* and *The Begum's Fortune*.[36] In 1905, soon

Figure 5 The astronomers in the Selenite palace in Georges Méliès's *A Trip to the Moon* (1902).

[35] Sandner, 'Shooting', 5.
[36] Cubitt, 'Phalke', 120–21.

after *A Trip to the Moon*, Méliès released a film titled *The Palace of the Arabian Nights*. Images of the orient arguably influenced the depiction of the Selenite serai, which features crescents and a king surrounded by beautiful women.

It is unclear how many Muslims saw Méliès's *A Trip to the Moon* and when. However, the movie was a global success. In addition to showing the film in Paris, Méliès marketed it through a company in London. Moreover, several American producers distributed unauthorized copies. Reportedly, these copies had originated from a print that Méliès had sold for exhibition in Algeria. Within less than three years, *A Trip to the Moon* was also marketed in Germany and Italy.[37] In 1952, El-Sayyed Hassan Gomaa, a film critic from Alexandria, remembered that Méliès had 'surprised the world at the beginning of the twentieth century with films based on deception'. He had done so especially with films 'derived from the *One Thousand and One Nights*'.[38]

Even if few Muslims watched Méliès's own films, other orientalist productions were popular. They were initially more in the genre of fantasy than science fiction. The *One Thousand and One Nights* occupied a prominent place in early cinema across the world. One of India's first features, released in 1903, was *Ali Baba and the Forty Thieves*, for instance. It was directed by Hiralal Sen, a photographer and filmmaker from near Dhaka in Bengal. The 1920s saw several hits that drew on the *Arabian Nights*. In 1922, *Princess Budur* by J. J. Madan, a theatre magnate from Bombay, appeared on screens. Raoul Walsh's *Thief of Bagdad*, a Hollywood production of the same decade, inspired further Indian films.[39]

Probably only a small fraction of Muslims frequented movie theatres during the first half of the twentieth century. Yet, through the writings of critics such as El-Sayyed Hassan Gomaa, readers of Arabic could stay informed about developments in global cinema. Beginning in the late 1920s, Gomaa published articles in *Al-Hilal* on various aspects of the medium. One of them concerned the 'past, present and future' of sound film.[40] The critic also advertised the religious and scientific benefits of filmmaking. Another piece on 'Cinema in the Service of Religions' discussed Cecil DeMille's film *The Ten Commandments* and Fred Niblo's *Ben-Hur: A Tale of the Christ*. Gomaa was particularly impressed by the construction of an ancient Egyptian town in California for the former.[41] In another piece, he explained the use of

37 Solomon, 'Introduction', 2–3.
38 Jumʿah, 'Alf laylah', 95.
39 Kaur, 'The Fictions', 285.
40 Jumʿah, 'Al-sīnimā al-nāṭiqah'.
41 Jumʿah, 'Al-sīnimā fī khidmat al-adyān'.

the movie camera in scientific observations and teaching. Botanists could film the growth of a plant, while astronomers may track planets.[42]

Soon, critics like Gomaa were also able to write about domestic productions. During the 1930s, Egypt developed the largest film industry in the Arab world, creating a 'Hollywood on the Nile'.[43] Cairo and Alexandria, like Los Angeles, benefited from clear skies and bright sunlight for much of the year. Filmmakers could thus shoot in the open on almost any day without the need for a studio.[44] Nevertheless, capitalists financed a sophisticated infrastructure. In 1935, Talaat Harb, the founder of Banque Misr, established a studio with the same name. With funds from the bank, it was able to purchase up-to-date equipment and employ actors, directors and technicians on permanent contracts. Studio Misr was in competition with Studio Al Ahram and others that were founded.[45] Distributors like Behna and Nahas brought their products to cinemas in Egypt, the wider Middle East and beyond.[46]

Beginning in the early 1940s, the Egyptian film industry produced notable works of speculative fiction. Like in France and India, orientalism influenced some of these productions. Togo Mizrahi from Alexandria directed *One Thousand and One Nights* and *Ali Baba and the Forty Thieves*,[47] which starred the comedian Ismaïl Yassein from Suez. Yassein also appeared in *Naduga*,[48] a jungle adventure resembling Tarzan.[49] Nahas Film brought out this film plus another one entitled *The Vanishing Cap* in 1944. For the latter, the director Niazi Mostafa had studied the special effects in James Whale's *The Invisible Man*. Similar to its American model, *The Vanishing Cap* was popular enough to be remade twice over the next fifteen years.[50] Initially, Egyptian films about invisibility were more fantasy than science fiction. Yet, by the early 1950s, they displayed elements that were more recognizable as science than as magic. Such was the case with *Where Did You Get This?*, which was also directed by Niazi Mostafa. In this iteration, the means of becoming unseen was no longer dusty headgear, but a serum developed by a professor and his student in a medical

42 Jumʿah, 'Al-thaqāfah al-sīnimāʾīyah', 580, 582.
43 Tartoussieh, 'Pious Stardom', 34.
44 El-Mazzaoui, 'Film', 248.
45 Gaffney, 'The Egyptian Cinema', 56–57.
46 El-Mazzaoui, 'Film', 250.
47 Mizrāḥī, *Alf laylah*; *ʿAlī Bābā*.
48 Fawzī, *Nādūjā*.
49 Wass, 'Where Did You'.
50 Ibid. Muṣṭafá, *Ṭāqiyat al-ikhfāʾ*; *Sirr ṭāqiyat al-ikhfāʾ*.

laboratory. Yassein appeared in this film as the scientist's valet. A second actor was Edmond Tuema, an Egyptian of Lebanese origin.[51]

Less than thirty years after its establishment, the Egyptian film industry looked with excitement to its own future. In 1950, *Al-Hilal* dedicated an issue to imaginations of life in the year 2000. Anwar Ahmed, one of the contributors, envisioned a 'Hollywood of the East' with studios and elegant mansions for the stars along the road to the pyramids. Films would be produced in Arabic and English for export to Europe and America, with Egypt's multilingual actors becoming global celebrities. Even ministers would be proud to see their daughters perform on screen. The author further portrayed luxurious, air-conditioned cinemas in Cairo. Audiences entirely dressed in European clothes would watch a feature about pharaonic Egypt in a calm manner without cries or laughter.[52]

Space exploration also featured prominently in the future that *Al-Hilal* was imagining. Its issue from 1950 included a conversation with the British writer Arthur C. Clarke under the title 'We will travel to the Moon'. Clarke assumed that any inhabitants of other planets would be peaceful. 'They are superior to us from the perspective of humanity', he said, and 'preceded us in the stages of the ladder of sophistication'. When asked why the inhabitants of other planets had not communicated with Earth, he compared them to a man who runs at great speed along a beach without checking every grain of sand.[53] A similar view of advanced and peaceful extraterrestrials appeared in 'A Bride from Mars' by El-Sayyed Hassan Gomaa. Written like a play, this story was shaped by the author's experience with cinema. Each section begins with a brief description of the locations: a rocket, 'a square on Mars' and a 'throne hall in the palace of the Queen of Mars'. In the beginning, the protagonist Farid 'is looking at a white screen like a cinema screen placed on top of the control system' of the rocket. This surface shows the way to Mars as recorded by the 'magic lens'.[54]

After Gomaa had written about the construction of an ancient Egyptian town for an American movie, he imagined a similar place in 'Bride from Mars'. The rocket pilot Farid and his assistant John land on a square surrounded by buildings in 'pharaonic style'. There, they encounter hundreds of Martians in the 'garb of ancient Egyptians'. Their commander explains to Farid and John

51 Wass, 'Where Did You'; Muṣṭafá, *Min ayna laka hādhā?*
52 Anwar Aḥmad, 'Al-sīnimā'.
53 Klārk, 'Sa-nusāfir', 98.
54 Jumʿah, 'ʿArūs'.

that more than 5,000 years prior, one of their scientists had travelled to Earth and created the 'City of Mars' or Cairo. The tombs of Martian leaders appear to the visitors from Earth as large versions of the pyramids of Giza and Saqqara, which had been designed by that same ancient space traveller.[55]

After introducing similarities, Gomaa drew a contrast between the societies of both planets, criticizing the racism and sexism of his fellow earthlings. Similar to Arthur C. Clarke's imagination, Mars was free of wars, and its inhabitants formed one people. 'There are no differences between an Easterner or Westerner, or between white and black', the commander chides the visitors. 'This is your thing, oh people of Earth. You differentiate between your races and colors. The big one eats the small one.' As a result, Earth has experienced wars 'without interruption'. In order to protect themselves from the 'spirit of evil', the Martians avoid communication with their neighbours in the solar system. Nevertheless, the Martian queen requests to meet the visitors. As the commander explains, the Martians have a female monarch out of 'respect' for her gender. Because women are mothers, wives, sisters and daughters, men ought to sanctify and obey them.[56]

Martian matriarchy marginalizes marriage, but – fortunately for the reader – does not prevent romance in Gomaa's imagination. The commander first explains that traditions normally forbid a queen from having a spouse. However, whoever happens to be queen at the turn of every millennium has the right to wed the first person entering the capital. This happens to be Farid, as he left the rocket before John. The marriage is meant to give the queen the opportunity to take a break before dedicating herself to politics again. After having a child with Farid, the queen is expected to divorce him. Instead, she escapes her palace and flies to Earth with Farid, their child and John. She chooses Luxor as a landing site and becomes the first Martian to arrive on Earth in thousands of years.[57]

Despite Gomaa's long experience with cinema, his 'Bride from Mars' was not adapted into a film. However, another Egyptian love story about a man from Earth and a woman from the red planet made it onto the stage. In 1951, the Modern Egyptian Theater group performed *A Nymph from Mars*. One of the actresses was Zahrat El-Ola from Alexandria, who would go on to act in Ismaïl Yassein movies.[58] Reportedly, the play was first submitted under the title

55 Jumʿah, ''Arūs', 140–41.

56 Ibid., 141–42.

57 Ibid., 144–46.

58 Muṣṭafá Zakī, *Wurūd lā tubdhal*, 61–62.

A Nymph from Paradise to a conservative censor in the Ministry of Interior. The Arabic word for 'nymph' in the title, *ḥūrīyah*, denotes a virgin pleasing a believer in the hereafter. 'May God save us', responded the censor. His objection forced the change from paradise to Mars. Once performed, the play was well-received by critics. One of them compared it to the 'famous Greek myth Pygmalion', in which a goddess grants a man's wish for a perfect wife.[59]

A Nymph from Mars owed inspiration not just to Islamic and Greek mythologies, but also to contemporary films. Rifʿat, the main male protagonist, is tired of the problems he has with his wife, Ihsan. One day, while Ihsan is out at a movie theatre, her husband sees three fairies from Mars. He falls in love with one of them, and God gives her to him. As one critic explained, this fairy appears in the 'clothes of Western nymphs' or 'sports clothes'. She is nice, beautiful, blind in her obedience and in total agreement with his views. Unlike in his marriage to Ihsan, Rifʿat faces no quarrels or fights. However, in this quiet new relationship, Rifʿat again longs for Ihsan. He explains this to the nymph, who then restores the connection between the two spouses. In the end, Rifʿat wakes up from what turns out to have been a dream, as his wife returns from the cinema.[60]

Interest in space and its creatures only increased over the course of the 1950s. Prompted by the launch of *Sputnik-1*, *Al-Hilal* dedicated a special issue to the 'satellite age' in January 1958. The minister of endowments contributed an article arguing that Islam supports space launches as a force of science.[61] In another piece Anwar Ahmed pointed out that Hollywood had preceded the Soviet conquest of space. He discussed several films from the decade, including *Destination Moon*, *Forbidden Planet* and *The Day the Earth Stood Still*.[62] Also part of the issue were translated short stories by H. G. Wells and Robert Heinlein plus a discussion of the question 'To whom belongs the Moon and which laws govern its inhabitants?'[63]

Spread by *Al-Hilal* and other media, the enthusiasm for space and science fiction was shared by one of Egypt's most prominent playwrights, Tawfiq al-Hakim. Inspired by scripture, he ventured into the fantastic early in his career. In 1933, he published the play *The People of the Cave*, which was based on the tradition of the Seven Sleepers of Ephesus. The play follows Christians who escape Roman persecution by sleeping in a cave and wake up 300 years

59 Ṣalāḥ, 'Ḥūrīyah'; Khiḍr, 'Al-adab'.
60 Ṣalāḥ, 'Ḥūrīyah'; Khiḍr, 'Al-adab'.
61 Al-Bāqūrī, 'Al-Islām'.
62 Anwar Aḥmad, 'Al-sīnimā'.
63 Atallah, 'Modernism', 1225.

later after the triumph of their religion. In al-Hakim's adaptation, however, the protagonists are dissatisfied with the new era and take refuge once more.[64] After World War II, the Egyptian playwright moved his plots to a technological future. In 1947, he published a short story under the title 'In the Year One Million'. In his vision, death, disease and gender discrimination have all been eradicated. Love and poetry are equally missing, however. Discontented with this dystopia, the people overthrow the state and destroy its laboratories and scientific instruments. In the end, fear, illness and death return to the world, but also religion, sexuality and the arts.[65]

As the space age began, Tawfiq al-Hakim explored the idea of immortality on another planet. In 1958, he published the play *Voyage to Tomorrow*. The two leading characters leave Earth on a rocket and crash-land on an 'unknown planet'. This celestial body consists of an 'unknown metal' and is 'saturated with electricity'. Under its cloudless, violet sky, the men feel no hunger, thirst, heat or cold. Their hearts stop beating and their lungs breathing, but they do not die. They communicate telepathically and are 'creatures that live on electricity', 'like radios'.[66] However, just like their counterparts 'In the Year One Million', the protagonists despair over the loss of meaning brought about by immortality. They thus repair their rocket and return to Earth, which during the intervening 300 years has similarly reached an unsatisfactory state. Advances in science and medicine have prolonged life and eradicated hunger. At the same time, automation has caused rampant unemployment.[67]

Tawfiq al-Hakim's utopias could be interpreted as critiques of the modernizing projects that governments like his own were engaged in. However, by setting his plays in worlds distant in time and space, he also made any such criticism less direct and obvious. Unlike many other members of the Egyptian elite, he survived the revolution against the monarchy unscathed. He worked as director general of the Egyptian National Library from 1951 until 1956. Thereafter, he served as a member of the Supreme Council of Arts, Literature, and Social Sciences and as his country's representative to UNESCO. In 1963, the Tawfiq al-Hakim Theater opened in Cairo. When his patron Gamal Abdel Nasser died at the end of the decade, the playwright published a eulogy.[68]

64 Long, 'Taufīq al-Ḥakīm'.
65 Rani, 'Science Fiction'.
66 Al-Ḥakīm, *Riḥlah*, 83–87.
67 Rani, 'Science Fiction'.
68 Hutchins, *Tawfiq al-Hakim*, xiv–xv.

From texts and stages, Egyptian imaginations of life in space soon hit the silver screen. In 1959, the movie *Journey to the Moon* was released. It was written and directed by Hamada Abdel Wahab, an experienced maker of popular films. A graduate of the English department at Cairo University, he had begun working in the industry in the 1940s. Among other roles, he was assistant director of *Ismaïl Yassein in the Ghost House* in 1951.[69] Subsequently, Abdel Wahab became director of two other productions starring the comedian: *The Noble Thief* and *Ismaïl Yassein Meets Rayya and Sakinah*.[70] It was Yassein who then gave Abdel Wahab the idea for *Journey to the Moon*.[71] Besides him, Abdel Wahab recruited Edmond Tuema and Roushdy Abaza, another well-known Egyptian actor. Much of the film was shot in the desert, which was used to represent the lunar surface. Other scenes were shot at Studio Misr, with Behna Films becoming the distributor.[72]

With Ismaïl Yassein in one of the main roles, *Journey to the Moon* was as much a comedy as science fiction. However, it also had a darker subplot that reflected Cold War anxieties. The heroes of *Journey to the Moon* are the journalist Roushdy, his driver Ismaïl, and the German scientist Sharvin, played by Edmond Tuema. The three accidentally take off from the Helwan Observatory near Cairo in a rocket designed by Sharvin. After landing on the Moon, they encounter the robot Otto, who hypnotizes them and leads them into a bunker. There they meet an elderly man named Cosmo, who through a device enables them to 'breathe in any atmosphere and endure any pressure'. Cosmo introduces himself as a former director of nuclear laboratories during a war that had devastated the Moon.[73] Moreover, he acquaints the travellers with other survivors: his daughter Stella and other beautiful young women named Luna, Zona, Venus, Marsia, Terra and Astra. For their return to Earth, the travellers retrieve atomic fuel from the dark side while encountering maimed and scarred soldiers. Once refilled, the rocket lands in Egypt with Roushdy, Ismaïl, Sharvin and their lunar companions all on board.[74]

Like Gomaa, Abdel Wahab played with the concept of matrimony, but added sex appeal. His lunar women are young, slim and fair with hair in different colours. They also bare much skin and perform a futuristic ballet. While Ismaïl

69 Faṭīn ʻAbd al-Wahhāb, *Ismāʻīl Yas*.
70 Ḥamādah ʻAbd al-Wahhāb, *Al-liṣṣ al-sharīf*; *Ismāʻīl Yas*.
71 Ṣumaydah, ʻMin qiṣaṣ al-ʻushshāqʼ.
72 Ḥamādah ʻAbd al-Wahhāb, *Riḥlah ilá al-Qamar*.
73 Ibid.
74 Ibid. Westfahl, *The Spacesuit Film*, 270–72.

is enjoying himself with several of them, Roushdy and Stella slowly fall in love with one another. The journalist introduces her to smoking cigarettes and to the idea of marriage, which she has trouble understanding. She is more comfortable with kisses, which they exchange passionately on the lunar surface. At the end of the movie, Roushdy says that he was returning 'from the Moon with guests like the Moon', using the satellite as a common metaphor for beauty. After landing, Stella agrees to become Roushdy's wife. As for her companions, they attract the lustful gazes of crowds of men welcoming the space travellers.[75]

Although it formed part of a whole wave of science fiction globally, in Egypt specifically *Journey to the Moon* neither spawned a sequel nor a similar film. This was arguably due to drastic changes in the institutional landscape that had supported the movie. The socialist government of Gamal Abdel Nasser continued to back astronomical research at the Helwan Observatory. At the same time, it took control of the major media companies, which had been tied to capitalist elites under the previous regime. In 1960, the government nationalized Studio Misr. Its competitors, including Al Ahram, soon followed, as did the large distribution companies. *Al-Hilal* suffered the same fate and came under a new editorship in 1961. Two years later, the Ministry of Culture and National Guidance took over the entire film industry. A bureaucracy that included few filmmakers resulted in inefficiencies and a decline in quality. Moreover, because of political tensions, the export market in other Arab countries shrunk. Egypt's output dropped to about five or six films per year by the early 1970s.[76] In this situation, Hamada Abdel Wahab moved his focus from cinema to television. Ismaïl Yassein appeared in few films after 1960. He went into debt, suffered from heart disease and died in 1972.[77]

While Egyptian cinema declined, theatre continued, sometimes criticizing in subtle ways the bureaucracy that was constraining the arts. A pertinent example is Ali Salem's play *The People of the Eighth Heaven*, which was written in the mid-1960s. It describes a rocket engineer who flees the injustice of Earth and lands on a distant planet. He encounters a people ruled by an emperor and controlled by scientists in accordance with rational laws. Children have their love glands removed in order to subdue their passions. However, the scientific bureaucracy burdens itself by making simple problems overly complicated. An absurd amount of effort is dedicated to freeing the emperor's son's hand, which

[75] Ḥamādah ʿAbd al-Wahhāb, *Riḥlah ilá al-Qamar*.
[76] Gaffney, 'The Egyptian Cinema', 59–60.
[77] Ṣumaydah, 'Min qiṣaṣ al-ʿushshāq'.

is stuck in a jar of cheese. The rocket engineer comes close to having his own love glands operated on, but is saved by a revolution.[78]

Despite its subversive potential, *The People of the Eighth Heaven* was put on stage. In 1965, the play even won the first prize in a competition run by Cairo's Tawfiq al-Hakim Theater. This award was worth 100 Egyptian pounds (around 230 dollars). However, Ali Salem claimed that he did not receive the money. Ironically, this was due to administrative restructuring, as the Egyptian government was moving all theatres to be under the supervision of the Ministry of Culture. Nevertheless, the play was published and sold for three piasters (around seven cents) per copy. Subsequently, it was performed in the towns of Damanhur and Kafr El Sheikh. Salem considered the show in Damanhur a 'failure'. According to him, the director had tried to make 'every sentence' and 'every scene' funny, thereby creating a 'disaster'. In contrast, the playwright considered the performance by a different group in Kafr El Sheikh 'a huge success'. 'I counted forty-two articles in all the newspapers and magazines praising the beauty of the show.'[79]

The Egyptian state was thus not just curbing the scientific imagination. It also stimulated it in many instances, even if inadvertently. Through its support for the Helwan Observatory and a rocket programme, Gamal Abdel Nasser's government provided both a location and inspiration for *Journey to the Moon.* State educational institutions continued to produce actors and directors. In 1978, Elham Shahin, a seventeen-year-old student from Cairo, began an acting career with a role in a new production of the play *A Nymph from Mars*, for instance. Her father objected to her calling, hoping that she would become a physician instead. Nevertheless, she completed her bachelor's degree from the Higher Institute of Dramatic Arts in 1982. Thereafter, she starred in numerous films. Whereas the relationship with her father remained broken, she expressed loyalty to the leadership of the state that had supported her. She defended President Hosni Mubarak and would oppose the revolution of 2011 that eventually toppled him.[80]

Even in cases of severe state repression, Egyptians were able or even forced to create highly imaginative plays. One of those cases was Ahmed Raef who had studied history at Cairo University and worked briefly in contracting. After an attempt on Gamal Abdel Nasser's life in 1965, he was imprisoned along with many people associated with the Muslim Brotherhood. Over several years,

[78] Badawi, *Modern Arabic Drama*, 197–98.
[79] Sālim, 'Ḥīn fashilat'.
[80] Qāsim and Wahbī, *Dalīl al-mumaththil al-ʿArabī*, 24; Al-ʿAjmī, 'Ilhām Shāhīn'.

he had intense contact with other political prisoners. To celebrate the tenth anniversary of the Suez War, the prison authorities encouraged the performance of a play written by Raef. Although this was meant to be a one-off, it inspired him to write a second one titled *The Fifth Dimension*. As proper writing materials were banned, the original version was scribbled on cigarette packets.[81] Following Raef's release, the play was first printed in Dubai in 1972.[82] During the subsequent decades, liberalizations allowed for more competition between Islamist and secular voices in the Egyptian media. This enabled Raef to publish *The Fifth Dimension* as well as histories of the Muslim Brotherhood in Cairo.[83]

The Fifth Dimension was an explicit work of Islamic science fiction. His most important mentor in jail was his fellow inmate Muhammad Qutb, who also wrote a preface to the play in 1968. He was the younger brother of the influential ideologue Sayyid Qutb, who had been executed at the order of Abdel Nasser two years earlier. In his preface, Muhammad argued that the Islamic perception of the universe encompassed all of existence – 'the Creator' and 'the creatures'. Therefore, Islamic art could treat 'absolutely every topic'. The Islamist lauded Ahmed Raef as a 'Muslim artist of broad and diverse culture'. *The Fifth Dimension* was a work that followed God's path instead of the 'ignorance' of either capitalism or communism.[84]

While the author was Muslim, his main characters were not. Like *Journey to the Moon*, *The Fifth Dimension* followed the space journey of a trio, including a German scientist and a journalist. The protagonists are the physicist Reinhard, the reporter Merhart, and Lydia, who is Reinhard's niece and Merhart's fiancée. Dissatisfied with Albert Einstein's model of four dimensions, Reinhard suggests the existence of a fifth, metaphysical and spiritual one. Regretful of his previous work for the Nazis, the scientist is unwilling to serve the American nuclear programme. He and the two others thus escape Earth on a rocket. Upon their arrival on Mars, they are welcomed by the planet's king, his wife and his viceroy. Subsequently, the American astronaut Scott and the Soviet cosmonaut Sukhalov join the Martian community. After a nuclear war devastates Earth, the human protagonists repopulate it in the end.[85]

Before returning to Earth, Raef's space travellers encounter a utopia on Mars that was based on the ideals of the Muslim Brotherhood. Drawing on Sayyid

81 Rā'if, *Al-buʿd al-khāmis*, 49; Szyska, 'On Utopian Writing', 97.
82 Tsīskā, 'Ḥawla al-kitābah al-ṭūbāwīyah', 117.
83 Rā'if, *Al-bawwābah al-sawdā'*; *Al-buʿd al-khāmis*; *Sarādīb al-Shayṭān*.
84 Quṭb, 'Muqaddimat al-masraḥīyah', 29–30, 33.
85 Szyska, 'On Utopian Writing', 98–99, 102.

Qutb's concept of an Islamic government, legislation is derived from the revelation of the last prophet. Wine, for instance, is forbidden. The interconnected principles of Martian society are religion, scientific progress, and honesty. Progress is predicated on an internalization of the sharia through education. In turn, technological progress serves moral ends. A special invention allows Martians to swim in their normal clothing, thus avoiding nakedness. The king is obliged to swear an oath 'to obey the laws of God, not to be unjust, and not to follow personal interests that may cause him to deviate from divine guidance'. The ruler is freely elected, and every citizen has the right to initiate proceedings to depose him. The executive is further controlled by a council of 100 wise people.[86]

The Fifth Dimension offered not just an alternative to Nasserism, but also to the ideologies of the Cold War superpowers. On Mars, the American astronaut reviews the history of his country. After escaping persecution in Europe, his Puritan ancestors had tried to build a new society based on divine rules. Yet, Scott realizes that his forefathers failed because of errors in Christian scripture. Similarly, his Russian counterpart first admires the Martian way of life as a realization of communism. However, after being questioned by Reinhard and his companions, he realizes that he had been misled by Soviet propaganda. Reinhard, Merhart, Lydia, Scott and Sukhalov thus all convert to Martian Islam. As the only human survivors of Earth's nuclear war, they compare themselves to passengers on Noah's ark.[87]

Although the Egyptian film industry was unable to adapt most science fiction plays for the silver screen, writers continued contributing to the genre. In 1972, Tawfiq al-Hakim published two plays entitled 'Lunar Report' and 'A Poet on the Moon'. In the former, invisible lunar beings demand information from two astronauts. In the latter, a poet encounters genderless humanoids on Earth's natural satellite. Like some of the fantastical characters in his earlier plays, these beings know neither birth nor death. They consist of 'energies of thought and feelings'. They dissipate and renew themselves 'like light' and 'spirit'.[88] While raising philosophical questions about immortality, such utopian plays lacked the romance, action or comedy of Hamada Abdel Wahab's *Journey to the Moon*. Perhaps as a result, works like 'A Poet on the Moon' were not made into films, despite al-Hakim's high position in his country's cultural bureaucracy.

86 Ibid., 106–9.
87 Ibid., 109–11.
88 Al-Ḥakīm, *Majlis al-ʿadl*, 50, 101, 107.

Turksploitation

Before it went into decline during the 1960s, Egypt's film industry was leading not just among Arab countries, but in the Middle East in general. Turkey, despite its comparable size, was lagging behind. Under Kemal Atatürk, local production companies and studios received little state support. The government considered the import of American and European films sufficient for its Westernization efforts. Persistent popular interest in oriental themes was satisfied through screenings of Egyptian and Indian productions. Only in the 1940s did local film producers succeed in lobbying the government to grant them a tax break. This resulted in a tripling in the production of Turkish films from six in 1946 to eighteen two years later.[89]

After a slow start, Turkey's film industry rapidly expanded during the 1950s and 1960s. The numbers of films made reached 116 in 1961. Eleven years later, this number peaked at 298.[90] The surge was in part due to better relations with the United States. After World War II, fears of further Soviet expansion across Eurasia brought the Turkish and American governments closer together. Considered a front-line state against communism, Turkey was one of the first recipients of aid under the Marshall Plan. In 1952, the country also acceded to the North Atlantic Treaty Organization. Under Western influence, Turkey liberalized its economy and political system. At the same time, increasing electrification allowed for the establishment of cinemas across the country. A profitable market for filmmakers was thus created. Turkey gained its own Hollywood, named Yeşilçam (Green Pine) after a street in Istanbul.[91]

While Turkish filmmakers had more economic opportunities, they still faced ideological constraints. A regulation from 1934 required all movies to avoid 'propagating religion' and 'political, economic and social ideologies which contradict the national regime'. Soviet productions were largely banned, and even American ones were examined by the Turkish Board of Censorship. This body rejected the remake of *The Ten Commandments* from 1956 over its religious content, for instance. On the other hand, William Wyler's *Ben-Hur* was accepted, as the board did not find 'any evidence of representing Christianity as superior to Islam'. The United States Information Agency for its part sought to 'present a favourable impression of America'. It supported the export of selected

89 Gürata, 'Tears'.
90 Erdoğan and Göktürk, 'Turkish Cinema', 535.
91 Yorulmaz and Blizek, 'Islam', 3–4.

Hollywood productions, excluding those 'not considered worthy examples of American life and character'. However, science fiction films mostly slipped through the double Turkish and American censorship.[92]

Like their counterparts in Egypt and India, Turkish directors and screenwriters were thus quick to adapt Western speculative fiction. *Dracula in Istanbul* was released in 1953, and *The Invisible Man in Istanbul* two years later. In order to appeal to Turkish audiences, such adaptations included local cultural and religious references, despite censorship. Garlic replaces the cross in *Dracula in Istanbul*. The lawyer Azmi counts on his faith in God when entering the vampire's castle against all warnings. Humour lightens the scary plot. A young woman suffering from a bite by Dracula is told that it will pass once she is married. Later in the movie, a woman protests her husband's discarding of all garlic: 'But I was supposed to cook *imam bayıldı*.' The name of this aubergine dish with olive oil literally means 'the imam fainted'.[93]

One of the first Yeşilçam productions about aliens was the comedy *Flying Saucers over Istanbul*, which was directed by Orhan Erçin. Released in 1955, the film arrived five years after the first American feature on the topic, Mikel Konrad's *The Flying Saucer*. The main characters in the Yeşilçam version are two failing journalists named Şapşal (sloppy) and Kaşar (slut). In the beginning, both men report about a 'lonely-heart club' of wealthy spinsters in search of husbands. However, the reporters are soon scolded by their editor for ignoring the big news about flying saucers. They thus sneak into the Istanbul University Observatory and make radio contact with a spacecraft. The journalists subsequently meet a group of beautiful Martians descending from the silvery ship. Thanks to an elixir, they have reached the age of several hundred years. Nevertheless, similar to the members of the 'lonely-heart club', they are looking for husbands due to the lack of men on their home planet. Şapşal and Kaşar promise to bring more men to them in exchange for the youth elixir. After much action, however, only the two journalists leave Earth with the Martian women.[94]

Like other exploitation films, Yeşilçam's products sought to attract large audiences with minimal budgets. To create a fog scene in *Dracula in Istanbul*, more than thirty people were brought in to smoke.[95] The makers of *Flying*

[92] Erdoğan and Kaya, 'Institutional Intervention', 52, 54, 56.
[93] Dönmez-Colin, *The Routledge Dictionary*, 129.
[94] Erçin, *Uçan Daireler*; Wass, 'Ucan daireler'.
[95] Dönmez-Colin, *The Routledge Dictionary*, 129.

Saucers over Istanbul compensated for the lack of expensive special effects with comedic and sexual content. Carrying an oversized camera, the journalists immediately look funny. In the Istanbul University Observatory, they distract a guard by handing him photographs of nude women. The Martian ladies are sexy too, wearing tight clothes that reveal most of their legs. Some of them do cover their hair, but with futuristic headgear rather than a scarf. The film also contains multiple belly dances by scantily-clad women from Earth. In one scene, the Martians turn on a 'man-detection machine' and order Şapşal and Kaşar to 'undress'. Although attracted to the Martians and mischievous in various ways, the journalists adhere to the Turkish Republic's ban on polygamy. Both of them refuse to marry more than one Martian.[96]

Despite the oriental dances, *Flying Saucers over Istanbul* arguably drew more on Hollywood than on any Islamic tradition. The divine is largely restricted to basic phrases, such as *Allah'ım* (oh God) and *Allah'a ısmarladık* (good bye). This was at best a subtle suggestion that Martians are Muslims. In their visual language, the filmmakers adopted many recognizable elements of global cinema. The alien ladies – like the ones in the Egyptian *Journey to the Moon* – are accompanied by a boxy robot. Their outfits include leotards, cloaks and ray guns. With its Amazon-like extraterrestrials, the film displays similarities to *Cat-Women of the Moon* and *Devil Girl from Mars*. Another borrowing from Hollywood is a Marilyn Monroe lookalike. Later in the film, she comes to Istanbul to dance in the 'lonely-heart club'. However, she gets frozen by a ray gun in the middle of her performance.[97]

American influence on science fiction persisted, as Turkey imported not just weapons but also cultural products from its Cold War ally.[98] At the same time, and like other developing countries, it sought to keep costs to a minimum by ignoring international treaties on copyright protection.[99] This gave Turkish directors considerable opportunity and freedom to adapt Western fiction for local consumption. Relatively liberal laws regarding the depiction of nudity and violence made the production of exploitation films easy. The belly dancer Özcan Tekgül, one of the actresses in *Flying Saucers over Istanbul*, gained roles in dozens of new productions, while also appearing naked in men's magazines. She became infamous as the 'queen of disgrace and scandal'.

96 Erçin, *Uçan Daireler*.
97 Erçin, *Uçan Daireler*; Wass, 'Ucan daireler'.
98 Karademir, 'Turkey'.
99 Smith, '"Beam Me up, Ömer"', 7–8.

Yet, she was still considered for a medal for her service to Turkish cinema.[100] Overall, hundreds of films categorized as 'Turksploitation' were produced between the 1950s and 1980s.[101]

Although the label 'Turksploitation' was mainly applied to movies, it had a parallel in the world of comics. The adaptation of Western science fiction images on paper even preceded their counterparts on film. The American comic strip *Flash Gordon* was first published in Turkish in the 1930s in the magazine *Çocuk Sesi* (Children's Voice). The title of the comic was subsequently changed to *Baytekin.*[102] *Jungle Jim*, another strip by Alex Raymond, was adapted as *Avcı Baytekin* (Hunter Baytekin). These adaptations were to serve patriotic as well as commercial ends. The heroes were given Turkish looks, including dark hair, whereas villains, such as Ming, retained their foreign looks and names.[103] Propaganda slogans, such as 'Strengthen our Air Force', were added to the pages.[104]

Baytekin remained popular well into the Cold War. In 1967, the series gave rise to *Baytekin: Battle in Space*, which was directed by Şinasi Özonuk from Ankara.[105] In this movie, aliens kidnap Baytekin and take off in a flying saucer. Like the original *Flash Gordon*, the hero soon becomes involved in a galactic war and seeks to prevent Emperor Ming the Merciless from conquering Earth. After being captured, the alien queen tries to seduce him. The hero, however, is able to escape with the help of a rebel prince. He continues the fight against Ming and ultimately kills him. On the way, Baytekin encounters humanoid extraterrestrials in capes and shorts and carrying laser guns. He further fights sandmen in a desert and a cactus-shaped, man-eating monster that resembles the Muppets.[106]

As in *Flying Saucers over Istanbul*, few characters in *Baytekin: Battle in Space* appear distinctly Islamic. Men and women wear tight sports clothes and show much skin. Religious expressions are again limited to common phrases, such as *inşallah* (God willing). However, the film represents a form of local machismo. Baytekin is attracted to almost any woman he encounters. When the queen attempts to seduce him, she complains to him that men on her planet have

[100] Wass, 'Ucan daireler'.
[101] Maack, 'Türkische B-Movies'.
[102] Özçınar, 'A Cornerstone', 166.
[103] Aksoy, 'The Adventures', 5.
[104] Glaser, 'Turkish Flash Gordon'.
[105] Özonuk, *Baytekin.*
[106] Ibid. Glaser, 'Turkish Flash Gordon'.

no interest in women. The hero is surprised and responds that Turkish males would even kill for a female. Later in the movie, he falls in love with a virtuous princess. Unlike the evil queen, the princess tells him that she has to keep her virginity until marriage in accordance with tradition.[107]

Turkish filmmakers not only adapted, but also satirized Western franchises. After *Baytekin: Battle in Space*, the next major appropriation of American science fiction was *Tourist Ömer in Star Trek*. This film from 1973 was produced soon after Turkish Radio and Television (TRT) had begun broadcasting the original series created by Gene Roddenberry. The Turkish version, which was directed by Hulki Saner from Istanbul, thus also preceded the first American *Star Trek* motion picture by six years. Simultaneously, Saner's movie completed its own series, which included titles like *Tourist Ömer in Germany* and *Tourist Ömer among the Cannibals*. In each of these comedies, Ömer makes irreverent comments about the strange people and places he sees.[108]

For his *Star Trek* parody, Hulki Saner inserted Ömer into a recreation of the 1966 episode 'The Man Trap'. He followed the original down to the details, replicating set design, costumes, characters and dialogue. The director also used Roddenberry's credit sequence and theme song, while superimposing his own titles. Rather than filming in a studio, however, many scenes were shot in the ruins of Ephesus. This was not just cheaper, but also led to more spectacular effects. Yet, the most important difference lies in Ömer's appearance. In the beginning of the film, he finds himself forced at gunpoint to marry a pregnant woman in Istanbul. He prays to God to save him from this fate and is promptly transported to a planet three million light years away. From there, Ömer is brought aboard the starship *Enterprise* for testing as a sample of an underdeveloped species. 'He doesn't have the attributes of a monster', Spock concludes, 'There are no monsters that stupid!' For the rest of the film, Ömer makes fun of the Vulcan and the rest of the crew. At one point, Spock says, 'On my planet rationality is everything, logic comes first.' Ömer replies, 'Well, don't forget, on my planet food comes first.' By the end of the movie, both have taken on characteristics of the other. Spock takes pleasures in a little irrationality, and Ömer has learned the Vulcan nerve pinch. After being transported back to his wedding in Istanbul, he employs this technique to escape once more.[109]

107 Özonuk, *Baytekin*.
108 Smith, '"Beam Me up, Ömer"', 5–6.
109 Ibid., 6–11.

Faithfully replicating much of the original American show, *Tourist Ömer in Star Trek* can hardly be described as Islamic science fiction. However, religion is given more space, even as it is made fun of. God does respond to Ömer's prayer in the beginning, just in an absurd way. A womanizer, Ömer pats the bare legs of one of the female crewmembers of the *Enterprise* and says, 'God bless you!' Later, he approaches an alien who has taken on the shape of a woman in a bikini. He greets her with *selamün aleyküm* (peace be upon you). She starts to touch his face and chest and licks her fingers. 'What are you doing?' he asks her, 'Are you performing an ablution?' He thus exposes his lower arms and legs too, as if to wash them in preparation for a formal prayer. Ömer then comes to view her behaviour as a kind of foreplay and starts to touch her in return.[110]

Cinematic circulations

The initial distribution of *Tourist Ömer in Star Trek* was largely restricted to Turkey. Hence, there was little incentive for Gene Roddenberry and his collaborators to sue for copyright infringement. Perhaps the American producers were not even aware of the Turkish remake. As a result, inspiration largely went one way.[111] However, the landscapes and cultures of the Muslim world contributed significantly to other popular American franchises, such as Frank Herbert's *Dune*. Herbert was influenced not just by authors of science fiction, such as H. G. Wells and Robert Heinlein, but also by orientalists. T. E. Lawrence's book *Seven Pillars of Wisdom* and its film adaptation *Lawrence of Arabia* had an especially strong effect on Herbert's vision of a desert planet.[112]

Through the – albeit distorting – medium of orientalist works, Herbert borrowed extensively from Muslim societies in constructing an exotic and plausible desert world. The Fremen, natives of the planet Arrakis, are modelled on Arab nomads. They are also called *Ichwan Bedwine*, wear long robes, form tribes and are deeply religious. The men are circumcised and polygamous, value honour and bravery, and practise vendetta. Their most deadly weapon is the 'crysknife', which was inspired by the Southeast Asian dagger *kris*. The Fremen's language closely resembles Arabic and includes much Islamic vocabulary. The Fremen believe in 'Shari'a', the existence of 'jinn', and 'jihad'.

110 Saner, *Turist Ömer*.
111 Smith, '"Beam Me up, Ömer"', 8.
112 Kennedy, 'Epic World-Building', 101; Hoda Zaki, 'Orientalism', 183.

The Fremen's religious manual is called the 'Kitab al-Ibar', like the work of the fourteenth-century historian Ibn Khaldun. (*Kitāb al-ʿibar* means 'the book of lessons'.) Other words in *Dune* are evocative of Arabic. The great sandworm on Arrakis has many names, including 'Shai-Hulud'. This name probably derives from *shayʾ* (thing) and *khulūd* (immortality). Appendices include an 'Almanak en-Ashraf' (Selected Excerpts of the Noble Houses). The word 'almanac' is itself of Arabic origin, and *ashrāf* is the plural of *sharīf* (noble).[113]

In addition to his linguistic and ethnographic borrowings, Frank Herbert drew on the history of Muslim lands. *Dune*'s plot retraces both the rise of Islam in the seventh century and the increase in Arab power after the establishment of the Organization of the Petroleum Exporting Countries (OPEC) in 1960. The planet Arrakis is the only source for the mélange, a substance essential for interplanetary navigation. It thus plays a similar role to oil in the economy of the twentieth century. As mélange is also called 'spice', the struggle over it is further reminiscent of early modern attempts to control the Indian Ocean trade. Paul Artreides, one of the main characters in *Dune*, is a figure similar to the prophet Muhammad. Although he comes from outside Fremen society, he is soon called the 'Mahdi' (guided one). Another name for him is 'Lisan al-Gaib' (tongue of the unseen). Artreides unifies the Fremen and leads them in a holy war to conquer the galaxy.[114]

Attempts to adapt *Dune* as a film had already begun in the early 1970s, but theatrical release only occurred in 1984. This delay allowed *Star Wars*, as another franchise involving a desert planet, to surpass *Dune* in popularity. George Lucas borrowed far less from the Arabic language than Frank Herbert did. Yet, he still owed much to Muslims, the Middle East and their stereotypes. Parts of different *Star Wars* films were shot in Tunisia, with many contributions from locals. Lucas borrowed the name of Luke Skywalker's home planet, Tatooine, from a southern Tunisian town. This planet is home to the Tusken Raiders or Sand People. Reminiscent of long-standing Western views of Middle Eastern peoples, the nomadic Tuskens are depicted as primitive and savage. They are covered from head to toe, and females wear what resembles a burqa.[115]

Star Wars thus formed part of the wider circulation of science fiction between the United States and Muslim-majority countries. Even Iranian theatres exhibited the first movie of the franchise both during and after the revolution. Soon after George Lucas's film received its Oscars in 1978, it was shown in

113 Kennedy, 'Epic World-Building', 101–4; Hoda Zaki, 'Orientalism', 181–83.
114 Kennedy, 'Epic World-Building', 104–5; Hoda Zaki, 'Orientalism', 182.
115 Charbel, 'Deconstructing', 143.

Tehran's Shahre Farang Cinema. The name of this establishment means 'peep show' and more literally 'European City'. In 1980, the theatre was renamed Azadi (Freedom). Other cinemas, which were associated with the shah's regime, were given new names, shut down or destroyed by revolutionaries. After the severance of diplomatic relations with the United States, imports of American movies were reduced, but did not stop. In 1983, both *Star Wars* and Spielberg's *Close Encounters of the Third Kind* were screened.[116]

Although the Iranian Revolution did not prevent the import of American science fiction blockbusters, it did severely restrict the production of local exploitation films. After the initial chaos, the state began to formally regulate and support many filmmakers during the 1980s. However, two kinds of cinema were the main beneficiaries. The first was a populist cinema that emphasized Islamic and revolutionary values. The second kind was a quality cinema that tended to critique in subtle ways the social conditions under the new regime.[117] Many of these films were entered in international festivals and won high praise. Yet, both kinds were subject to censorship, especially regarding erotic content. This included belly dancing, a common motif in pre-revolutionary Persian films.[118] A queen of scandal like Özcan Tekgül would have been as unwelcome as the exiled widow of the last shah.

As a result, few bare-legged aliens appeared in Iranian productions of the following decades. The silvery humanoids in Davoodi's *I Love Earth* are fully clothed. One female dons a futuristic black cloak, headcover and laser-shooting gloves. The only exemption from modest dress codes was granted to a creature with tentacle-like ears, a single leg and more than a dozen hands.[119] Much skin (pink this time) was also shown by the main puppet character of *Zizigulu Tales*. This television series from the mid-1990s was directed by Marzieh Boroumand from Tehran. However, the alien from the planet Ta-Be-Ta is childlike and entirely unerotic.

While the Iranian Revolution brought religious and social restrictions at home, it also strengthened a diaspora that comprised many filmmakers. A creative exile community in Los Angeles had already formed during the last shah's rule. One of its members was the futurist and transhumanist writer Fereidoun M. Esfandiary, who changed his named to FM-2030.[120] Also part of

[116] Naficy, 'Islamizing Film Culture', 126, 134.
[117] Naficy, 'Iranian Cinema', 549.
[118] Rekabtalaei, 'Cinematic Revolution', 585.
[119] Dāwudī, *Man Zamīn rā dūst dāram*.
[120] Naficy, *The Making*, 10.

the diaspora was the prolific television director Reza Badiyi, who had moved to the United States in the 1950s. He directed episodes that would have been virtually impossible to produce in post-revolutionary Iran, such as for the series *Baywatch*. Badiyi also made episodes of several science fiction series, including *The Six Million Dollar Man*, *The Incredible Hulk*, *Star Trek: Deep Space Nine* and *Sliders*. During this time, the exile community grew substantially. In 2007, it gave rise to the annual Noor Iranian Film Festival in Los Angeles. Two years later, this festival bestowed upon Badiyi a Lifetime Achievement Award.[121]

Iranians contributed to American science fiction franchises not just by directing, but also by acting. One of them was Shohreh Aghdashloo, who was born in Tehran in 1952. Growing up, she and her brothers had watched the original *Star Trek* series in Persian. 'What we loved about it', Aghdashloo said, 'was not only that it was futuristic, but also that we could understand it'. She added that the series 'wasn't beyond our education' and, 'when you're kids, your imagination is huge'. In the 1970s, she began her acting career, which continued in the United States following the Iranian Revolution. In 2016, she played Commodore Paris, the commanding officer of Starbase Yorktown, in *Star Trek Beyond*. In addition, Aghdashloo played a United Nations official in the television series *The Expanse*.[122]

In Turkey, a coup d'état in 1980 also brought turmoil and led to the arrest and exile of many politicians and intellectuals. However, most Turksploitation films, which were neither politically nor intellectually challenging, were unaffected. One of the most prolific directors was Çetin İnanç from Ankara, who became known as a 'jet filmmaker'. During the 1970s and 1980s, he churned out countless B-movies. They ranged from adaptations of Westerns and cartoons to sex films. As censors became more accepting of religious content, he also made conservative movies to be shown during Ramadan. He became notorious for shooting movies in one to ten days. Despite having only minimal technical facilities, he was not deterred from making science fiction either.[123]

The circulation of global hits thus continued to spawn local adaptations. One of them was *The Man Who Saved the World*, which was directed by İnanç. It was mainly shot in the Anatolian region of Cappadocia, but reused footage from the first *Star Wars* movie. The director later confessed to having stolen the reels from a cinema overnight and cut the scenes before returning them in the

[121] McLellan, 'Reza Badiyi'.
[122] StarTrek.com, 'Beyond's Commodore Paris'.
[123] Dönmez-Colin, *The Routledge Dictionary*, 184.

morning. His crew even confiscated a helmet from a random motorcyclist for use by a fighter pilot.[124] İnanç was thus able to show special effects, including battles in space, at next to no cost.[125] Furthermore, his film used music from another Lucasfilm production: Steven Spielberg's *Raiders of the Lost Ark*. Partly set in Egypt, this first Indiana Jones movie had been shot at some of the same Tunisian locations as *Star Wars* – and contains its own orientalist imagery. The James Bond movie *Moonraker*, the 1980 edition of *Flash Gordon* and other hits provided further scores. The sheer number of copyright infringements made the Turkish film iconic.[126] Like other films considered so bad that they are good, İnanç's production eventually acquired a cult following even in the USA.[127]

While in many ways unique, *The Man Who Saved the World* was similar in its plot to *Baytekin: Battle in Space*. The Turkish warriors Ali, and Murat, who is played by Cüneyt Arkın, seek to defend Earth against a powerful wizard. Following a battle, their spacecraft lands on an arid planet. In the belief that only women inhabit it, they wolf-whistle, but attract hostile skeletons instead. The wizard's forces subsequently capture the heroes, and the alien queen attempts to seduce Ali. The latter remains captive, but Murat manages to escape after an extended fight. With the help of an unnamed beauty and her father Bilge, Murat finds a lightning-shaped sword and a golden brain with magical powers. Much of the remaining movie is made up of further battles. Ali is killed in an explosion, after which Murat melts the sword and brain into powerful gauntlets. With his new gear, he finally kills the wizard and leaves the planet in the *Millennium Falcon* from *Star Wars*.[128]

Although Çetin İnanç used footage of Tatooine, he adopted hardly any images of nomadic people from George Lucas's universe. The circulation of orientalism in global science fiction thus had its limits. Besides black skeleton costumes, aliens in the Turkish production wear metal armour and pink and brown fur, but no veils or burqas. The alien queen who tries to seduce Ali covers herself with little other than underwear and a crown, while the nameless female has long blonde hair and no headgear. The wizard who seeks to destroy Earth does wear a long black beard. Yet, overall, he is perhaps more reminiscent of *Flash Gordon*'s Emperor Ming the Merciless than of characters in Middle Eastern history.[129]

[124] Kaya, *Remake*.
[125] Özçınar, 'A Cornerstone', 170–71.
[126] İnanç, *Dünyayı Kurtaran Adam*.
[127] Glaser, 'Long-Lost 35mm Print'.
[128] İnanç, *Dünyayı Kurtaran Adam*.
[129] Ibid.

Although the characters do not dress in distinctly Islamic ways, religion was given more attention in *The Man Who Saved the World*. This was part of a wider resurgence of Islam in Turkey's public sphere during the 1980s. Murat finds the sword and brain in the tomb of Hacı Bektaş-ı Veli, a thirteenth-century Alevi mystic. This tomb, together with other underground caves, is said to have broken away as a fragment from Earth '1000 space years ago'. Bilge explains to Murat the importance of his religion, which 'is the sign of civilization'. 'Islam has begun with the last prophet, Muhammad, and has been the guide of righteousness and humanity for centuries', expounds the old man. 'Each Muslim is the messenger of Islam and defender of religions. As the villains moved away from their God and religions, the wars began, and the world has been the target of all evil in space.' The Qur'an, the old man elaborates, is a book about the world, space, the phases of human civilization and 'all creatures that have ever existed'.[130]

Although Islam received more space in Turkish films, some adaptations continued to be irreverent. One of them was the 1987 movie *Homoti*, directed by Müjdat Gezen from Istanbul. It represented a low-budget parody of Steven Spielberg's recent blockbuster *E.T. the Extra-Terrestrial*. However, as the title suggests, the main character is a homosexual alien. The E.T. lookalike crash-lands in Istanbul in a flying saucer from Homon, one of 'millions of planets'. The tabloid journalist Ali encounters him by chance, as he is faking photographs of UFOs by throwing pot lids in the air. Ali takes Homoti home to interview him and protects him from criminals. The alien falls in love with Ali and, with his special powers, helps him record an interview with an Arab sheikh on a flying carpet. Celebrating their feat with a bottle of champagne, Homoti gets drunk and confesses his feelings for his host. However, as he watches on television what appears to be Spielberg's *Jaws*, he becomes scared and decides to leave Earth.[131]

Although largely a light form of entertainment, *Homoti* offered a critique of authoritarianism after years of repression in the wake of the coup d'état in 1980. In the interview in Ali's home, Homoti confesses that he cannot return to his planet, because he would be punished. 'Why?' asks Ali. 'Because there is a dictatorship in our place.' 'What would happen to you if they find you?' inquires the journalist. Homoti explains that the punishment would be 'very harsh. I cannot leave my home for one whole day'. Ali confirms sarcastically, 'Wow, it is very harsh!' He probes further, 'What if you frankly speak your mind?' The alien reassures him the planet's dictator would not care about that as 'he speaks

130 Ibid.
131 Gezen, *Homoti*.

as he wishes too'. Homoti then asks, 'What kind of ruling system do you have?' The Turk responds overconfidently, 'Democracy, of course.' Homoti exclaims, 'How nice!' Ali sighs and confirms with irony, 'It's nice.'[132]

While providing some political commentary, Turkish science fiction films continued to focus on comedy and action after the resumption of greater pluralism. In 2006, Çetin İnanç's movie received a sequel in *The Son of the Man Who Saved the World.* Set fifty years in the future, the film again starred Cüneyt Arkın as Murat as well as a younger generation of actors. The new Turks in space are Murat's twin sons, Kartal and Şahin. The extraterrestrial villain Uga kidnaps Şahin and raises him as his own son under the name Zaldabar. Both brothers grow up to command spaceships and come to engage each other in combat. Zaldabar's ship damages Kartal's, causing it to crash-land on a planet whose surface resembles, again, Cappadocia. Later, Zaldabar learns about his kidnapping by Uga, kills the villain and is reunited with his brother. In the end, Earth is saved from a missile launched by Uga's deputy.[133]

Like previous Turkish productions, *The Son of the Man Who Saved the World* satirized *Star Trek* and *Star Wars*, featuring comical fights with lightsabres and laser guns. Some of the uniforms resemble those of Starfleet, and one room is reminiscent of the Jedi Temple on the planet Coruscant. This time, all the footage is original.[134] This was perhaps the result of greater enforcement of copyright laws following negotiations with the European Union.[135] These very negotiations are parodied as well, however. In the beginning of the movie, the Orion Union votes against accepting the state of Lunatika as a new member. The reasons given are that Lunatika displays backward elements of Turkish culture, such as oil wrestling.[136]

Both Islam and Turkish nationalism were more pronounced in *The Son of the Man Who Saved the World.* Yet, they were also exaggerated to the point of ridicule. The opening sequence gives a long historical account of Ottoman and Turkish victories that ends with the Galatasaray football club winning the UEFA Cup in 2000. Kartal's spaceship is named *Ulubatlı Hasan* after a soldier who climbed the walls of Constantinople with the Ottoman flag in 1453. Following his crash on a planet, Kartal similarly plants a Turkish flag. He also uses some common phrases invoking God. In general, however, few characters appear

132 Ibid.
133 Tibet, *Dünyayı Kurtaran Adam'ın Oğlu.*
134 Ibid.
135 Smith, '"Beam Me up, Ömer"', 7.
136 Tibet, *Dünyayı Kurtaran Adam'ın Oğlu.*

pious in either speech or dress. In the otherwise Turkish movie, one woman shouts in English, 'Fuck you, crazy man, fuck you!' The only crewmember of the *Ulubatlı Hasan* who is wearing a hijab is the cleaner. When asked by the captain why she was scrubbing the already spotless floor of the bridge, she responds that 'cleaning comes from faith'. She also once asks in panic for the direction of Mecca before the end of the prayer time.[137]

The Son of the Man Who Saved the World was not the only such Turkish movie during the 2000s, as demand for science fiction comedies continued. An even greater hit of the same decade was *G.O.R.A.: A Space Movie*. It starred Cem Yılmaz, a stand-up comedian from Istanbul. He played the carpet salesman Arif who is abducted by aliens from the planet G.O.R.A. Subsequently, he thwarts the evil plans of the planet's psychopathic security chief Logar. *G.O.R.A.* once again satirizes *Star Wars*, but also Luc Besson's *The Fifth Element* and the Wachowskis' *The Matrix*. All aliens converse in Turkish and conduct trade in lira.[138] At some point, Arif looks into the camera and says, 'Hollywood, this goes to you. For decades you've misrepresented the aliens to us. But don't forget, a human is a human even if he's an alien.'[139]

G.O.R.A. was extremely successful for a Turkish production, earning a record $30 million worldwide.[140] A sequel, *A.R.O.G: A Prehistoric Film*, was thus quickly produced. It again starred Cem Yılmaz and was co-directed by him. As the title suggests, the film is about time rather than space travel. After having saved the planet G.O.R.A., Arif settles back on Earth. However, Logar seeks revenge and tricks him into a time machine. Sent a million years back into the past, Arif fights against a Tyrannosaurus rex and cavemen. In the end, he helps one tribe triumph over another in a prehistoric soccer match. Logar also warps into the past, but becomes stranded there.[141]

Most science fiction films produced in the Muslim world were light in content. Popular ingredients included the fight by a hero against a villain, romance between handsome men and beautiful women, and comedic elements. Borrowings from Hollywood were hard to miss, be they ubiquitous UFOs or ray guns. In turn, Western productions drew on Middle Eastern cultures and landscapes. Veiled aliens appeared in both American and Iranian productions. Science fiction movies from Muslim-majority countries were thus part of

137 Ibid.
138 Smith, '"Beam Me up, Ömer"', 3.
139 Sorak, *G.O.R.A.*
140 Dönmez-Colin, *The Routledge Dictionary*, 8.
141 Yılmaz and Baltacı, *A.R.O.G.*

global cinema, even as they contained local religious and ethnic elements and occasional political commentary. The politics of religion of individual countries still affected the size and shape of a local film industry. However, in many cases, circulations and conversations transcended divides between Islamic and secular states.

Just as global as science fiction filmmaking was an endeavour that was at least intended to be more serious: ufology or the study of unidentified flying objects. Universal images of the flying saucers as shown by *Shanee* or *I Love Earth* appeared in the illustrations of numerous books and magazines. However, rather than offering light entertainment, many of these publications promoted dark and complex conspiracy theories. Some of the most elaborate accounts combined Middle East politics with Qur'anic exegesis and space research. Yet, such complexity did not diminish the audiences of ufological books, which were often as large as those of many space operas.

4

Islamic UFO Religions

'I want to believe'

– *The X-Files*

In November 1978, sightings of unidentified flying objects over Kuwait made news even in distant places. The 'first-ever flying saucer' in the country 'came without sound'. It 'was as big as a jumbo jet, cylindrical, with a huge dome and a flashing red light. After seven minutes in a Kuwaiti oilfield, it took off without a trace'. This was the testimony of seven Kuwait Oil Company technicians, including one American. It formed part of a news item by United Press International, which was printed in papers as far apart as America's *Schenectady Gazette* and South Africa's *Rand Daily Mail*. The witnesses were 'frozen with horror' and hesitated to approach the object. They later insisted that the entity 'definitely was not a helicopter'. The agency further reported that the UFO temporarily disrupted telecommunications and the operations of an oil pumping station.[1]

Not just the media, but also officialdom paid attention to the sightings. The events 'caused security concern in Kuwait', noted the US ambassador, Frank Maestrone. An investigatory committee of the Kuwait Institute for Scientific Research produced a report that described eight sightings in late 1978. It rejected the claim that the UFOs were 'espionage devices but remained equivocal about whether they were of extraterrestrial origin'. A representative of the committee confessed that it 'did not know enough about the phenomena to say with certainty that they weren't "spaceships"'. Maestrone concluded that 'even those who are not inclined to believe in visitors from outer space do tend to think something strange has been going

1 Schenectady Gazette, 'Arabs'; Flying Saucer Review, 'Kuwait'.

on in Kuwaiti airspace'. The diplomat mentioned speculations about aircraft or hovercraft bringing refugees and money out of revolutionary Iran.[2]

The overthrow of Iran's monarch did coincide with a wave of sightings over the Gulf countries. In December 1978, a police car and a patrol boat in Dubai tracked a UFO. A young man even took a picture of a disc with a dome in the middle and a tail of light. As the *Gulf Weekly Mirror* reported, he had not previously believed in flying saucers or extraterrestrial life.[3] A couple of months later, people in Sharjah made a similar observation.[4] In yet another incident, the crew of two Kuwait Airways flights spotted 'a huge ball of bright light' around ten miles in diameter in September 1980. It was moving north-west of Kuwait City at around the same altitude as the aircraft.[5] The accumulation of such incidents over the years led a local newspaper to declare that 'flying saucers prefer Kuwait'.[6]

Whatever turmoil the end of the 1970s brought on the ground and in the air, its UFOs were far from the first over the Muslim world. From 1946 onwards, such objects had developed into a global phenomenon.[7] By the end of the 1950s, they had been sighted over virtually every country in the world.[8] In 1958, American officials investigated a 'fast moving orange light' that moved out of Syria and zigzagged across the sky over Adana in southern Turkey. The US Air Force reported that 'the light appeared to stand still for a brief period; and that there was an apparent absence of sound'. Based on similar incidents, the Americans explained the event as a possible sighting of 'jet exhausts and particularly afterburners' at night. They concluded that there was 'no reason to believe that the "unknown light" observed was anything other than a high-altitude jet aircraft from a neighboring "Eastern Bloc" country'.[9]

While the US Air Force preferred the term 'unidentified flying object', journalists and artists across the world popularized the term 'flying saucer'. Equivalents in other languages often appeared as direct translations of the English term. The concept was thus as global as the phenomenon. 'Flying saucer' translates as *soucoupe volante* in French, *fliegende Untertasse* in German and *platillo volador* in Spanish.[10] Other translations in languages of

[2] Fawcett and Greenwood, *UFO Cover-Up*, 90; Maestrone, '"UFO" Sightings'.
[3] Yates, *Catastrophes*, 144.
[4] Hellyer, 'Book Review'.
[5] Fawcett and Greenwood, *UFO Cover-Up*, 91.
[6] Al-Shāhid, 'Al-aṭbāq al-ṭā'irah'.
[7] Eghigian, '"A Transatlantic Buzz"'.
[8] Geppert, 'Extraterrestrial encounters', 338.
[9] Hanania, 'UFOs'.
[10] Geppert, 'Extraterrestrial Encounters', 336.

Muslim-majority countries include *ṭabaq ṭā'ir* (or *ṣaḥn ṭā'ir*[11]) in Arabic, *piring terbang* in Malay and *bushqāb-i parandah* in Persian. *Uçan daire* became the Turkish version of the term, and *uṛan ṭashtarī* the Urdu one. However, the English abbreviation UFO was also used. The term 'ufology' appeared as *ufoloji* in the title of a Turkish book as early as 1977.[12] At the same time as filmmakers were developing a new visual language, writers almost everywhere gained convenient words to distinguish alien spacecraft from ordinary ones.

Although a recurrent phenomenon in the skies and on screen for over two decades, UFO sightings in Muslim-majority countries substantially increased in the years before the Kuwait incidents. This arguably had to do with broader public consciousness of the phenomenon and denser normal air and space traffic. In 1975, the Algerian military spotted unidentified objects on radar and in the air as shapeless bright light. The following year, Middle Eastern skies seemed more crowded. In August, Tunisian authorities observed similar incidents and found them 'completely unexplainable'. The subsequent month, two F-4 fighters belonging to the Imperial Iranian Air Force chased a bright object over Tehran at night. The pilots lost instrumentation and communications as they approached the object, but saw their systems restored upon withdrawal.[13]

UFOs came with trails of paper as much as of light. Following the Tehran incident, the Iranian government invited a lieutenant colonel of the US Air Force for a debriefing. Neither he nor the Central Intelligence Agency solved the mystery, but they produced much written material for ufologists to exploit.[14] Also in September 1976, King Hassan II requested information from the US embassy in Rabat regarding a luminous object over Morocco. Secretary of State Henry Kissinger told his ambassador that such a sighting could be explained in various ways: 'in terms of local balloon, aircraft, or satellite activity; by meteorological and atmospheric conditions, including meteor events; and by astronomical objects'. He added that he was unaware of any relevant 'US aircraft or satellite activity'.[15] As it would turn out decades later, the light was probably caused by a Soviet booster engine re-entering the atmosphere.[16]

11 'Umrān, *Al-'ālam*, 116.
12 Sarıkaya and Bergil, *Ufoloji*.
13 Fawcett and Greenwood, *UFO Cover-Up*, 79–86; Bigliardi, *La mezzaluna*, 122–23.
14 Dunning, 'The Tehran 1976 UFO'.
15 Fawcett and Greenwood, *UFO Cover-Up*, 86–87.
16 Stuster, 'WikiLeaked'.

By the late 1970s, governments anywhere could thus hardly ignore flying saucers. They discussed the phenomenon not just on secret military channels, but also at United Nations fora. At a session of the General Assembly in 1977, representatives of various Muslim-majority countries listened to a recommendation by the prime minister of Grenada to establish an agency for the study of UFOs. Indonesian officials were especially interested. The previous year, its foreign minister Adam Malik had invited J. Allen Hynek, the editor of the *International UFO Reporter*, to lecture at the University of Indonesia and Bosscha Observatory. The government of the island nation also proposed the search for extraterrestrial civilizations to the UN Committee on the Peaceful Uses of Outer Space. In 1977 as well, the *Voyager 1* and *Voyager 2* spacecraft were launched, each carrying a Golden Record with numerous languages. 'Greetings to our friends in the stars. May time bring us together', said the Arabic recording. Kurt Waldheim, as secretary general of the UN, provided an additional salutation 'on behalf of the people of our planet'. 'We step out of our Solar System into the universe seeking only peace and friendship', he said, 'to teach if we are called upon; to be taught if we are fortunate'.[17]

The proposed UN UFO agency was not realized, which was in part due to the overthrow of Grenada's prime minister in a coup in 1979.[18] However, even in the absence of an intergovernmental organization, knowledge about flying saucers crossed borders. By 1979, Ahmad Jamaludin from Kuantan, for instance, served as West Malaysia Representative for the US-based Mutual UFO Network (MUFON).[19] Two years later, the British *Fortean Times* introduced him as one of its 'Special Correspondents'.[20] Jamaludin further edited the *Malaysian UFO Bulletin*[21] and served as a consultant for the British *Flying Saucer Review* (*FSR*), covering Southeast Asia. In parallel, the *FSR* also had a consultant for the Middle East, the Damascus-based engineer Khaled Hamsho. In 1987, he published an Arabic translation of a Spanish work by Antonio Ribera, yet another *FSR* correspondent. The magazine advertised it as the 'first Arabic book on UFO abductions'.[22] Probably seeking Islamic legitimacy for the topic, Hamsho began his translation with four verses from the Qur'an that speak of the 'heavens and Earth'.[23]

17 Othman, 'Supra-Earth Affairs', 693–94; International UFO Reporter, 'UFO Interest'.
18 Speigel, 'WikiLeaks'.
19 Jamaludin, 'Humanoid Encounters', 7.
20 Jamaludin, 'Tales'.
21 Eberhart, *UFOs*, 657.
22 *Flying Saucer Review* 33, no. 2, iv.
23 Rībīrā, *Al-mukhtaṭifūn*.

Ufologists from the Muslim world not only translated Western literature, but also participated in global knowledge production about flying saucers. In 1983, the *Flying Saucer Review* printed the Qur'anic verse 55:33: 'Jinn and mankind, if you can pass beyond the regions of the heavens and Earth, then do so: you will not pass without Our authority.' Alongside this quotation, the editor, Gordon Creighton, added the following statement: 'In the Islamic world, just as in China and other countries of further Asia, more and more people are awakening to the reality and the significance of the UFO problem, and we are glad to see that FSR has an increasing number of readers in the Muslim lands.' The *FSR* continued, 'We are fully appreciative of the particular contribution which they are in a position to make to our studies.'[24]

Muslims offered new perspectives to global UFO discourses based on different geographies and traditions. In several articles in the *MUFON UFO Journal* and the *FSR*, Ahmad Jamaludin reported on sightings of tiny humanoids in Malaysia. Measuring only three to six inches, these beings formed 'a class of their own', he claimed in 1979. 'Why do Malaysian encounters (the UFO and the humanoids) come only in tiny sizes when compared to other parts of the world?' he asked. As a reason, he suggested Malaysia's lack of magnetic and seismic anomalies, which UFOs use to operate.[25] In 1985, the ufologist also speculated about the effects of local culture. 'Inhabited as it is by peoples of three different stocks and cultures (Malays, Chinese, and Tamils) Malaysia is a land rich in religious and traditional features', he explained. 'Many people still cling to the older folk-lores and traditions, and one belief that is still adhered to by many individuals of the older generations concerns the question of mysterious abductions of humans by mysterious entities.'[26]

While the belief in tiny aliens may have had specific cultural roots in Malaysia, the existence of another kind of entity was widely acknowledged across the Muslim world. These were the jinn, creatures that formed the subject of chapter 72 of the Qur'an. In another issue of the *Flying Saucer Review* from 1983, Gordon Creighton discussed them in an article on the 'true nature of the UFO entities'. He argued that 'study of all the great world-religions – and notably of Islam – would yield valuable clues as to the true nature of the so-called "UFO Phenomenon" and would rapidly eliminate much of the fatuous "Space-Age Mythology"'. He went on to list 'parallels' between jinn and 'UFO entities'. They include

[24] *Flying Saucer Review* 28, no. 6, 8.
[25] Jamaludin, 'Humanoid Encounters', 9.
[26] Jamaludin, 'The Malaysian UFO Scene', 11.

invisibility, shapeshifting, abductions, sexual relations with humans, teleportation and telepathy. The editor stressed, 'In official Islam – and this cannot be over-emphasized – the existence of the Jinns has always been completely accepted, even legally, and even to this day, in Islamic jurisprudence.'[27]

While Creighton was based in England, his views resonated with readers in Muslim-majority countries. Khaled Hamsho wrote to the editor, 'I had thought that I was the first person in the world to perceive that the Jinn are behind the "UFO Phenomenon," but am glad to see now that you had thought of it too.' The Syrian added that the Qur'an includes a 'clear reference' to 'cross-breeding' between humans and extraterrestrials.[28] Adil Al-Nahhas of the Institute of Radiology and Nuclear Medicine in Baghdad concurred. 'I could not find in any of my reference sources a better explanation for the UFOs than yours', he wrote in a letter. 'I will be greatly honoured to cooperate with you at any level', he offered. 'Although a person in my position may have the right to be afraid of local ridicule, I still have the courage to introduce this thorny subject of the UFOs in various ways among my fellow-countrymen of Iraq.'[29]

Not just engineers and doctors, but also scholars with more traditional credentials came to relate jinn to UFOs. In 1985, the *Flying Saucer Review* reported on an address given to Muslims in London by Sheikh Nazım al-Haqqani of the Naqshbandi Sufi order. He described jinn as the operators of the aerial vehicles. They subject the human race by secretly causing wars, strife, disasters and disturbances. The sheikh also believed that contemporary UFO activity was preparatory to the end of the world.[30] This resonated with Gordon Creighton who believed in the apocalypse as well. Editorials in the *FSR* from the early 1990s were entitled 'We Shall See the Four Horsemen' and 'Countdown to Satanic Victory?'[31]

The aerial phenomena witnessed over Kuwait and elsewhere thus stimulated the imagination of influential figures. Their visions fed not only ufological studies, as published in books and periodicals, but in some cases entire UFO religions. Such new movements often combined science, scripture and conspiracy theories in original, if controversial ways. Whether uncanny or uncomfortable, many visions of alien spacecraft were certainly creative and

27 Creighton, 'A Brief Account'.
28 Hamsho, 'World Control'.
29 Al-Nahhas, 'The UFO Entities'.
30 Flying Saucer Review, 'A Turkish Religious Leader'.
31 Creighton, 'We Shall See'; 'Countdown'.

unconventional. Some of those who combined Islam with belief in UFOs were denounced as criminals and detained or even killed. However, even when they were labelled terrorists, they were also futurists. Ideologues of Hamas and Al-Qaeda may have been extremists, but some of their views were also products of the scientific imagination.

Black uplifts

Arguably, some of the most inventive leaders of Islamic UFO religions emerged outside of Muslim-majority countries. In the USA, religious freedoms combined with racial oppression made many black Americans seek alternatives to Christianity – the faith of the former slaveholders. Some new groups sought salvation in science and technology, including advanced and mysterious flying saucers. Afrofuturists were especially attracted by non-Western cosmologies and mythologies that were seen as distant from mainstream white culture. Extraterrestrial, ancient Egyptian, Jewish and Islamic civilizations all served as sources for the spiritual and social empowerment of African Americans.

One of the most prominent African American movements combining Middle Eastern traditions with beliefs in UFOs was the Nation of Islam (NOI). Founded by the mysterious Wallace Fard Muhammad in 1930, the NOI attracted tens of thousands of followers in the decades after World War II. Under the leadership of Elijah Muhammad and Malcolm X, the black nationalists competed with the civil rights movement in their efforts to end white supremacy. Civil rights activists in turn used the Nation of Islam as a foil and depicted the group's hatred of whites as the unfortunate byproduct of racial segregation and conflicts.[32] Whether the approaches of these different movements were separatist or inclusive, they suffered from violence, including the assassinations of some of their leaders.

While drawing on the Qur'an and the Bible, the Nation of Islam developed a distinct scientific imagination. Elijah Muhammad's catechisms included 'actual facts' from astronomy. Powerful ancient scientists play crucial roles in his mythology. One of them split the Moon from Earth in a gigantic explosion. Later, another by the name of Yakub was exiled from Mecca to the island of Patmos in the Aegean Sea, which was closely associated with the Book of Revelation. There, Yakub created the devilish white race through a multigenerational

[32] Curtis, 'Science', 17.

breeding programme. Black babies were killed at birth, and brown children whitened over time. The Nation of Islam's mythology thus resembled the eugenics programmes in Nazi Germany and the United States.[33]

As an icon of popular culture, the flying saucer also entered the cosmology of the Nation of Islam. Even though Yakub's white devils enslaved the original black race, they would eventually face annihilation brought about by bombs from the Mother Plane. This vehicle is a wheel-shaped wonder under the control of black Muslim scientists. It is able to defy Earth's gravity, lift up mountains and generate its own oxygen and hydrogen. In his imagination, Elijah Muhammad drew on scripture as well as descriptions of UFOs. Especially influential was the vision of God's four-wheeled throne 'chariot' (*merkabah*) in the Book of Ezekiel. With reference to the Qur'an, the religious leader described the scientists aboard the Mother Plane as knowing 'what you are thinking before the thought materializes'. Thanks to this divine prescience, the Mother Plane can destroy any fighter jets sent against it by white governments.[34]

While original, Elijah Muhammad's syncretism was controversial and came to alienate many of his followers. Malcolm X broke with him in 1964 and embraced a more mainstream version of Islam. The following year, after a pilgrimage to Mecca and travel to Africa, Malcolm X was assassinated by members of the Nation of Islam. However, after Elijah Muhammad's death in 1975, his own son sought to bring the movement closer to Sunnis elsewhere. In the meantime, Louis Farrakhan, a former competitor of Malcolm X, held on to Elijah Muhammad's thought, thus splitting the movement. Farrakhan's splinter group continued to include science and technology in its mythology. The Mother Plane was preserved as a Mother Ship or Mother Wheel. Farrakhan claimed to have been abducted by this craft while on a visit to Mexico in 1985. On board, he encountered Elijah Muhammad, who informed him about a secret war planned by the US government. On the surface, the White House was fighting Muammar Gaddafi's Libya, which had friendly relations with the NOI. On a deeper level, the administrations of Ronald Reagan and George Bush were seeking to exterminate black people under the guise of the 'war on drugs'.[35]

The science fiction elements of the Nation of Islam even facilitated an otherwise unlikely alliance with the Church of Scientology in the twenty-first century. Previously, the church had been widely associated with wealthy

[33] Ibid., 10–16.
[34] Ibid., 19–24. See also Lieb, *Children*.
[35] Finley, 'The Meaning', 439–46.

white people, notably the actor Tom Cruise. The nation, in contrast, recruited mostly poorer black people. However, both movements shared a belief in extraterrestrials. In the church's thought, the galactic dictator Xenu had brought billions of people to Earth on a plane-like spacecraft in order to kill them with hydrogen bombs. Like the leaders of the Nation of Islam, L. Ron Hubbard, the founder of Scientology, promised his followers enhancement and salvation through science and technology. Both groups were also similar in the amount of opposition and controversy they created.[36]

In 2010, Louis Farrakhan even started encouraging his followers to engage in auditing. A core practice of Scientology, it involved the recalling of negative situations in one's life as a way to free oneself. 'How could I see something that valuable and know the hurt and sickness of my people and not offer it to them?' the minister asked in 2012. For the Church of Scientology, the alliance with the Nation of Islam enabled it to expand and renew its following. In order to become 'hip', the group had to infiltrate the 'ghetto', explained one Scientology defector. 'I'm speaking of those who truly set cultural trends', stated David Miscavige, the organization's leader. 'Most white folks wouldn't have a clue of what it means to be cool if it weren't for black America.'[37]

While the Church of Scientology penetrated black communities in the 2010s, the Nation of Islam did not disappear, but remained an independent UFO religion. Despite health problems, the ageing Farrakhan held on to his leadership of the movement and its ideology. In a speech in 2011, he described the Mother Wheel again as the bringer of destruction. The circular plane is made of a kind of steel unknown in the USA. 'Like the universe', it consists of 'spheres within spheres'. Each of the 1,500 smaller wheels within the Mother Wheel carries three bombs. This Mother Ship remains in proximity to Earth, ready to save the Nation of Islam. In 2014, Farrakhan called on President Barack Obama to 'open up' the classified Air Force facility of Area 51 in Nevada. This would reveal the secrets of UFOs and the 'sign of the presence of God'.[38]

Although the Nation of Islam was perhaps the longest-lasting Muslim UFO movement, it had its rivals. A notorious competitor of Elijah Muhammad and Louis Farrakhan was Dwight York. Involved in a New York gang during his teens, he spent time in prison during the 1960s. Following his release, he

36 On the relationship between both movements, see Bigliardi, 'What Would Ron Choose' and King, 'Clearing the Planet'.

37 Gray, 'The Mothership'.

38 Hallowell, 'Farrakhan'.

began attending the Islamic Mission of America founded by Daoud Faisal. The latter had embraced a more widespread version of Sunni Islam and criticized the Nation of Islam for claiming the divinity of its founder, Wallace Fard Muhammad. York enjoyed a warm relationship with Faisal, but soon departed from his mentor's tradition. In 1967, he established his own syncretic circle by the name of Ansaar Pure Sufi. The group's symbol consisted of an intertwined crescent, Star of David and ankh. The following year, York changed the name to Nubian Islaamic Hebrews. His followers wore African robes, black fezzes and nose rings. York himself adopted the title 'Imam Isa', using the Qur'anic name for Jesus.[39]

In the 1970s, Dwight York followed the paths of black internationalists, but went much further. During that time, he abandoned some of the Jewish symbolism and renamed his community Ansaaru Allah (God's helpers). In 1973, he travelled to Egypt and Sudan. Like many members of the Nation of Islam, he had his photograph taken at the tomb of the nineteenth-century Nubian ruler Muhammad Ahmad. The latter was known by his adopted title of the Mahdi. York also met with the ruler's descendants, in whose company he had further pictures taken. Upon his return to the United States, he claimed to have received a doctorate in Islamic law and experienced a mystical visitation in Sudan. More than that, he considered himself the great-grandson of Muhammad Ahmad, which made him Dr Isa al-Mahdi. His male disciples began to wear the long white robes and turbans of Sudan, while the women put on modest gowns and face veils.[40]

Despite its transnational connections and more conservative appearance, the Ansaaru Allah soon came into conflict with other Muslims. York condemned previous translations of the Qur'an and only considered his own 'nineteenth' version as valid. He also criticized other Muslims for 'hiding the fact' that the prophet Muhammad had been black. He rejected the succession of the 'Caucasian' Abu Bakr as the first caliph and traced the prophet's lineage via Muhammad Ahmad through to himself. In response, imams in Brooklyn denounced the community as a dangerous cult.[41] In 1988, the Jamaican-born Bilal Philips came to the same conclusion in a book published in Riyadh. Based on a master's thesis at King Saud University, the book contextualized the Ansaaru Allah within a long history of 'esoteric' sects that had sought to destroy Islam

39 Susan Palmer, *The Nuwaubian Nation*, 5–7.
40 Ibid., 46–47.
41 Ibid., 67.

'from within'. These groups included the Shia, Druze and Baha'is.[42] American authorities were no less hostile towards the Ansaaru Allah. They investigated York's movement for arson, welfare fraud and extortion.[43]

The escalation of tensions with other Muslims and the state caused the Ansaaru Allah to leave New York for rural Georgia, abandoning much of its Islamic symbolism in the process. Dwight York defended himself against 'orthodox Sunni Muslims' and denounced the Saudis as hypocrites.[44] After escaping an assassin in 1992, he distanced himself further from other Muslims. He announced that he was now 'The Lamb, Liberator of Women'. He instructed the female members of his community to take off their veils and permitted them to wear shorts. The movement also rapidly changed names to Holy Tabernacle Ministries and the United Nuwaubian Nation of Moors. York distinguished his Nuwaubians from the 'Nubians', African Americans outside his movement. 'Nuwaubian' was also reminiscent of *nabī* and *nubūwah*, Arabic words for 'prophet' and 'prophecy'.[45] A further association was with 'Nawab', an honorific title of Muslim rulers in India.

As the Nuwaubian Nation relocated to the state of Georgia, it took on the characteristics of a UFO religion. Around 1993, its leader, under the name Dr Malachi Z. York, published a booklet or 'scroll' titled *Man from Planet Rizq*. He announced that he was an extraterrestrial by the name of Yaanuwn. He also described himself as an 'angelic being', an 'Eloheem' and 'Anunnaq'. He further called himself an 'avatar', using the Arabic words *ilāh mutajassid* (incarnated god). York proclaimed that he had come from the eighth planet Rizq in the nineteenth galaxy called Illyuwn. Drawing on the beliefs of the Nation of Islam, he claimed to have arrived on a passenger craft from the Mother Plane called *Merkabah*. Despite his embrace of such a powerful vehicle, he ironically denounced Earth's inhabitants for having built weapons of mass destruction themselves. 'These are the kind of things you do with the little bit of intellect and technology that you have been given.'[46]

While York distanced himself from many Muslims, he continued to use the Qur'an in support of his claims. His movement thus retained Islamic aspects, even as it came to focus on extraterrestrials. The religious entrepreneur published another 'scroll' entitled *Rizq and Illyuwn: Fact or Fiction?* 'I have been labeled

42 Philips, *The Ansar Cult*, i.
43 Bailey, 'The Final Frontier', 306.
44 York, *360 Questions*.
45 Susan Palmer, *The Nuwaubian Nation*, 6, 8, 68.
46 York, *Man*, 23, 122.

"a liar, a false prophet, etc."', he acknowledged. Yet, he promised, 'It would only take a sincere believer of the facts to do a little research to find out that what I am teaching you is true.' Rizq was related to *al-razzāq* (the provider), one of God's names. Illyuwn appears in the Qur'an as *'illīyīn* and refers to the seventh and highest heaven. 'So I say, no I did not make RIZQ, or ILLYUWN, up, it is real', York concluded. 'If you accept the QUR'AAN you will have to accept RIZQ and ILLYUWN. It is your heavenly home where your God ALLAH lives as ANU or YAHWEH.' He added, 'it is real, not a fabrication of my mind'.[47]

After York's group had already experienced conflicts in Brooklyn, with its racial and religious diversity, tensions only escalated in rural Georgia. The black separatists sought their own sovereignty as the Yamassee Native American Moors of the Creek Nation. York himself took on the tribal name Chief Black Eagle and now claimed descent from Pocahontas. He and around a hundred disciples constructed a theme park-like Egyptian village called Tama Re, complete with pyramids and a sphynx. However, he and his followers immediately attracted suspicions of being a 'cult'. Their compound was considered in violation of zoning and building regulations. After mounting hostilities with the surrounding communities and their sheriff, agents of the Federal Bureau of Investigation raided the community in 2002. York was arrested on multiple charges, including child molestation, and sentenced to 135 years in a federal prison. The Egyptian village, which the Nuwaubians also called the 'Mecca in the West', was demolished and the land sold at auction.[48]

Despite state repression, the Nuwaubian Nation survived in the urban environments in which it was born. Hip-hop artists, such as Philadelphia's Lost Children of Babylon, incorporated Nuwaubian themes into their work.[49] A network of bookshops in different cities as well as websites belonging to the movement continued to sell York's publications.[50] In Brooklyn, the All Eyes on Egipt Bookstore (Figure 6) adorned with an ankh and crescent was also advertising weekly spiritual and 'family fun' nights. When I visited the temple-like building in 2019, a large poster on the facade was calling upon the Republic of Liberia to 'repatriate Consul General and Diplomatic Agent Dr. Malachi York'. In the now gentrified neighbourhood, the shopkeeper still expressed admiration for the incarcerated leader of her 'tribe'. She even credited him with having 'cleaned up' the area, which used to be 'very rough'.

[47] York, *Rizq*.
[48] Susan Palmer, *The Nuwaubian Nation*, 71–121.
[49] Imarisha, 'Right Rhyming'.
[50] Bahler, 'The Alien Race'.

Figure 6 All Eyes on Egipt Bookstore in Brooklyn, 2019. Courtesy of the author.

Muslim ufology

The Nation of Islam and the Nuwaubians were among the most notorious and imaginative Islamic UFO religions during the twentieth century. However, outside of the United States, many Muslims also produced long treatises on UFOs and, in a few cases, their own eccentric and syncretic movements. The treatises drew on an increasing archive of journalistic writing in local languages about flying saucers during the 1960s and 1970s.[51] Another major source for Muslim ufology were theses about the extraterrestrial origins of ancient civilizations. Pioneered by Robert Charroux and Peter Kolosimo, such theories were further popularized by Erich von Däniken.[52] He had experienced an intense extraterrestrial vision during the mid-1950s and began publishing about ancient astronauts the following decade.[53] Von Däniken in turn influenced Zecharia Sitchin, a Jewish American author who was born in Azerbaijan and raised in Palestine. Sitchin's own popular books about aliens in history then shaped the mythology of the Nuwaubian Nation.[54] Although von Däniken and Sitchin's texts were frequently described as pseudoscientific, pseudohistorical or fringe, they proved popular.

51 Examples from the 1960s include Ismāʿīl, 'Al-aṭbāq al-ṭāʾirah' and Badr, 'Al-aṭbāq al-ṭāʾirah'.
52 Bigliardi, 'La paleoastronautica', 39.
53 Lieb, *Children*, 52.
54 Nuruddin, 'Ancient Black Astronauts', 137.

Theories about ancient astronauts flourished not just in the liberal publishing environments of Western Europe and North America, but even in the Soviet Union. During the Khrushchev Thaw, debates about gods as extraterrestrial visitors provided individuals with the opportunity to delve into religious topics.[55] Atheist officials perhaps tolerated such activities because they saw them as curbing religious sentiments through the replacement of the divine by intelligent aliens. The Russian Matest Agrest, for instance, suggested that the Baalbek temple complex in Lebanon had served as a launch pad and that nuclear explosions had destroyed Sodom and Gomorrah. Alexander Kazantsev from Kazakhstan also believed in the possibility that archaeological findings and mythology reveal contact with aliens. These writers then influenced Erich von Däniken who visited Moscow in 1968.[56]

Circulating globally like science fiction films, literature about ancient astronauts quickly reached Cairo, one of the centres of Arabic publishing. As early as 1969, the Egyptian Abdul Razzak Naufal referred to von Däniken's claims of alien landings in his book *Heaven and the People of Heaven*.[57] Soon thereafter, the journalist Anis Mansour wrote *Those Who Descended from the Sky*. It was first published by Dar El Shorouk in Cairo and Beirut in 1971.[58] Like his peers, Mansour took scripture and archaeological evidence to suggest contact between human and extraterrestrial civilizations throughout history. He began his account by quoting ancient sources that suggest space travel. They included the Qur'an, the Bible, the Book of Enoch, an Egyptian papyrus in the Vatican and the Epic of Gilgamesh. Mansour used them as evidence that intelligent beings had come to Earth. 'We are not alone in the universe, and our ancestors are not from among the apes!' Mansour stressed. Instead, Adam and Eve had migrated to Earth from other planets. Overall, the journalist sought to confirm scripture, but with more modern interpretations, like the destruction of Sodom and Gomorrah by nuclear weapons. The Egyptian also inserted a chapter about 'flying saucers', which 'suddenly filled the world in 1947', into his longer story.[59]

Although Mansour challenged notions of human evolution, he sought validation from scientists. In 1977, the journalist published a sequel, *Those Who Returned to the Sky*, also with Dar El Shorouk.[60] The title resembles von

55 Schwartz, 'Wunder', 106.
56 Schwartz, *Die Erfindung*, 94–95; Eghigian, '"A Transatlantic Buzz"', 290.
57 Nawfal, *Al-samā'*, 120.
58 Manṣūr, *Alladhīna habaṭū*.
59 Manṣūr, *Alladhīna habaṭū*, 25, 131.
60 Manṣūr, *Alladhīna 'ādū*.

Däniken's book *Return to the Stars*, which was first published in German in 1969.[61] In his introduction, Mansour related a conversation on a plane with the Egyptian-American geologist Farouk El-Baz, while both were accompanying President Anwar El-Sadat on a trip to the USA. El-Baz was tired, but agreed to correct or confirm information. The journalist fed him the contents of *Those Who Descended from Heaven*, including the principal hypothesis that the 'inhabitants of other planets had come to this Earth and had left their traces here'. Mansour claimed that El-Baz had responded multiple times with the word 'okay'. Whether the scientist was, in fact, convinced is not clear. In any case, both of Mansour's books became bestsellers, turning him into an Arab von Däniken. Eighteen editions of *Those Who Descended from Heaven* had appeared by 2001. As for *Those Who Returned to Heaven*, fifteen editions had gone to press by 2003.[62]

As extravagant theories about flying saucers caught on, some scientists and officials felt obliged to counter them with more cautionary accounts. However, one especially influential scientist was himself very enthusiastic about space and perhaps inadvertently lent legitimacy to the topic. This was the Saudi geologist Mohamed Abdu Yamani. He had studied under religious scholars in Mecca's grand mosque and later completed degrees at King Saud University (KSU) and Cornell University. After earning his doctorate in 1968, he became a faculty member and soon the director of KSU. During that time, he accompanied American astronauts on tours of Saudi Arabia[63] and developed a friendship with Farouk El-Baz.[64] Yamani continued his interests in space as minister of information from 1975 onwards. A few years into this role, he wrote a book entitled *Scientific Views on the Conquest of Space*.[65] He was further invited to give a lecture that resulted in another book with the title *Flying Saucers: Truth or Fiction?*[66]

With his combined religious and scientific training, Yamani was able to assess the phenomenon from diverse perspectives. His English sources included books by prominent supporters of the existence of flying saucers, such as the American aviator Donald Keyhoe and the Irish peer Brinsley Le Poer Trench. The official balanced these sources with writings by critics, such as the astronomer Donald Menzel. His Arabic references included the Qur'an, traditional exegetical works

61 Däniken, *Zurück zu den Sternen*.
62 Manṣūr, *Alladhīna ʿādū*, 5–8.
63 Yamānī, *Al-aṭbāq al-ṭāʾirah*, 6.
64 Bates, 'Space-Age Immigrant', 25.
65 Yamānī, *Naẓarāt*.
66 Yamānī, *Al-aṭbāq al-ṭāʾirah*, 8.

and books by Muhammad Ghamrawy and Abdul Razzak Naufal.[67] With this combination of sources, the minister of information set out to present 'science from an Islamic perspective'.[68] 'From our point of view, as Muslims', he declared, Qur'anic verses 'do not contradict the probability of life in God's vast universe'. He cautioned, however, that it 'is a life whose essence only God knows'.[69] Printed in bold, one of his sentences makes clear that 'there is no proof or scientific evidence for the existence of humans like on Earth on any planet of the various solar systems'. The geologist added that there was 'no evidence for the existence of any life like on Earth'.[70] However, he accepted UFOs as an 'existing phenomenon'. It did not matter 'whether the objects are flying saucers or not and whether these flying saucers are spacecraft coming from other worlds or are terrestrial secret weapons'.[71] He further called upon his readers to seek to define their 'essence' and 'nature'.[72]

As the minister's account left many possibilities open, it may have inspired rather than satisfied his readers' curiosity. The book certainly did not exhaust the growing demand for Arabic texts on UFOs. In 1980, the Egyptian journalist Ragy Enayat published *The Secret of the Flying Saucers* with Dar El Shorouk. This volume was part of his series *Stranger than Fiction*, which also included titles like *The Curse of the Pharaohs: Illusion or Truth?* and *Dream Interpretation and Astrology*.[73] *The Secret of the Flying Saucers* was less thoroughly researched than Yamani's work and based on fewer sources. Nevertheless, growing public interest in paranormal events made *Stranger than Fiction* a commercial success. Enayat's text went through seven editions within fifteen years.[74]

Even Qatar, a country with a tiny population and publishing industry, saw enough interest in UFOs for the production of a book. In 1981, the magazine *Aldoha* published a positive review of Yamani's *Flying Saucers: Truth or Fiction?*[75] Four years later, Mahmud Muftah, a researcher with Qatar Petroleum, brought out his own book on *The Sky and Flying Saucers*. For the cover, the Qatari artist Hassan Al Mulla, a graduate of the University of Baghdad, painted a yellow round spacecraft with red lights. Building on the previous

67 Ibid., 185–89.
68 Ibid., 8.
69 Ibid., 143.
70 Ibid., 50.
71 Ibid., 167.
72 Ibid., 164.
73 Snir, 'The Emergence', 268.
74 'Ināyat, *Sirr al-aṭbāq al-ṭā'irah*, 123.
75 Al-'Anānī, 'Al-aṭbāq al-ṭā'irah'.

Arabic literature, Muftah referred to Anis Mansour and Ragy Enayat as well as Yamani.[76] The Qatari author stated that the news of UFOs had 'reached everybody' and had become 'of interest to many individuals'.[77] He cautioned, however, that the phenomenon and 'the existence of intelligent creatures other than human beings' require 'material evidence'. Like other writers before him, he concluded, 'God knows best.'[78]

If Qatar was at one extreme in the extent of its publishing activity, Turkey was at the other. The transcontinental country perhaps led the Muslim world in terms of sheer numbers of ufological books, as it did with science fiction films. One of the most popular authors in Turkish, as in other languages, was Erich von Däniken. Among his first translators was Zeki Okar, a graduate of the Istanbul Academy of Economic and Commercial Sciences. During the 1970s, he translated *Chariots of the Gods?* and *Return to the Stars*, probably on the basis of the English versions.[79] Subsequently, others went back to the original German.[80] These translations were not particularly Islamic, however. Von Däniken's astronaut 'gods' appear as *tanrılar*, a Turkish word related to the Central Asian religion of Tengrism. This was in contrast to the Arabic *Allah*.

Several of von Däniken's books became bestsellers in Turkey too. Okar's rendering of *Chariots of the Gods?* had appeared in seventy editions by 1997.[81] The translation of *Return to the Stars* did not sell nearly as well, but still went through six editions by 1999.[82] What may have helped von Däniken's popularity in the Middle East was his coverage of regional heritage. The Swiss author speculated that ancient astronauts had been involved not just in the construction of the Great Pyramid of Giza, but also in the creation of the Piri Reis world map. Although von Däniken was implicitly belittling the historical capabilities of non-Europeans, his theories were sensational. Ideas that Middle Eastern peoples had been in contact with powerful beings in the past could even have served to compensate for contemporary feelings of weakness vis-à-vis Western states.

With probably many thousands of readers, von Däniken had a significant influence on Turkish popular culture. Orhan Duru from Istanbul referred to the Swiss author in his short story 'The Poor Are Coming'. One of the protagonists

76 Muftāḥ, *Al-samā'*, 121–24.
77 Ibid., 24.
78 Ibid., 109.
79 BBC, 'Zeki Okar'; Däniken, *Tanrıların Arabaları*; *Yıldızlara Dönüş*.
80 Däniken, *Tanrının Ayak İzleri*; *Yoksa Yanıldım Mı?*
81 Däniken, *Tanrıların Arabaları*.
82 Däniken, *Yıldızlara Dönüş*.

is the extraterrestrial agent E.V.D., author of *Chariots of the Gods?* He is described as enriching himself through his book sales, while helping prepare an alien invasion. At the end of the story, the Ottoman navigator Piri Reis appears. A visitor from space shows him a globe, which enables him to create his map.[83] Von Däniken further appeared in Zafer Par's film *Buddy* from 1983. This was another adaptation of Steven Spielberg's *E.T. the Extra-Terrestrial* besides *Homoti*. In one scene, several children are reading the Turkish translation of *Chariots of the Gods?* The Swiss and the Turks who drew on him thus also filled a need among local audiences to be part of the exciting world of science fiction. 'Why do they always come to Americans?' says one of the characters in *Buddy* about alien visitors. 'Let them come to us once.'[84]

However, the attractiveness of ideas about Middle Eastern contacts with aliens was not just about countering Hollywood and Western hegemony. Belief in extraterrestrials also fitted well with other activities often described as fringe or pseudoscience, such as Spiritism. In the late nineteenth and early twentieth centuries, the French astronomer Camille Flammarion had promoted not only ideas of the plurality of worlds and Martian canals. He had also engaged in psychical research. His work then influenced the Turkish physician Bedri Ruhselman,[85] who founded a Metapsychic Investigations and Scientific Research Society in 1950. More than two decades later, several former members of this society established the Science Research Group in Istanbul. The group's leader, Halûk Sarıkaya, was the author of a book on *Aliens and Flying Saucers*.[86] By 1978, he and his associates had set up their own publisher, called the Science Research Center, which brought out dozens of volumes over the next few years.

While signifying authority, the name of Sarıkaya's group hid the full spectrum of its activities. The Science Research Center published in such areas as esotericism, theosophy, philosophy, ufology, parapsychology and spirituality. It classified all these fields under a supreme Book of Knowledge or Book of Truths. In the hierarchy of scriptures, this text stands below the Preserved Tablet, the timeless heavenly record of the Qur'an. Yet, it ranks above man-made copies of the Islamic scripture as well as the Torah, Gospel, Vedas and Popol Vuh. Its 'truths' include Earth's extraterrestrial guidance in the form of the Sirius Mission

83 Duru, *Sarmal*, 301–15.
84 Par, *Badi*.
85 Ruhselman, *Ruh*.
86 Sarıkaya, *Uzaylılar*.

and the imminent golden age and day of resurrection. From Turkey, the Science Research Center predicted, 'paradise' would spread to the rest of the planet.[87]

As Sarıkaya's home country played a special role in the eschatology of the Science Research Center, figures in Anatolian history appeared prominently in its literature. The ascended masters included several prominent medieval mystics, namely Rumi, Hacı Bektaş-ı Veli, Hacı Bayram-ı Veli and Yunus Emre. Poems by these Sufis were printed in several books. Also in the list of celestial guides were Kemal Atatürk and Bedri Ruhselman. The former was celebrated for liberating Turkey and defending it against imperialism, capitalism and fascism. The Turkish War of Independence was thus presented as a divine mission in the service of the 'lord of the worlds'. The cosmic masters come from other planets and the underground state of Agartha.[88]

The Science Research Center combined its Sufi theosophy with socialism. In its cosmology, the latter has already been achieved by the superior inhabitants of other planets and should be the goal of humans. Accordingly, Sarıkaya and his comrades claimed that they did 'not pursue a capitalist purpose'.[89] Their centre was a 'a non-profit organization which spends all of its earnings in publishing further books'.[90] Quotations from Friedrich Engels, Lenin and Che Guevara all appeared in their texts.[91] In one reprinted newspaper article, Fidel Castro describes Jesus as a 'great revolutionary' and reassures that there is no contradiction between Christianity and Cuban socialism.[92] The books also included poetry by the Turkish communist Nâzım Hikmet, who had died in exile in Moscow in 1963.[93] Perhaps because of the persecution of people like Hikmet by the Turkish government, the Science Research Center kept a low profile. Copies were sold largely by mail order rather than in bookshops. The members also rejected many requests by readers to meet them.[94]

As Sarıkaya and his associates located the source of their spiritual guidance outside Earth, they had a special interest in spacecraft and life on other planets. In their research, they relied heavily on ufological studies in European languages. As a result, their books exhibited the influence of various traditions outside of

87 Bilim Araştırma Merkezi, *Sirius Misyonu*, 38–39, 64, 67.

88 Ibid., 31, 35–36.

89 Sarikaya et al., *UFO & Apollo*, 105, 111.

90 Sarikaya et al., *Ekminezi*, 2.

91 Bilim Araştırma Merkezi, *İnsan*, 2; Sarikaya et al., *UFO & Apollo*, 102; Bilim Araştırma Grubu, *Kozmos'dan Dünyalılara*, 4.

92 Bilim Araştırma Merkezi, *Dünya Öğretmeni*, 43.

93 Ibid., 42. Sarikaya et al., *UFO & Apollo*, 101.

94 Bilim Araştırma Merkezi, *Uzaylılar*, 64.

Islam. One volume was dedicated to the Israeli psychic Uri Geller and his alleged connection to the planet Hoova.[95] Another one, entitled *Vimana: Prehistoric Spacecraft*, focused on flying palaces or chariots in Hindu and Jain texts. The bibliography consists entirely of works in English, except for a book in German by von Däniken.[96] Halûk Sarıkaya also corresponded with the editors of the *Flying Saucer Review*. In 1982, he reported on a 'UFO flap', which he 'related to the Supreme Function Turkey is going to carry out in the very near future'.[97] The same sightings made it into a *Turkey UFO Report* from 1985, which drew on the *International UFO Reporter* and the German *UFO-Nachrichten*, as well as local sources. Seeking additional authority, the *Turkey UFO Report* included an interview with Hakkı Ögelman, a Cornell-educated astrophysicist at the Middle East Technical University in Ankara. 'There are about a hundred billion more Milky Ways', Ögelman is quoted as saying. Assuming that life only exists on our planet was therefore as arrogant as the ancient claim that Earth was the centre of the universe.[98]

Broad in its spiritualism, the Science Research Center drew on Islamic history as well. In the *Turkey UFO Report*, Sarıkaya claimed that a 'Spiritual Guide', via a 'Spiritual Office', was using UFOs to deliver messages to humanity. The Black Stone of Mecca's Kaaba may have been sent to Earth with a spacecraft, the author suggested. *Buraq*, which carried Muhammad to the heavens, was a spacecraft rather than an animal. It was travelling at the speed of light, as its name derived from *barq*, the Arabic word for 'lightning'. Turkish history specifically is also filled with UFO incidents. One of them was a strange light that appeared over the Hagia Sophia during the Ottoman siege of Constantinople in 1453.[99]

The Science Research Center remained an active publisher for less than a decade, with the *Turkey UFO Report* being one of its last volumes. However, parts of the group's mythology were continued by the World Brotherhood Union, a new religious movement started by Bülent Çorak in Istanbul. Çorak, a doctor's wife and mother of a daughter, saw herself as the reincarnation of the mystic poet Rumi. She thus took on his honorific, Mevlana (our master). In the early 1980s, she claimed to have received extraterrestrial messages.[100] These communications were subsequently combined as fascicles in *The Knowledge*

[95] Bilim Araştırma Merkezi, *Spektra*.
[96] Bilim Araştırma Merkezi, *Vimana*, 54.
[97] Sarikaya, 'UFO Flap', 27.
[98] Sarıkaya, *Türkiye UFO Raporu*.
[99] Ibid.
[100] Harley and Melton, 'World Brotherhood Union Mevlana Supreme Foundation'.

Book, which was published by the World Brotherhood Union Mevlana Supreme Foundation a decade later. Central to the movement was again the Sirius Mission, which sought to unite humanity and bring about a golden age through UFOs. The mission's focal point was once more Atatürk's Turkey. Reminiscent of the Nation of Islam's mother plane, a central 'mother ship' was in connection with Mevlana. Like the NOI and the Nuwaubians, the World Brotherhood Union distanced itself from other Islamic traditions. Nevertheless, *The Knowledge Book* still revered the Qur'an and Muhammad alongside Jesus and Moses.[101]

While mother ships played a central role in different Islamic UFO movements, the World Brotherhood Union was particularly feminist. 'Sex discrimination exists only in Your Galaxy', says a message received by Çorak in 1984, 'This astonishes Us.'[102] The crews of the Sirius Mission's special surveillance ships always consist of women as well as men.[103] Although *The Knowledge Book* emphasized that the Spirit had no sex, women and especially mothers like Çorak herself were preferred. 'By the Command of God, all the Goodwill and Love in the entire Universe is given to the Woman who is going to be a Mother.'[104] In terms of salvation, women come before men.[105] *The Knowledge Book* also contained the following extraterrestrial warning: 'Undeveloped Societies will be annihilated in proportion with the torment they cause for women. Do not ever forget this.'[106]

With organizations like the Science Research Center and the World Brotherhood Union, Turkey was exceptionally prolific in the production of ufological literature. Nevertheless, the reception of English literature on UFOs was not confined to Muslim-majority countries that had good relationships with Western powers. Despite being under US sanctions since 1979, Iran still imported much American literature. The war with Saddam Hussein's Iraq even stimulated interest in UFOs. In the summer of 1980, just before the outbreak of the conflict, Bahman Rouhizad from Tehran wrote to J. Allen Hynek's Center for UFO Studies in Evanston, Illinois. He had just finished reading the novel version of Spielberg's *Close Encounters of the Third Kind*. Rouhizad reported that in recent weeks 'there has been an almost daily report on observing unknown … star-like objects with yellow, orange, pink and greenish colors, mainly in cities near the south and west

[101] Çorak, *The Knowledge Book*.
[102] Ibid., 4.
[103] Ibid., 103.
[104] Ibid., 22.
[105] Ibid., 14.
[106] Ibid., 23.

borders of Iran'. He added that 'because of the present problems of Iran with the United States and Iraq, the Iranian guards have become suspicious of a new trick by the above-mentioned countries and (have been) shooting towards these objects'. Finally, he hoped that this 'political problem is not going to block my way for obtaining your monthly scientific work and reports'.[107]

Iranians interested in UFOs did not just correspond with Western peers, but also translated their books relatively quickly. In 1987, for instance, the American author Whitley Strieber published *Communion: A True Story*. This book describes an encounter with an alien whom the author likened to the ancient Mesopotamian goddess Ishtar. Four years later, in 1991, a Persian translation had appeared under the title *The Secrets of the Flying Saucers (UFOs)*. The chemist Dariyush Adib traced his motivation behind the translation back to an incident in 1988. That year, a young man had photographed UFOs in Tehran's Abbas Abad park. At the time, the site hosted a heavily-guarded camp for Iraqi prisoners of war. While observing the objects over several days, the man became schizophrenic according to Adib. He hoped that after developing a telepathic connection with them, the UFOs would take him to his American dreamland and specifically to Los Angeles.[108]

Despite tense relations with the United Kingdom, Dariyush Adib corresponded with Gordon Creighton of the *Flying Saucer Review* over the Abbas Abad incident. After receiving the photographs and negatives, the editor confirmed with a Kodak scientist that there were 'no signs of flaws in the emulsion or of any kind or trickery'. Adib rejected an explanation by the Islamic Revolutionary Guard Corps that the UFOs were 'American spying devices'. 'They are assuredly not of our dimensions, since they could appear and disappear in the twinkling of an eye. And no radar equipment could trace them.' Adib and Creighton concurred that the occupants of these craft were jinn and part of an eschatological plan. 'I strongly believe that the world is coming very rapidly to its end', Adib declared. 'We feel this here in the Middle East. Look at Saddam Hussein and the prophecies that World War III would commence from Iraq.'[109]

Although heightened by the war with Iraq, Iranian interest in UFOs was also part of a longer engagement with the metaphysical. As early as the 1890s, before Bedri Ruhselman was born, Mirza Khalil Khan Saqafi, a young Iranian physician, had travelled to Paris and learned about Spiritism. Subsequently, he

[107] Rouhizad, 'Correspondence'.
[108] Istrībir, *Asrār-i busqāb'hā-yi parandah*, 11–12.
[109] Creighton, 'UFOs Photographed'.

translated and popularized works by Camille Flammarion and other psychical researchers. In the 1920s, Saqafi founded the Society of Experimental Spirit Science in Tehran. This group regularly hosted seances with the souls of prominent Europeans as well as Iranians. Among them were Flammarion himself, the medieval polymath Ibn Sina, plus the poets Hafez and Saadi.[110]

If American literature could be imported to Iran, the reception of Erich von Däniken as a Swiss was even less problematic. By the time of the revolution in 1979, a Persian translation of *Chariots of the Gods?* had already appeared in three editions. Lending authority to the translation, the mathematician Mohsen Hachtroudi contributed a preface. A prominent science popularizer, Hachtroudi had served as president of the University of Tabriz and dean of the Faculty of Science at the University of Tehran. Adding Islamic legitimacy, the Qur'anic verse 55:33 was attached to the beginning of the first chapter: 'Jinn and mankind, if you can pass beyond the regions of the heavens and Earth, then do so: you will not pass without Our authority.'[111] Despite von Däniken's potentially blasphemous rendering of deities as aliens, *Chariots of the Gods?* remained in circulation under the post-revolutionary regime. In 1983, a fifth edition by a different publisher and translator had appeared. Perhaps indicating a level of acceptance of the work, this version appeared without the verse.[112]

As many Iranians embraced New Age practices, von Däniken's other books were popular too. In the 1990s, the liberalization after the devastating war with Iraq made space for new spiritual entrepreneurs.[113] In this context, a translation of *In Search of Ancient Gods* was published in Tehran with a print run of 5,000 copies. Like the Turkish Science Research Center, the translators Homayoun Khorram and Reza Ramez had broad interests in esoteric topics beyond Islam. They would bring out books with equal print runs on yoga and energy therapy.[114] Nevertheless, the Iranian publisher of *In Search of Ancient Gods* defended the book in Islamic terms. After quoting the first verse of the Qur'anic chapter *al-Qalam* (The Pen), the press praised God for giving humans the ability to talk and write. This was followed by an emphasis on books as a means of spreading knowledge.[115]

110 Doostdar, 'Empirical Spirits', 326–29.
111 Danīkin, *Arrābah-i khudāyān*, 11.
112 Dānīkin, *Arrābah-i khudāyān*.
113 Doostdar, *The Iranian Metaphysicals*, 11.
114 Khurram and Rāmiz, *Yawgā darmānī*; *Āmūzish-i inirzhī darmānī*.
115 Dānīkin, *Ilah'hā-yi guẕashtagān*, 3.

The popularization of Erich von Däniken in Iran was not only similar to Turkey, but went in part via its neighbour. A prolific translator of his books from Turkish to Persian was the linguist Ghadir Golkarian from Tabriz. In the 1980s, he completed bachelor's and master's degrees in his hometown before moving to Ankara University for his doctorate. Following a stint in Azerbaijan during the early 1990s, he returned to Islamic Azad University in Tabriz, where he became director of a research centre. In this position, he came to be credited as the translator of more than a dozen of von Däniken's books between 1996 and 2000. Most of them were issued in several thousand copies by the Tehran publisher Elmi (Scientific).[116]

Flying saucers as jinn

Books with extravagant claims by the likes of Erich von Däniken and Anis Mansour often enjoyed greater commercial success than cautious accounts. Nevertheless, Mohamed Abdu Yamani also continued to find venues for his ideas. In 1992, the former minister of information was invited to speak at Beit Al Qur'an in Bahrain, a complex dedicated to Islamic art. His lecture was published as a book entitled *Are We Alone in this Universe?* He further asked, 'Do we really face an invasion from other worlds? Where are the unidentified flying objects that invade Earth coming from? Are they from other planets like ours, from solar systems close to ours or from worlds far from us?'[117]

Unlike many UFO religionists, Yamani posed more questions than he provided answers. Yet, he still shared the wider association of flying saucers with extraterrestrial life. In contrast, a significant number of Muslims also considered UFOs as belonging to Earth. Even Istanbul's Science Research Group dedicated a book to man-made vehicles under the title *Global Construction of Flying Saucers*. Relying on literature in English, French and German, the work focuses on different North American and European designs. They include the VZ-9 Avrocar by Avro Canada, a photograph of which made it onto the book's cover page.[118]

While *Global Construction of Flying Saucers* was primarily technical, other works explored terrestrial origins of UFOs with more emphasis on religion. This

[116] E.g., Danīkin, *Asrār-i ahrām-i Miṣr*; *Yādgārān-i guẕashtah*.
[117] Yamānī, *Hal naḥnu waḥdanā*, 90.
[118] Bilim Araştırma Merkezi, *Dünya Yapısı Uçan Daireler*.

was especially the case with texts by a number of Arab and Pakistani authors. Prominent among them was the itinerant Jordanian scholar Umar al-Ashqar who had studied sharia in Saudi Arabia. While subsequently teaching at Kuwait University, he worked on a series of Arabic books on the Islamic creed, in which he promoted Sunni views in general and the Salafi tradition in particular. In 1978, he published a volume on *The World of the Jinn and Devils*, which comprised a section on 'Jinn and flying saucers'. The book was reprinted multiple times and translated into many languages, including English, French and Persian.[119]

In *The World of the Jinn and Devils*, al-Ashqar was critical of astrobiological research. 'Humans today spend billions of dollars with which they could build cities or countries and end poverty in the farthest reaches of the world', he complained. 'Instead, they spend that money on research to discover whether there is life or whether life is possible on nearby planets.' The scholar urged his readers to turn their attention to beings closer to home: 'What about an existence that is known to be living and thinking and that lives right here with us on our earth?' Jinn 'live in our houses and they eat and drink with us. In fact, they even spoil our thoughts and our hearts'. The scholar continued, 'These creatures drive us to destroy our own selves and to spill each others' blood. They make us worship them or any other creature so that we will be deserving of the anger and wrath of our Lord.'[120]

Writing during the late 1970s, al-Ashqar was well aware of the global reach of flying saucers. 'Many times we hear about the sightings of unidentified flying objects', he stated. 'Perhaps a week cannot go by without hearing of one person or a group of people who have reported a sighting.' The Jordanian mentioned that the later US president Jimmy Carter had seen a UFO in 1973. Al-Ashqar argued that this incident and Spielberg's *Close Encounters of the Third Kind* had convinced the US government to devote funds to the search for extraterrestrial intelligence. The scholar further referred to a Kuwaiti magazine report that China's Mao Zedong believed in non-human beings inhabiting other planets.[121] Al-Ashqar also considered flying saucers to be real, but identified them as jinn rather than as objects from other planets. 'There is no scope to deny the existence of strange creatures that are not human', he acknowledged. However, he was 'certain that those beings are from the species of the jinn that reside on this earth'. They possess 'superior abilities', such as speed faster than light and shape-shifting.

[119] Al-Ashqar, *'Ālam al-jinn*; Al-Ashqar, *The World*; Al-Achqar, *Le monde*; Ashqar, *Dunyā-yi jinn'hā*.
[120] Al-Ashqar, *The World*, 1.
[121] Al-Ashqar, *The World*, 165–66.

In an age of 'scientific progress' and space exploration, jinn had assumed the form of UFOs and aliens 'in order to mislead and deceive mankind'.[122]

Umar al-Ashqar was extraordinarily influential. As a professor, he educated generations of Islamic thinkers in Kuwait and subsequently in Jordan. He also became a key figure in the emergence of Hamas. Yet, he was not exceptional in linking flying saucers to demons on Earth. The Egyptian journalist Muhammad ʿIsa Dawud proposed a similar, but more conspiratorial theory. After having studied literature at Cairo University, he pursued a career in journalism. He joined the newspaper *Akhbar El-Yom* and also worked for *al-Nadwah* in Saudi Arabia. In 1991, he published a book entitled *Beware of the Antichrist Who Invades the World from the Bermuda Triangle*.[123] Dawud claimed that he received hundreds of letters in response, only two of which challenged the book's contents. This positive feedback apparently encouraged him to publish another book with some confirmations and corrections: *The Hidden Threads between the Antichrist, the Secrets of the Bermuda Triangle, and the Flying Saucers*.[124]

Like al-Ashqar, Dawud was sceptical of extraterrestrial explanations of UFOs. Because of the distances to other stars, he argued, an alien civilization would have to be very advanced in order for its spacecraft to reach Earth. Why would the inhabitants of other planets cross many light years in order to 'steal some crops and chickens or undertake some secret experiments on samples of humans'? If 'men from other planets' possessed superior technology by hundreds of years, why would they not take control of the entire globe? The 'truth from a Muslim mind', the author claimed, was that behind the flying saucers were not 'Gog and Magog'. Instead, their owners were humans with 'dreams to rule the world' and to 'control it technologically and scientifically'. These people, the Egyptian journalist argued, were in turn possessed by the 'king of evil', the 'devil'. Dawud announced to 'all mankind that the Bermuda Triangle is the base for the launch and return of flying saucers'. On this base, the devil commands workers, 'administrative staff' and 'individual evil minds'. The journalist said he reached this truth 'after extensive research, long travels, numerous meetings with officials and specialists, and adventures'.[125]

Dawud's devilish elucidation of flying saucers was soon developed further by his fellow Egyptian, Mansoor Abdul Hakim. Trained as a lawyer, he published

[122] Ibid., 166–67.
[123] Dāwud, *Uḥdhurū al-Masīkh al-Dajjāl*.
[124] Dāwud, *Al-khuyūṭ al-khafīyah*.
[125] Dāwud, *Al-khuyūṭ al-khafīyah*, 151.

more than 100 Arabic books on historical, political and religious topics. One of his best-known works was entitled *Women Who Deserve to Go to Hell*, which appeared in English translation in Karachi. It includes sections on the 'woman who adorns herself', the 'indecent woman' and the 'disobedient wife', among others.[126] In other texts, Abdul Hakim combined eschatology with conspiracy theories and paranormal events. In 1998, he brought out a book titled *The Throne of the Devil, the Bermuda Triangle, and the Flying Saucers*. The author relied on both al-Ashqar's *The World of the Jinn and Devils* and Dawud's *Beware of the Antichrist*. Combining theology and ufology, Hakim further referred to Brinsley Le Poer Trench's book *Mysterious Visitors* and the Qur'an. He also drew on prophetic traditions collected by Muslim ibn al-Hajjaj and Muhammad al-Bukhari in the ninth century.[127]

In part, Abdul Hakim's book reproduced Western conspiracy theories regarding UFOs, while adding reports about incidents in the Middle East. The lawyer explained that the American writer Morris Jessup had died in what was deemed a suicide, as he was about to reveal secrets about UFOs. Similarly, the physicist James McDonald was determined to continue Jessup's research, but was found dead in 1971. Hakim added the story of a boy from Upper Egypt who encountered a flying saucer on a farm in 1990. Creatures with three green eyes undertook experiments on him that gave him special powers, including the ability to eat glass and razor blades in front of television audiences. Hakim further mentioned sightings of flying saucers in Kuwait and Algeria.[128]

In a similar way to Dawud, Abdul Hakim linked these incidents to evil beings on Earth rather than from other planets. However, he disagreed about their precise geographical source. The lawyer argued that 'the owners of the flying saucers are the soldiers of the devil and the Antichrist, that is, they are the demons of the jinn and humans'. In other words, 'the flying saucers are the air force' of the Antichrist and 'under his personal command'. In contrast to Dawud's claim about Bermuda, Hakim argued that they originate from the Formosa Triangle in the Pacific. This area around Taiwan was the Antichrist's 'principal base and permanent residence'. As evidence, the lawyer referred to a tradition by Muslim ibn al-Hajjaj.[129]

126 Abdul Hakim, *Women*.
127 ʿAbd al-Ḥakīm, *ʿArsh Iblīs*.
128 ʿAbd al-Ḥakīm, *ʿArsh Iblīs*, 25, 44–47.
129 Ibid., 24, 47–48.

Like Abdul Hakim's views on women, Muhammad ʿIsa Dawud's ufology circulated not just in Arab countries, but also reached South Asia. The Indian-born and Pakistan-based writer Asim Umar was aware of both of Dawud's titles: *Beware of the Antichrist* and *The Hidden Threads*. Umar cited these works in a book of his own, which he published in Karachi in 2009: *The Bermuda Triangle and the Antichrist*. It contained a long chapter entitled 'Flying Saucers'. In another global conspiracy narrative, Umar linked UFOs to satanism, Marxism, and biological weapons such as the human immunodeficiency virus (HIV). In his imagination, the Taliban and other Muslim forces fight the Antichrist and his Jewish and American allies. Following Dawud, Umar locates the origin of the satanic saucers in the North Atlantic as well.[130]

It is unclear whether Umar's book on *The Bermuda Triangle and the Antichrist* was a commercial success. However, the overall oeuvre of which it was part earned the author recognition among people who also saw themselves engaged in a larger Muslim struggle. In 2007, Umar published a book with the title *World War III and the Antichrist*, in which Western organizations conspire to depopulate Muslim countries ahead of an eschatological battle.[131] During the same year, the American private military company Blackwater received notoriety for a massacre of civilians in Baghdad. This event then fed into another book entitled *The Army of the Antichrist: Blackwater*.[132] In addition to his publishing, Umar preached in Pakistani mosques and madrasas. Although his reputation was more that of an ideologue than of a fighter, the Al-Qaeda leader Ayman al-Zawahiri declared him 'emir' for the Indian subcontinent in a video message in 2014.[133] Five years later, he was reportedly killed in a joint US and Afghan raid on a Taliban compound in Helmand province.[134]

The propagation of conspiracy theories about flying saucers and the devil in Pakistan was not restricted to Al-Qaeda circles. Abdul Aziz Khan, a Virginia-based journalist with the Voice of America's South Asia Division, was equally interested in such connections. He gained experience in writing about flying saucers as a field reporter for the Mutual UFO Network. In 2008, he published a book entitled *UFOs in the Quran*. This work drew on al-Ashqar's *The World of the Jinn and Devils* and von Däniken's *Chariots of the Gods?* Khan was also influenced by books on freemasonry and websites on conspiracy theories.

[130] ʿUmar, *Barmūdā tikon*.
[131] ʿUmar, *Tīsrī jang-i ʿaẓīm*.
[132] ʿUmar, *Dajjāl Kā Lashkar*.
[133] Tanveer and Golovnina, 'Al Qaeda's Shadowy New "Emir"'.
[134] BBC, 'Key al-Qaeda Leader'.

A further source was the popular work *The Bible, the Quran, and Science* by Maurice Bucaille, a French physician to King Faisal of Saudi Arabia.[135]

Following Bucaille, Abdul Aziz Khan took the Qur'an as a source of scientific knowledge. 'Right now at this very moment', he claimed, 'there exists a book fourteen centuries old that not only contains things we have only recently discovered, but also things that are too advanced for today's mind (such as UFOs and their origin)'.[136] Islamic scripture, Khan argued, uses the term 'jinn' for unidentified flying objects. These entities have the ability to neutralize gravity and teleport objects. With their help, King Solomon had been able to surprise the Queen of Sheba by transporting her throne into his palace. The Qur'an also describes ancient Arabs as worshippers of jinn – or 'sky gods' in von Däniken's account. Khan thus urged fellow Muslims to take flying saucers seriously. In the journalist's opinion, Qur'anic confirmation of the phenomenon even implied that 'in order to be Muslims they must believe in UFOs'.[137]

Having identified jinn with UFOs, Khan read aliens into stories about Jesus and Muhammad. According to Muslim ibn al-Hajjaj, jinn had once taken Muhammad away from his community. Khan considered this incident an 'abduction' and thus a close encounter of the fourth kind. Another attempt failed, in which a jinni had 'tried to burn his face with a light'. What Ibn al-Hajjaj had described as light or fire was, in Khan's assessment, 'the same stun beam that abductees describe in modern cases of alien abduction'.[138] During Muhammad's ascension to heaven, he had been followed by Satan in a 'jet of flame'. Khan suggested that this phrase could describe the 'afterburners of a spaceship'. Similarly, a common Muslim view was that Jesus had been 'lifted up' by God instead of dying on the cross. The ufological interpretation of the Qur'an raised the question whether Jesus was 'taken into the skies by technologically advanced visitors'.[139] However, such abductions had targeted not just prophetic figures. Khan equally drew on accounts by the medieval scholars Ibn Taymiyah and al-Suyuti. Both had been convinced that humans and jinn frequently have sex and beget children. Khan took this as evidence of 'sexual abductions'.[140]

Like other authors, Abdul Aziz Khan associated UFOs with the devil. This made worshippers of the sky gods satanists. The journalist translated the Arabic

135 Abdul Aziz Khan, *UFOs*, 191–92.
136 Ibid., 101.
137 Ibid., 116–23.
138 Ibid., 123–26.
139 Ibid., 142, 145–47.
140 Ibid., 135.

word *kāfir*, which Muhammad used for a 'pagan', as 'the one who conceals or withholds information'. Therefore, the prophet's mission was to eradicate 'concealment' or 'cover-up' (*kufr*). In other words, spreading Islam was to reveal the truth about aliens. When Muhammad and his followers conquered Mecca in the year 630, they entered the Kaaba and took down the statues of 'astral deities', that is, 'alien astronauts'. At this point, in Khan's words, the prophet announced, 'The truth is here and "cover-up" has been eliminated!' After Muhammad's death, Muslim armies conquered other lands of 'astronaut deities'. In a 'universal war', Muslims fought 'concealment' in Mesopotamia, Egypt and India.[141]

This reinterpretation of Islamic history was combined once more with conspiracism. Despite the Muslim conquests, cover-up of UFOs continued throughout history in Khan's account. During the Middle Ages, many people were fascinated with the magical powers of the jinn. Aladdin in the *One Thousand and One Nights* used an 'alien connection' to operate outside of the law and enrich himself. During the crusades, the Assassins possibly handed the 'secrets of alien contact' to the Knights Templar. The latter thus became 'associated with occultism and devil worship'. Subsequently, the knights changed their name to Freemasons. In the twentieth century, Khan, similar to Asim Umar, considered the possibility that AIDS was caused by a 'biologically engineered alien virus'. In the future, the journalist predicted a clash between two ideologies: 'The first is the Secular Order, which has obvious roots in alien worship and Satanism.' The second ideology is Islam, which seeks to eliminate UFO 'cover-up'. The author concluded, 'May God give us all the wisdom to see the truth and the courage to accept it when we see it.'[142]

Such associations between UFOs and demonic creatures on Earth spread across the Muslim world, reaching Turkey too. A prominent proponent of the idea of jinn as aliens was Farah Yurdözü. She described herself as 'Turkey's first female UFO researcher'.[143] Yet, paranormal interests had run in her family for generations. She claimed that her great-grandfather, a teacher of French and mathematics in Istanbul, had been visited by reptilians. After this incident, several of his descendants had become psychics. Yurdözü saw her first UFO while in high school, initially in a dream and then in the skies.[144] Subsequently, she studied Spanish at Istanbul University and learned about an encounter with

[141] Ibid., 164–66.
[142] Ibid., 143, 167–89.
[143] Yurdözü, 'Farah Yurdozu'.
[144] Yurdozu, 'A Paranormal Family Tradition'.

a flying saucer from the planet Ummo in Madrid.[145] From 1990, she dedicated herself to investigating UFOs. She did so initially from Turkey, but moved to the United States in 2002.[146]

In her investigations of UFOs, Yurdözü drew on hypotheses of ancient astronauts as well as Central Asian spiritual traditions. In 2006, she posted a blog entry entitled 'Visitors from the Stars in Ancient Shamanic Turkish Tribes'. The ufologist claimed that her ancestors 'knew that we are not alone in the universe, that life and intelligent people can be found in other stars'. For that reason, 'in modern Turkish society UFO sightings or abduction cases are considered normal'. In the mythology of the Göktürks, the 'original Turks', contact with people from the sky was 'very important', she explained. One commentator on Yurdözü's blog was very excited. 'We need to bring this religion back to life in Turkey', the reader urged, 'this is our true way, not Islam'.[147] In 2008, Yurdözü posted another entry claiming that the ancient Hittites had formed the first hybrid half-human, half-extraterrestrial civilization in Turkey.[148]

Yurdözü's ufology overall was thus less Islamic than that of many of her Arab and Pakistani peers. However, she also connected aliens with jinn. In 2008, she also blogged about *Semum*, a Turkish horror film about a young woman who is possessed by a servant of the devil. The ufologist commented that in a behind-the-scenes picture, what looks like a grey alien appears in a fire. 'According to our belief system' jinn are created from fire, she explained. These beings 'have been doing everything that Grey aliens do with human society'. She thus speculated about a 'Jinn-Grey existence in the paranormal dimension'.[149]

In 2009, Yurdözü gathered many ideas from her blog in an English book entitled *Confessions of a Turkish Ufologist*. This work included a chapter on 'The Genie's Bottle: A Spacecraft?' She again drew parallels between reports of jinn encounters and alien abductions, such as paralysis and the staining of bodies and clothes. Rather than an Islamist, she was a Kemalist, however. 'I confess to having a crush on someone', Yurdözü wrote in a chapter titled 'The First Exopolitician'. According to her, Atatürk was also 'the first world leader to see the extraterrestrial origin of his own people'. He built a democracy based on the system of government of the lost continent Mu, from whose alien inhabitants

145 Yurdozu, 'The UMMO Letters'.
146 Yurdözü, 'Farah Yurdozu'.
147 Yurdozu, 'Visitors'.
148 Yurdozu, 'Hittites'.
149 Yurdozu, 'Mysterious Beings'.

the ancient Turks had descended. However, Yurdözü alleged that 'some dark forces didn't want to disclose one of the world's biggest and most significant secrets'. For that reason, Atatürk was poisoned and his Mu files sealed or lost.[150]

In addition to Kemalism and conspiracism, Yurdözü's book exhibited a continuation of the spiritualism of Istanbul's Science Research Center. She reiterated theses by Halûk Sarıkaya, whom she praised as a 'pioneering Turkish UFO investigator'. Like him, she believed in a profound connection between Earth and Sirius, whose 'vibrations' exert powerful effects on human life and destiny. The star 'is accepted as a spiritual sun in my native country', she explained. Sirius's role was already documented by the ancient Egyptians and Sumerians, she added with reference to Zecharia Sitchin. The use of stars in international brands, such as Mercedes-Benz and Starbucks, was further evidence of the power of the stars over humanity.[151]

As more work by Middle Eastern ufologists became available in English, it further drew American writers to connections between aliens and jinn. Until the 2000s, associations between the space age and the *One Thousand and One Nights* had been rare. A notable exception was the 1960s sitcom *I Dream of Jeannie*, in which the main male character is an astronaut. Yet, Jeannie is obliging, well-meaning and harmless. Similarly benign and helpful is the Genie in Disney's *Aladdin*.[152] However, in 2008, the jinn featured in a book by the American researcher Philip Imbrogno under the title *Interdimensional Universe: The New Science of UFOs, Paranormal Phenomena and Otherdimensional Beings*.[153] He subsequently co-authored a book entitled *The Vengeful Djinn* with fellow American Rosemary Ellen Guiley. First published in 2011, it referred to an English translation of Umar al-Ashqar's *The World of the Jinn and Devils*.[154]

In the 2010s then, more American ufologists came to share the conclusions of their Middle Eastern counterparts. 'Islamic scholars describe the djinn as glowing objects that can change their shape and at times take on a physical form', wrote Guiley and Imbrogno in *The Vengeful Djinn*. They considered it plausible that the jinn 'prefer using the extraterrestrial guise in order to hide their true identity'.[155] In 2013, Guiley expanded on this argument in a book entitled *The Djinn Connection*. She drew on Farah Yurdözü's writing on the relationship

[150] Yurdozu and Gore, *Confessions*, 17, 22–26.
[151] Ibid., 32, 62, 64.
[152] Guiley and Imbrogno, *The Vengeful Djinn*, xx.
[153] Imbrogno, *Interdimensional Universe*.
[154] Guiley and Imbrogno, *The Vengeful Djinn*, 253.
[155] Ibid., 170.

between jinn and extraterrestrials, but went further. The American claimed that aliens were only one of many forms that jinn could assume. In addition, jinn were 'likely to account for archons, the Watchers or Sons of God, the Nephilim, the Anunnaki, and many reptilian, fairy and demon encounters'. She concurred with her Muslim peers that jinn have 'hostile intent toward humans'[156] and can produce infertility.

Nevertheless, despite demonic associations, flying saucers still made for benign hoaxes as well. One morning in 2013, pupils of Al Mushrif School in Abu Dhabi were surprised to find a strange, car-sized, pentagon-shaped object on their playground, sealed off by the police. Alistair Bond, the principal, had built it at home with plywood, duct tape, paint and plastic tarpaulin. The purpose was an elaborate creative writing exercise, in which the students were asked to interview witnesses and produce a newspaper article and a script for television. 'As adults, we're often guilty of not allowing our imagination to be set free', Bond commented. 'The children are naturally creative, they're imaginative, they're inquisitive. Having days like this encourages them to increase their curiosity to have their imagination stimulated, but it's also something they'll remember for the rest of their lives.'[157]

Whether flying saucers were seen as shape-shifting jinn or not, they were flexible enough to be employed by various people for diverse purposes. Signifying superior and mysterious science and technology, they lent themselves to the leaders of entire new religious movements from New York to Istanbul. Although associated with fringe beliefs, these spacecraft commanded a powerful place within global popular culture. As such, they were also attractive to officials, ideologues and educators of many different persuasions. As proof of the existence of UFOs remained elusive, these individuals – from ministers to militants – were highly imaginative and creative.

To what extent the UFO hoax at the Al Mushrif School contributed to raising a new generation of speculative writers in the United Arab Emirates remains to be seen. However, during the 2010s, literary imagination about life in the universe was already thriving among adults who perhaps had not enjoyed as experimental an education as Bond's pupils. One of them was Noura Al Noman from Sharjah, who had studied English at the United Arab Emirates University during the 1980s. She attributed her fascination with science fiction to having caught the trailer of the first *Star Wars* film. She was further introduced to world-

[156] Guiley, *The Djinn Connection*, viii.
[157] Pennington, '"UFO" Spotted'.

building by Tolkien's *Lord of the Rings* and Frank Herbert's *Dune*.[158] After her studies, Al Noman worked as a censor with the Ministry of Information and Culture. However, this did not close her mind towards science fiction. On the contrary, she 'got paid to read books all day'.[159]

Eventually, patronage by members of Sharjah's ruling family enabled Al Noman to create her own fiction. From 2002 onwards, she worked as director general of the executive office of Jawaher Al Qasimi, the wife of Sharjah's ruler. The sheikha's daughter Bodour specifically encouraged Al Noman to write.[160] More than that, she issued two children's books by Al Noman about a cat and a hedgehog through her publisher Kalimat (Words). In 2012, Al Noman was able to publish her first science fiction novel for young adults, *Ajwan*.[161] The title referred to the heroine's Arabic name, which means 'small sea' and 'gulf'.[162] In 2013, the novel won an Etisalat Award for Arabic Children's Literature.[163]

Although Noura Al Noman had herself once been part of a repressive apparatus, she took inspiration from Arab politics for her writing. Ajwan is a young water breather and refugee from a planet destroyed by natural disaster. Leaving her dead husband behind, she engages in an interstellar quest to rescue her son from an evil organization that seeks to turn him into a super-soldier. In creating the water breather, Al Noman was indebted to the American television series *Man from Atlantis* from the 1970s. Regarding the main plot line, however, the author acknowledged: 'I was inspired by issues from my part of the world: disenfranchised and marginalized people, and how unscrupulous power hungry individuals may use such groups to further their own agenda through terrorism and violent acts.' As a special power, Ajwan has empathy, of which Al Noman believed there was not enough in the world.[164]

When *Ajwan* was published, Noura Al Noman still felt that she was unusual as both a female and an Emirati science fiction writer. 'I think Arabs would find it strange that a woman is writing SF – an Emirati woman writing SF is even stranger', she said in 2012. 'What would a woman in an abaya know about science, creating worlds filled with aliens and building action filled plots?' Despite her previous work with Bodour Al Qasimi's press Kalimat, she

[158] Jurado, 'An Interview'.
[159] Muhammad Aurangzeb Ahmad, 'Interview'.
[160] Al-Khaṭīb, 'Nūrah al-Nūmān'.
[161] Al-Nūmān, *Ajwān*.
[162] Yūsuf, 'Nūrah al-Nūmān'.
[163] Zriqat, 'Portrait'.
[164] Jurado, 'An Interview'.

struggled to find a publisher for *Ajwan* in her home country. She thus went with Nahdet Misr, a press from Greater Cairo that had brought out an Arabic translation of *The Lord of the Rings*.[165] In order to support her genre in the UAE, Al Noman also founded Manuscript 5229, a publisher specializing in science fiction and fantasy.[166]

Although Al Noman was a pioneer in the United Arab Emirates, in the Muslim world as a whole she was not. As early as 1905, Begum Rokeya, a Bengali feminist, had published a utopian story entitled *Sultana's Dream*. Set in a technologically advanced future, the story inverts traditional gender roles and counters stereotypes. In Ladyland, women are the main public actors, while men live in seclusion. Since then, women as well as men from Morocco to Indonesia have produced science fiction short stories and novels. They did so often under more repression and economic constraints than in the twenty-first-century UAE. However, much of their writing emerged not against postcolonial states, but in tandem with them.

165 Muhammad Aurangzeb Ahmad, 'Interview'.
166 Zriqat, 'Portrait'.

5

Building Nations and Worlds

In 2012, Noura Al Noman still felt lonely. 'There's hardly any SF in the Arab World', the Emirati writer stated, 'until only recently, I actually believed there was none'. Because she found so few examples, she herself struggled to create a terminology. She had to figure out the Arabic equivalents of words like 'worm holes' and 'plasma drives' by reading the subtitles of movies.[1] Al Noman partly blamed Arab education systems for the underdevelopment of her genre. They were not creating enough interest among young people in a scientific career. 'Without science, there can be no science related writings and, of course, no readers either.' The result, she argued, was little science fiction and few patents.[2]

Based in the UAE, where English was the dominant language of business and science, Al Noman seemed unaware of the hundreds of Arabic stories that were published in Syrian magazines alone around the same time. Syrian writers had the advantage of an education system that taught the natural sciences in Arabic at all levels. In addition, Taleb Omran stood out through the sheer amount of state patronage that he was able to secure for his genre. However, elsewhere, Arabic science fiction grew even under challenging political and economic circumstances. In Egypt, hardship and repression arguably inspired more than stifled speculative fiction. Dystopian novels set in Cairo became popular with readers of English as well as Arabic in the twenty-first century. Examples include such titles as Jamil Nasir's novel *Tower of Dreams*, Mohammed Rabie's *Otared* and Basma Abdel Aziz's *The Queue*. Set in the near future, these works exaggerated present-day inequalities, segregation and oppression.[3] Rather than asking what might be, they could merely state what is.[4]

1 Jurado, 'An Interview'.
2 Muhammad Aurangzeb Ahmad, 'Interview'.
3 Madoeuf and Pagès-El Karoui, 'Le Caire'; Murphy, 'Science Fiction'.
4 Murphy, 'Science Fiction'; Moore, '"What Happens"', 195.

Dystopian novels were especially attractive to critics, as they appeared as a form of literary resistance against authoritarian governments. In *The Queue*, for instance, citizens of a near-future Egypt depend on a centralized authority called 'the Gate' for permission to fulfil their basic needs. However, the gate never opens, and the number of people waiting in line only grows and grows. The plot centres on the futile quest of a sales representative to gain the approval for surgery to remove a bullet from his gut. Basma Abdel Aziz's novel thus offered a critique of a controlling state that fails to provide even the most essential services. It was inspired by the author's own observation of unmoving lines outside a closed government building in Cairo.[5] However, her book also resonated with international audiences and was compared to George Orwell's *Nineteen Eighty-Four*.[6]

Dystopias like *The Queue* were especially popular in the 2010s, as they seemed to speak to the disappointments of the Arab Spring. However, such works only represented a fraction of science fiction novels and short stories from the Muslim world. Many other publications were at least ostensibly more aligned with the aims of postcolonial states. *Al-Hilal*'s special issue on the 'satellite age' from 1958, for instance, expressed the Egyptian regime's desire to develop rockets and join the global space race.[7] Widely-distributed magazines like *Al-Hilal* were, of course, under special scrutiny, if not direct control, by their governments. However, individual authors also shared – and further spread – the popular enthusiasm for the space age. Many of them arguably responded to market forces at least as much as to government directives. By the late twentieth century, mass literacy, itself the product of state-sponsored mass education, had created demand for genre fiction in most major languages of the Muslim world.

However, caterers to interest in science fiction were not equally distributed. Several authors from Pakistan, Bangladesh, Egypt and Indonesia stood out through the sheer quantity of novels and short stories they churned out. Writers of Arabic, Bengali, Malay and Urdu benefited from large national as well as regional markets. Nevertheless, in order to make a living from writing, some of them still had to contribute to more than one genre. Popular authors produced spy fiction, fantasy and even romance alongside science fiction. At times, they also combined these genres, writing about secret agents who avert extraterrestrial threats.

5 Moore, '"What Happens"', 196.
6 Alter, 'Middle Eastern Writers'.
7 Atallah, 'Modernism', 1224.

When adapting the likes of *James Bond* and *Star Wars*, authors from the Muslim world also expressed perspectives on world politics from the global South. International as well as interstellar relations thus featured in their texts. Many novels and short stories critiqued the militarism and imperialism of the superpowers, for instance. Moreover, even if critical of the actual power or development of their countries, many popular authors expressed aspirations of the newly independent states. They created national heroes who used futuristic science and technology to fight for their countries. With such figures, much science fiction in former colonies was equally concerned with nation-building as it was with world-building. In other words, the scientific imagination also contributed to the national imagination.

National space

Soon after gaining independence in 1947, Pakistan gave rise to several series of popular books that contained elements of detective, spy and science fiction. One of the most important authors was Asrar Ahmad, who used the pen name Ibne Safi (Son of the Pure One). This pseudonym mirrored the literal meaning of Pakistan as 'land of the pure'. Yet, just like his adopted country, Ibne Safi had a mixed heritage. Born near Allahabad in northern India in 1928, he had grown up with both South Asian and European fiction. As a child, he read the Urdu epic *Tilism-e-Hoshruba* and Henry Rider Haggard's adventure novel *She*.[8] The latter had itself been shaped by orientalism, as it features a femme fatale named Ayesha, who is ruling over an African kingdom.[9] These texts, combined with *James Bond* movies,[10] fed into two series of Urdu thrillers, which Ibne Safi published over decades: *Spy World* and *Imran*.

Despite Ibne Safi's embrace of purity, his postcolonial fiction was in part nostalgic about the united Indian subcontinent in which he had grown up. Riots related to the partition of India in 1947 had interrupted his studies at Aligarh Muslim University. He subsequently completed a bachelor's degree at Agra University. In 1952, he followed other Muslims to Pakistan, but maintained connections to his previous home. Many of his novels were simultaneously published in Karachi and Allahabad. Appealing to audiences on both sides of

8 Nisar and Masood, 'The Nostalgic Detective', 35–36.
9 Rodgers, 'Restless Desire'.
10 Varma, 'The Son'.

the border, a frequent setting was an unnamed Hindustani country. Reminiscent of colonial India as much as of Pakistan, English and Urdu are spoken in Ibne Safi's stories. The main characters carry Muslim as well as Christian names such as Ahmad Kamal Faridi, Ali Imran, Joseph Mugonda and Juliana Fitzwater. However, Ibne Safi's Asian country is not a colony, but an independent nation defending itself against foreign powers and international criminals.[11]

Reflecting India more than Pakistan, the state that Ibne Safi's agents are defending is secular rather than Islamic. His heroes are virtuous, yet their faith is a private matter. Faridi and Imran are wealthy, but not excessive in their behaviour. They obey the law, avoid unnecessary violence and neither consume alcohol nor gamble. Unlike James Bond and the heroes of many Turksploitation films, they seem immune to the temptations of beautiful women. Ibne Safi's agents do not impose their behaviour and beliefs on others, however.[12] In one of the novels, Imran first praises the virtues of being a Muslim and then tells his colleague to feel free to drink his heart out. Joseph Mugonda and Juliana Fitzwater never convert to Islam. However, they appear as loyal to their Hindustani homeland as the Muslim characters. Although Ibne Safi had taken Pakistan as his home, his novels contained little support for making Islam a state religion.[13]

Ibne Safi's nostalgia for religious pluralism was coupled with an excitement about technological futures. Ali Imran himself is a scientist with a doctorate in chemistry from the University of Oxford. A novel from 1956 presents a villain who controls his organization through a global television system. In a subsequent book, scientists manipulate the weather in order to create floods. Readers also encounter a robot walking the streets, managing traffic and settling minor disputes. In *Jungle Fire*, published in 1960, a villain builds a machine that turns three crippled beggars into a gorilla. Ibne Safi's novels further featured ray guns and even brain transplants.[14]

Although Ibne Safi did not make extraterrestrial life a major theme of his work, he shared the global excitement about unidentified flying objects. In 1968, he published *Space Battle*.[15] In this novel, the villain Theresia captures Imran and transports him to Zeroland, where zombie-like inhabitants serve her. In prison, Imran meets a scientist who is forced to build spacecraft. Together, they escape and in a climactic scene win over six enemy flying saucers. Around

11 Nisar and Masood, 'The Nostalgic Detective'; Dutta, 'The Return of X-2'.
12 Sardar, 'Ibn-e-Safi, BA', 135–36.
13 Nisar and Masood, 'The Nostalgic Detective', 46, 48.
14 Omar Ahmed Agha, 'The Man with the Golden Pen'; Sardar, 'Ibn-e-Safi, BA', 136.
15 Ibn-i Ṣāfī, *Faẓā'ī hangāmah*.

2000, the novel was republished in a collection whose cover depicts a yellow flying saucer, a grey alien and the Klingon character Worf from *Star Trek*.[16] Posthumous editions of other novels from the *Imran* series similarly display images of the starship *Enterprise* on their covers.[17]

While Ibne Safi catered to the demand for genre fiction in Urdu, readers of Bengali did not have to wait long for an equivalent to *Imran*. In 1963, Qazi Anwar Hussain, son of a professor at the University of Dhaka, established a press for pulp fiction under the name Sheba Prokashoni. This publisher would later also bring out books about flying saucers and the Bermuda Triangle. However, arguably Hussain's most popular creation was the *Masud Rana* series. Also inspired by Ian Fleming's *James Bond*, the titular character was an agent of Pakistan and later Bangladesh Counter-Intelligence. As another hero of the postcolonial nation, Rana also defended his home country against geopolitical threats. Employing several ghost writers, Hussain's Sheba Prokashoni published hundreds of *Masud Rana* novels over decades. Although not explicitly science fiction, the series featured much imaginary technology. In one of the early novels, an Indian spymaster threatens Pakistan's harvest with biologically modified locusts in an attempt to starve the country into submission. Rana foils this plan by entering the Indian locust breeding centres with a super-pesticide prepared by a scientist at the University of Dhaka.[18]

Qazi Anwar Hussain followed Ian Fleming in situating his novels in the actual geographies of the Cold War more than in fictional domains, such as Zeroland. *Masud Rana* was also closer to *James Bond* than *Imran* was in that the series included more sex. This was a profitable, but risky move for Hussain, especially before the Bangladesh Liberation War. After Hussain published the third *Masud Rana* novel, the journalist and rival publisher Gazi Shahabuddin Ahmed wrote that he should be publicly whipped and his hands burned. Hussain responded with a defamation case against him, which the court dismissed on the basis that the book in question had already been banned. After 1971, however, Sheba Prokashoni benefited from a secular reputation that reflected that of newly independent Bangladesh.[19]

During the 1970s, Qazi Anwar Hussain was joined by more writers who shared his secular outlook. Among the most prominent were two brothers who were trained scientists. Their lives were indelibly marked by Bangladesh's war

16 Ibn-i Ṣāfī, *Shūgar benk*.
17 Ibn-i Ṣāfī, *Zīrolenḍ*; *Thirīsiyā kī wāpsī*.
18 Mukharji, 'Technospatial Imaginaries'.
19 Kibria, 'Masud Rana's Qazi Anwar Husain'.

of independence, as their father, a police officer, had been killed in the struggle against Pakistani forces. The older brother, Humayun Ahmed, first studied at the University of Dhaka and then completed a doctoral dissertation in chemistry at North Dakota State University in 1982.[20] He subsequently returned to Dhaka to teach, before dedicating himself fully to creative pursuits. He became one of the most prolific Bengali authors of all time, publishing more than 200 books, including more than a dozen science fiction novels. Like Hussain, Ahmed often dealt with sexuality, but shied away from explicit descriptions.[21]

Emerging in the aftermath of Bangladesh's independence struggle, Humayun Ahmed's science fiction was hardly Islamic. Many Muslim characters do appear, but so do a few Hindus, reflecting the country's demography. However, religion is not a major theme of his stories. Instead of the relationships between different faiths, Ahmed preferred to explore those between humans, robots, plants and extraterrestrial beings. This was in line with successive governments that sought to develop the country scientifically and technologically, while excluding Islamists from power. In addition, the secular nature of his novels was perhaps meant to appeal to a wider Bengali readership stretching to neighbouring India.

Even more dedicated to both science fiction and secularism was Ahmed's younger brother Zafar Iqbal. Born in Sylhet in 1953, he studied at the Bogra Zilla School, which also educated Ziaur Rahman, the founder of the Bangladesh Nationalist Party.[22] After completing a bachelor's degree in physics at the University of Dhaka, he went to the University of Washington in 1976. He undertook research at the Nuclear Physics Laboratory there and completed a doctoral dissertation on the hydrogen atom in 1983.[23] Next, Iqbal worked at the California Institute of Technology and Bell Communications Research, where he contributed to several patents.[24] In 1994, he and his wife and fellow physicist Yasmeen Haque returned to Bangladesh to join the recently established Shahjalal University of Science and Technology in Sylhet. He taught computer science and became head of the department of electrical and electronic engineering. Unlike his brother, he retained his faculty position, while publishing dozens of novels in Bengali.[25]

20 Humayun Ahmed, 'Adsorption'.
21 Bari, 'Tears'.
22 Rahman, 'A Successful Seat'.
23 Muhammed Zafar Iqbal, 'Search', 209.
24 E.g. Brackett et al., 'System'.
25 Rana, 'Muhammad Zafar Iqbal'.

Much of Iqbal's work was devoted to building a strong and independent Bangladeshi nation. 'Our education system is in a mess', he wrote in a newspaper article in 2004. To alleviate this situation, he proposed the teaching of basic science in Bengali rather than English.[26] His writing of fiction in his mother tongue was also a means of translating and popularizing scientific knowledge. As a secular nationalist, he was hostile towards the Jamaat-e-Islami, a party that had opposed Bangladeshi independence and collaborated with the Pakistani army. Iqbal supported the banning of the party in 2013 and the trial of its leaders for war crimes. In his view, promoters of violence had no right to participate in elections. He also attacked newspaper editors and other representatives of civil society for favouring the Jamaat-e-Islami. Moreover, he complained that European diplomats in Dhaka were not paying tribute to the 'martyrs' of the liberation war on Victory Day.[27]

Zafar Iqbal's hostility towards political Islam also shaped his science fiction. His novels often had characters with Muslim names, but few other references to religion. Such was the case with *Peril in Space*, a novel published in 1977 for which he drew on his knowledge of nuclear physics. Four scientists and engineers named Hasan, Jahid, Jasmine and Kamal seek to defend Earth against Harun Hakshi and his aide Turner, a nuclear specialist. Hakshi, a convicted murderer, had fled from prison and built the space laboratory *Plutonik* and the flying saucer *Phobos*. The latter attacks other spaceships in an attempt to take over the world. Jahid, Jasmine and Kamal are detained and controlled by a computer that predicts the near future. In desperation, Jasmine contemplates suicide. However, Kamal and Jahid are able to trick Hakshi and destroy *Phobos* with a nuclear explosion.[28]

Even as a secular writer, Iqbal occasionally employed his religious imagination. One example is his novel *Triton is a Planet's Name* from 1988. The plot follows five humans and their robot assistant onboard a spaceship as they investigate whether Triton bears life. As the ship approaches the planet, all passengers are gripped by terror. An astronomer explains that Triton might be hell, a sphere in which sinners are burnt. Although the scientists cannot hear the wrongdoers' screams, they might still be able to feel their fear. It turns out that the planet as a whole is a living being whose progeny could devour Earth. The scientists communicate with the planet via

26 Muhammed Zafar Iqbal, 'Doing Science'.
27 Daily Star, 'Zafar Iqbal Slams'.
28 Ikabāla, *Mahākāśe Mahātrāsa*.

neutrinos. In that process, Triton's reading of trillions of such particles from a nearby star cause it to overheat slowly and explode.[29]

Personal piety appears in Iqbal's stories about space as well, but rather as an exception. One example is his novel *The Lonely Planetary Traveler*, which was first published in 1994. The story again involves a spaceship with humans and robots who are exploring a distant planet. This planet is similar to Earth, but located between two stars whose radiation periodically produces extreme temperatures. The animals on the surface have each of their organs spread out through their entire body, which allows them to survive otherwise fatal wounds. The explorers also find a sole human called Suhan, a descendant of earlier visitors. Kiri, the spaceship's robot captain, decides to kill and dissect Suhan in order to discover how his body has adapted to the environment. Laina, the human co-pilot, however, feels sympathy and ultimately love for Suhan. She thus prays to God to save Suhan from the devil Kiri. This is the first prayer in her life, and she starts to feel inner peace. In the end, Suhan manages to destroy Kiri, and the two humans are united.[30]

Despite some positive depictions of piety, Zafar Iqbal remained controversial as an 'anti-Islamist'. His wife insisted that none of his books contained 'anything that goes against the Islamic sentiment'. Nevertheless, one blogger argued that 'a lot of Iqbal's writings, especially the ones written for children, are of propagandist nature'. A bearded or religious man often turns out to be the villain. Iqbal's hostility towards the Jamaat-e-Islami made him close to the ruling Awami League, but also a target for its enemies. One political analyst said that Iqbal's rhetoric 'looks at the country through the simplistic narrative of pro versus against Liberation War'. Dawah Ilallah, an internet forum of the banned Ansarullah Bangla Team (ABT), went so far as to label Iqbal an atheist and hosted discussions on possible ways to kill him.[31] In 2016, he and his wife received death threats via messages on their phones. 'Welcome to our new top list! Your breath may stop at anytime. Abt', read the text to Yasmeen Haque. 'Hi unbeliever! We will strangulate you soon', said the note to Iqbal.[32] In response, a police detail was assigned to both around the clock.[33]

29 Ikabāla, *Trāitana*.

30 Ikabāla, *Nisḥanga grahachāri*.

31 Mahmud, 'Bangladesh'.

32 Serajul Islam, 'Prof Zafar Iqbal'.

33 bdnews24.com, 'Police'.

Galactic Mamluks

What made Zafar Iqbal a target was not just his outspokenness, but also his prominence. In addition to his dozens of novels, he wrote numerous newspaper columns. Most other science fiction writers in the Muslim world did not reach his status as a public figure. However, they were still successful critically or commercially. One of the best known was the Egyptian Nehad Sherif, who early in his life already had privileged access to scientific and literary works. Born in Alexandria, he completed his primary and secondary education in Helwan, the location of Egypt's leading observatory at the time. His imagination was further developed with the help of his family. When he was a child, his grandmother told him stories from the *One Thousand and One Nights*. He also attended the cultural salons hosted by his father, a prominent artist. The young Nehad further benefited from the big and diverse library of his great-grandfather Mohamed Sherif Pasha, who had served as prime minister of Egypt three times. Nehad first read children's books by the Egyptian Kamel Keilany and subsequently works by the medieval authors al-Maʿarri and Ibn Tufayl as well as by Jules Verne and H. G. Wells. At night, Nehad loved watching the stars from Helwan. One of his relatives who worked at the observatory allowed him to visit and converse with astronomers, including the leading Abdel Hamid Samaha.[34]

Despite his familiarity with the Helwan Observatory, Sherif did not become an astronomer himself. Instead, he pursued broad interests across the arts and sciences. He initially studied medicine at the request of his father, but pneumonia prevented him from completing his degree. He thus switched to history, earning a licentiate from Cairo University in 1956. At the beginning of his career, he worked as a science journalist with the magazine *Akher Saa* (The Last Hour), which was published by *Akhbar El-Yom*. However, he soon took up positions in the bureaucracy that left him with more time to write fiction. For his first novel, *Time Conqueror*, he was said to have read 300 books.[35] Similar to Tawfiq al-Hakim's plays, *Time Conqueror* explored the idea of immortality. The plot centres on the journalist Kamil and the scientist Halim who conducts experiments freezing people in a villa close to the Helwan Observatory.[36]

34 Al-Shārūnī, 'Nihād Sharīf', 52; Al-Shaymī, 'Nihād Sharīf'; Maʿāṭī, 'Rajul', 86–88; Sārah, 'Nihād Sharīf', 79.

35 Al-Shārūnī, 'Nihād Sharīf', 52; Al-Shaymī, 'Nihād Sharīf'.

36 Maʿāṭī, 'Nihād Sharīf', 16.

Although *Time Conqueror* was not about aliens, astronomy appeared prominently. The narrative is bracketed by an explanation by a researcher from the twenty-fourth century that the rest of the text was found in the ruins of the Helwan Observatory. Before discovering the cryogenics experiments at the nearby villa, the journalist Kamil undertakes research on the history of Egyptian astronomy. Among other scientists, he is interested in the tenth-century Ibn Yunus and the nineteenth-century Mahmoud Hamdi. In addition, the journalist writes about the work of the twentieth-century Ra'uf, a fictional researcher at the Helwan Observatory and an old friend of his.[37] *Time Conqueror* engages in such explorations of the past with a view towards the national future. Sherif dedicated his novel 'to a potential tomorrow in which Egypt reclaims scientific glory'. It was his 'wish' that 'the Egyptian takes his place within his heritage as the first builder of the oldest civilization known in history'.[38]

Time Conqueror was not just an expression of Sherif's pride in Egyptian science, but also of his fascination with English and French fiction. At the beginning of the novel, one of the characters praises Egyptian literature as 'noble, grandiose, and eternal'. After having become tired of its realism and traditionalism, however, he turned towards writing that follows the 'method of science' and possesses 'wider horizons'. 'I read Jules Verne, Wells, Huxley and other writers, and with them I live in those mysterious worlds of theirs, travel in a world that no longer exists, witness the war of planets and rediscover the continent of Atlantis', explained the protagonist. 'Then, I plunge into the centre of the Earth, taste godly food, look for the invisible man, look out from Huxley's new world.'[39]

While acknowledging European influences, Sherif did more than imitate Western science fiction. His work also reflected the debates over the relationship between science and religion, which had developed in the context of competition between Christian and Muslim missionaries. 'Couldn't cryogenics be considered an obvious interference in God's will?' Kamil asks Halim in the novel. 'God is bigger than any power we know', the doctor responds, 'It's in his power to grant us, or to not grant us, the insight to discover what we discover day after day.' In the past, dissection of the human body, the claim of Earth as round, and ascending to the heavens had been denounced as 'unbelief', 'atheism' or 'apostasy'. However, 'the near future will witness the arrival of humankind on

37 Ian Campbell, *Arabic Science Fiction*, 120, 128–29.
38 Sharīf, *Qāhir al-zaman*, 6.
39 Barbaro, 'Where Science Fiction', 33.

the moon, and Venus and Mars and other planets', the physician predicted. 'Trust that all of this will only happen by the command of God and his perfect will.'[40]

Continuing to pursue his interests in astronomy and space exploration, Sherif soon incorporated extraterrestrials into his writing. In 1969, he completed a short story that would also form the title of a collection released five years later: 'Number 4 Commands You'. In the year 1990, in his imagination, a mysterious voice appears globally, addressing all people in their own languages. It sends a 'statement' from planet number 4, that is Mars, to planet number 3 or Earth. The Martians scold their neighbours for their 'selfishness' and 'intellectual backwardness' compared with their own 'advanced civilization'. The Martians go on to accuse the earthlings of 'criminal acts' peaking with the nuclear explosion over Hiroshima in 1945.[41]

'Number 4 Commands You' was similar to other science fiction stories about the unprecedented threats of the Cold War and the nuclear age. Yet, in Sherif's imagination, the accusations and dire warning also had an explicit religious dimension. The Martians argue that Earth's inhabitants have 'challenged God's wisdom in His creation'. Earth's arsenals of hydrogen bombs pose a threat not only to planet number 3, but also to its neighbour. The Martians recall the fate of the 'fifth planet' between Mars and Jupiter, whose existence had been suggested by the German astronomer Johann Elert Bode. The voice explains that the planet was 'the most magnificent and wealthiest in the solar system' and its civilization 'extremely advanced and prosperous'. However, a nuclear war led to its explosion and disintegration into tens of thousands of asteroids more than one million years ago. In order to avoid a similar disaster, the Martians call upon Earth's governments to dismantle their atomic arsenals and related technology.[42]

Earth's inhabitants are unconvinced, which gives Sherif the opportunity for further world-building. The very idea of life existing on the red planet is described as a 'lie' that has been denied by American scientists for decades. However, the Martians stress that 'we', the 'inhabitants of planet number 4', and 'not the Russians or the Americans' are behind the statements. They do not live on their planet's surface, but in underground cities and tunnels up to nine kilometres deep. There, they had sought refuge from the thousands of meteoroids caused by the fifth planet's explosion. They breathe ammonia and have phosphorescent light and ultraviolet rays to compensate for the lack of solar radiation. Livestock

40 Ian Campbell, *Arabic Science Fiction*, 122.
41 Sharīf, *Raqm 4*, 31–32.
42 Ibid., 32–35.

are raised in 'animal cities' and fish in underground lakes, but birds are extinct. On the surface, farms with red plants are irrigated with water from the poles. The detailed explanations come to naught, however. As Earth's governments do not comply with the Martian orders, thousands of flying saucers suddenly appear. In meetings in Cairo, Earth's great powers unite, but their weapons fail. In the end, Earth's nuclear technology vanishes, and the spaceships return home.[43]

Nehad Sherif's imagination of Egypt as a centre of science and politics was attractive, even though – or perhaps because – it contrasted with actual failures of Gamal Abdel Nasser's government. Disappointment spread rapidly after the defeat against Israel in the Six-Day War of 1967. At the same time, Sherif's science fiction quickly gained acceptance and a level of 'canonization'.[44] This was arguably facilitated not just by the quality of his writing, but also by his connections and loyalty to the Egyptian state. During the 1960s, he worked in public relations for different government agencies, including as spokesman for the Ministry of Agricultural Reform.[45] In 1969, his first novel, *Time Conqueror*, won first prize in a competition of the Egyptian Story Club.[46] It was published by Dar Al-Hilal, which produced the magazine of the same name. Sherif's stories were adapted for radio as well. In 1974, he was appointed a member of the Supreme Council of Arts, Literature, and Social Sciences.[47] Within the council, he was responsible for editing and publishing and later for competitions.[48] In addition, he supervised different scientific and literary associations. In 1975, he also became a founding member of the Writers' Union of Egypt.[49]

Crucial for Sherif's career was also the patronage of Youssef El-Sebai, an influential member of the regime. An army officer and a writer, he served as editor-in-chief of *Akher Saa*, chairman of Dar Al-Hilal and minister of culture. He played a key role in the creation of the Story Club and the Writers' Union. He 'was the godfather of all novelists in Egypt and we felt secure when he was around', said Fathi Salama, secretary of the union, later. He recalled that El-Sebai used to intercede with Nasser, when journalists or novelists were arrested.[50] El-Sebai himself also published a space-themed science fiction novel

43 Ibid., 37–44.
44 Snir, 'The Emergence of Science Fiction', 274.
45 Al-Sayyid, 'Nihād Sharīf', 138.
46 Maʿāṭī, 'Nihād Sharīf', 16.
47 Al-Shārūnī, 'Nihād Sharīf', 52.
48 Al-Sayyid, 'Nihād Sharīf', 138.
49 ʿĀmir, 'Ḥiwār', 40.
50 Wren, 'Egypt'.

entitled *You Are Not Alone*.[51] It was he then who, as minister of culture, brought Sherif into the Supreme Council of Arts, Literature, and Social Sciences.

Occupying prominent positions in the Egyptian literary landscape, Sherif quickly became recognized as a leader of Arabic science fiction. Other members of the Supreme Council of Arts, Literature, and Social Sciences mostly contributed to other genres.[52] This allowed Sherif to outshine even such giants as Tawfiq al-Hakim when it came to sci-fi. In 1976, Taleb Omran described him as one of the 'most enjoyable' Arab writers of the genre.[53] In 1984, Sherif travelled to Jordan to record two television episodes about his work.[54] During the same year, the Egyptian critic Mahmoud Kassem compared him to Jules Verne. Even though Sherif had only published two novels by this point, he was further likened to twentieth-century authors who had 'succeeded' in combining 'scientific, ideological, political, and cultural contemplation'.[55] *Aldoha* magazine published several of Sherif's short stories and hailed him as 'the pioneer of science fiction in Arabic literature'.[56]

Encouraged by his successes, Sherif kept publishing new stories about aliens in particular. In 1983, the writer brought out an entire collection entitled *I and the Space Beings*.[57] His narratives contained many ingredients of global science fiction, such as flying saucers, but also specific references to Egypt and its Arab neighbours. 'Encounter with Khufu's Granddaughter' features a descendant of the commissioner of the Grand Pyramid of Giza, who was also known as Cheops. Thousands of years ago, in Sherif's imagination, ancient Egyptians had migrated to one of Uranus's moons before returning to Earth in modern times. Another story is set in 1999, when a spaceship with Arab scientists reaches Jupiter. Gelatinous beings who live in the planet's atmosphere come to examine them.[58]

The appeal of Sherif's stories arguably derived not just from his imagination of Egyptian and wider Arab achievements. Another factor behind their popularity was an element of romance. In *Time Conqueror*, the journalist Kamil falls in love with Halim's sister-in-law.[59] More alluring was 'A Woman in a Flying Saucer',

51 Al-Sibā'ī, *Lasta waḥdak*.
52 Goldschmidt, *Biographical Dictionary*, 68.
53 'Umrān, *Al-'ālam*, 126.
54 Sharīf, 'Muqaddimah', 3.
55 Qāsim, 'Al-taqārub', 116.
56 Sharīf, 'Al-hijrah'; Sārah, 'Nihād Sharīf'.
57 Sharīf, *Anā*.
58 Ibrāhīm, 'Nihād Sharīf', 123–24.
59 Barbaro, 'Marginality', 47.

another story in *I and the Space Beings*. An astronomer at Egypt's Kottamia Observatory has an experience reminiscent of the 'mystical vision' of classical Sufi literature. In the desert, he encounters a beautiful young woman. She takes him to her spacecraft, whose interior is similar to the 'computer centers' in Cairo. She is described in sexual terms, having 'red-wine skin', 'rosy lips' and 'full and round breasts'. An illustration shows her wearing long black hair and a very short dress. As the story unfolds, the scientist saves her life and those of her companions.[60] The visitor tells him that they are from the moon Deimos, which he has long had a vague feeling that it was 'inhabited'.[61]

Sherif combined passion with a political message similar to the one in 'Number 4 Commands You'. The woman warns the astronomer once again of the danger of a nuclear war. Such a conflict could destroy Earth and with it a metal that the inhabitants of Deimos require to live. In the past, they had prevented such disaster by annihilating the technologically advanced, but warmongering people of Atlantis. 'Two-hundred neutron missiles' had killed all of them, but left Earth's 'peaceful, primitive peoples' untouched. Over the course of Sherif's story, the astronomer slowly falls in love with the woman, whose home he describes as a place more respectful of God's creation. Before the flying saucer departs, the two protagonists sensually touch. In the end, the astronomer wishes, 'If only this creature remained on my Earth.'[62]

Even though Sherif imagined romantic encounters that were extramarital as well as extraterrestrial, he sought to provide moral guidance for his readers in accordance with his faith. His aliens appear as 'messengers of love, peace and cooperation',[63] but also as quasi-divine punishers. In an interview for *Aldoha* in 1985, he was asked about the 'religious, social, and political issues' in his novel *Time Conqueror*. He made clear that he stood 'against the use of humans in scientific experiments'. However, like his central character, he did not consider the freezing of bodies itself as interfering with God's will. He argued instead that God, 'who created us', gave us the ability to discover. Therefore, 'whatever scientific achievements we reach will not be in violation of God's will'. The author sought to contribute to such achievements with his writings. By offering a 'personal' and 'local' view, he wanted to confront the scientific 'backwardness' of the 'Arab nation'.[64]

60 Snir, 'The Emergence of Science Fiction', 276; Sharīf, *Anā*, 11.
61 Sharīf, *Alladhī taḥaddá*, 147.
62 Ibid., 152.
63 Ibrāhīm, 'Nihād Sharīf', 125.
64 Sārah, 'Nihād Sharīf', 82.

Sherif's writings about aliens specifically were also part of a religious quest. 'Why has God created me, you, and all of us?' he asked at the beginning of *I and the Space Beings*. 'Why did He make us on this rocky sphere swimming, hanging in its eternal corner of the universe?' The writer then asked whether He had populated other planets with humanlike beings. The answer, he said, requires 'a long period of careful study in the books of religions and the works of philosophers, thinkers and scientists'. He also acknowledged several friends who had 'watched the sky' and examined its 'worlds' with him since his youth. They included two engineers, a scientist, a diplomat, a fellow writer, plus the filmmaker Kamal El-Sheikh, but interestingly no theologian.[65]

Although coming from outside a clerical circle, the Islamic elements of Sherif's work were perhaps as much appreciated as his patriotism. In 1987, a movie adaptation of *Time Conqueror* directed by Kamal El-Sheikh was released.[66] The critic Ahmad ʿAbd Allah lauded the picture as a 'bold step', especially in light of the financial and technical challenges of the Egyptian industry. He emphasized that the film did not take a 'materialist form that is contrary to our religious and spiritual values'. Instead, the work linked 'science fiction to our cultural and religious heritage'. The reviewer also noted that 'the film stressed the importance of religion in more than a scene'. The physician's daughter is shown with a copy of the Qur'an 'more than once'. The doctor himself quotes the scripture, thus confirming that his cryogenic experiments would succeed or fail 'only by God's will'.[67]

Despite the contrast between Sherif's imagination and the actual state of Arab science, the Egyptian government continued to support his work. It did so even after his patron Youssef El-Sebai was assassinated in 1978 for his support for peace with Israel. In 1989, the General Egyptian Book Organization published another novel of his under the title *The Thing*. The title could have been a borrowing of the adaptations of John W. Campbell's novella *Who Goes There?* However, Sherif's aliens come to the Egyptian desert in place of the Arctic. Instead of violent and terrifying, they are pacifist. They have concluded treaties of friendship with neighbouring planets and hope to do the same with Earth. Their flying saucer, called 'the thing', only engages in self-defence. As it hovers over Egypt in the year 2007, it disrupts the engines of approaching fighter jets and deflects missiles.[68]

65 Sharīf, *Anā*, 3–4.
66 Al-Mawjī and al-Shaymī, 'Aflām al-khayāl al-ʿilmī al-miṣrī'.
67 ʿAbd Allāh, 'ʿIndamā yatawaqqaf al-zaman', 69.
68 Sharīf, *Al-shay*'; Snir, 'The Emergence of Science Fiction', 278–79.

Sherif's *The Thing* was Egyptian not just in the setting, but also in its religious references. One scholar of Islamic jurisprudence in Cairo worries that Earth's people have lost their religion as a result of the arrival of the flying saucer. In response, he reminds them that God is the 'Creator of the heavens and the creatures of the heavens'. He advises that 'in your true religion and in the recourse to God, you have security, safety and peace'. Meanwhile, an American astronomer discovers references to 'the thing' in hieroglyphs. One of his Egyptian peers confirms that his ancestors had been capable of space flight and built pyramids not just on Earth, but also on the Moon and Mars. At the end of the story, which spans over seven days, the aliens turn out to have names from the ancient Egyptian religion. Three robotic occupants of 'the thing' are named Ra, Horus and Thoth. Another one is called Ka, probably after a part of the soul. These robots send a message to the sole ruler of their 'great planet' in the 'galaxy of cold light'. He is the 'son of Amun the Renewer'. Their message concludes with 'peace and God's mercy and blessings'.[69]

Whether the divinity was Islamic or ancient Egyptian, Sherif framed contact with aliens in religious terms for the rest of his career. One of his last novels, published by Nahdet Misr in 2008, was entitled *The Son of the Stars.* It was dedicated to 'the first Earthly human' and the 'first being from another celestial body' who meet and 'end the heavy isolation'. In his introduction, Sherif stressed that 'it is important to believe what we have already felt in our unconscious'. He added that 'we have discovered it mentioned in our heavenly books – all of them without exception – ending with our great Holy Qur'an'. He explained that just like man is a 'social being', 'Earth is a social planet in need of others'. Such worlds 'represent the torches of light from the divine'.[70]

Such religious inclusivism together with a privileging of Islam was in line with the Egyptian government, which sought to serve and control a Muslim majority as well as minorities. Perhaps this made Sherif an ideal science fiction writer for his regime. That he persisted in putting Egyptian science and technology at the centre of his stories added to his appeal. *The Son of the Stars* continued this hallmark of his work. The plot, which is set during the mid-1990s, shares elements with Carl Sagan's novel *Contact* and its movie adaptation. One of the main characters is a radio astronomer who has received an extraterrestrial radio

69 Sharīf, *Al-shay'*, 74, 107–8.
70 Sharīf, *Ibn al-nujūm*, 3, 5–6.

message, but who is met with doubt and ridicule. However, in Sherif's novel, he is called Dr Najati, and the telescope is installed at the Kottamia Observatory.[71]

By the time of his death in 2011, Sherif had cemented his position as a leader of Arabic science fiction, even as recognition of the genre as a whole was still limited. In 2007, he was honoured at the opening of the Lucian the Syrian Symposium in Damascus.[72] In an obituary from 2011, the Saudi-owned newspaper *Asharq Al-Awsat* (The Middle East) called Sherif the 'dean of Arabic science fiction'. The paper further compared him to Robert Heinlein in the USA.[73] However, in 2013, Sherif's daughter Iman also acknowledged the world-builder's failures as an institution builder. He had fought for the creation of a committee for scientific culture as part of Egypt's Supreme Council for Culture as well as for the establishment of science fiction clubs. Yet, he had been frustrated by the number of obstacles caused by the Ministry of Culture and the Writers' Union. Iman also complained that the Supreme Council for Culture and the General Egyptian Book Organization had not kept their promises of reissuing her father's books after his death.[74]

As exceptional as Sherif was in his success among critics, he was unusual in his dependence on state patronage. This was especially the case after the 1980s, when mass literacy and liberalizations expanded the market for writers of popular fiction. The Egyptian public, like their counterparts in Pakistan, demanded stories with local heroes rather than mere translations of *James Bond* or *Tintin*. Science fiction writers included not only journalists, but also physicians who were themselves the product of mass higher education. The medical profession offered not just day jobs that could sustain aspiring writers. Some inspiration also came directly from the doctors' work, which regularly combined science and narratives.

The Modern Arab Establishment became one of the main suppliers for the demand for Egyptian genre fiction. After initially focusing on educational books, this publisher shifted towards entertainment. In 1984, the company, which was owned by Hamdi Mustafa, advertised for writers of science fiction novels.[75] One of those hired was the young physician Nabil Farouk, who had long written stories, but failed to convince other presses. He was equally frustrated with the

71 Sharīf, *Ibn al-nujūm*.
72 Al-Shammās, 'Al-nadwah al-ūlá', 425.
73 Salāmah, 'Raḥīl ʿamīd al-khayāl al-ʿilmī al-ʿArabī'.
74 Fuʾād, 'Ibnat al-riwāʾī Nihād Sharīf'.
75 Fārūq, *Rajul al-mustaḥīl*, 14.

Egyptian public health system. Because of 'ridiculous bureaucratic problems' involving the governorates of Qena and Tanta, he had stopped receiving his salary.[76] He also described himself as a non-governmental being who 'gets refreshed by freedom and corrupted by routine'.[77] He thus resigned from the Ministry of Health and worked for private clinics instead. Released from the constraints of state service, the offer to become a professional writer with the Modern Arab Establishment was especially attractive to him.

As unhappy as Nabil Farouk was with the Egyptian state in his medical work, he was committed to his nation as a writer. Born into a middle-class family in Tanta in 1956, he had grown up reading much Western genre fiction. This included texts by Jules Verne, H. G. Wells and Arthur C. Clarke as well as the detective and crime fiction of Arthur Conan Doyle, Maurice Leblanc and Agatha Christie.[78] Like many people, he loved the plots involving Arsène Lupine, Sherlock Holmes and Miss Marple. 'We were dazzled by the ideas of their stories and the extreme excitement in every page', Farouk later recounted, 'despite the fact that they completely contradicted all the values, morals and principles that we were raised on'. While in medical school in Tanta, he was inspired to create heroes 'with authentic Egyptian and Arab values befitting our belief and our society'.[79] This inspiration was in part the result of a wave of patriotism that had swept Egypt in the aftermath of the war of 1973 against Israel.[80] Emphasizing the national character of the series that they sought to publish, Mustafa and Farouk created the brand *Egyptian Pocket Novels*.[81]

Farouk's writing was shaped not just by nationalism, but – like Sherif's – also by his faith. In the doctor's case, religious genre fiction was likely the result of his professional environment and the response to a market niche. As royalties from the Modern Arab Establishment were meagre at first, he supplemented his income by practising in a specialist clinic of the Sidi Ahmad El Badawi Charitable Association in Tanta. This organization was named after a thirteenth-century mystic and saint who had died in the city. Although Farouk's passion lay in writing, he was committed enough to the clinic to become its director and make it profitable.[82] As he was settling into family life and had children, he

76 Fārūq, 'Ḥarb qalam', 25.
77 Fārūq, *Rajul al-mustaḥīl*, 42.
78 Fārūq, 'Ḥarb qalam', 23.
79 Gratien, '"Man of the Impossible"', 41; Fārūq, *Rajul al-mustaḥīl*, 7.
80 Fārūq, 'Ḥarb qalam', 23.
81 Fārūq, *Rajul al-mustaḥīl*, 41.
82 Ibid., 46–47.

also became interested in writing modest romance. As with other genre fiction, he found the romantic novels available on the Egyptian market to be 'contrary to our traditions, our religion, and our society'. In 1986, Farouk proposed to his publisher 'a clean series that talks about love as a sublime emotion and as a feeling that should not be polluted'. Mustafa was convinced and developed a slogan: 'The only romance series that parents are not ashamed to have at home.'[83]

Farouk's most successful novel series combined conservative morality with action and nationalism in a way similar to Ibne Safi's *Spy World* and *Imran*. It began in 1985 under the brand of *Egyptian Pocket Novels* and was entitled *Man of the Impossible*. It featured Adham Sabri, a secret agent who defends Egypt against Israel and Western powers. Like Faridi and Imran, Sabri has the strength of James Bond, but not his promiscuity. He does not drink alcohol either and refrains from excessive violence. He is referred to as a man 'with the bravery of the ancient Egyptians in his blood and the courage of the Arab knights, a man who fears not the impossible'.[84] Illustrations by the artist Ismail Diab showed much action, but hardly any nudity. The Egyptian equivalents of Bond girls thus generally do not appear in bikinis (but not in headscarves either).

In addition to *Man of the Impossible*, Farouk launched two series of books that were explicitly science fiction. They were also published by the Modern Arab Establishment and entitled *Future File* and *Cocktail 2000*. The former, which also started in 1985, involved members of the Egyptian Scientific Intelligence. The latter, which had its debut four years later, featured a mix of material, including short stories with different characters. Continuing an earlier interest of the Modern Arab Establishment, both series were intended to be educational as well as entertaining. *Future File* bore the subtitle of 'a series of science fiction detective stories for the youth'.[85] Back covers of *Cocktail 2000* promised 'a peak in suspense and excitement'. However, the prefaces also claimed to offer 'tomorrow's culture for today's youth'. As the twenty-first century was approaching, Farouk predicted that knowledge would become as necessary 'as water and air'. With 'the fast development of science, art, and literature', *Cocktail 2000* was meant as a gateway to 'knowledge' and 'civilization'.[86]

As in Sherif's work, extraterrestrials played significant roles in Farouk's fiction. However, to serve as a foil for the heroes, these roles tended to be more

83 Ibid., 45.
84 Gratien, '"Man of the Impossible"', 43–44.
85 Fārūq, *Ikhtifāʾ ṣārūkh*, back cover.
86 Fārūq, *Al-nubūʾah*, back cover, 4; Fārūq, *Al-tajribah al-rahībah*, back cover, 4.

negative, especially in *Future File*. Volume 58 of the series was titled *Battle of the Planets*. The main protagonist Nur al-Din and fellow Egyptian agents defend Earth against the empire of Arghuran. Both planets are similar in size and climate, but the latter has just one continent and two suns. Its inhabitants, red-skinned and snake-eyed humanoids, had already developed space technology half-a-million years ago and created an empire that stretches over dozens of light years.[87] Against all odds, the Egyptians defeat Arghuran, but only to find it replaced by another empire, that of the planet Glorial.[88] Five volumes of *Future File* describe the Egyptian-led human fight against the green-skinned, red-eyed soldiers of Glorial's emperor. The titles themselves signpost the stages of Earth's war of liberation: *Occupation*, *Resistance*, *Struggle*, *Confrontation* and *Victory*.[89]

Adding to their epic character, Farouk coloured these conflicts between Egypt and alien empires in religious language. The opening of *Battle of the Planets* sees Nur al-Din in his fighter 'cutting through that majestic, divine sea' that is space.[90] In the following novel, Arghuran is described as 'the planet of curses' and 'hell'. On its surface, Nur al-Din and his companions, including Ramzi, encounter 'death at every step'. Once, a plant grabs Ramzi's leg with one of its branches and tries to cut his throat with a sword-like leaf. Then, the heroes face a huge black humanoid with silvery eyes, a long tail and a 'body like a devil from the depths of hell'. The Egyptians frequently shout 'oh God'. In the end of *The Hell of Arghuran*, they also express the deepest gratitude to Him for their safe return to Earth.[91]

With God on their side, the son of Satan is one of the Egyptians' fiercest enemies in Farouk's space opera. At the end of one of the volumes of *Future File*, the heroes send this devil into the black hole closest to Earth. This turns out to be a 'space time gap' that transports him to Arghuran. Following the empire's defeat at the hands of the Egyptians, the son of Satan takes on the shape of the emperor of Glorial. In the novel *Victory*, he reveals himself to Nur al-Din again. 'It's me, little Beelzebub, Lucifer junior, or any name that pleases you, among my many names.' He explains to Nur al-Din, whom he calls the 'descendant of Osiris', that he had initially planned to destroy Earth completely. Instead, he decides to turn the planet into 'a horrible hell'.[92] Glorial's soldiers

87 Fārūq, *Maʿrakat al-kawākib*, 8–9.
88 Fārūq, *Al-naṣr*, 158–59.
89 Snir, 'The Emergence', 270.
90 Fārūq, *Maʿrakat al-kawākib*, 5.
91 Fārūq, *Jaḥīm Arghūrān*, 39, 41, 50, 52, 119.
92 Fārūq, *Al-naṣr*, 157–60.

take away 'progress', 'freedom' and 'civilization'. People are executed simply for listening to music.[93] Fortunately, at the end of the volume *Victory*, Nur al-Din and his companions vanquish the devil once more.[94]

Nabil Farouk's fiction included not just fallen, but also fake angels. In another volume of *Future File*, titled *Prison of the Moon*, Nur al-Din and his colleagues encounter winged humanoids with white skin and clothes. The tender creatures bring the Egyptians to their underground city Luna, a 'paradise' full of diamonds, gold, silver and marble. The inhabitants of Luna do not think of themselves as supernatural beings, however. Actual angels consist of 'pure light' and are a special creation of God, explains the Great Wise, the city's leader. Previous generations of humans had mistaken the Moon's inhabitants for angels, when they visited Earth in their spaceships.[95]

The people of Luna turn out to be the survivors of a civilization that had almost annihilated itself. As much as Farouk celebrated Egyptian strength and heroism, he also criticized militarism. As with Nehad Sherif, this critique arguably responded to Cold War competition and arms races. The Great Wise explains that, several million years ago, the Moon had been a planet with an atmosphere, seas, cloud-filled skies, and plants. Intelligent life had evolved even more rapidly than on Earth. Then 'greed found its way into the hearts of the leaders of our civilized states'. The Great Wise continues, 'Every state thought that it could win the planet's leadership, and the result was the destruction of all.' Weapons annihilated the planet's atmosphere, forcing the survivors underground, where they became peaceful and united. However, at present, they worry about their Earthly neighbours, who have not developed 'spiritually' to the same extent. The inhabitants of Luna are also afraid that humans would covet their precious stones and wage war over them.[96]

Although Farouk dealt with similar themes as Sherif, he remained less recognized in Egypt's literary scene. Early on in his career, other publishers had rejected his manuscripts on the grounds that they were too focused on 'individual heroism'. Even though *Future File* was more about teamwork than *Man of the Impossible*, critics remained dissatisfied. Some of them mistook his books for children's literature based on the format and then argued that they did not suit kids. Against so much resistance, it took him fourteen years to join the

[93] Fārūq, *Al-muqāwamah*, 5–6.
[94] Fārūq, *Al-naṣr*, 176–78.
[95] Fārūq, *Sijn al-Qamar*, 95–96, 101.
[96] Ibid., 93–98.

Writers' Union of Egypt. Some of its members dismissed his novels as 'take-away'. Although Farouk described Sherif as his 'teacher at all levels', he had to wait for others to advocate for him. Even when he won a State Encouragement Award for Literature, one critic congratulated him on having received the prize for children's literature.[97] The doctor was, however, invited to contribute two monthly pages on espionage for the magazine *al-Shabāb* (Youth), which belonged to the leading newspaper *Al-Ahram*.[98]

Although less respected by the literary establishment than Sherif was, Farouk became more popular and successful commercially. Over the course of twenty years, his hundreds of books came to reach millions of readers across the Arab world. The Modern Arab Establishment not only paid him cash, but gave him a loan to buy his first car and later provided him with an office and an apartment in Cairo. He earned additional income by writing stories for the Saudi magazine *Basim* as well as articles for various periodicals. In the end, he made enough money to leave the medical profession. He thus became one of few science fiction writers who were able to support themselves and their families mostly through book sales.[99]

The demand for national genre fiction was large enough for the Modern Arab Establishment to enlist other authors as well. One of them was Ahmed Khaled Towfik, a physician of a similar middle-class background as Nabil Farouk. Towfik was born to a cotton trader and a university secretary in Tanta in 1962. As a teenager, he began devouring British, American and Russian books in his father's library. He too studied medicine at Tanta University, but unlike Farouk practised it for most of his life. A specialist in tropical diseases, he became a professor at his alma mater. Beginning in the 1990s, the Modern Arab Establishment published three series by him under the titles *The Supernatural*, *Safari* and *Fantasy*. They included thrillers, horror and science fiction. Rifʿat Ismaʿil, the hero of *The Supernatural*, is a doctor similar to the author himself.[100]

Although Towfik had a good scientific training, he was not bound by it in his imagination. *Fantasy* is 'the land of dreams that do not end', 'where everything is possible', he wrote. '*Fantasy* is the paradise of the lovers of the imagination.' In volume four of the series, *Empire of the Stars*, the heroine discovers Galactica, a world without gravity or atmosphere. In one of the planet's areas, 'everything is

[97] Fārūq, 'Ḥarb qalam', 24, 26.
[98] Fārūq, *Rajul al-mustaḥīl*, 78.
[99] Fārūq, *Rajul al-mustaḥīl*.
[100] Yaqoob, 'Ahmed Khaled Towfik'.

metal – buildings, streets, and people'. Visitors from other worlds need to bring their respective gases for breathing. They include nitrogen, methane, xenon and – in the rare case of Earthly beings – oxygen. Nevertheless, characters are able to speak in the vacuum. A footnote reminds the reader: 'On a planet without an atmosphere, sound cannot be transmitted, but we are in *Fantasy*, where everything is possible.'[101]

In addition to publishing his own novels, Towfik collaborated with Farouk in translating foreign works for the Modern Arab Establishment. In the early 1990s, Farouk began editing a series of *Global Pocket Novels*, complementing the larger brand of *Egyptian Pocket Novels*. The new series focused on works of speculative fiction and especially those with successful cinematic versions. The first four volumes were translations of *Flash Gordon, King Solomon's Mines, Dr. No* and *Star Wars*.[102] As Farouk became preoccupied with his own writing, Towfik took over the series in 1996. Science fiction, including stories about extraterrestrial life, continued to feature in this collection. Volume ten was Steven Spielberg's *Close Encounters of the Third Kind*.[103] After *Jurassic Park* had been a global success, Towfik translated Michael Crichton's earlier novel *The Andromeda Strain*.[104] Other issues included Arthur C. Clarke's *2001: A Space Odyssey* and Robert Heinlein's *Stranger in a Strange Land*.[105] Like other novels published by the Modern Arab Establishment, the Arabic translations contained their own illustrations, which were typically less racy than the originals. Flash Gordon's fellow adventurer Dale Arden, herself a prototype for Princess Leia in *Star Wars*, appears in long dresses with her arms and legs covered.[106]

In addition to translating global science fiction, Towfik borrowed from it in his own novels. In a volume of *Fantasy* entitled *Earth, Moon, Earth*, the Egyptian physician paid homage to both Jules Verne and H. G. Wells. He asked the reader to choose between either the 'French' or the 'English' way of travelling to the Moon. The former was by means of a cannon, as conceived in Verne's *From the Earth to the Moon*. The latter was by means of a weightless sphere, as imagined by Wells in *The First Men in the Moon*.[107]

101 Tawfīq, *Imbarāṭūrīyat al-nujūm*, 5, 40–44.
102 Rāymūnd, *Flāsh Jūrdun*; Hājārd, *Kunūz al-malik Sulaymān*; Fliminj, *Duktūr Nū*; Lūkās, *Ḥarb al-nujūm*.
103 Sbīlbirj, *Liqāʾāt*.
104 Krishtūn, *Sulālat Andrūmīdā*.
105 Klārk, *Ūdīsā al-faḍāʾ*; Hāynlāyn, *Gharīb*.
106 Rāymūnd, *Flāsh Jūrdun*.
107 Tawfīq, *Arḍ*.

Occasionally, Towfik adapted American cultural productions to criticize US imperialism. *Empire of the Stars* from 1995 makes clear references to *Star Wars*. At the same time, the novel condemns American military operations against Iraq. The name of the dominant state, Galactica, is reminiscent not just of the franchise *Battlestar Galactica*, but also of the Galactic Empire in *Star Wars*. Borrowing from George Lucas's universe, Towfik's novel features lightsabres and a rebel princess called Leia.[108] Towfik associated Galactica strongly with the United States, however. Its fighter jets are called F-1600, in reference to the F-16, which flew in combat operations during the Gulf War. (In fact, American pilots called the F-16 'Viper' because of its resemblance to the Colonial Viper spacecraft in *Battlestar Galactica*.[109]) In Towfik's novel, a screen with the CNN logo shows a 'successful campaign' that turns the rebels' planet into a 'big grave'. The princess denounces this operation as a 'massacre'. Yet, one of Galactica's computers compares it to the 'necessary' removal of a tumour.[110]

Although the United States and Egypt were allies at the time – and both used F-16s – Towfik thus rendered the USA as an evil empire. In other works, like in Nabil Farouk's pulp, more explicitly diabolic themes appear. The texts Towfik translated included Washington Irving's short story 'The Legend of Sleepy Hollow' and Stephen King's novel *Misery*. As the Arabic title for the latter, the Egyptian chose *The Female Satan*.[111] The series *The Supernatural* features demons, ghosts and vampires. They too are of extraterrestrial origin, arriving through gaps from a parallel world called 'Side of the Stars'. At least one of these openings exists in Egypt, and 'as the legend goes', no less than seven in Romania. Through one of them, Dracula entered 'our world'.[112]

Outside the Arab region, Towfik became better known for his imagination of an Earthly dystopia than of other worlds. When he took over the series of *Global Pocket Novels* from Nabil Farouk, he had already thought about translating George Orwell's *Nineteen Eighty-Four*.[113] His Arabic rendering eventually appeared in two volumes. However, before that, Towfik also translated Ray Bradbury's *Fahrenheit 451*.[114] In 2008, Towfik published his own dystopia, entitled *Utopia*.[115]

[108] Tawfīq, *Imbarāṭūrīyat al-nujūm*, 46–47.
[109] Güvenç and Yanik, 'Turkey's Involvement', 118.
[110] Tawfīq, *Imbarāṭūrīyat al-nujūm*, 40.
[111] Īrfinj, *Usṭūrat Slībī Hūlū*; Kīnj, *Al-shayṭānah*.
[112] Tawfīq, *Fī jānib al-nujūm*, 27–28.
[113] Ūrwīl, *1984*, 10.
[114] Brādbūrī, *451 fahrinhāyt*.
[115] Tawfīq, *Yūtūbiyā*.

Set in Egypt in the 2020s, it describes class inequality, corruption and brutality. 'Utopia' is the name of an enclave, in which American troops guard the Egyptian elite against the impoverished masses. The novel thus came to be seen as diagnosing some of the conditions that led to the Egyptian revolution of 2011. In the same year, Bloomsbury Qatar Foundation Publishing brought out an English translation. As the Arab Spring unfolded, the book received critical acclaim and scholarly attention far beyond Middle Eastern audiences. Towfik was interviewed by *Locus* magazine, and his work discussed in various academic journals. In 2012, the work was shortlisted for the Science Fiction and Fantasy Translation Awards, which were administered by a charity in California. By the time of his death in 2018, Towfik was thus also included among the recognized Muslim science fiction authors globally. On what would have been his fifty-seventh birthday the following year, he was even honoured with a Google Doodle.[116]

While most novels published by the Modern Arab Establishment were conservative, they were hardly Islamist. Farouk and Towfik's heroes fought for the Egyptian nation rather than an Islamic state. Nevertheless, religious references abound in the *Egyptian Pocket Novels*. Another major contributor to this brand was Raouf Wasfi, a graduate of the American University in Cairo. He taught in Egypt, Iraq and Kuwait and popularized science on radio, television and in print. His non-fiction includes books on *The Universe and Black Holes*[117] and *The Computer*.[118] He further translated H. G. Wells's novels *The Invisible Man* and *Men Like Gods* into Arabic.[119] However, he was perhaps best known for his series *Nova*, which included short stories, novels and poems.

Nova also drew on Western science fiction as well as on older stories from the Middle East. The second volume of *Nova* included 'Adventure on the Planet Jupiter', 'after a story by Isaac Asimov', as the Egyptian acknowledged. Although Wasfi did not specify Asimov's piece, it was probably 'Victory Unintentional'. In both stories, three human-built robots resist the superior inhabitants of Jupiter.[120] In a more original creation titled 'Planet of Terror', Wasfi described 'a thing that only exists in nightmares'. He likened it to 'a scary giant emerging from one of the stories of the *One Thousand and One Nights*'.

116 Towfik, *Utopia*; Morgan, 'A Conversation'; Ian Campbell, 'Prefiguring Egypt's Arab Spring'; Madoeuf and Pagès-El Karoui, 'Le Caire'.

117 Waṣfī, *Al-kawn*, 257.

118 Waṣfī, *Al-ḥāsib al-ālī*.

119 Waylz, *Al-rajul al-khafī*; *Bashar*.

120 Waṣfī, *Al-insān al-ālī al-qātil*, 121–40.

It was 'a mythical monster' from 'the depths of popular tales'.[121] In yet another story, visitors from Sirius display a sword similar to those in the Arabic epic of Abu Zayd al-Hilali.[122]

Although the format of *Nova* was similar to other series by the Modern Arab Establishment, Wasfi's preface was already more religious than Farouk and Towfik's. He called upon his readers to open their minds to 'everything' they would not have believed before. 'If we allow our minds, our imagination, to set out without limits', the science popularizer explained, 'we begin to envisage part of this magnificent panorama, which we call the universe'. 'Faith', he argued, emanates from the 'greatness and splendor of the universe'. By looking at the sky, 'the human mind succumbs to the divine power'. It 'surrenders completely in reverence and worship' to 'the eternal divine coordination of every atom in the universe' and to the 'Creator's wisdom'.[123]

Wasfi's scientific imagination was, indeed, very broad and included a plethora of extraterrestrial life forms. His creatures exist on a broad spectrum between pacifist and warmongering, primitive and advanced. They appear humanlike, animal-like, plant-like or in a combination of them. In one of his stories, a meteorite brings seeds to Earth that first grow into plants and subsequently into green humanoids.[124] Among extraterrestrial animals, the writer imagined dinosaurs, crocodiles and other reptiles. One of his stories describes an interplanetary zoo on board a spaceship that lands on Earth once a year. It exhibits 'huge three-legged creatures of Venus', 'long, thin beings from Mars', and 'scary, snake-like lifeforms from one of the planets of Alpha Centauri'.[125] If one considers ghosts to be life forms, they too exist in the space of the Egyptian's imagination.[126]

As was the case with other science fiction, Wasfi's diverse aliens are very frequently described as 'creatures', even if the 'Creator' goes unmentioned. Occasionally, God is also invoked clearly. One example was the mystical poem 'Playing on the Strings of the Universe'. It starts, 'I, a tiny atom left over from the beginning of the Big Bang during the creation of the universe fifteen billion years ago.' The narrator continues, 'It would have been possible that I remained

[121] Waṣfī, *Al-ḥubb al-mustaḥīl*, 93–94.

[122] Waṣfī, *Sirr kitāb al-mawtá*, 112.

[123] Waṣfī, *Ghazw*, 4.

[124] Waṣfī, *Al-ḥubb al-mustaḥīl*. This story was republished under the title 'Love Comes from the Depths of the Universe'. Waṣfī, 'Al-ḥubb ya'tī'.

[125] Waṣfī, *Shawāṭi' al-abadīyah*, 64.

[126] Waṣfī, *Ashbāḥ*, 5–18.

somewhere in space as a particle.' 'But thanks to God', the voice says, 'I enjoy life. I was born, I breathe and feel, and I love.'[127] In another story entitled 'Hell and Chemical Weapons', a horned Satan appears, 'laughing in madness' and bringing about the end of the world.[128]

Wasfi's Creator was not necessarily an Islamic one. However, occasionally other terms with Islamic connotations appear as well. One example is his story 'The Awesome Journey', in which humans have spread to the other planets of the solar system and formed the 'Space Empire'. As the sun turns into a red giant, it brings about 'the strangest event in the history of the solar system': 'the migration of the nine planets to another location'. Here, Wasfi used the word *hijrah*, which also refers to the 'migration' of the prophet Muhammad from Mecca to Medina in the year 622. In Wasfi's story, delegates from the different planets gather. The one from Venus says, 'All the peoples in the Space Empire pray to God that the plan will be accepted.'[129]

Adding to words with religious connotations, Wasfi made heavy use of prominent Muslim figures in his world-building. In different stories in *Nova*, Wasfi gave the name al-Farabi to a spaceship and station.[130] He thus honoured a scholar from Central Asia who was known in Latin as Alpharabius. Several other spacecraft are called Ibn al-Haytham.[131] Wasfi took this name from a pioneer in optics from Basra who had become known in Europe as Alhazen. Al-Biruni, al-Qazwini, al-Razi, Ibn Battuta and Ibn Hayyan also appear among the names of different vessels. Ibn Rushd and Ibn Sina are commemorated in similar ways.[132] Names of Muslim rulers appear in Wasfi's work too. His novels *Space Princess* and *Battle between the Stars*, which are set in Andromeda, feature an Empire of the Center of the Galaxy. This polity with its capital Sheliak is democratic and monarchical at the same time. The emperor is called Namiq Khan, and his sons Timur and Karim.[133]

Wasfi drew on personalities from across the Islamic lands. Yet, like other literary nation-builders and world-builders, he also inserted rulers of Egypt specifically into his stories. This gave his science fiction a patriotic flavour as well. In 'Planet of Terror', human visitors encounter not just a 'scary giant' but also Mamluks, complete with swords, turbans and silk shirts. 'God save the

[127] Waṣfī, *Ruʿb*, 86, 88.
[128] Waṣfī, *Ashbāḥ*, 158.
[129] Waṣfī, *Al-riḥlah al-rahībah*, 6–7.
[130] Waṣfī, *Mudhannab al-dimār*, 6; *Thawrat al-rūbūt*, 6.
[131] Waṣfī, *Sirr kitāb al-mawtá*, 102; Waṣfī, *Qīthārat al-mawt*, 56; Waṣfī, *Ashbāḥ*, 6.
[132] Waṣfī, *Ightiyāl kumbiyūtir*, 87, 91; *Qīthārat al-mawt*, 84; *Thawrat al-rūbūt*, 90, 92, 102, 126.
[133] Waṣfī, *Amīrat al-faḍā'*, 26–27.

Sultan!' shouts one of them. Qalawun, the sultan, claims that an alien spaceship had abducted their ancestors during a battle against the Tatars. After having been dropped on the new planet, their descendants had preserved their dress and customs. A battle between the human visitors and the aliens ensues, in which the former are saved by the spaceship *Hittin*. This ship's name itself referred to the site of a defeat of Crusaders at the hands of Saladin in 1187.[134] References to pre-Islamic personalities abound too. In a story entitled 'Adventure on the Dinosaur Planet', Captain Samir Karim commands an 'Egyptian space shuttle' named Ramesses III.[135] Similarly, a story with the title 'Adventure on a Primitive Planet' features the spaceship *Zoser*, again referring to a pharaoh.[136] Other ancient Egyptian names of spacecraft include Amenhotep, Ahmose and Khafra.[137] By projecting different strands of heritage into the future, Wasfi arguably promoted both an Islamic and a pharaonic nationalism for Egypt.

Eliza in wonderland

Thanks to the authors of the Modern Arab Establishment, Egypt had become one of the leading producers of science fiction novels in the Muslim world. The Cairo publisher had access not only to a large domestic market, but also to the pan-Arab one. Around 2000, Nabil Farouk and Ahmed Khaled Towfik's series were sold in places as different as elegant bookshops in Abu Dhabi, supermarkets in Riyadh and second-hand bookstalls in Sanaa.[138] In the following years, many hundreds of volumes were scanned and uploaded to various websites.[139] Alongside piracy, legal sales continued. Despite around ten years of blockade by Israel and Egypt, a bookshop in Gaza, for instance, was still selling volumes of *Future File* and *The Supernatural* in 2016.[140]

As Egypt exported books to Arabic speakers worldwide, its production of science fiction even surpassed that of the more populous Indonesia. Nevertheless, in the latter country, mass literacy and increasing wealth also expanded the market for genre fiction from the 1970s. Science fiction specifically received

134 Waṣfī, *Al-ḥubb al-mustaḥīl*, 83–102.
135 Waṣfī, *Ashbāḥ*, 83.
136 Waṣfī, *Al-riḥlah al-rahībah*, 123.
137 Waṣfī, *Al-vayrūsāt al-dhakīyah*, 58; *Ruʿb*, 63, 123.
138 Olsa, Jr and Obadalová, 'SF', 46.
139 Gratien, '"Man of the Impossible"', 39.
140 Al-Ghoul, 'Do Gaza's Melting-pot Markets'.

inspiration from the Indonesian government's technological ambitions. The New Order regime of President Suharto initiated a series of 'lighthouse' projects to mark the development of the nation. In 1976, the country became the first in the developing world to have its own satellite system. Suharto celebrated its launch with replicas of a traditional dagger or *kris* as well as phone calls to remote parts of the archipelago.[141]

The enthusiasm for large technological projects was shared not just by politicians and engineers, but also by writers. One of the most important was Djokolelono from East Java. Like Nabil Farouk, he wrote across a variety of genres and often targeted young people. He also translated much children's literature by authors including Enid Blyton. However, he became equally known for a number of science fiction books. In 1976, when the Indonesian satellite *Palapa* was launched, he published a novel entitled *Falling into the Sun*. In Djokolelono's imagination, his country participates in a multinational effort to colonize Venus in the year 2048. To that aim, Indonesians join Americans, Indians, Japanese and Russians aboard the space station *Sagan*. In the meantime, an experimental fuel throws the spacecraft *Hermes-1* on a dangerous course towards the sun. Sweta Kamandalu, a cadet of the Indonesian Space Academy, seeks to save *Hermes-1* from destruction against all odds.[142]

While similarly patriotic as the *Egyptian Pocket Novels*, Djokolelono's books tended to be less Islamic. *Hermes-1* referred to a god in ancient Greek religion rather than a Muslim figure. The Indonesian author continued such borrowing in his series *Space Explorer* beginning in 1985. Greek letters provided the names for the planets Epsilon and Tau Ceti, for instance. He also shared with writers of English science fiction the use of the Latin word 'Terra'. To be sure, other strange-sounding names, such as Sartach, Dach and Noch, still made Djokolelono's work distinctive.[143] Yet, despite the influence of Indonesian nationalism, his science fiction was hardly independent of the genre's global tradition.

With prolific authors like Djokolelono, science fiction in Indonesia was dominated by men during the twentieth century, as it was in Egypt and many other countries. However, during the twenty-first century new female voices rose to prominence. In Indonesia, this was facilitated by a shake-up of the publishing industry during the financial crisis in 1997. Many large publishers shut down and went dormant, giving way to smaller presses with new editorial

[141] Barker, 'Engineers'.
[142] Djokolelono, *Jatuh ke Matahari*.
[143] Merawati, 'Perkembangan Fiksi Ilmiah Karya Pengarang Indonesia', 146.

attitudes. The monetary crisis also led to the resignation of Suharto as president in 1998 and the fall of his New Order. The ensuing period known as *Reformasi* was marked by an expansion of freedom of expression.[144]

Although the reform era also saw the strengthening of Islamism, this current did not come to dominate Indonesian science fiction. Instead, the new voices reflected the huge diversity of the country, which stretched over thousands of islands. One of the most prominent authors of the genre in the twenty-first century, Dee Lestari, was not even Muslim. Born in Bandung in West Java in 1976, she had been raised in a strict Christian family. She regularly attended a Protestant church of which her mother was a board member. When the New Order fell, she graduated in international relations from Parahyangan Catholic University. However, rather than applying her knowledge of politics directly under the post-Suharto presidencies, she pursued an artistic career as a singer and writer. While opposed to 'fundamentalists', she developed a 'love' for Buddhism and an interest in Kabbalah, she said.[145]

Lestari's broad spirituality shaped her first science fiction novel, *Supernova*, which she completed in 2001. 'We will follow the movement of something that moves faster than light', announces the prologue. 'We will deal with things that can only be dimly grasped by abstract faith yet nevertheless live deep down in the shriveled-up cells of our minds.' However, the author cautioned that her novel was neither an 'occult text', nor 'a religious institution', nor 'a course in philosophy'.[146] Despite the subtitle *The Knight, the Princess, and the Falling Star*, the work was not a fairy tale-like space opera either. *Supernova* did not stay within the bounds of mainstream morality, whether Christian or Islamic. Instead, the book is about a brilliant gay couple creating their own novel centred on a high-class prostitute named Diva. As her alter ego Supernova, Diva gives advice about life and science via the internet.

Both morally and intellectually exciting, *Supernova* appealed to critics and broader audiences alike. Despite being self-published, Lestari's first novel turned out to be a huge success with 7,000 copies being sold within two weeks.[147] The work also emerged among 350 as a finalist of the inaugural Khatulistiwa Literary Award. Named after the equator, this prize had a jury of forty-five members with oversight by the firm Ernst & Young.[148] Lestari had thus garnered

[144] García, 'The Indonesian Free Book Press', 129–30.
[145] Junaidi, 'Dewi "Dee" Lestari'.
[146] Lestari, *Supernova*, 9–10.
[147] Flyn, 'The Best Contemporary Indonesian Literature'.
[148] Ian Campbell, 'Some Developments', 54.

enough interest for the creation of an entire series, which counted six volumes by 2016. The fourth, entitled *The Particle*, deals extensively with UFOs and crop circles. Contact with aliens is made through magic mushrooms rather than space technology, however.[149]

Covering many unorthodox topics, the *Supernova* series was as controversial as it was successful. Lestari's fiction and that of other young urban women was given the label 'fragrant literature'. This term was opposed to 'the old image of Indonesian literature that had been dominated by male authors who were poor and unkempt', Lestari explained. However, 'fragrant literature' was also used to question the quality of female writing – whether it was 'mere instant sensation'.[150] One reviewer of *The Particle* named Arfian Agus wished it had 'more science, less pseudoscience and less romance'. Meeting an extraterrestrial intelligence by being 'high' on mushrooms was laughable to him.[151]

Lestari's interest in fungi was part of her growing concern for the environment. Alarmed by the effects of the livestock industry on global warming, she became a vegetarian. She further nurtured her spirituality through meditation, yoga and marriage to a holistic healer.[152] Agus observed that Lestari had 'become some kind of a buddhist-hippie'. Yet, he recognized that her writing resonated with many people. He even felt compelled to start his review of *The Particle* with an apology to 'all Dee fans'.[153] In 2014, the first *Supernova* novel was adapted as a film. By 2019, 1.8 million people were following Lestari on Twitter and 300,000 on Instagram.

Lestari was exceptional in her popularity. However, Indonesian women of Muslim backgrounds enjoyed great success as writers of science fiction as well. Eliza Vitri Handayani was among the voices emerging after the fall of the New Order. She was born on Eid al-Fitr in 1982, but her mother did not want her to be named like many other children. She thus slightly changed her middle name from Fitri to Vitri. The first book she received was about her namesake: *Alice in Wonderland*, translated into Indonesian as *Elisa di Negeri Ajaib*. As a child, Handayani also listened to audio plays about giants and magic kingdoms. Stories told by her mother about witches and princes metamorphosing into rivers or flowers further stimulated her imagination.[154] She developed her

[149] Lestari, *Supernova Episode: Partikel*.
[150] Flyn, 'The Best Contemporary Indonesian Literature'.
[151] Lestari, 'Partikel (Supernova #4)'.
[152] Candra Malik, 'Dewi "Dee" Lestari'.
[153] Lestari, 'Partikel (Supernova #4)'.
[154] Handayani, 'Between Languages'.

own creative skills at Taruna Nusantara, an elite boarding school in Java, and subsequently at Wesleyan University in Connecticut.

Although Handayani grew up in an Islamic and nationalist environment, she was critical of authority. 'God is watching you, always, although you can't see Him', her parents told her. 'Like a demon', she thought. To her mother's chagrin, she liked to combine the Indonesian words *Tuhan* (God) and *Hantu* (demon) as *Tuhantu.* In primary school, her Islamic teacher said, 'All night angels rain curses on a woman who refuses her husband's advances.' 'Did your wife refuse your advances last night?' she wanted to ask. She also sympathized with Hindu students who were uncomfortable with mentioning God, when reciting the preamble of the constitution during the weekly flag raising ceremony: 'With the blessings of Allah the All Powerful, we the Indonesian people declare our independence.' Handayani admired the bravery of one kid who changed the word 'Allah' into the ecumenical *Tuhan.*[155]

Like so many of her peers in the Muslim world, the young Eliza also grew up with much Western genre fiction. Early on, she read Enid Blyton's *The Famous Five* and Robert Arthur's *The Three Investigators.*[156] In secondary school, the American television series *The X-Files* inspired what would become her first novel. Entitled *Area X*, it was set in a technologically advanced Indonesia in the year 2015. By that point, humanity had already taken photographs of several Earthlike planets through the Terrestrial Planet Finder telescope. In response to the threat of overpopulation and a global energy crisis, Indonesia's government had constructed research areas, the tenth of which had 'ultra top secret status'. The plot follows two students, Elly and Yudho, who investigate mysterious incidents, such as the landing of a flying saucer, near this Area X on the outskirts of Jakarta. They discover an Indonesia UFO and Curious Aerial Phenomena Studies (IUCAS) centre and a failed project to create an alien-human hybrid. In the end, the military arrest Elly and Yudho and attempt to erase their memory, as Area X is destroyed.[157]

Despite her critical thoughts, Handayani was forced to adhere to some Islamic precepts. She initially submitted the novella to a screenwriting competition organized by the National Film Center in 1999 and won first prize in the action category. She also gained the support of Taufiq Ismail, one of Indonesia's most prominent poets, who had first met her during a visit of her boarding

[155] Handayani, 'Islam', 51–53.
[156] Handayani, 'Between Languages'.
[157] Handayani, *Area X*.

school. He published the novella in his magazine *Horison* and helped bring out an expanded version as a book in 2003. He also included an excerpt in an anthology of Indonesian literature under the title *From Fansuri to Handayani*. At the same time, he and others censored her work. They objected to scenes in which her main male and female protagonists were holding hands, kissing, or talking alone in a room. Ismail also illustrated the main character as wearing a hijab, even though Handayani had wanted her to have no discernible religious identity. Despite thus being more conventional in its morality than *Supernova*, *Area X* equally became a bestseller. It also won an award in the young-adult category of the Indonesian Publishers Association in 2004.[158]

After *Area X*, Handayani shied away from science fiction. She regretted not just her submission to her editors, but also her 'montage of laughably impossible world events' that had allowed Indonesia to become so advanced. Instead of imagining political events in the near future, she became more interested in writing about the archipelago's recent past.[159] In 2014, she published a novel about the *Reformasi* period entitled *From Now On Everything Will Be Different*. This time, she challenged censorship. Not only did she write about sexuality, but she defied the cancellation of her book launch at the Ubud Writers & Readers Festival in Bali in 2015. The police had advised the removal of 'sensitive issues' from the programme, including 'those related to the Indonesian Communist Party, or to race, religion, ethnicity, and other identity groups'. Her book was considered controversial, as it described anti-Chinese riots and rapes during the fall of the New Order in 1998. In protest, Handayani wore t-shirts printed with excerpts from her novel each day of the festival.[160]

Despite her turn to actual Indonesian politics, Handayani retained visions of extraterrestrial life. In 2017, she published a personal narrative entitled 'Islam and I'. In a section on the 'afterlife', she referred to some scientists' suggestions that 'either civilizations become advanced enough to create lifelike simulations, or they perish'. Because one advanced civilization alone could create billions of simulations, 'odds are overwhelmingly on the side that we are living inside a simulation – a game in an alien kid's computer. A kid with blue furs and golden eyes'. Such a view of God made sense to Handayani. 'Why many of his rules seemed arbitrary or egocentric, why sometimes I felt the universe was watching

158 Handayani, 'Between Languages'; 'Tentang'; Sarah Malik, 'Navigating Sex'.
159 Handayani, 'Between Languages'.
160 Handayani, 'A Bloody Past'.

over me and other times I felt completely alone', she wrote. 'He is, after all, just a child.' As this alien is able to simulate the end of the world, He can revive her, judge her, or toss her 'into another simulation – a red world with spiky red hills awash with red clouds'.[161]

The fantastic worlds that Muslim novelists and short story writers built were as diverse as the nations to which they belonged. As with films and plays, fiction books betrayed the influences of various religious and cultural traditions – from the pharaonic to the Islamic mystical. At the same time, many Muslim authors were also part of the global mass cultural genre system. They translated and adapted science fiction from other parts of the world, often using similar icons and conventions. However, as literary entrepreneurs whose main markets were national and regional, they also tended to localize their heroes and plots. This included addressing the specific geopolitical anxieties of different countries. Many authors of speculative fiction struggled to gain recognition among critics. Yet, in their combination of local and global popular culture, they were still very creative and imaginative. This allowed at least some of them to be commercially successful in economically and politically challenging contexts. The Emirati Noura Al Noman certainly had advantages working in a stable and prosperous country. Nevertheless, such an environment was in no way a necessity for achieving fame as a science fiction writer.

In the twenty-first century, digital technologies further lowered barriers to publishing and inspired new content. In many ways, the likes of Dee Lestari and Eliza Handayani were heavily influenced by computers. Yudho in *Area X* is a computer science student. The author herself wrote the first version in a computer lab at her boarding school – while her male classmates were surfing porn.[162] Nabil Farouk, in contrast, resisted the use of PCs until the late 1990s, when he was in his early forties. By that point, much science fiction already appeared on computer screens rather than on paper. Farouk's own children loved video games, while he shied away from them.[163] Increasingly, many Muslims not just consumed such games, but also produced them. Digital world-building took place even in Iran, where science fiction cinema had previously struggled. Moreover, such games were part of a growth in forms of artistic expression. An ever greater range of Muslim creative entrepreneurs employed the scientific imagination to visualize the future of humanity and the universe.

[161] Handayani, 'Islam', 56–57.
[162] Handayani, 'Between Languages'.
[163] Fārūq, 'Al-abnā''.

6

Muslim Futurisms

In 2018, Zafar Iqbal expected to retire from Shahjalal University of Science and Technology in Sylhet. However, in March of that year, the Bangladeshi was almost killed there, despite police protection. He was delivering a speech at 'Robofight', a two-day event organized by the Department of Electrical and Electronic Engineering. Suddenly, he was stabbed – by a human, not a robot. With wounds on his head, back, and left hand, he was first rushed to a hospital in Sylhet and then transferred to Dhaka for further treatment. 'Do not beat him', the professor told the crowd, 'Check if he is my student.' The assailant was hit anyway and subsequently detained and interrogated by counterterrorism specialists. Faizur Rahman identified himself as a local madrasa student. He justified his action by claiming that Iqbal was an 'enemy of Islam'.[1] According to officials, the attack bore the hallmarks of Ansar al Islam, which was previously known as the Ansarullah Bangla Team. Prior to this attempted murder, the group had monitored other activists on social media and hacked them to death.[2]

Iqbal did not lose consciousness during the incident. He even performed some calculations in his head to confirm that his brain was still working.[3] Nevertheless, the attack sparked condemnation and demonstrations across Bangladesh. Thousands of people formed chains in Sylhet and Bogra. 'The attack is an assault on the core of free-thinking', said Syed Hasanuzzan, the president of the teachers' association at Iqbal's university.[4] 'Those who are committing these crimes are fanatics', Prime Minister Sheikh Hasina stated during a ceremony for the awarding of research fellowships. 'They think by

1 bdnews24.com, 'Don't Hurt Him'.
2 Chowdhury, 'It Bears Hallmarks'.
3 Mahmud, 'Explaining the Attack'.
4 Daily Star, 'Attack'.

killing a person they will go to heaven', she explained. Instead, 'they'll suffer in the hell'. Sheikh Hasina took this occasion as an opportunity to warn against wider threats against her society. 'We want to make the country free from militancy, terrorism and drug abuse', declared the politician. 'These three social menaces are just destroying children.'[5]

On the surface, the attack could be read as an example of Islamist opposition to science fiction. Indeed, some newspapers stressed Iqbal's identity as a writer of the genre in their coverage of the event. 'Popular science fiction writer Zafar Iqbal stabbed in Bangladesh', was the title of an article in *The Hindu*.[6] 'Top Bangladesh sci-fi writer Zafar Iqbal stabbed in head at seminar', stated Singapore's *Straits Times*. The latter explained that 'Islamist extremists' had been targeting secular and atheist writers and bloggers. While the Islamic State had claimed responsibility for an attack on a Dhaka cafe in 2016, Ansar al Islam had been blamed for most of the violence. The *Straits Times* further mentioned that the Bangladeshi group was linked to Al-Qaeda in the Indian subcontinent.[7]

Nevertheless, it was Iqbal's prominence as a secular activist rather than as a science fiction writer that had made him a target for religious extremists. The attack was thus far from representative of the relationship between Islam and science fiction. Influential religious scholars did object to novels or movies they considered blasphemous or harmful to society. Yet, many advocates of political Islam were similarly imaginative about science and technology as Iqbal. Asim Umar, head of Al-Qaeda in the Indian subcontinent, had himself promoted conspiracy theories involving flying saucers. Ahmed Raef as a writer linked to the Muslim Brotherhood had imagined an Islamic utopia on Mars. Even the Islamic State in Iraq and Syria (ISIS) favoured aesthetics comparable to Italian Futurism, which was itself associated with fascism. ISIS propaganda glorified speed and technology, including cars and weaponry. The organization's videos included effects reminiscent of popular action movies and games, such as the 'bullet time' of *The Matrix* and *Max Payne*.[8] While many Islamist futurists were hostile to competing religious and secular entrepreneurs, such competition forced them to be creative.

Whatever the fate of individual activists like Iqbal, a future decline of secularism and rise of Islamism is thus unlikely to spell the end of the scientific

5 Daily Star, 'Zafar Iqbal's Attackers'.
6 Haroon Habib, 'Popular Science Fiction Writer'.
7 Straits Times, 'Top Bangladesh Sci-Fi Writer'.
8 Botz-Bornstein, 'The "Futurist" Aesthetics'.

imagination in all its forms in the Muslim world. Between the nineteenth and twenty-first centuries, this imagination became firmly rooted. Its products came to encompass an ever greater range, including new digital forms more recently. Just as diverse were the themes of futurisms from Muslim-majority countries. Whereas some aesthetics were explicitly Islamic, those of many other activists and revolutionaries were more national. Some artworks were utopian, others dystopian, and perhaps the best ones ambiguous. In the short film *A Space Exodus* from 2009, for instance, the artist Larissa Sansour travels to the Moon. There, she plants a Palestinian flag before drifting back into space and calling repeatedly for 'Jerusalem'. Although only a few minutes long, *A Space Exodus* gave critics and scholars much material to look for meanings.[9]

Amid their diversity, many futurists shared a concern for empowerment, whether of individuals, countries or the entire Muslim community. Uplift was planned from the top down as well as from the bottom up. Some endeavours overlapped with Afrofuturism, a movement at the 'intersection of imagination, technology, the future, and liberation'.[10] In contrast, a 'paternalistic futurism' in Egypt or the Arabian Peninsula represented the visions of governments rather than activists. Grand projects enticed subjects to place their trust in an authoritarian, but benevolent leadership.[11] In the 'futuristic state' of Qatar, for instance, citizens and foreign residents were made to live in anticipation of big events, like the 2022 FIFA World Cup, for years.[12] There and elsewhere, entire populations were urged to contribute to centrally planned national visions.

What fed the various futurisms from the Muslim world were not just new technologies on Earth, but also research beyond our planet. Part of 'paternalistic futurism' was the United Arab Emirates' plan to establish a city on Mars by 2117, for instance.[13] This particular vision seemed far-fetched when it was first announced in 2017. However, Muslim-majority countries have long produced leaders in solar system exploration and other areas of space science, even if they had to migrate in certain cases for their professional advancement. Despite its international isolation at times, Iran gave rise to an especially important diaspora. This migration was in part due to Islamic and authoritarian politics.

9 Hochberg, 'Jerusalem', 38.
10 Womack, *Afrofuturism*, 9.
11 Mneimneh, '"Futurism"'.
12 Maziad, 'Qatar', 125.
13 Mneimneh, '"Futurism"'.

Iranian aliens

Although their country's relationship with the United States was fraught with tension for decades, numerous Iranians chose to settle there. In 1952, when Mohammad Mosaddegh was prime minister, Tehran-born Ebrahim Victory went to the USA. While Mossadegh was overthrown in a coup d'état orchestrated by the Central Intelligence Agency, Victory attended the Massachusetts Institute of Technology. After completing degrees in mechanical engineering, he participated in research programmes for the US Air Force, Navy and NASA. In addition, he wrote popular science articles on such topics as life in the universe and the exploration of Mars. While he lost his proficiency in Persian over the decades, others translated his writings for him. They appeared in the Los Angeles-based magazine *Rah-E Zendegi* (Way of Life) and in a book entitled *The Wonders of the Universe.*[14]

In 1979, the Islamic Revolution helped grow the Iranian community in such creative centres as California even more. Another space age migrant was Firouz Naderi from Shiraz. After arriving in the USA in 1964, he studied first at Iowa State University and subsequently at the University of Southern California. Under the guidance of Nasser Nahi, another electrical engineer from Iran, he completed a doctoral dissertation on image processing in 1976.[15] Upon his return to Iran, Naderi formed part of an Engineering Research Group belonging to National Iranian Radio and Television (NIRT).[16] He worked at the Mahdasht Satellite Receiving Station, which was constructed and operated under contract with General Electric. In 1979, however, Sadegh Ghotbzadeh, a close aide of Ruhollah Khomeini, took over NIRT and sought to bring it in line with the new regime. One of those purged was Naderi.[17] 'This is not your country', he was told. 'You are free to leave.' So he did and joined NASA's Jet Propulsion Laboratory (JPL) in Pasadena.[18]

In exile, Naderi channelled his efforts towards a managerial career at NASA. Rather than specializing in a certain area of space exploration, he moved between different technologies. For most of the 1980s, he worked on communications satellites, first at the JPL and then at NASA Headquarters in Washington. At the end of the decade, he returned to the JPL to lead the development of a

[14] Victory, *The Wonders*.
[15] Naderi, 'Estimation'.
[16] Naderi and Sawchuk, 'Detection', 2883.
[17] Tarikhi, *The Iranian Space Endeavor*, 89–92.
[18] Birnbaum, 'Iranian Scientist'.

scatterometer, which studied ocean winds from space.[19] He won the confidence of his superiors, especially the Lebanese-American Charles Elachi, a fellow electrical engineer and immigrant. 'He knew how to write NASA management plans', said Donald Burnett, one of his collaborators. 'He had NASA drooling about his management plans.'[20] In 1996, Naderi was appointed head of NASA's Origins Program, which studied the beginnings of life and the universe.[21]

While Naderi had impressive administrative skills, he was less interested in education and outreach. Burnett claimed that because Naderi did not take such activities 'very seriously', one of his mission proposals had lost in a NASA competition.[22] However, in 1999, the Iranian-American did give two public lectures about the Origins Program at the JPL and Pasadena City College. The title was 'The Search for Our Cosmic Roots and … Galactic Cousins?'[23] He explained that his programme sought 'answers to two fundamental questions': 'How Did We Get Here?' and 'Are We Alone?' Through an array of observatories, NASA was looking for 'the "smoking gun" that would indicate biological activity on some extra-solar planets'.[24]

As life outside of our solar system was difficult to detect, Naderi switched to environments closer to Earth. After NASA's efforts in Martian exploration had suffered setbacks during the 1990s, Naderi took charge. In 2000, he was named manager of the newly-created Mars Program Office.[25] Four years later, the rovers *Spirit* and *Opportunity* successfully landed on the planet. In recognition of his leadership, Naderi earned NASA's highest honour, the Distinguished Service Medal. In 2005, Charles Elachi, by then director of the JPL, made Naderi his associate director for programmes and strategy.[26] Continuing a pattern, in which he changed positions about every five years, Naderi became director of solar system exploration in 2011.[27] In this position, he was responsible for all missions to bodies orbiting around the sun except Mars. They included the *Cassini* and *Juno* probes to Saturn and Jupiter respectively. *Dawn*, another spacecraft, studied Vesta and Ceres, two of the largest objects in the asteroid belt.[28] At his

19 Fattahyani, 'To Mars', 14.
20 Sears, 'Oral Histories', 1725.
21 Hardin, 'JPL Names Naderi'.
22 Sears, 'Oral Histories', 1726.
23 Platt, 'Public Lectures'.
24 Naderi, 'NASA's Origins Program'.
25 Hardin, 'JPL Names Naderi'.
26 Webster, 'JPL's New Associate Director'.
27 Platt, 'JPL Announces'.
28 Fattahyani, 'To Mars', 10.

retirement party in 2016, the Iranian-American learnt that asteroid 5515 had been named 'Naderi' in his honour. 'Fortunately, it is not an Earth crosser', the scientist commented, adding that 'its orbit is a little more eccentric than most asteroids in the main belt'.[29]

In his last position as director of solar system exploration, Naderi turned his interests to the moons of Jupiter and Saturn. 'Finding life on Europa is more exciting than finding life on Mars', he said in 2013. A meteorite from Earth could have seeded life on the red planet and vice versa. However, 'If we were to find life under the crusty ice of Europa, that would be a definite second genesis of life in the solar system.'[30] In the search for microbes, the JPL thus planned the *Europa Clipper* mission. In 2018, an international team, including JPL researchers, reported the detection of complex organic material on Saturn's moon Enceladus. The compounds had been ejected from the ocean beneath the moon's icy surface and collected by *Cassini*. Two founding members of the Astrobiology Network of Pakistan, Nozair Khawaja and Fabian Klenner, were among the co-authors of the paper announcing the discovery.[31] Khawaja explained that Enceladus thus fulfilled three conditions of 'life anywhere in the universe': liquid water, a source of energy and organic molecules.[32]

Firouz Naderi had put more effort into administering programmes to reach the stars than into becoming a celebrity in his own right. Nevertheless, his distinguished career at NASA made him well-known among Iranians worldwide. In 2017, the director Asghar Farhadi asked Naderi and the space traveller Anousheh Ansari to accept the Academy Award for Best Foreign Language Film on his behalf. Farhadi himself boycotted the ceremony in protest against an executive order by President Donald Trump that was known as the 'Muslim ban'. Farhadi had not previously met either Naderi or Ansari. 'We know of each other because of our work', explained the engineer. Standing next to him at the ceremony, Ansari read out a statement by Farhadi, 'My absence is out of respect for the people of my country and those of six other nations whom have been disrespected by the inhumane law that bans entry of immigrants to the US.'[33]

Naderi's appearance at the Oscars ceremony added to his fame. However, his stand-in for an Iranian filmmaker also caused 'an avalanche of trash by professional mudslingers', as he put it. The main accusation was that he had

[29] PressTV, 'Asteroid'.
[30] Fattahyani, 'To Mars', 13.
[31] Postberg et al., 'Macromolecular Organic Compounds'.
[32] Saadeqa Khan, 'Pakistan's Man'.
[33] Birnbaum, 'Iranian Scientist'.

failed to denounce the Iranian regime while on stage. Naderi responded that he had remained faithful to Farhadi's statement and that the allotted time by the Academy had been forty-five seconds. On Facebook, however, the scientist clarified that he favoured 'a democratically-elected, secular government, observing full civil liberties and human rights with separation of "church" and state'. He also rejected the label 'royalist', but praised the last shah as a 'patriot' and expressed 'enormous respect' for his widow. 'I have no religious affiliation', Naderi added, 'although I consider myself a spiritual person, believing in "something" beyond himself. My religion is do good, and do well by others'.[34]

Despite his criticism of theocracy, Naderi rejected military action against Iran. 'Do I support bombing Iran? Hell no', he continued on Facebook. People who do 'have forfeited their right to be called Iranians'. Even after decades of living on the other side of the globe, he still had a strong attachment to his place of origin. 'America is my country, and Iran is my homeland', he explained. 'And how blessed I am to be rooted in an ancient civilization with a rich culture, and at the same time a proud American living in this young nation that has lifted me on her shoulders, allowing me to reach for the stars.' Describing himself as a 'liberal democrat', he was against Donald Trump's executive order and wider Iran policy. Instead, he endorsed the nuclear deal reached in 2015 as 'good for both countries'.[35]

Firouz Naderi not only represented a prominent filmmaker. Contributing further to the arts, he also advised a fellow Iranian-American in the writing of science fiction. Alexandra Monir, a Los Angeles-based author of novels for young adults, considered him a 'personal hero'. A friend of her parents, Naderi read the manuscript of her novel *The Final Six*, which was published in 2018. It is set in a near future in which Earth is largely destroyed by climate change. In an attempt to save humanity, the United Nations sends six astronauts to create a new settlement on Europa. One of them is a young, female Iranian-American genius by the name of Naomi Ardalan. Naderi corrected the scientific contents of Monir's book and helped her choose the route of her spacecraft.[36]

If Naderi as an engineer and administrator was able to contribute to science fiction, researchers specializing in extrasolar planets have perhaps even greater potential to inspire future imaginations of alien life specifically. Several astronomers working in Muslim-majority countries have made important advances. The Qatar Exoplanet Survey led by Khalid Alsubai discovered ten

34 Naderi, *Facebook*.
35 Ibid.
36 Monir, 'Author's Note'; Parsonson, 'Author Alexandra Monir'.

planets between 2010 and 2019.[37] During the same decade, Khalid Barkaoui and Zouhair Benkhaldoun from the Oukaïmeden Observatory in Morocco participated in the detection of seven Earthlike planets around the nearby dwarf star TRAPPIST-1.[38] Although researchers like Alsubai and Benkhaldoun identified as astrophysicists rather than biologists, they stressed the connection of their work to the study of life. 'The primary motivation for the search for extrasolar planets is identifying how frequent habitable worlds and life may be within the Galaxy', said Benkhaldoun in 2018.[39]

Alsubai, Barkaoui and Benkhaldoun were based in their home countries. However, exoplanet hunters, like other space scientists, were found in the diaspora as well. Especially prominent was the Iranian-American Nader Haghighipour. He had earned a bachelor's degree in physics at the University of Tehran in 1989. Thereafter, he worked as an instructor and laboratory manager before embarking on further studies at the University of Missouri. Under Bahram Mashhoon, yet another Iranian-American, he completed a doctoral dissertation on planetary dynamics in 1999.[40] His subsequent career took him to the University of California, Irvine, Northwestern University and the University of Hawai'i. In 2015, Haghighipour became president of the International Astronomical Union's Division F, which dealt with planetary systems and bioastronomy.[41]

One of the foci of Haghighipour's research was planets orbiting binary stars. He contributed to the discovery of Kepler-453b in 2015, which the *Huffington Post* likened to Tatooine in *Star Wars*. Haghighipour had imagined such planets with two suns for much of his career. 'For me, it's personal', he said. 'For 20 years, I've been saying these things exist, and now we are discovering them.'[42] He situated his quest within a context that transcended specific religious communities. In a book chapter from 2010 he stated, 'How our planet was formed, how life came about, and whether life exists elsewhere in the universe are among some of the long-standing questions in human history.' The astronomer added, 'It is now certain that our planetary system is not unique and many terrestrial-size planets may exist throughout the universe.'[43]

37 Alsubai et al., 'Qatar-1b'; Alsubai et al., 'Qatar Exoplanet Survey'.
38 Gillon et al., 'Seven Temperate Terrestrial Planets'.
39 Osman, 'Morocco Observatory'.
40 Haghighipour, 'Resonance Lock', 121.
41 Haghighipour, 'Nader Haghighipour'.
42 D'Angelo, 'New "Tatooine"'.
43 Haghighipour et al., 'Planetary Dynamics', 285.

While Haghighipour saw his own research as part of a broader human endeavour, he maintained connections to his country of origin specifically. In 2009, he gave lectures on extrasolar planets at the University of Tehran and Sharif University of Technology. In the following years, sanctions created obstacles for further travel to Iran. However, Skype allowed him to give presentations about planet detection and the space observatory *Kepler* to audiences in Tehran remotely. Haghighipour also fed knowledge about Iranian initiatives back to the US community. The most important was the Iranian National Observatory (INO), a planned installation with a 3.4-metre telescope. The astronomer gave a presentation about it at a meeting of the American Association for the Advancement of Science in Washington in 2016.[44]

Haghighipour used the construction of the Iranian National Observatory as an occasion to engage in scientific diplomacy. He did so in the wake of the nuclear deal, the implementation of which had begun in January 2016. In March of that year, Haghighipour published an article on the website of the American Astronomical Society entitled 'An Astronomical Thaw'. He wrote that the INO would not only 'enable Iranian astronomers to have significant contributions'. By 'being available to the international astronomical community it will also offer an invaluable opportunity for collaboration in observational as well as theoretical projects'. Haghighipour thus hailed the new installation as a 'fantastic opportunity'.[45]

Science under sanctions

The Iran deal, formally the Joint Comprehensive Plan of Action, did not defrost diplomatic relations. The United States continued to impose sanctions over Iran's ballistic missile programme and withdrew from the agreement in 2018. Furthermore, the Central Intelligence Agency revived a secret programme to sabotage Iranian rockets. The Iranian military and scientific community were resilient, however. In 2016, Brigadier General Amir Ali Hajizadeh vowed that his country's missile programme would never stop 'under any circumstances'.[46] 'There is no sanction on knowledge', said Reza Mansouri, a former project director of the Iranian National Observatory, in 2018.[47] Major American presses

44 Haghighipour, 'Nader Haghighipour'.
45 Haghighipour, 'An Astronomical Thaw'.
46 Sanger and Broad, 'U.S. Revives'.
47 Mansouri, 'Impact'.

had long agreed and published articles by Iran-based authors, citing freedom of speech in their defence.[48] Mansouri, who had also served as deputy science minister, even claimed that sanctions had generally been beneficial for science in Iran. The government had increased funding, encouraged local problem-solving, and supported institutional development. International collaboration was only 'mildly affected', and cooperation with other countries in the region even increased. Scientists did find their international mobility restricted. At the same time, determination to overcome 'obstacles' increased.[49]

Even under sanctions, scientists based in Iran were able to participate in international exoplanet research. One of the most visible was Sohrab Rahvar, an astrophysicist of the same generation as Haghighipour. Born in 1974, he first became interested in other worlds in his childhood, as his mother and aunt were reading *Alice in Wonderland* and scientific books to him. He subsequently completed a bachelor's degree in physics at the University of Tabriz. From there, he went to Sharif University of Technology in Tehran, where he earned his doctorate under Reza Mansouri in 2001. Rahvar kept Tehran as his base during his subsequent career, working first at the Institute for Research in Fundamental Sciences and later at Sharif University of Technology. In addition, he held several visiting positions in Europe and North America. Together with the Qatari astrophysicist Khalid Alsubai and many others, he formed part of MiNDSTEp, the Microlensing Network for the Detection of Small Terrestrial Exoplanets.[50] Together with his collaborators, Rahvar detected at least nine planets between 2010 and 2018 alone. Despite US sanctions, four of these discoveries were reported in the American Astronomical Society's *Astrophysical Journal*.[51]

Sohrab Rahvar's exoplanet research aimed to find not just physical objects, but also intelligence. In 2016, he published an article in the *Astrophysical Journal* on 'Gravitational Microlensing Events as a Target for the SETI Project'. 'Are we alone in the universe? This is one of the deepest questions of mankind', he wrote. At the same time, he acknowledged that 'the detection of signals from a possible extrasolar technological civilization is one of the most challenging efforts of science'. He conceived of 'an Earth-like civilization that is producing electromagnetic waves at the same frequency range and the same power that

48 Brumfiel, 'Publishers Split'.
49 Mansouri, 'Impact'.
50 Rahvar, 'Curriculum Vitae'.
51 Batista et al., 'MOA-2009-BLG-387Lb'; Miyake et al., 'A Sub-Saturn Mass Planet'; Muraki et al., 'Discovery'; Bachelet et al., 'MOA 2010-BLG-477Lb'; Kains et al., 'A Giant Planet'; Skowron et al., 'OGLE-2011-BLG-0265Lb'; Rattenbury et al., 'Faint-source-star Planetary Microlensing'; Ryu et al., 'OGLE-2016-BLG-1190Lb'; Udalski et al., 'OGLE-2017-BLG-1434Lb'.

we are'. The mass from a star could bend and magnify these waves, thereby allowing them to be received by observatories on Earth. 'Natural telescopes' composed of one or more stellar lenses could amplify radio signals as far away as the centre of the Milky Way.[52]

Even as Donald Trump's administration became more punitive towards Iran, it failed to isolate scientists like Sohrab Rahvar completely. The astrophysicist did complain about the devaluation of the Iranian currency and travel restrictions to the USA. However, he was still able to give presentations in neighbouring countries. In late 2018, he lectured at Istanbul Technical University, Koç University and Sabancı University. In April 2019, he further participated in a Workshop of High Energy Physics at Sultan Qaboos University in Oman. During the same month, a poster co-authored by him was presented at a meeting of the American Physical Society in Denver, Colorado. This poster discussed the use of microlensing for exoplanet detection through NASA's Spitzer Space Telescope. He praised this instrument as 'performing extremely well, returning excellent scientific data'.[53]

Through his international connections, Rahvar was able to draw on global science and fiction in his imagination of extraterrestrial life. In 2014, he gave a presentation about exoplanets at a conference at the Institute for Research in Fundamental Sciences. He talked in Persian, but wrote his slides in English. 'Are we alone in the universe?' he asked. Based on understanding of extremophiles on Earth, he argued that 'in our solar system there must be such a simple form of life'. Subsequently, he introduced the Kardashev scale of planetary, stellar and galactic civilizations. Rahvar also noted the Fermi paradox that advanced civilizations must exist in the Milky Way, but for some reason have not been discovered. He illustrated these ideas with an artist's concept of a Dyson sphere, a hypothetical megastructure that encompasses a star and captures its energy. Another image in his slides was taken from the television series *Star Trek: Voyager*.[54]

In 2012, Reza Roosta Azad, the chancellor of the Sharif University of Technology, confessed that his greatest wish was to hold a collective prayer on another planet.[55] Nevertheless, for many astronomers, the quest for exoplanets was largely separate from religion. Neither Haghighipour nor Rahvar made

52 Rahvar, 'Gravitational Microlensing Events'.
53 Bagheri et al., 'Exoplanet Detection'.
54 Rahvar, 'Exoplanets'.
55 Tarikhi, *The Iranian Space Endeavor*, 201.

many references to Islam in their publications. The same was true for members of the generation who were born after the revolution of 1979. They include Sedighe Sajadian, who completed a dissertation on exoplanet detection under Rahvar at Sharif University of Technology in 2011. Like her supervisor, she remained in Iran, working first as a postdoctoral researcher in Tehran and later as assistant professor at Isfahan University of Technology. However, the most overt reference to religion in her presentations, whether in Iran or Italy, were the words 'In the name of God' on the first slides.[56]

The increasing rate of exoplanet discoveries also brought space scientists working in other fields into discussions about astrobiology. In January 2010, Martin Dominik, who was a collaborator of Alsubai, Haghighipour and Rahvar, organized a meeting at the Royal Society of London. The title was 'The detection of extra-terrestrial life and the consequences for science and society'. Among the speakers were the Malaysian astrophysicist Mazlan Othman, who then served as director of the United Nations Office for Outer Space Affairs. At this point, she had little direct experience with exoplanet research, but was still excited about its advances. 'Rapid developments in the detection of extra-solar planets augur well for those hoping to detect planets that would provide the right ecosystems for life', she stated. 'The continued search for extra-terrestrial communication, by several entities, sustains the hope that someday humankind will receive signals from extra-terrestrials.'[57]

During Othman's tenure at the UN, the organization also served as an important intermediary for Iran amid sanctions. In the wake of the revolution of 1979, Iran's participation in the United Nations Committee on the Peaceful Uses of Outer Space had been suspended for several years. However, from 2000 onwards, the Islamic Republic contributed to the committee again regularly.[58] In 2016, the United Nations Office for Outer Space Affairs co-organized a Workshop on the Use of Space Technology for Dust Storm and Drought Monitoring in the Middle East Region. Hosted by the Iranian Space Agency in Tehran, the workshop included speakers from Africa, Europe and South America, as well as Asia.[59]

If sanctions and sabotage did not stop space research in Iran, they arguably had even less effect on science fiction. While Iran faced difficulties importing

56 Sajadian, 'Simulation'; 'Detecting Planetary Microlensing Events'.
57 Othman, 'Supra-Earth Affairs', 699.
58 Tarikhi, *The Iranian Space Endeavor*, 82.
59 United Nations Office for Outer Space Affairs, 'Programme'.

technical equipment, it was able to absorb ideas with ease. In the early twenty-first century, Hossein Shahrabi from Tehran, for instance, not only translated older texts by Isaac Asimov, Ray Bradbury and Arthur C. Clarke – he was also quick to publish Persian editions of Andy Weir's *The Martian* and novels by John Scalzi. The American television series *Ancient Aliens*, which premiered in 2010 on the History channel, soon spawned an Iranian website with the same name. It went beyond selling copies of the different seasons to Iran-based customers by offering Persian translations of various books, by Erich von Däniken and other writers, about ancient astronauts and UFOs.[60]

Iranians were not just able to import, but also to produce their own science fiction under sanctions. In the 2000s, the country's Physics Society, over which Reza Mansouri presided at the time, organized competitions for the best science fiction short stories. The declared goals were to promote science, enrich Persian literature and foster the imagination.[61] In the following decade, the Ayaz Astronomical Society in Tabriz started national contests for paintings and short stories under the name 'My Galactic Dream'. These activities were part of the World Space Week,[62] an annual event initiated by the United Nations General Assembly. Faculty members at Tabriz Islamic Art University served as judges of the paintings during the second contest in 2017. This particular competition saw the submission of 133 stories and 97 visual artworks from across the country. Mansouri's monthly magazine *Nojum* (Astronomy) sponsored the event[63] and published the winning story, 'The Last Ring of Slavery' by Mujtaba Ghaffari. This tale centred on conflict between humans and robots on an alien planet.[64]

Despite the tense diplomatic climate, Iranian promoters of science fiction used Western authors and entrepreneurs as models. Ghaffari himself had read Arthur C. Clarke, Isaac Asimov and Jules Verne from the age of ten.[65] Accompanying 'The Last Ring of Slavery' in *Nojum* was an article by Hossein Shahrabi. 'Why should you read science fiction?' asked the prolific translator, 'Almost all the celebrities in the world of technology and science, from Elon Musk and Bill Gates to Stephen Hawking and Carl Sagan are interested in science fiction', he pointed out. 'Writers such as Isaac Asimov, Arthur C. Clarke, Neal Stephenson, and Andy Weir are for many scientists more famous and beloved than the stars of cinema

60 Bīgānigān-i Bāstānī, 'Bīgānigān-i bāstānī'.
61 Iranian Students' News Agency, 'Anjuman-i Fīzīk-i Īrān'.
62 Iranian Students' News Agency, 'Musābaqah-i naqqāshī va dāstān-i ʿilmī takhayyulī'.
63 Fakhīmī, 'Raqābat-i adabīyāt va hunar'.
64 Ghaffārī, 'Ākharīn ḥalqah-i bardigī'.
65 Fakhīmī, 'Raqābat-i adabīyāt va hunar', 10.

and music.' References to science fiction were thus also part of the language of scientists. This genre opens our minds and helps us better understand science, he argued. Therefore, it could serve as an 'extremely useful' educational tool.[66]

To be sure, Iran's international situation hampered mobility across borders for artists, as it did for scientists. However, diplomatic conflicts also contributed to keeping talented creators of science fiction inside Iran. Such was the experience of the Bandar Abbas-based filmmaker Ali Pourahmad, who had planned to move to the United States. In 2010, he was admitted to the Academy of Art University in San Francisco. However, he was unable to obtain his student visa. In 2018, I asked him whether he was trying again. However, at that point he was forty-seven, which he considered too old. He also had more than thirty years of experience in fine arts, including computer-generated imagery and visual effects. Rather than starting another bachelor's degree, he preferred to focus on making films. Similar to the experience of astrophysicists, remaining in Iran did not prevent him from collaborating with Americans entirely. The New York-based model and actress Cheyenne Lutek appeared – without head cover – in a trailer for his space movie *Towards the Future*.[67]

Science fiction filmmaking still faced restrictions in Iran, but these were often unrelated to the sanctions. Pourahmad repeatedly faced religious objections and failed to get permissions from local authorities. 'We just have to make films that are in perfect conformity with the orders of Islam', he complained to me. Science fiction films, in contrast, 'tell of the future and fundamental changes'. Showing a woman's hair was also 'considered a big sin in Iran', he explained. Distributing short films and trailers over the internet was no problem. However, finding sponsorship for longer movies or showing them in public without a licence was risky or even impossible.[68]

Nevertheless, even amid such constraints, a whole science fiction series consisting of seventy episodes was released on Iranian television in 2009. Entitled *Mosaferan* (Travellers), it was produced by Rambod Javan from Tehran. The plot centres on aliens who explore Iran by disguising themselves as a family from Sweden. They often misunderstand local culture, leading to many funny situations. Similar to many Turkish comedies, *Mosaferan* thus also satirizes contemporary society. Still, the series adhered to many prevailing norms: the aliens wear hijab, and episodes begin with 'In the name of God'. At the same time,

66 Shahrābī, 'Chirā bāyad ʿilmī takhayyulī khvānad?'
67 Ali Pourahmad, messages via LinkedIn, 24 and 27 January 2018.
68 Ali Pourahmad, messages via LinkedIn, 20, 24 and 28 January 2018.

Javan's production adapted global science fiction. The soundtrack combines the main theme from *Star Wars* with traditional Iranian music, for instance. Given the absence of formal relations between the Islamic Republic and the USA, Javan arguably had little reason to worry about copyright enforcement.

What helped the development of science fiction was the spread of computer-generated imagery. In the twenty-first century, the Iranian government itself helped broaden the use of animation for information as well as entertainment. Short films about traffic regulations reached general audiences through national television. One of their makers, Bahram Azmi, subsequently gained municipal support for a feature entitled *Tehran 2121.* Well-known actors inspired further confidence in the project by lending their faces and voices to the cartoon characters. The Ministry of Culture and Islamic Guidance ultimately approved a film that had many elements of global science fiction. They include a flying car reminiscent of the time machine in *Back to the Future.* However, in this vision of the twenty-second century, not just women, but even a female robot dons a headscarf. In a street scene, the android is even told to extend her mechanical manteau to cover more of her metal legs.[69]

The Iranian video game industry benefited from the increasing expertise in computer graphics. However, it struggled perhaps more than scientists and filmmakers under the sanctions. Major European publishers were reluctant to sign deals with Iranian developers out of fear of American penalties. Without such publishers, Iranian companies faced difficulties in distributing their products internationally. They were unable to access the Google Play Developer Console with Iranian internet protocol addresses. When attempting to create Apple IDs, they could not find Iran in the drop-down menu. People inside the Islamic Republic could disguise their location with virtual private networks, but these were not completely reliable. In order to enter such marketplaces as the App Store and repatriate profits, Iran-based firms had to set up foreign front companies and broker complex and costly bank transfers.[70]

Overall, however, as with scientific research, sanctions probably helped more than hindered the emergence of a resilient national community. In 2007, a group of developers submitted a plan to the Ministry of Culture and Islamic Guidance, which resulted in the creation of the Iran Computer and Video Games Foundation. This was followed by the establishment of the Iranian Game Development Institute in 2012. In its first year, 300 students enrolled at the

69 Amir Shahkarami, 'The Pre-Production Phase'; ʿAẓīmī, *Tihrān 1500.*

70 Elmjouie, 'The Game Industry'.

institute.[71] In order to make local games competitive with pirated ones from abroad, the Iran Computer and Video Games Foundation collected fees on the sale of the latter. For copies of foreign games to be legally sold in Iranian stores, they had to receive holographic stickers issued by the foundation.[72]

Government support for video games also came with regulation and censorship. The foundation did not issue stickers for games it deemed 'un-Islamic', such as *Grand Theft Auto*. Stores selling unstickered games risked being shut down.[73] Furthermore, the foundation rated games for different age groups in accordance with social norms and religious values. Violence, drug use, sexual behaviour and horror all affected the rating.[74] An adventure game about crime and corruption titled *Devil in the Capital* was recommended for the age group 15+, for instance. *The Look of Evil*, another dark adventure game, received the rating 18+. In contrast, the sports management game *Footcardia* was deemed suitable for anybody over the age of two.[75]

The Iran Computer and Video Games Foundation also supported science fiction. In the early 2010s, Tehran-based Simulator Developer produced two editions of the online strategy game *Asmandez* (Sky Fortress). The second one won a Massively Multiplayer Online (MMO) game award in Germany in 2013.[76] The game is set in the twenty-ninth century, when humans flee from robots to a new planetary system. Female characters still cover their hair so far into the future – though with helmets rather than headscarves. Around the same time, Raspina Studio, another Tehran developer, produced the game *E.T. Armies*. This first-person shooter was set in a post-apocalyptic world, in which human survivors fight against an enemy called the Forsaken.[77]

Like novelists, video game developers drew on global science fiction and national heritage in their world-building. One of the locations depicted in *E.T. Armies* are the ruins of Persepolis. In *Asmandez II*, the Persium Mine is among the structures that players can build. The ancient stories of Gilgamesh and Bozorgmehr influenced the quests that Simulator Developer created for the players. However, modern writings shaped the world of *Asmandez* as well. One of the main characters is 'FM-2830'. He represents the futurist FM-2030, who

71 Ahmadi, 'Iran', 277–78.
72 Elmjouie, 'The Game Industry'.
73 Ibid.
74 Ahmadi, 'Iran', 280–81.
75 Iran Computer and Video Games Foundation, 'Devil in Capital'; 'The Look of Evil'; 'Footcardia'.
76 PressTV, 'Iran Online Game'.
77 Ahmadi, 'Iran', 287.

has woken up after hundreds of years of cryopreservation. Farzam Molkara, the founder of Simulator Developer, further acknowledged inspiration by Arthur C. Clarke, Fred Saberhagen and Stanisław Lem. Lem's novel *The Invincible* with its clouds of alien microrobots gave rise to dark fog in the universe of *Asmandez*.[78]

Despite continued American sanctions, the Iranian nuclear deal opened up new European partnerships for Iranian developers. Raspina Studio, in collaboration with the British publisher Merge Games, released *E.T. Armies* on the distribution platform Steam in 2016. This made it easily purchasable for the global gaming community.[79] The same year, Iranian developers participated in the trade fair Gamescom in Cologne, Germany. The Iranians were conscious of their international competition, but also confident in their own value propositions. 'I think we should focus on providing unique content – content based on our own culture, our language, a unique message and artistic styles', said one developer. 'This would be interesting for people who haven't seen this kind of content before.'[80]

All tomorrows

Given the Islamic Republic's resilience in the arts and sciences over the decades, any future sanctions are unlikely to stifle Iranian creativity. An escalation of conflicts to the point of open war could also be stimulating as much as it would be destructive. World War II, which encompassed an Anglo-Soviet invasion of Iran, had already resulted in the production of science fiction. In 1941, Abdolhosain Sanatizadeh wrote *The Angel of Peace*. In this work for adolescents, a girl criticizes the conflict and loses her life bringing peace to her country.[81] Similarly critical was the book *No Heaven for Gunga Din* by Ali Mirdrekvandi, which was first published in 1965. The author drew heavily on his experience working in an officers' mess in occupied Tehran. The story follows British and American soldiers and their servant Gunga Din trekking across the Milky Way in search of heaven. When they reach heaven's gate, they find it guarded by military police who demand Freedom Passes. To earn these, the group must go to the Judgement-Field.

78 Farzam Molkara, emails, 19 December 2018.
79 Chalk, 'ET Armies'.
80 Abbany, 'Post-Nuclear'.
81 Ghaeni, 'The History', 468.

Eventually, the Western officers receive forgiveness for their sins and are saved. Gunga Din, however, is condemned to hell for minor offences.[82]

More recently as well, war has been productive for science fiction in the Middle East, even in cases where it has been devastating in many areas of life. This was the case with the American-led wars against Iraq during the 1990s and 2000s. Bombings not only killed people directly, but also destroyed vital electricity and sewage infrastructure. On top of that, the Americans' widespread use of depleted uranium poisoned soil and water, causing unprecedented levels of birth defects. Many inhabitants of Iraq thus faced a 'dystopian environmental future'.[83] Pessimistic visions soon also appeared in literary form. In 2016, the filmmaker and writer Hassan Blasim edited a book under the title *Iraq+100: Stories from a Century after the Invasion.* For this project, he assembled a number of peers who all imagined their country's state long after the campaign of 2003.[84]

Iraq+100 was not only a response to one particular American war. It was also a form of creative resistance against stereotypes that had fed Western interventions in the Middle East. 'Arabs tend to get portrayed in western culture as conmen, religious fanatics or terrorists', complained Hassan Abdulrazzak, one of the contributors. 'I wanted to show authentic Arabs, the kind of people I know and grew up with, who are interested in the arts, who drink and smoke, and whose social relationships are not governed by taboos.'[85] However, *Iraq+100* also sought to challenge conservative forces in the Muslim world. 'Inflexible religious discourse has stifled the Arab imagination', wrote Blasim in his foreword. 'Pride in the Arab poetic tradition has weakened the force and freedom of narration, while invaders and occupiers have shattered the peace that provided a home for the imagination.'[86]

Like the invasion of 2003 itself, *Iraq+100* came with shock and horror. Abdulrazzak's story in the collection is titled 'Kuszib', a combination of *kus* (cunt) and *zib* (cock). Kuszib is also the name of one of the main characters, a hermaphrodite alien. It is one of many tentacle-bearing creatures from outer space who have occupied Earth in the author's vision. The aliens consider it a sport to hunt and eat humans. They find it especially exciting to observe a couple having sex and to pierce them with a harpoon as they are about to reach orgasm. The blood of these humans is the 'ultimate aphrodisiac'. At the end of

[82] Hanif and Rezaei, 'Ins and Outs'.
[83] Jones, 'Toxic War', 797.
[84] Blasim, *Iraq+100*.
[85] Henley, 'The Other Side'.
[86] Blasim, *Iraq+100*, ix.

the story, two aliens named Ona and Ur themselves make love for hours, while Kuszib feeds them the chopped-up corpses of two human lovers.[87]

Turning Americans into violent and hedonistic aliens, 'Kuszib' satirizes their attitudes. 'What was surprising is that humans failed to grasp the inevitability of their defeat', as one alien professor recounts the history of Earth's invasion. 'They actually put up a fight!' The academic further seems to mimic the arrogance of Western leaders. 'I mean how hard is it to work out that having crossed vast distances to reach this Sector, we are the superior race technologically, and therefore their betters?' the professor tells his students. This is followed by a trivialization of human art as 'repetitive' and science as 'laughably limited'. 'You can call it what you like but civilisation it was not.' Still, Ona, a former student, has doubts. 'I know they're just humans but they have feelings, don't they?' She worries about possible divine punishment, but her lover Ur is dismissive. Abdulrazzak writes, 'Ur had always found Ona's belief in the "Setter of the Cosmological Constant," with his powers to punish and reward, endearingly anachronistic but right then it irritated him immensely.' In the end of the story, Ona still feels sorry for the humans, but is happy that their meat and blood rekindle her love to Ur.[88]

Despite contents that were hard to stomach, Iraqi science fiction inspired by the war resonated beyond Muslim-majority countries. The newspaper *The Guardian* and the bookseller Barnes & Noble named *Iraq+100* one of the best science fiction and fantasy books of 2016.[89] The magazine *World Literature Today* listed it among seventy-five 'notable translations' of the same year.[90] The book also received favourable coverage by America's National Public Radio (NPR) and in the magazines *In These Times* and *Strange Horizons*.[91] Based on this remarkable reception, the publisher, UK-based Comma Press, brought out a similar collection in 2019: *Palestine+100: Stories from a Century after the Nakba*.[92] It imagines diverse possible futures for the occupied territories, where life already appeared dystopian. One contributor solved the Arab–Israeli conflict by having two parallel worlds in the same geographic space. Another writer proclaimed a 'right to digital return' for Palestinian refugees. However, *Palestine+100*'s editor Basma Ghalayini still struggled against censorship. She

87 Abdulrazzak, 'Kuszib', 132, 137.
88 Ibid., 122–23, 128–29, 137–38.
89 Roberts, 'The Best SF and Fantasy Books'; Cunningham, 'The Best Science Fiction & Fantasy Collections'.
90 Johnson, '*World Literature Today*'s 75 Notable Translations'.
91 El-Mohtar, '"Iraq + 100"'; Qualey, 'Sci-Fi Iraq'; Saleem, 'Iraq+100'.
92 Ghalayini, *Palestine+100*.

complained about the silencing of pro-Palestinian voices through accusations of anti-Semitism in Western countries, for instance. Nevertheless, even before its publication, *Palestine+100* won a PEN Translates award and NPR selected the volume as one of its Favourite Books of 2019.[93]

Of similar success was the novel *Frankenstein in Baghdad* by Ahmed Saadawi. First published in Arabic in 2013, the story follows a junk dealer who collects mortal remains after bombings and stitches them together. The patchwork body comes alive and takes revenge on those who have turned Baghdad into a slaughterhouse. The titular reference to Mary Shelley's work arguably helped Saadawi's novel to quickly earn recognition from critics. In 2014, *Frankenstein in Baghdad* won the International Prize for Arabic Fiction, which was supported by the Emirates Foundation in Abu Dhabi.[94] Four years later, an English translation was shortlisted for the Man Booker Prize.[95]

Sanctions and wars were not the only potential challenges for the scientific imagination in the Muslim world. Of a similar magnitude, albeit of a different quality, could be hostility towards the theory of evolution. Limiting the teaching of one of the central theories of modern biology could inhibit research in the life sciences. This is especially the case with disciplines that concern themselves with the origin and long-term development of life, such as astrobiology. It was perhaps no coincidence that the Astrobiology Network of Pakistan arose in a country in which evolution was taught widely.[96] On the other hand, evolutionism's replacement by creationism, with its belief in an all-powerful God, could also facilitate the imagination of myriad worlds with different inhabitants.

Evolution has been on the minds of both scientists and science fiction writers even in the Islamic Republic of Iran. This was helped by an education system that was more open to Darwin's theory than that of Saudi Arabia, for instance.[97] The astrophysicist Sohrab Rahvar was convinced that the 'discovery of life outside earth would be a great revolution in human history'. It would prove that the 'universe is not designed for us' and that we are just 'minuscule evolved-intelligent-animals' in one corner of it.[98] While Rahvar was still chasing extraterrestrial intelligence, the writer Iraj Fazel Bakhsheshi already imagined the evolution of life on other planets in his novels. In *The Sons of the Sun* from 2011,

93 Qualey, 'Future-focused "Palestine +100"'; Brady, 'What Palestine Might Be Like'.
94 Perry, 'Frankenstein'.
95 Kaplan, 'Man Booker Prize International 2018 Shortlist'.
96 Asghar et al., 'Evolution'.
97 Burton, 'Teaching Evolution'.
98 Sohrab Rahvar, email, 6 August 2019.

for instance, natural selection has produced one-eyed, Paleolithic humans on a 'second Earth'. Advanced visitors from the first Earth seek to dominate them by pretending to be the pharaoh and the sun goddess. In employing the figure of the cruel ancient Egyptian ruler, Bakhsheshi drew on a long-standing Islamic image taught as extensively in Iranian schools as evolution.[99]

While evolutionists in Iran and Pakistan enjoyed considerable influence, their peers in Turkey came to face a strong backlash. During the heyday of secularism between the 1930s and early 1970s, Darwinian evolution was an essential part of the science curriculum. In the following decades, various Islamists campaigned for creationism.[100] Prominent among them was Adnan Oktar, who used the name Harun Yahya. He rejected not just notions of the evolution of species, but also the idea that aliens could have seeded life on Earth. He argued against what he called 'space religion'. 'Out of pride, egocentricity and arrogance', authors such as Richard Dawkins 'find it more appropriate to submit themselves to aliens, since they do not want to submit themselves to Allah'.[101] In 2017, anti-Darwinist campaigns culminated in the removal of evolution, though not yet of adaptation or mutation, from Turkish textbooks.[102] The following year, however, in the context of the purges of President Erdoğan's opponents and rivals, Oktar and more than 160 associates were arrested on charges of fraud and sexual abuse.[103]

Despite limits on the teaching of evolution, the theory persisted in the mythology of the World Brotherhood Union. 'An entity which was once a Cat, a Dog, an Ape, a Bird can become one day a Human Being', said *The Knowledge Book*. 'Do not ever forget that the theory of Darwin can never be underestimated.' In Bülent Çorak's imagination, evolution is progressive, teleological and theistic. 'God has designed an Evolutionary Tableau in accordance with His System of Creation', her scripture explained. 'The Single Cell which came into existence is always on the Evolutionary path which leads it to becoming a Human Being.'[104]

It is, of course, possible that evolutionist UFO religions like the World Brotherhood Union will meet similar repression from Turkish authorities as Adnan Oktar's creationist group. Oktar headed an organization called the Science Research Foundation, using a similar name to Halûk Sarıkaya's earlier

[99] Bakhshishī, *Farzandān-i Khūrshīd*. On the figure of the pharaoh in Islamic historiography, see, e.g., Hirschler, 'The "Pharao" Anecdote'.
[100] Peker et al., 'Three Decades', 740–41.
[101] Yahya, 'Dawkins'.
[102] Altuntaş, 'Turkey's New School Year'.
[103] Erkoyun, 'Turkish Police'.
[104] Çorak, *The Knowledge Book*, 155–56.

Science Research Center. Çorak's movement already attracted suspicion and hostility in the mid-2000s. Ramazan Biçer from the Theology Faculty at Sakarya University described the World Brotherhood Union as a 'heretic New Age/Ufo sect' and a 'cult'. He compared it to Raëlism and Hasan-i Sabbah's medieval order of Assassins.[105] He also stated that *The Knowledge Book* contained 'many unacceptable claims about Islam' and 'assaults' against Muslims.[106]

Amid such hostility, the World Brotherhood Union expanded into other countries, making it less dependent on the Turkish political environment. The English translation of *The Knowledge Book* had already appeared in a second edition by 1998.[107] Eight years later, a Swedish version was published and soon gave rise to a group called the Gulls of Lake Siljan.[108] The World Brotherhood Movement even made inroads into Russia, where it faced opposition from the Orthodox Church. In 2017, two preachers were fined in Chelyabinsk Oblast for distributing a Russian edition of *The Knowledge Book* without permit. Another missionary was punished after the local diocese had reported that a 'Turkish sect' advocating suicide was operating in the region.[109]

Nonetheless, even in Turkey itself, heavy-handed treatment by the government is unlikely to extinguish the imaginations of movements like the World Brotherhood Union entirely. The creativity of some heterodox groups could have a legacy lasting hundreds of years. This is the lesson of the Dönmeh, crypto-Jews who had publicly converted to Islam in the seventeenth century. The sect only lost its distinct identity very slowly. In the 2010s, one of their descendants, Cevdet Mehmet Kösemen, still documented the Dönmeh's unique artistic legacy. They include photographs of the deceased that were displayed on tombstones, in contrast to the practices of other Muslims.[110]

Amid the rise of Erdoğan's Justice and Development Party, Kösemen himself also created original art, which drew on evolution. In 2002, he completed an International Baccalaureate programme at the private Koç School in Istanbul. During the following years, he studied at Cornell University, Sabancı University in Istanbul and Goldsmiths, University of London. His focus was on the visual arts, but he took additional courses in history and biology. Thereafter, he was employed in marketing and communications, practising art on the side. Many

[105] Biçer, 'Heretik Bir New Age Tarikati', 27.
[106] Biçer, 'Kutsal Kitaplar Üstü Apokrif Kutsal', 15.
[107] Çorak, *The Knowledge Book*.
[108] Frisk and Åkerbäck, *New Religiosity*, 157–59.
[109] Sibireva, 'Freedom', 116.
[110] Kösemen, *Osman Hasan*.

of his sketches showed encounters with creatures that inhabit parallel universes, such as demons and grey aliens. 'I have never had such "visions" nor am I a believer in such experiences', he explained. 'My work is grounded in research and scientifically-plausible speculation.'[111] He acknowledged, however, that his portrayal of serpents and horned beings might be connected to the mystical Kabbalistic symbolism of his Dönmeh forebears.[112]

Early in his career, in 2004, Kösemen published a book containing an elaborate vision of the evolution of life throughout the Milky Way. The title was *All Tomorrows: The Myriad Species and Mixed Fortunes of Man* (Figures 7 and 8). Covering billions of years, the work tells how humans first split into earthlings

Figure 7 Cover of *All Tomorrows* (2004). Courtesy of Cevdet Mehmet Kösemen.

111 Kosemen, *Tangent Worlds*, 4.
112 Garcia, 'The Accidental Dönmeh'.

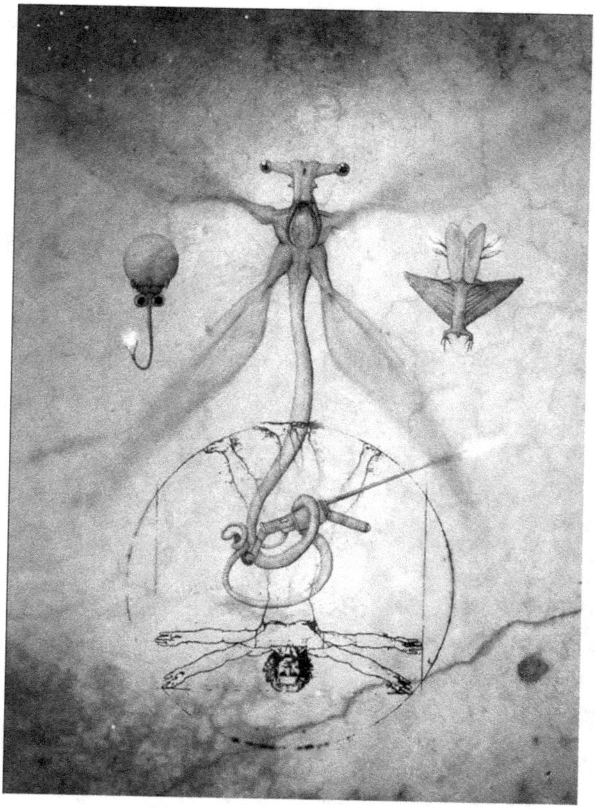

Figure 8 'Qu triumphant in the fall of Man', incorporating Leonardo da Vinci's *Vitruvian Man*. Courtesy of Cevdet Mehmet Kösemen.

and Martians and are reunited as star people. After spreading over a spiral arm of our galaxy, this species suffers from a devastating encounter with advanced nomadic aliens called Qu. Masters of genetic engineering and nanotechnology, the Qu consider themselves gods. They defeat almost all human descendants and turn them into 'worms', 'swimmers' and 'flyers', among others. After the Qu depart, the survivors evolve independently from one another on different planets and become 'snake people', 'tool breeders', 'pterosapiens', etc. One group of star people escapes by hiding inside asteroids-turned-spaceships. These 'spacers' then evolve into 'asteromorphs' and 'god-like forms'. While Kösemen used words like 'god' to describe these creatures, he maintained that 'nothing was sacred in the evolutionary process'. At the end of the book, all descendants of humanity become extinct.[113]

[113] Kosemen, *All Tomorrows*.

After the publication of *All Tomorrows*, which covers numerous worlds, Kösemen turned to a more detailed description of a particular one called *Snaiad*. This project began as a website in 2007. It was influenced by the American Wayne Barlowe's book *Expedition: Being an Account in Words and Artwork of the 2358 A.D. Voyage to Darwin IV.*[114] *Snaiad* describes the human arrival on a distant planet eight billion years old. 'Life on Snaiad is similar to life on many other planets; inconceivably old and diverse, and full of surprises', Kösemen wrote. Besides dinosaur-like vertebrates, the artist imagined 'Arthrognathans, Elastozoans, Trilateralans, Terrabivalves and weird animal-plant symbiotes'.[115] The artist explained that his project 'explores how life could evolve on a planet that is roughly similar to Earth'.[116]

Even as religion was given more space under the Justice and Development Party, Kösemen's world-building was hardly Islamic. The artist explained that his human colonists did not find a 'second Garden of Eden, but an unusual new world they had to understand and adapt in order to survive'.[117] He also denied that he was 'playing God' by depicting a new planet and the evolution of creatures on it. 'I did it for fun and intellectual fulfillment', he said. 'Real nature is far more complicated and old', Kösemen added. 'It took more than four billion years of evolution for life on Earth to get to its current state.' Evolution itself did not follow a designer's plan either, he clarified. 'There is currently no evidence suggesting an intelligent agency in this process.' In contrast to Bülent Çorak, Kösemen rejected teleology. 'Evolution depends more on chance and accidents than most people assume.' He commented on the absence of intelligent creatures other than the human colonists on Snaiad: 'Intelligence is not a "goal" of the evolutionary process, nothing is.'[118]

Kösemen continued his work, even as evolution became more controversial in Turkey. He neither worried about accusations of 'blasphemy' nor felt the 'need to self-censor', he told me in 2018.[119] Two years earlier, he had self-published a second edition of sketches under the title *Tangent Worlds*. Among other creatures, he described scorpion-like beings that had evolved on a dry planet. They believe in a 'Bad God' who is cruel and 'spoils everything'. In their religious rituals, the scorpion people respond with curses and insults. 'Die, Bad

114 Kosemen, 'Links'.
115 Kosemen, 'Life on Snaiad'.
116 Kosemen, 'Frequently Asked Questions'.
117 Kosemen, 'Snaiad'.
118 Kosemen, 'Frequently Asked Questions'.
119 C. Mehmet Kösemen, email, 19 March 2018.

God, for you are a shit. May I tear the claw-mouths off of your mother. May I piss on your eggs.'[120] As an independent artist, Kösemen was largely unaffected by the Turkish government's purges or its removal of evolution from curricula. In 2018, Kösemen participated in a group exhibition at the Science Museum of Virginia titled *Evolution!*[121] During the same year, he was the subject of a documentary film directed by Kevin Schreck and titled *Tangent Realms*.

Apart from this documentary, Kösemen's books have not yet been turned into feature films. However, the 2010s did see the production of other, more serious Turkish science fiction films alongside comedies. Cinematic creativity has thus persisted amid repression and will likely continue into the future. In 2012, the television series *Turkish Space Test* offered jokes along the lines of the hit *G.O.R.A.* Satirizing the Turkish economy, two characters in front of an ATM on board a spacecraft discuss whether they should withdraw money to invest it in gold or keep it in the bank to earn interest.[122] On the serious side of the genre was the psychological drama *Ivy*, which was directed and written by Tolga Karaçelik and released in 2015. It was less successful at the box office, but better received by critics and festival judges than previous Turkish science fiction productions. Rather than a spacecraft, it featured a freight ship stuck on the waters of the Mediterranean. Because the vessel's owner has gone bankrupt, the captain and five crewmembers have to wait on board for the settlement of legal questions. Without purpose, isolated and running out of food, water and drugs, the captain slowly loses control. Alien organisms in the form of snails and fast-growing ivy suddenly appear and cover parts of the ship. They haunt the sailors who hunt one another.[123]

Despite censorship, *Ivy* enjoyed critical success in Erdoğan's Turkey. This may have been in part because of the political interpretations for which it allows. Karaçelik explained that he wanted to explore what happens to authority figures when they lose their purpose. The captain whose ship is going nowhere can easily be taken to represent the Turkish government, while his five crewmembers stand for different parts of society: workers, pious Muslims, young people, leftists and Kurds.[124] At the 52nd Antalya Film Festival in 2015, Nadir Sarıbacak won the best actor award for his role as a drug-addicted sailor. However, the pro-government broadcaster A Haber cut off Sarıbacak's speech

[120] Kosemen, *Tangent Worlds*, 69.
[121] Kosemen, 'CV'.
[122] Güneyer, *Türk'ün Uzayla İmtihanı*.
[123] Karaçelik, *Sarmaşık*.
[124] Sadar, 'Turkish Film Sarmasik'.

after he mentioned a popular alcoholic drink in calling for Turkish unity: 'Only brotherhood and conversation will save us. A glass of rakı or a tea …'[125]

Although Turkey has been a leading producer, the production of science fiction films in the Muslim world will not depend on the fate of Yeşilçam alone. In the twenty-first century, the United Arab Emirates also emerged as an important contributor to the genre. Foreign producers of big-budget films received financial incentives to shoot in an attempt to turn locations into tourist attractions. Abu Dhabi's Rubʿ al-Khali thus posed as the desert planet Jakku in *Star Wars: The Force Awakens*.[126] *Star Trek Beyond* turned Dubai's towers into Starbase Yorktown. Its producers found not just generous subsidies there, but also architecture that fitted their 'world of the future'.[127] Cinemagoers could further see the Burj Khalifa crash into London in Roland Emmerich's *Independence Day: Resurgence*. Initially, the world's tallest building was supposed to be thrown by the alien invaders onto Paris. However, terrorist attacks in the French capital in 2015 changed this plan. The director 'felt it wasn't right to have the Burj Khalifa crashing on the Eiffel Tower'.[128]

With its desert landscapes and futuristic cityscapes, the UAE came to host not just major global productions, but also smaller local ones. In Dubai, the Pakistani director S. A. Zaidi found a suitable setting for an apocalyptic film titled *The Sons of Two Suns*. Produced by the Emirati Ghanem Ghubash, it was unrelated to Iraj Fazel Bakhsheshi's novel of a similar name. The film depicted a city at the end of the world, whose skyline is slowly burned by the heat from two stars.[129] Zaidi and Ghubash's next movie, *Aerials*, focused on alien spacecraft appearing over Dubai's towers. 'As kids Ghanem and I watched a lot of sci-fi alien invasion films', said Zaidi. 'Watching massive space ships taking over the city of New York or hovering over the city of Los Angeles, we always wondered what would happen if aliens actually visited this part of the world.'[130] Zaidi and Ghubash's films had small budgets and were mostly self-funded. 'We were literally emptying our banks out', said Zaidi. The Dubai Film and TV Commission provided some support, but mainly in the form of permissions to shoot on sites like Sheikh Zayed Road.

[125] Hürriyet Daily News, 'Antalya Film Fest'.
[126] Lorraine Ali, 'The Harsh Reality'.
[127] Holmes, 'The Real Reason'.
[128] Reyes, 'Where Dubai'.
[129] Merchant, 'Dubai's First Sci-Fi Film'.
[130] Jalal, 'These Guys'.

After three years of work, *Aerials* was released in 2016. To the producers' relief, their picture was in Emirati cinemas before Emmerich's *Independence Day: Resurgence*.[131]

Unlike in Emmerich's film, the aliens in *Aerials* do not destroy the Burj Khalifa or other buildings in Dubai. The size of the budget was one reason; respect another. 'Our families and our friends will see this – we don't want them asking why we wanted to destroy everything they know and love', explained Zaidi. Thus, the huge spaceships bring about a standstill by disrupting electronics, telecommunications and transportation. While different inhabitants of the city ask about the aliens' intentions, a domestic drama ensues. Confined to their home, an Emirati man and his disabled Western wife explore their cultural differences, which have become more pronounced. They try to understand the reason behind the aliens' arrival and experience strange encounters at home.[132]

Beyond futuristic architecture, Dubai's cosmopolitanism probably contributed to sci-fi renderings of meeting the Other. In the UAE's similarly diverse neighbours, young people made an increasing number of science fiction films. Moreover, they engaged more seriously with what they called 'Gulf futurism'. The Qatari-American artist Sophia Al-Maria discussed this phenomenon in a blog from 2008 under the title 'The Gaze of Sci-Fi Wahabi'. It was subtitled 'A Theoretical Pulp Fiction and Serialized Videographic Adventure in the Arabian Gulf'. Al-Maria drew a contrast between the concern for privacy on the one hand and its intrusion by technology on the other. This was symbolized by the omnipresence of both veils and camera phones in Dammam, Doha and Dubai. 'The volatile forces of a regressive Islam, foolhardy futurism and sudden wealth jettisoned the oil-states through this fresh temporal portal into a prophetic unreality.'[133]

Growing up between Qatar and the United States, Sophia Al-Maria often considered herself to be an alien. Her father was of Bedouin background and met her mother while on a Qatari government scholarship to learn English in the state of Washington. When having to declare her ethnicity in official documents during her high school years, Al-Maria always checked the box for 'other'. When asked to 'specify', she wrote 'Klingon', thus identifying with the warrior

[131] Newbould, 'Aerial Assault'.
[132] Ibid.
[133] Al-Maria, 'Introduction'.

species from *Star Trek*. In 2012, she published a memoir under the title *The Girl Who Fell to Earth*.[134] The title itself was a reference to David Bowie's film *The Man Who Fell to Earth*.[135]

The same year as her memoir came out, Al-Maria was involved in the making of a short film in which Qatar forms the centre of an extraterrestrial threat. The artist served as creative producer of *Topaz Duo: Cosmic Phoenix*, a musical comedy. With support from the Doha Film Institute, it was largely shot in the city's futuristic Sheraton hotel. Designed by the American architect William Pereira, the hotel had already hosted Al-Maria during her childhood.[136] In the movie, the Egyptian lounge singers Ahmed and Nahla Topaz fight the former's ex-wife Kaluza who has been possessed by an eleventh-dimensional demon from outer space. Kaluza turns the hotel guests into energy demons and seeks to open a stargate to attract more creatures and bring about the end of the universe. However, with the power of love and frying pans – that's right – the Topaz Duo defeat the demons. In the end, Ahmed and Nahla go through the gate, turn into firebirds and fly into the eleventh dimension (where the bald Ahmed hopes his hair will regrow).[137]

Al-Maria's own feeling of being like an alien was shared by other Gulf artists of her generation, such as Monira Al Qadiri. The daughter of a Kuwaiti diplomat, she was born in Senegal in 1983. Because she and many others in Kuwait went to English schools, they were called 'chicken nuggets': 'brown on the outside, white on the inside'. Al Qadiri consumed much American popular culture, including junk food and alien abductions. At the same time, she experienced the arrival of American expansionism and cultural hegemony as an 'alien invasion'.[138] However, the Kuwaiti became equally obsessed with Japanese culture, especially cartoons, at an early age. This obsession led her to complete a doctorate at Tokyo University of the Arts in 2010.[139]

As another artist between different worlds, Monira Al Qadiri included extraterrestrial themes in her work. In two projects entitled *Alien Technology*, she created gigantic sculptures of oil drills, which she described as foreign to the 'ecology, economy and history' of the Gulf.[140] In 2017, she exhibited a

134 Al-Maria, *The Girl*, 199.
135 Kleinman, 'On Sophia Al-Maria's The Girl Who Fell to Earth'.
136 Al-Maria, *The Girl*, 84–85.
137 Robinsoni, *Topaz Duo*.
138 Gasworks, 'Interview'.
139 Kretowicz, 'Positive Realism'.
140 Kunak, 'An Interview'.

video entitled *The Craft*, which was based on a childhood dream. In the opening scene, her father, the Kuwaiti ambassador to Senegal, leaves the residence in Dakar to go to work. The voice-over cautions, 'everything is not as it seems. You start to question reality, the world as a whole'. The voice asks, 'Are we really where we think we are? Are we there? Are we really us?' A few minutes later, the viewer learns that the embassy is actually a spacecraft, in which aliens plot to subdue humanity and to plunder Earth. The inside of their vessel looks like an American diner, and children's drawings of hamburgers, hot dogs and sandwiches are filling the screen.[141]

Leading futurists from the Gulf were privileged in their access to wealthy patrons. However, money itself was not a guarantee for successful productions. In the 2010s, the Qatari director Ahmed Al Baker partnered with the Emmy Award-winning Arab Telemedia Group to produce a series entitled *Medinah*. It is set in near-future Qatar after the catastrophic failure of a rocket mission that was meant to offset climate change by spraying sulphur dioxide into the stratosphere. Featuring dialogue in both English and Arabic, the show had a diverse international cast, including Oscar nominee Eric Roberts and Tahmoh Penikett, who was known for *Battlestar Galactica*. Very optimistic, the producers brought *Medinah* to the San Diego Comic-Con in 2017 despite lacking a distributor.[142] However, by that time, the show had already run into disputes. In 2016, a blog had been created with the declared aim of shaming 'Arab Telemedia and/or Ahmed Al Baker into paying the former crew the $500,000+ in wages plus damages that they are owed'. The website would only be taken down on 'the day the entire crew is rightfully compensated for being abused, threatened, exploited, lied to, and not paid'. As of 2019, the blog was still up, and the show unreleased.[143]

Medinah was perhaps as unexpected a title for a work of science fiction as 'Mecca' would have been. Nevertheless, despite its historical hostility towards cinemas, Saudi Arabia too might soon follow the smaller Gulf states in producing futurist films. Under Crown Prince Mohammed bin Salman, the government made news reminiscent of science fiction. As part of the Future Investment Initiative in 2017, the kingdom surprised critics of its human and women's rights records by granting citizenship to a robot named Sophia.[144]

[141] Muller, 'Tomorrow Girls', 120–21.
[142] Kay, 'Comic-Con'.
[143] Medinah Show Uncut, 'About'.
[144] Parikka, 'Middle East and Other Futurisms', 46.

At the same time, the government planned Neom, a new solar-powered city that relies on robots and self-driving cars for many of its functions.[145] The name itself was a combination of the Greek prefix *neo-* (new) and the Arabic *mustaqbal* (future).[146] These projects were part of the Saudi Vision 2030, a plan to reduce the kingdom's dependence on oil and to create jobs in the service sector, including recreation and tourism. Repressing opposition to its social and economic reforms, the regime arrested many conservative clerics, including Muhammad al-Munajjid.[147]

As part of its new vision, the kingdom ended its long ban on public cinemas. One of the first films shown was the Afrofuturist *Black Panther* produced by Marvel Studios. Men and women were seated together during a screening in Riyadh, and the censors only cut two kisses and a curse.[148] The movie is set in Wakanda, a fictional advanced nation in sub-Saharan Africa. It was formed by the first Black Panther, a warrior who had gained superpowers thanks to the effect of vibranium, a metal from a meteorite. This imaginary substance is a rendering of uranium, which was mined and exported by such countries as Muslim-majority Niger. Whereas most Nigeriens remained poor, in the Marvel Comics fantasy, the Wakandans have benefited technologically and financially from their possession of the metal.[149]

Even if the liberalization of the Saudi entertainment sector is reversed, this would not bring the variety of Muslim futurisms to an end. Artists in the diaspora would probably continue their work regardless of the political situation in their countries of origin. This goes not just for people from affluent Gulf countries but also for people with backgrounds in poorer states. A pertinent example is Pakistan-born artist Saks Afridi. His father worked for Pakistan Airlines, making his family 'change countries, houses, schools, languages, and cultures, on a regular basis'. Looking back after settling in New York, Afridi said that he had lived the life of an 'Insider Outsider'. By this, he meant 'achieving a sense of belonging while being out of place and finding happiness in a state of temporary permanence'. 'Insider Outsider' was then also the title of a series of artworks from 2016 – handmade wool rugs whose inner patterns form UFOs.[150]

145 Saif, 'Blade Runner'.
146 Al Arabiya, 'What does Saudi Arabia's Mega Project "NEOM"'.
147 Al-ʿArab, '5 iʿtiqālāt jadīdah'.
148 Jovanovic, 'This Is a Historic Moment'.
149 Hecht, *Being Nuclear*, 17–19.
150 Plackis-Cheng, 'Saks Afridi'.

Like his peers from the Gulf region, Afridi explored distinct kinds of futurism. He explained that the 'combination of Eastern traditional craftsmanship and Western contemporary sensibilities' led him to the category of 'Sub-Continental Futurism'.[151] In 2018, he created a series of sculptures entitled 'SpaceMosque', merging the aesthetics of spacecraft and traditional Islamic architecture (Figures 9 and 10). In Afridi's 'parafictional' narrative, every human being on the planet has their prayers answered through a strange mosque-like vessel from outer space. Mixing mysticism with technology, he called his approach 'Sci-fi Sufism'. Drawing on Afrofuturism, he also situated it under the umbrella 'IslamoFuturism'. Among his influences, he acknowledged Arthur C. Clarke's novel *Childhood's End* and art by Hiroshi Sugimoto, as well as Muhammad's

Figure 9 'SpaceMosque'. Courtesy of Saks Afridi.

[151] Ibid.

Figure 10 'SpaceMosque'. Courtesy of Saks Afridi.

ascension to heaven. He furthermore considered 'SpaceMosque' as part of the same 'parafictional genre' as Damien Hirst's documentary *Treasures from the Wreck of the Unbelievable*.[152]

Not only South Asia, but also sub-Saharan Africa is likely going to give rise to more migrant Muslim futurists. Drawing on the more established category of Afrofuturism could even be more straightforward for them. A recent example is the Somali-Canadian artist Riya Jama. Growing up, she felt that people like herself were absent from popular representations. She loved *Harry Potter*, but wondered why it did not encompass any Somali witches or wizards.[153] Jama had a similar experience studying fine art: 'I was force fed European artists as the only prime example of what artistic brilliance looked like. Art that never reflected anyone who looked like me.'[154] Only when she was invited to an Afrofuturism conference in New York did she find a satisfying way to describe her own work.[155]

[152] Breitsameter, 'In Conversation'.
[153] Baker, 'This Toronto Artist'.
[154] Dietz, 'Centering Muslim Black Women'.
[155] Baker, 'This Toronto Artist'.

Toronto-based Jama thus made black Muslim women the focus of her futurist art. Because she did not wear a hijab, she often found her Muslim identity overlooked within the black community, while her black identity was underappreciated by other Muslims. She was in the 'limbo of intersection', as she said on the occasion of her first solo exhibition in 2018. This show had the Somail title *Riyadii Farxiyo* (dreams of Farhiya). It featured mixed-media portraits of dark-skinned women and girls against a background of space. 'There's something poetic about making a Black woman the mother of the universe', she explained.[156] In contrast to her own preference, she even depicted the women as wearing headscarves. 'It is essential to me that Hijabs exist in space too', Jama said in 2017. 'I want a young Muslimah to know that she too exists and to also value her Black skin more because it is celebrated in my various universes.'[157]

Not all Muslim futurisms-to-come are likely to reflect on Islam. However, explicitly Islamic science fiction will be among future imaginations by Muslims. One of those spearheading this subgenre was the Pakistani data scientist Muhammad Aurangzeb Ahmad, the editor of the website *Islam and Science Fiction*. In 2008, he co-edited a book entitled *A Mosque Among the Stars*.[158] Eight years later, this was followed by *Islamicates Volume I: Anthology of Science Fiction Short Stories Inspired from Muslim Cultures*. The collection was the result of a competition with seventy-eight submissions.[159] In 2018, Ahmad launched another project: the quarterly magazine *Takwin*. 'We are looking for original works of Sci-Fi in English with great characters, inspired by Islamic history, Islamic theology and Islamic cultures', the scientist announced. 'Anything that can be construed as offensive according to Islamic ethos will not be accepted.' Within these constraints, *Takwin* was open to a variety of contributions: short stories, poems, micro-fiction of two to five sentences, graphic designs, reviews and essays.[160]

Although Islamic, such science fiction was neither necessarily opposed to, nor separate from, Western productions. Even smaller works were similarly global in their inspiration as large franchises, such as *Star Trek* and *Star Wars*. Alex Kreis, one of the contributors to *Islamicates Volume I*, lived in Boston, but described himself as a world traveller. 'He's stayed in a castle in Scotland, bought an ill-fitting sweater on the black market in Moscow, and got terribly

156 Ibid.
157 Dietz, 'Centering Muslim Black Women'.
158 Ahmad and Khan, *A Mosque*.
159 Muhammad Aurangzeb Ahmad, ed., *Islamicates*, i.
160 Muhammad Aurangzeb Ahmad, 'Launching Takwin'.

lost in Cairo.' He furthermore 'climbed to the top of Temple IV in Tikal just to see where George Lucas shot the Rebel Base' in *Star Wars*.[161] In parallel to *Takwin*, Ahmad pursued another project, *Desi Star Trek*, combining Pakistani truck art with images of the starship *Enterprise* (Figure 11).[162]

Some combinations of Islam and Western science fiction will probably remain controversial, as they have been in the recent past. In 2017, Scott Neidich, a biologist at Duke University in North Carolina, published an article in which he laid out 'Why the Star Trek films are the wrong place for the Hijab'. He argued that 'Placing a hijab on the bridge of the Enterprise would imply that Islam had survived to the 23rd century, while we have no reason to believe any other modern human religion can claim similar.'[163] The risk of violating Starfleet dress codes did not deter the African American activist Blair Imani from dressing up as Geordi La Forge at the San Diego Comic-Con in 2017. The addition of a headscarf to her costume riled up 'trolls'. However, La Forge's

Figure 11 *Desi Star Trek* (2018). Courtesy of Muhammad Aurangzeb Ahmad.

[161] Kreis, 'Calligraphy', 1.
[162] Muhammad Aurangzeb Ahmad, 'Star Trek Pakistani Truck Art'.
[163] Neidich, 'Why the Star Trek Films'.

actor LeVar Burton called it the 'best cosplay of Geordi, EVER'. Imani herself stated that 'It's just exciting to think of a future that includes everybody, which includes Muslims.'[164]

Of course, if predicting the future is close to impossible, foreseeing all possible futurisms is even closer. One can merely guess what products of the scientific imagination might come out of the Muslim world over the next century. Forget about the large interdisciplinary field of astrobiology! Forecasting the progress of more confined endeavours, such as the search for extraterrestrial intelligence (SETI), is hard enough. Nevertheless, Muslim-majority countries and their diasporas have established solid bases for the production of speculative texts and images of all kinds. Free thinking flourished even in very repressive and conservative contexts. More than that, authoritarian governments and Islamists were often themselves highly creative producers of futuristic visions. Lack of censorship can be helpful for movie industries and UFO religions alike. However, constraints have also been enabling in many cases too. Even if authoritarianism and conservatism prevail, this would be unlikely to stifle the scientific imagination completely and end the competition of ideas.

Products of the scientific imagination are in turn likely to feed into concrete space programmes that various Muslim-majority countries have been setting up. Although only Iran among them had its own launch capacity in 2019, many states possessed the financial resources and international connections to lift payloads into orbit. Even poorer countries, like Morocco, came to command their own satellites. Whether more ambitious projects, like the UAE's city on Mars, will be realized remains to be seen. However, the combination of immense wealth, technological ambitions, and almost limitless imagination makes many missions conceivable. Taleb Omran's novel *The Search for Other Worlds*, with its Arab spaceship heading for Alpha Centauri, could one day be more than fiction.

[164] Donnelly, '"Star Trek" Costume'.

Bibliography

Interviews

Muhammad Aurangzeb Ahmad, Doha, 20 October 2018, and via Facebook Messenger, November and December 2018

Syed Muneeb Ali, via Facebook Messenger, August and September 2018

Ahmed Salah Al-Mahdi, via Twitter, October 2018

Noura Ahmed Al Noman, via Twitter, September and October 2018

Khalid Alsubai, Doha, 3 and 10 January 2018

Gugun Arief, via Facebook Messenger, November 2018

Iraj Fazel Bakhsheshi, via LinkedIn and email, December 2018 to February 2019

Emad El-Din Aysha, via email, March to September 2018

Riawani Elyta, via email, September 2018

Hosam Elzembely, via email, March and April 2018

Nabil Farouk, via email, March 2018

Rama Firmansyah, via Facebook Messenger, November 2018

Ghadir Golkarian, via Twitter, October 2018

Ali Hakim, via Facebook Messenger, November and December 2018

Eliza Vitri Handayani, via Instagram, September and October 2018

Ayham Jabr, via Instagram, June 2018

Azrul Jaini, via Facebook Messenger, June and July 2018

Stefani Jovita, via Facebook Messenger, November 2018

Nozair Khawaja, via Skype, 17 October 2019

Cevdet Mehmet Kösemen, via email, March 2018

Kaushani Majumder, via Goodreads, August 2019

Reza Mansouri, Doha and via email, February to May 2018

Jamal Mimouni, via email, September 2018

Farzam Molkara, via email, December 2018

Ali Pourahmad, via LinkedIn, January and February 2018

Ahmad Sufiatur Rahman (Sufi Arthur), via Facebook Messenger and email, November 2018

Sohrab Rahvar, via email, August 2019

Sidra Ramzan, via Facebook Messenger, June and July 2019

Hanna Sabat, Doha, 23 September 2019

Asal Sadeghinia, via email, December 2018

Parviz Tarikhi, via LinkedIn, June to September 2018

Victor G. Tejfel, via email, June and July 2018

Ahmed Khaled Towfik, via email, March 2018

Primary sources

Abbany, Zulfikar. 'Post-nuclear: Video Games are "Blooming" in Iran and Some Make Up To "200k" a Day'. *Deutsche Welle*, 19 August 2016. http://p.dw.com/p/1JliR.

ʿAbd al-Ḥakīm, Manṣūr [see also Abdul Hakim, Mansoor]. *ʿArsh Iblīs wa-muthallath Birmūdā wa-al-aṭbāq al-ṭāʾirah*. Al-Qāhirah: al-Maktabah al-Tawfīqīyah, 1998.

ʿAbd Allāh, Aḥmad. 'ʿIndamā yatawaqqaf al-zaman fī Qāhir al-Zaman'. *Al-Qāhirah*, no. 69 (1987): 68–69.

ʿAbd al-Wahhāb, Faṭīn. *Ismāʿīl Yas fī bayt al-ashbāḥ* (Aflām al-Nīl, 1951).

ʿAbd al-Wahhāb, Ḥamādah. *Al-liṣṣ al-sharīf* (Miṣr lil-Tamthīl wa-al-Sīnimā, 1953).

ʿAbd al-Wahhāb, Ḥamādah. *Ismāʿīl Yas yuqābil Rayya wa-Sakīnah* (Al-Nīl lil-Sīnimā, 1955).

ʿAbd al-Wahhāb, Ḥamādah. *Riḥlah ilá al-Qamar* (Behna Films, 1959).

Abdulrazzak, Hassan. 'Kuszib'. In *Iraq+100: Stories from a Century after the Invasion*, edited by Hassan Blasim, 115–38. Manchester: Comma Press, 2016.

Abdul Hakim, Mansoor [see also ʿAbd al-Ḥakīm, Manṣūr]. *Women Who Deserve to Go to Hell*. Translated by Rafiq Abdur Rahman. Karachi: Darul Ishaat, 2004.

Abu Taleb Khan, Mirza. *Travels of Mirza Abu Taleb Khan in Asia, Africa, and Europe, during the Years 1799, 1800, 1801, 1802, and 1803*. Translated by Charles Stewart. Second edition. Vol. 1. Broxbourne: R. Watts, 1814.

Agence France-Presse. 'Saudi Mufti Warns of "Depravity" of Cinemas and Concerts'. *The National*, 14 January 2017. https://www.thenational.ae/world/saudi-mufti-warns-of-depravity-of-cinemas-and-concerts-1.636828.

Agha, Omar Ahmed. 'The Man with the Golden Pen'. *Pakistan Today*, 16 July 2015. https://www.pakistantoday.com.pk/2015/07/16/the-man-with-the-golden-pen/.

Aghā, Riyāḍ Naʿsān. 'Al-khayāl al-ʿilmī … li-mādhā?' *Al-Khayāl al-ʿIlmī*, no. 1 (2008): 4–5.

Aghā, Riyāḍ Naʿsān. 'Adab al-khayāl al-ʿilmī huwa adab al-mustaqbal'. *Al-Khayāl al-ʿIlmī*, no. 2 (2008): 4–5.

Aḥmad, Anwar. 'Al-sīnimā baʿda khamsīn ʿāman'. *Al-Hilāl* 58, no. 1 (1950): 148–52.

Aḥmad, Anwar. 'Al-sīnimā sabaqat ilá ghazw al-faḍāʾ'. *Al-Hilāl* 66, no. 1 (1958): 110–16.

Ahmad, Mirza Tahir. *Revelation, Rationality, Knowledge and Truth*. Tilford: Islam International Publications, 1998.

Ahmad, Muhammad Aurangzeb. 'Interview of Noura Al Noman'. *Islam and Science Fiction*, 30 October 2012. http://www.islamscifi.com/interview-noura-alnoman/.

Ahmad, Muhammad Aurangzeb. 'Islam Sci-Fi Interview with Hal. W. Hall'. *Islam and Science Fiction*, 21 March 2016. http://www.islamscifi.com/islam-sci-fi-interviewwith-hal-w-hall/.

Ahmad, Muhammad Aurangzeb. 'Star Trek Pakistani Truck Art'. *Islam and Science Fiction*, 9 March 2018. http://www.islamscifi.com/star-trek-pakistani-truck-art/.

Ahmad, Muhammad Aurangzeb. 'Launching Takwin – A Magazine of Islamicate Science Fiction'. *Islam and Science Fiction*, 30 October 2018. http://www.islamscifi.com/launching-takwin-a-magazine-of-islamicate-science-fiction/.

Ahmad, Muhammad Aurangzeb, ed. *Islamicates Volume I: Anthology of Science Fiction Short Stories Inspired from Muslim Cultures*. Lahore: Mirza Book Agency, 2016.

Ahmad, Muhammad Aurangzeb, and Ahmed A. Khan, eds. *A Mosque Among the Stars*. Central City: ZC Books, 2008.

Ahmed, Humayun. 'Adsorption of Water-Soluble Polymers on Clay and Water Transport through Water Soluble Acrylic Copolymer Films'. PhD thesis, North Dakota State University, 1982.

Akhtar, Jamshed. *In Search of Our Origins: How the Quran Can Help in Scientific Research*. CreateSpace, 2014.

Akhtar, Jamshed. *The Ultimate Revelations*. Updated and revised version. CreateSpace, 2015.

Akhtar, Jamshed. 'Press Reviews of the Book'. *Institute of Revealed Knowledge*. Accessed 8 January 2019. http://irk.co.in/documents/reviews_tur.html.

Akhtar, Jamshed. 'The Background'. *The Ultimate Revelations*. Accessed 9 January 2019. http://theultimaterevelations-jamshed.blogspot.com/p/background-of-book.html.

Al-Achqar, Omar Soulaiman. *Le monde des djinns et des démons*. Translated by A. M. Ghadi. Riyadh: International Islamic Publishing House, 2007.

Al-ʿAjmī, ʿAbd al-Fattāḥ. 'lhām Shāhīn. māta wāliduhā ghayr rāḍ ʿanhā wa-hādhihī ʿalāqatuhā bi-"Rāmī Lakaḥ"'. *Al-Taḥrīr*, 3 January 2018. https://www.tahrirnews.com/posts/860948/.

Al-ʿAnānī, Aḥmad. 'Al-aṭbāq al-ṭāʾirah: ḥaqīqah am khayāl?' *Al-Dawḥah* 6, no. 2 (1981): 116–17.

Al-ʿArab. '5 iʿtiqālāt jadīdah bi-al-Suʿūdīyah shamilat al-dāʿiyah Muḥammad al-Munajjid'. *Al-ʿArab*, 27 September 2017. https://www.alarab.qa/story/1259140/.

Al Arabiya. 'What Does Saudi Arabia's Mega Project "NEOM" Actually Stand for?' *Al Arabiya*, 24 October 2017. http://english.alarabiya.net/en/business/economy/2017/10/24/What-does-NEOM-mean-.html.

Al-Ashqar, Umar Sulaiman. *The World of the Jinn and Devils*. Translated by Jamaal al-Din M. Zarabozo. Boulder: Al-Basheer, 1998.

Al-Ashqar, ʿUmar Sulaymān. *ʿĀlam al-jinn wa-al-shayāṭīn*. Al-ṭabʿah al-rābiʿah. Al-Kuwayt: Maktabat al-Falāḥ, 1984.

Alavi, Omair. 'The Return of a Visionary'. *The News on Sunday*, 11 January 2015. http://tns.thenews.com.pk/pakistani-cinema-the-return-of-a-visionary.

Alavi, Suhayb. 'Super Hero's "Homecoming" Delayed!' *Geo.tv*, 30 July 2017. https://www.geo.tv/latest/151647-actress-noor-photos-with-wali-hamid-khan-photos-surfaced.

Al-Azzawi, Fadhil. 'Poems from a UFO Window'. *Banipal* 12 (2001): 52–55.

Al-Bāqūrī, Aḥmad Ḥasan. 'Al-Islām wa-al-ṣuʿūd ilá al-kawākib'. *Al-Hilāl* 66, no. 1 (1958): 15–20.

Āl Bassām, ʿAbd Allāh ibn ʿAbd al-Raḥmān ibn Ṣāliḥ, ed. *Khizānat al-tawārīkh al-Najdīyah*. Vol. 7. [Al-Riyāḍ:] ʿAbd Allāh ibn ʿAbd al-Raḥmān ibn Ṣāliḥ Āl Bassām [1999].

Al-Baṭāwī, ʿAbd al-Ḥamīd. 'Muḥammad Aḥmad al-Ghamrāwī min ahl a-tafsīr al-ʿilmī'. *Multaqá ahl al-tafsīr*, 15 May 2011. https://vb.tafsir.net/tafsir26359/#.W-FG3-JoRaQ.

Al-Bustānī, Buṭrus. *Dāʾirat al-maʿārif.* Vol. 3. Bayrūt: Maṭbaʿat al-Maʿārif, 1878.

Al-Ghamrāwī, Muḥammad Aḥmad. 'Al-nāḥiyah al-ʿilmīyah min iʿjāz al-Qurʾān'. *Al-Risālah* 15, no. 705 (1947): 36–37.

Al-Ghamrāwī, Muḥammad Aḥmad. 'Al-nāḥiyah al-ʿilmīyah min iʿjāz al-Qurʾān (Tatimmat mā nushira fī al-ʿadad al-māḍī)'. *Al-Risālah* 15, no. 706 (1947): 54–55.

Al-Ghamrāwī, Muḥammad Aḥmad. *Al-Islām fī ʿaṣr al-ʿilm: al-dīn, wa-al-rasūl wa-al-kitāb*. Edited by Aḥmad ʿAbd al-Salām al-Kardānī. Cairo: Maṭbaʿat al-Saʿādah, 1973.

Al-Ghoul, Asmaa. 'Do Gaza's Melting-pot Markets Reflect Identity Crisis?' *Al-Monitor*, 1 February 2016. http://www.al-monitor.com/pulse/originals/2016/02/gaza-markets-egypt-turkey-products-tunnel-demolition.html.

Al-Ḥakīm, Tawfīq. *Majlis al-ʿadl*. Cairo: Maktabat Miṣr, 1988.

Al-Ḥakīm, Tawfīq. *Riḥlah ilá al-ghad*. Cairo: Maktabat Miṣr, 1994.

Al-Hilāl. 'Al-ḥayāt fī al-kawākib wa-al-arḍ'. *Al-Hilāl* 31, no. 3 (1922): 297–99.

Ali, Lorraine. 'The Harsh Reality of Building a "Star Wars" Fantasy in Abu Dhabi'. *Los Angeles Times*, 3 December 2015. http://www.latimes.com/entertainment/herocomplex/la-ca-hc-star-wars-filming-abu-dhabi-20151206-story.html.

Al-Jammāl, Aḥmad. 'Ḥusām al-Zambīlī: al-iʿlām lā yahtamm bi-adab al-khayāl al-ʿilmī'. *Al-Jarīdah*, 31 August 2018. http://www.aljarida.com/articles/1535642872365098600/.

Al-Jeffery, Amina. 'Bridging Arab Mythology with Western Sci-fi'. *Arab News*, 19 May 2017. http://www.arabnews.com/node/1101736/art-culture.

Al-Khaṭīb, Mīrfat. 'Nūrah al-Nūmān: al-Shāriqah tushajjiʿ ʿalá al-qirāʾah wa-al-kitābah wa-al-thaqāfah'. *Al-Khalīj*, 18 November 2013. http://www.alkhaleej.ae/supplements/page/2c168687-4928-49c4-88ab-d04b2d9c2f39.

Al-Maria, Sophia. 'Introduction'. *The Gaze of Sci-Fi Wahabi: A Theoretical Pulp Fiction and Serialized Videographic Adventure in the Arabian Gulf*, 7 September 2008. http://scifiwahabi.blogspot.com/2008/09/introduction.html.

Al-Maria, Sophia. *The Girl Who Fell to Earth*. New York: HarperCollins, 2012.

Al-Mashriq. 'Fākihah'. *Al-Mashriq* 7, no. 23 (1904): 1128–29.

Al-Mawjī, Muná, and Hudá al-Shaymī. 'Aflām al-khayāl al-ʿilmī al-miṣrī. muḥāwalāt bāʾisah'. *Masrawy*, 11 January 2015. http://www.masrawy.com/Arts/cinema/details/2015/1/11/427045/.

Al-Miṣrīyūn. 'Najl rāʾid al-wasaṭīyah al-ʿArabīyah yataḥaddath li-"al-Miṣrīyūn"'. *Al-Miṣrīyūn*, 23 April 2015. https://www.almesryoon.com/story/724375/.

Al-Munajjid, Muhammed Salih. '3324: Reading Fiction and Watching Science Fiction Movies'. *Islam Question and Answer*, 2 June 1999. https://islamqa.info/en/3324.

Al-Muqtaṭaf. 'Al-Qamar'. *Al-Muqtaṭaf* 1, no. 1 (1876): 7–13.

Al-Muqtaṭaf. 'Al-Mushtarī'. *Al-Muqtaṭaf* 2, no. 4 (1877): 81–84.

Al-Muqtaṭaf. 'Al-ab Anjilū Sikkī'. *Al-Muqtaṭaf* 2, no. 12 (1878): 284–85.

Al-Muqtaṭaf. 'Ḍarar al-mā' al-muqaddas'. *Al-Muqtaṭaf* 22, no. 9 (1898): 717.

Al-Nahhas, Adil Mosa. 'The UFO Entities and the Jinns'. *Flying Saucer Review* 29, no. 4 (1984): iii.

Al-Nūmān, Nūrah Aḥmad. *Ajwān*. Cairo: Dār Nahḍat Miṣr, 2012.

Al-Shāhid. 'Al-aṭbāq al-ṭā'irah tufaḍḍil al-Kuwayt'. *Al-Shāhid*, 3 November 2016. http://www.alshahed.com.kw/index.php?option=com_content&view=article&id=11928.

Al-Shaymī, Hudá. 'Nihād Sharīf. mana'ahu maraḍuhu min dirāsat al-ṭibb fa-taḥawwala li-'amīd adab al-khayāl al-'ilmī'. *Masrawy*, 11 January 2015. http://www.masrawy.com/Arts/cinema/details/2015/1/11/427169/.

Al-Sibā'ī, Yūsuf. *Lasta waḥdak*. Al-Qāhirah: Maktabat Miṣr, 1986.

Alsubai, K. A., N. R. Parley, D. M. Bramich, R. G. West, P. M. Sorensen, A. Collier Cameron, D. W. Latham, et al. 'Qatar-1b: A Hot Jupiter Orbiting a Metal-rich K Dwarf Star'. *Monthly Notices of the Royal Astronomical Society* 417, no. 1 (2011): 709–716.

Alsubai, Khalid, Zlatan I. Tsvetanov, Stylianos Pyrzas, David W. Latham, Allyson Bieryla, Jason Eastman, Dimitris Mislis, et al. 'Qatar Exoplanet Survey: Qatar-8b, 9b, and 10b – A Hot Saturn and Two Hot Jupiters'. *Astronomical Journal* 157, no. 6 (2019): 224.

Alter, Alexandra. 'Middle Eastern Writers Find Refuge in the Dystopian Novel'. *New York Times*, 21 December 2017. https://www.nytimes.com/2016/05/30/books/middle-eastern-writers-find-refuge-in-the-dystopian-novel.html.

Altobelli, N., Frank Postberg, K. Fiege, M. Trieloff, H. Kimura, V. J. Sterken, H.-W. Hsu, et al. 'Flux and Composition of Interstellar Dust at Saturn from Cassini's Cosmic Dust Analyzer'. *Science* 352, no. 6283 (2016): 312–318.

Altuntaş, Öykü. 'Turkey's New School Year: Jihad in, Evolution out'. *BBC News*, 18 September 2017. http://www.bbc.com/news/world-europe-41296714.

Al-Ṭabīb. 'Al-khalā'iq al-ḥayyah fī al-sayyārāt'. *Al-Ṭabīb* 1, no. 19 (1884): 361–67.

Al-Ṭabīb. 'Al-khalā'iq al-ḥayyah fī al-sayyārāt'. *Al-Ṭabīb* 1, no. 22 (1885): 421–26.

Al-Zambīlī, Ḥusām 'Abd al-Ḥamīd. *Anṣāf al-bashar*. Jamā'at al-Wasaṭīyah, 2001.

Al-Zambīlī, Ḥusām. *Al-kawkab al-'ajīb: awwal ḥiwār ma'a fayrūs 'āqil*. Jamā'at al-Wasaṭīyah, 2001.

Al-Zambīlī, Ḥusām. *Amrīkā 2030: qiṣṣat inhiyār al-'ālam*. Jamā'at al-Wasaṭīyah, 2001.

Al-Ziriklī, Khayr al-Dīn. *Al-a'lām: qāmūs tarājim li-ash'har al-rijāl wa-al-nisā' min al-'Arab wa-al-musta'ribīn wa-al-mustashriqīn*. Al-ṭab'ah al-khāmisah. Vol. 1. Bayrūt: Dār al-'Ilm lil-Malāyīn, 1980.

'Āmir, 'Abbās Maḥmūd. 'Ḥiwār ma'a Nihād Sharīf ḥawla adab al-khayāl al-'ilmī'. *Al-Qāhirah*, no. 85 (1988): 40–43.

Ansari, Anousheh. 'Space Holds the Key to the Future of Humanity'. In *Planetary Echoes: Exploring the Implications of Human Settlement in Outer Space*, edited by Lukas Feireiss and Michael Najjar, 102–8. Leipzig: Spector Books, 2018.

Ansari, N. A. *Wahan Ke Log* (Bundel Khand, 1967).

Antoniadi, E. M. 'La planète Jupiter dans les petits instruments'. *L'Astronomie* 8 (1889): 75.

Antoniadi, E. M. 'Observation de Saturne'. *L'Astronomie* 8 (1889): 154.

Antoniadi, E. M. 'Curieuses déformations du soleil couchant'. *L'Astronomie* 12 (1893): 35.

Antoniadi, E. M. 'La merveille de basiliques: Sainte-Sophie de Constantinople'. *Je sais tout* 9, no. 2 (1913): 107–16.

Antoniadi, E. M. *The Planet Mars*. Translated by Patrick Moore. Shaldon: Keith Reid, 1975.

Ashqar, ʿUmar Sulaymān. *Dunyā-yi jinn'hā ū shayāṭīn*. Translated by Gurūh-i Farhangī-i Intishārāt-i Ḥaramayn. Aqeedeh, n.d.

Astrobiology Network of Pakistan. 'Core Team'. *Astrobiology Network of Pakistan*, 2018. http://www.astrobiopak.net/core-team/.

ʿAẓīmī, Bahrām. *Tihrān 1500* (Fīlmīrān, 2012).

Bachelet, E., I.-G. Shin, C. Han, P. Fouqué, A. Gould, J. W. Menzies, J.-P. Beaulieu, et al. 'MOA 2010-BLG-477Lb: Constraining the Mass of a Microlensing Planet from Microlensing Parallax, Orbital Motion, and Detection of Blended Light'. *Astrophysical Journal* 754, no. 1 (2012): 73.

Badr, ʿAbd al-Raḥīm. 'Al-aṭbāq al-ṭāʾirah'. *Al-Bayān*, no. 22 (January 1968): 40–44.

Bagheri, Fatemeh, Sedighe Sajadian, and Sohrab Rahvar. 'Exoplanet Detection by Spitzer via Microlensing Events'. *Bulletin of the American Physical Society*, 2019. http://meetings.aps.org/Meeting/APR19/Session/S01.36.

Baker, Allison. 'This Toronto Artist Uses Sci-fi and Space to tell her Story of Growing up Somali'. *Toronto Life*, 16 July 2018. https://torontolife.com/culture/toronto-artist-uses-sci-fi-space-tell-story-growing-somali/.

Bakhshishī, Īraj Fāẓil. *Firishtah-yi nigahbān*. Tihrān: Qaṣīdah Sarā, 2008.

Bakhshishī, Īraj Fāẓil. *Farzandān-i khūrshīd*. Mashhad: Ahang-i Qalam, 2011.

Bari, Rashidul. 'Tears for Humayun Ahmed: The Shakespeare of Bangladesh'. *Times of India*, 16 August 2012. https://timesofindia.indiatimes.com/nri/citizen-journalists/citizen-journalists-reports/rashidul-bari/Tears-for-Humayun-Ahmed-The-Shakespeare-of-Bangladesh/articleshow/15515838.cms.

Barker, Joshua. 'Engineers and Political Dreams: Indonesia in the Satellite Age'. *Current Anthropology* 46, no. 5 (2005): 703–27.

Bates, Brainerd S. 'Space-Age Immigrant'. *Aramco World* 27, no. 6 (1976): 18–25.

Batista, V., A. Gould, S. Dieters, S. Dong, I. Bond, J. P. Beaulieu, D. Maoz, et al. 'MOA-2009-BLG-387Lb: A Massive Planet Orbiting an M Dwarf'. *Astronomy & Astrophysics* 529 (2011): A102.

Baweja, Tehseen. 'New Prize for Pakistani Writers of Imaginative Fiction'. *The Asian Writer*, 20 December 2016. http://theasianwriter.co.uk/2016/12/new-prize-for-pakistani-writers-of-imaginative-fiction/.

Baweja, Tehseen. 'Science Fiction in Pakistan'. *The Salam Award for Imaginative Fiction*, 22 December 2016. http://thesalamaward.com/index.php/2016/12/22/science-fiction-in-pakistan/.

Baweja, Tehseen. 'I Set up the Salam Award to Encourage Creativity in Pakistan'. *Dawn*, 24 February 2017. https://images.dawn.com/news/1177142.

Baweja, Tehseen. 'Advisors'. *The Salam Award for Imaginative Fiction*. Accessed 16 June 2018. http://thesalamaward.com/index.php/the-award/advisors/.

Baweja, Tehseen. 'Rules'. *The Salam Award for Imaginative Fiction*. Accessed 16 June 2018. http://thesalamaward.com/index.php/rules/.

Bazykine, Victor. 'The New Science of Astro-Botany'. *South African Journal of Science* 56, no. 10 (1960): 229–31.

BBC. 'Zeki Okar (1954–2008)'. *BBC Turkish*, 21 March 2008. http://www.bbc.co.uk/turkish/news/story/2008/03/080317_zekiokar_obit.shtml.

BBC. 'Key al-Qaeda Leader "Killed in Afghanistan"'. *BBC News*, 8 October 2019. https://www.bbc.com/news/world-asia-49970353.

bdnews24.com. 'Don't Hurt Him, Check If He Is My Student: Zafar Iqbal on Attacker'. *bdnews24.com*, 4 March 2018. https://bdnews24.com/bangladesh/2018/03/04/dont-hurt-him-check-if-he-is-my-student-zafar-iqbal-on-attacker.

bdnews24.com. 'Police Couldn't Have Prevented Attack, says Yasmeen Haque'. *bdnews24.com*, 4 March 2018. https://bdnews24.com/bangladesh/2018/03/04/police-couldnt-have-prevented-attack-says-yasmeen-haque.

Bhatia, Gautam. 'An Interview with Doctor Hosam El-Zembely'. *Strange Horizons*, 28 January 2019. http://strangehorizons.com/non-fiction/an-interview-with-doctor-hosam-el-zembely/.

Bīgānigān-i Bāstānī. 'Bīgānigān-i bāstānī'. *Ancient Aliens*, 7 May 2018. http://www.ancientaliens.ir/.

Bilim Araştırma Merkezi. *Dünya Öğretmeni ve Altın Çağ Rehberliği*. Istanbul: Bilim Araştırma Merkezi, 1978.

Bilim Araştırma Merkezi. *Dünya Yapısı Uçan Daireler*. Istanbul: Bilim Araştırma Merkezi, 1981.

Bilim Araştırma Merkezi. *İnsan ve Kehanet: Kanıtlı Öngörümler*. Istanbul: Bilim Araştırma Merkezi, 1979.

Bilim Araştırma Grubu. *Kozmos'dan Dünyalılara: Ummo Planeti Misyonu*. Istanbul: Bilim Araştırma Merkezi, 1978.

Bilim Araştırma Merkezi. *Sirius Misyonu: Bildirge*. Istanbul: Bilim Araştırma Merkezi, 1979.

Bilim Araştırma Merkezi. *Spektra ve Urı Geller: Hoova Planeti Misyonu*. Istanbul: Bilim Araştırma Merkezi, 1978.

Bilim Araştırma Merkezi. *Uzaylılar: Genel Bilgiler*. Istanbul: Bilim Araştırma Merkezi, 1978.

Bilim Araştırma Merkezi. *Vimana: Tarih-Öncesi Uzay Araçları*. Istanbul: Bilim Araştırma Merkezi, 1980.

Birnbaum, Sarah. 'Iranian Scientist Who Accepted Oscar Says US Is Turning Away the Best and Brightest'. *Public Radio International*, 28 February 2017. https://www.pri.

org/stories/2017-02-27/iranian-scientist-who-accepted-oscar-says-us-turning-away-best-and-brightest.

Blaber, Phillippa, and Angélique Verrecchia. 'Cassini-Huygens: Preventing Biological Contamination'. *Space Safety Magazine*, 3 April 2014. http://www.spacesafetymagazine.com/space-exploration/extraterrestrial-life/cassini-huygens-preventing-biological-contamination/.

Blasim, Hassan, ed. *Iraq+100: Stories from a Century after the Invasion*. Manchester: Comma Press, 2016.

Brackett, Charles A., Gee-Kung Chang, and Muhammed Z. Iqbal. 'System for Wavelength Division Multiplexing/Asynchronous Transfer Mode Switching for Network Communication'. US patent number 5,550,818, filed 19 September 1994 and issued 27 August 1996.

Brādbūrī, Rāy. *451 fahrinhāyt*. Translated by Aḥmad Khālid Tawfīq. Al-Qāhirah: al-Muʾassasah al-ʿArabīyah al-Ḥadīthah, n.d.

Breitsameter, Sophie. 'In Conversation with New York-based Pakistani Artist Saks Afridi'. *Baku Magazine*, 25 June 2018. https://baku-magazine.com/art/sci-fi-sufi-the-art-of-saks-afridi/.

Brumfiel, Geoff. 'Publishers Split over Response to US Trade Embargo Ruling'. *Nature* 427 (2004): 663.

Buratti, B. J., P. C. Thomas, Elias Roussos, C. Howett, M. Seiß, A. R. Hendrix, P. Helfenstein, et al. 'Close Cassini Flybys of Saturn's Ring Moons Pan, Daphnis, Atlas, Pandora, and Epimetheus'. *Science* 364, no. 6445 (2019).

Chalk, Andy. 'ET Armies, a Sci-fi FPS Developed in Iran, is Coming to Steam'. *PC Gamer*, 17 February 2016. https://www.pcgamer.com/et-armies-a-sci-fi-fps-developed-in-iran-is-coming-to-steam/.

Chong, Gabriel, and Valerie Soo. 'Meet the Scientist: Datuk Dr. Mazlan Othman'. *Scientific Malaysian* 6 (30 December 2013). http://magazine.scientificmalaysian.com/issue-6-2013/interview-datuk-dr-mazlan-othman.

Chowdhury, Dwoha. 'It Bears Hallmarks of Ansar al Islam'. *Daily Star*, 5 March 2018. http://www.thedailystar.net/frontpage/attack-renowned-professor-dr-muhammad-zafar-iqbal-hallmarks-ansar-al-islam-there-1543534.

Çorak, Vedia Bülent (Önsü). *The Knowledge Book*. Second edition. İstanbul: World Brotherhood Union Mevlana Supreme Foundation, 1998.

Creighton, Gordon. 'A Brief Account of the True Nature of the UFO Entities'. *Flying Saucer Review* 29, no. 1 (1983): 2–6.

Creighton, Gordon. 'We Shall See the Four Horsemen'. *Flying Saucer Review* 36, no. 2 (1991): 1–2.

Creighton, Gordon. 'UFOs Photographed in Iran (1988)'. *Flying Saucer Review* 36, no. 4 (1991): 12–14.

Creighton, Gordon. 'Countdown to Satanic Victory?' *Flying Saucer Review* 37, no. 1 (1992): 1.

Cunningham, Joel. 'The Best Science Fiction & Fantasy Collections and Anthologies of 2016'. *The B&N Sci-Fi and Fantasy Blog*, 21 December 2016. https://www.

barnesandnoble.com/blog/sci-fi-fantasy/best-science-fiction-fantasy-collections-anthologies-2016/.

Daily Star. 'Zafar Iqbal Slams Media'. *Daily Star*, 5 January 2014. http://www.thedailystar.net/zafar-iqbal-slams-media-5496.

Daily Star. 'Attack on Zafar Iqbal: Protest Spread Countrywide'. *Daily Star*, 4 March 2018. http://www.thedailystar.net/country/attack-on-professor-dr-muhammad-zafar-iqbal-sust-students-continue-protest-1543291.

Daily Star. 'Zafar Iqbal's Attackers are Fanatics: PM'. *Daily Star*, 4 March 2018. http://www.thedailystar.net/country/professor-dr-muhammed-zafar-iqbal-attackers-are-fanatics-says-bangladesh-prime-minister-sheikh-hasina-1543300.

D'Angelo, Chris. 'New "Tatooine" Discovery Confirms Circumbinary Planets Aren't Just Science Fiction'. *Huffington Post*, 14 August 2015. http://www.huffingtonpost.com/entry/a-10th-tatoonine-discovered_us_55cccfc1e4b064d5910ac23a.

Däniken, Erich von. *Zurück zu den Sternen: Argumente für das Unmögliche*. Düsseldorf: Econ, 1969.

Däniken, Erich von. *Tanrıların Arabaları*. Translated by Zeki Okar. Tenth edition. İstanbul: Milliyet Yayınları, 1973.

Däniken, Erich von. *Yıldızlara Dönüş*. Translated by Zeki Okar. İstanbul: Milliyet Yayınları, 1974.

Däniken, Erich von. *Tanrının Ayak İzleri*. Translated by Halit Kakınç. Fourth edition. İstanbul: Cep, 1984.

Däniken, Erich von. *Yoksa Yanıldım Mı? (Gelecekten Taze Anılar)*. Translated by Halit Kakınç and Esat Nermi. Fifth edition. İstanbul: Cep, 1988.

Däniken, Erich von. *Tanrıların Arabaları*. Translated by Zeki Okar. Seventieth edition. İstanbul: Cep, 1997.

Däniken, Erich von. *Yıldızlara Dönüş*. Translated by Zeki Okar. Sixth edition. İstanbul: Cep, 1999.

Danīkin, Irīk fūn. *Arrābah-i khudāyān*. Translated by Muḥammad ʿAlī Najafī. Third edition. Tihrān: Andīshah, 1979.

Danīkin, Irīk fūn. *Asrār-i ahrām-i Miṣr (shawkah-i khudāyān)*. Translated by Qadīr Gulkāriyān. Tihrān: Intishārāt-i ʿIlmī, 1996.

Dānīkin, Irīk fūn. *Ilah'hā-yi guẕashtagān*. Translated by Humāyūn Khurram and Riẕā Rāmiz. Muʾassasah-'i Farhangī-i Intishārātī-i Muḥsinī, 1996.

Danīkin, Irīk fūn. *Yādgārān-i guẕashtah*. Translated by Qadīr Gulkāriyān. Tihrān: Intishārāt-i ʿIlmī, 1997.

Dānīkin, Irīk vun. *Arrābah-i khudāyān*. Translated by Siyāmāk Būdā. Fifth edition. Jāvīdān, 1983.

Dāwud, Muḥammad ʿĪsá. *Uḥdhurū al-Masīkh al-Dajjāl yaghzū al-ʿālam min muthallath Birmūdā*. Al-Qāhirah: al-Mukhtār al-Islāmī, 1991.

Dāwud, Muḥammad ʿĪsá. *Al-khuyūṭ al-khafīyah bayna al-Masīkh al-Dajjāl wa-asrār muthallath Birmūdā wa-al-aṭbāq al-ṭāʾirah*. Al-Qāhirah: Dār al-Bashīr, 1994.

Dāwudī, Abū al-Ḥasan. *Man Zamīn rā dūst dāram* (Sīnāfīlm, 1994).

Dietz, Stephanie. 'Centering Muslim Black Women in Sci-Fi Art'. *Griots Republic*, 6 July 2017. http://www.griotsrepublic.com/farhiya-jama/.

Djokolelono. *Jatuh ke Matahari*. Jakarta: Pustaka Jaya, 1976.

Donnelly, Erin. '"Star Trek" Costume with Hijab Sparks Debate: "You Bet I'm Islamifying These Looks"'. *Yahoo!*, 25 July 2019. https://www.yahoo.com/entertainment/star-trek-hijab-cosplay-geordi-laforge-185148207.html.

Duru, Orhan. *Sarmal: Toplu Öyküler*. İstanbul: Yapı Kredi Yayınları, 1996.

Dutta, Amrita. 'The Return of X-2'. *Indian Express*, 24 April 2011. http://indianexpress.com/article/news-archive/web/the-return-of-x2/.

El-Mohtar, Amal. '"Iraq + 100" Is Painful, But Don't Look Away'. *NPR*, 10 December 2016. https://www.npr.org/2016/12/10/503068002/iraq-100-is-painful-but-dont-look-away.

Elyta, Riawani, and Syila Fatar. *Gerbang Trinil*. Jakarta: Moka Media, 2014.

Erçin, Orhan. *Uçan Daireler İstanbul'da* (Birsel Film, 1955).

Erkoyun, Ezgi. 'Turkish Police Arrest TV Preacher and Followers Accused of Fraud, Sexual Abuse'. *Reuters*, 11 July 2018. https://www.reuters.com/article/us-turkey-security-operation/turkish-police-launch-raids-to-detain-islamic-figure-followers-media-idUSKBN1K10GT.

Express Tribune. 'SOS: Aliens to Attack Pakistan in Saeed Rizvi's Next'. *Express Tribune*, 20 October 2015. https://tribune.com.pk/story/976251/sos-aliens-to-attack-pakistan-in-saeed-rizvis-next/.

Fakhīmī, Maryam. 'Raqābat-i adabīyāt va hunar zīr-i chatr-i Nujūm'. *Nujūm*, no. 265 (2017): 48–49.

Fārūq, Nabīl. *Ikhtifāʾ ṣārūkh*. Al-Qāhirah: al-Muʾassasah al-ʿArabīyah al-Ḥadīthah, [c. 1985].

Fārūq, Nabīl. *Al-muqāwamah*. Al-Qāhirah: al-Muʾassasah al-ʿArabīyah al-Ḥadīthah, n.d.

Fārūq, Nabīl. *Al-naṣr*. Al-Qāhirah: al-Muʾassasah al-ʿArabīyah al-Ḥadīthah, n.d.

Fārūq, Nabīl. *Al-nubūʾah*. Al-Qāhirah: al-Muʾassasah al-ʿArabīyah al-Ḥadīthah, n.d.

Fārūq, Nabīl. *Al-tajribah al-rahībah wa-qiṣaṣ ukhrá*. Al-Qāhirah: al-Muʾassasah al-ʿArabīyah al-Ḥadīthah, n.d.

Fārūq, Nabīl. *Jaḥīm Arghūrān*. Al-Qāhirah: al-Muʾassasah al-ʿArabīyah al-Ḥadīthah, n.d.

Fārūq, Nabīl. *Maʿrakat al-kawākib*. Al-Qāhirah: al-Muʾassasah al-ʿArabīyah al-Ḥadīthah, n.d.

Fārūq, Nabīl. *Sijn al-Qamar*. Al-Qāhirah: al-Muʾassasah al-ʿArabīyah al-Ḥadīthah, n.d.

Fārūq, Nabīl. *Rajul al-mustaḥīl wa-anā*. al-Duqqī: Dār Līlá, 1998.

Fārūq, Nabīl. 'Al-abnāʾ yuʿallimūn al-ābāʾ!' *Al-Hilāl* 108, no. 9 (1999): 106–9.

Fārūq, Nabīl. 'Ḥarb qalam'. *Fuṣūl* 76 (2009): 22–27.

Fattahyani, Aryadad. 'To Mars and Beyond: Interview with Dr. Firouz Naderi, the Director Solar System Exploration at NASA JPL'. *Leonardo Times* 17, no. 3 (2013): 10–14.

Fawzī, Ḥusayn. *Nādūjā* (Naḥḥās Fīlm, 1944).

Fesenkov, V. G. 'Expedition of the Academy of Sciences of the USSR to Aswan, Egypt, for Observations of the Zodiacal Light and of the Optical Properties of the Atmosphere'. *Soviet Astronomy* 2 (1958): 276–85.

Fīrn, Jūl [see also Warn, Yūliyūs]. *Al-riḥlah al-ʿilmīyah fī qalb al-kurah al-Arḍīyah.* Translated by Iskandar Anṭūn ʿAmmūn. Al-Iskandarīyah: Maṭbaʿah Jarīdat al-Maḥrūsah, 1885.

Fliminj, Ayān. *Duktūr Nū*. Edited by Nabīl Fārūq. Al-Qāhirah: al-Muʾassasah al-ʿArabīyah al-Ḥadīthah, n.d.

Flying Saucer Review. 'Kuwait: Huge UFO Makes Silent Landing'. *Flying Saucer Review* 25, no. 2 (1979): 5.

Flying Saucer Review. 'A Turkish Religious Leader Speaks on UFOs'. *Flying Saucer Review* 30, no. 6 (1985): 25.

Flyn, Cal. 'The Best Contemporary Indonesian Literature Recommended by Dee Lestari'. *Five Books*, 2019. https://fivebooks.com/best-books/contemporary-indonesian-literature-dee-lestari/.

Fuʾād, Shaymāʾ. 'Ibnat al-riwāʾī Nihād Sharīf: Sūriyā naṣabat wālidī ʿamīd al-khayāl al-ʿilmī wa-ittiḥād al-kitāb tajāhalahu'. *Muḥīṭ*, 19 June 2013. http://m.moheet.com/2013/06/19/1783838/.

Garcia, Alfredo. 'The Accidental Dönmeh'. *Inspicio*, 2016. http://inspicio.fiu.edu/profiles/profiles-2016/the-accidental-donmeh/.

Gasworks. 'Interview with Monira Al Qadiri – The Craft at Gasworks'. *YouTube*, 28 March 2018. https://www.youtube.com/watch?v=LuTf73G_VRw.

Gezen, Müjdat. *Homoti* (Silverstar, 1987).

Ghaffārī, Mujtabá. 'Ākharīn ḥalqah-i bardigī'. *Nujūm* 267 (2018): 44–49.

Ghalayini, Basma, ed. *Palestine+100: Stories from a Century after the Nakba.* Manchester: Comma Press, 2019.

Ghānim, Zuhayr. 'Khayāl adab al-khayāl al-ʿilmī al-ʿArabī'. *Al-Khayāl al-ʿIlmī*, no. 1 (2008): 38–42.

Gillon, Michaël, Amaury H. M. J. Triaud, Brice-Olivier Demory, Emmanuël Jehin, Eric Agol, Katherine M. Deck, Susan M. Lederer, et al. 'Seven Temperate Terrestrial Planets around the Nearby Ultracool Dwarf Star TRAPPIST-1'. *Nature* 542, no. 7642 (2017): 456–60.

Guiley, Rosemary Ellen. *The Djinn Connection: The Hidden Links between Djinn, Shadow People, ETs, Nephilim, Archons, Reptilians and Other Entities*. New Milford: Visionary Living, 2013.

Guiley, Rosemary Ellen, and Philip J. Imbrogno. *The Vengeful Djinn: Unveiling the Hidden Agenda of Genies*. First edition, fifth printing. Woodbury: Llewellyn, 2017.

Güneyer, Tayfun. *Türk'ün Uzayla İmtihanı* 2 (2012).

Gupta, Supriya Das. 'India'. In *World Filmography, 1967*, edited by Peter Cowie and Derek Elley, 253–84. London: Tantivy, 1977.

Habib, Haroon. 'Popular Science Fiction Writer Zafar Iqbal Stabbed in Bangladesh'. *The Hindu*, 3 March 2018. http://www.thehindu.com/news/international/popular-science-fiction-writer-zafar-iqbal-stabbed-in-bangladesh/article22920210.ece.

Haghighipour, Nader. 'Resonance Lock and Planetary Dynamics'. PhD thesis, University of Missouri-Columbia, 1999.

Haghighipour, Nader. 'An Astronomical Thaw: A New Rise of Iranian Astronomy'. *American Astronomical Society*, 6 March 2016. https://aas.org/posts/story/2016/03/astronomical-thaw-new-rise-iranian-astronomy.

Haghighipour, Nader. 'Nader Haghighipour'. University of Hawai'i, 2016. https://www.ifa.hawaii.edu/users/nader/CV.pdf.

Haghighipour, Nader, Rudolf Dvorak, and Elke Pilat-Lohinger. 'Planetary Dynamics and Habitable Planet Formation in Binary Star Systems'. In *Planets in Binary Star Systems*, edited by Nader Haghighipour, 285–327. Dordrecht: Springer, 2010.

Hājārd, Rāydir. *Kunūz al-malik Sulaymān*. Edited by Nabīl Fārūq. Al-Qāhirah: al-Muʾassasah al-ʿArabīyah al-Ḥadīthah, n.d.

Hallowell, Billy. 'Farrakhan Begs for Big UFO Reveal: "President Barack Obama … Open Up Area 51"'. *TheBlaze*, 20 February 2014. https://www.theblaze.com/news/2014/02/20/farrakhan-begs-for-big-ufo-reveal-president-barack-obama-open-up-area-51.

Hamsho, Khaled. 'World Control by the Jinns'. *Flying Saucer Review* 30, no. 6 (1985): 29.

Hanania, Ray. 'UFOs Have Plagued the Arab World, Too'. *The Arab Daily News*, 21 January 2015. http://thearabdailynews.com/2015/01/21/ufos-plagued-arab-world/.

Handayani, Eliza V. *Area X: Hymne Angkasa Raya*. Bandung: DAR! Mizan, 2003.

Handayani, Eliza V. 'Tentang'. *Eliza Vitri Handayani*, 19 January 2014. https://elizavitri.com/tentang-biography/.

Handayani, Eliza V. 'A Bloody Past: On Censorship in Indonesia'. *Words Without Borders*, 17 December 2015. https://www.wordswithoutborders.org/dispatches/article/a-bloody-past-on-censorship-in-indonesia-eliza-vitri-handayani.

Handayani, Eliza V. 'Between Languages Between Worlds'. *Eliza Vitri Handayani*, 1 November 2016. https://elizavitri.com/2016/11/01/blbw/.

Handayani, Eliza V. 'Islam and I'. *Kill Your Darlings*, 31 July 2017, 51–57.

Hardin, Mary. 'JPL Names Naderi as New Head of Mars Program Office'. *Jet Propulsion Laboratory*, 7 April 2000. http://www.jpl.nasa.gov/news/news.php?feature=4944.

Hāynlāyn, Rūbirt. *Gharīb fī arḍ gharīb*. Translated by Aḥmad Khālid Tawfīq. Al-Qāhirah: al-Muʾassasah al-ʿArabīyah al-Ḥadīthah, n.d.

Henley, Jon. 'The Other Side of Baghdad'. *The Guardian*, 18 January 2008. https://www.theguardian.com/stage/2008/jan/18/theatre.

Holmes, Adam. 'The Real Reason Star Trek Beyond Decided to Shoot in Dubai'. *Cinemablend*, 14 December 2015. http://www.cinemablend.com/new/Real-Reason-Star-Trek-Beyond-Decided-Shoot-Dubai-99987.html.

Hoodbhoy, Pervez, and Stefano Bigliardi. 'Science Resolutely Refuses to Take Root in Muslim Countries'. *Newsline*, July 2017, 73–76.

Hsu, Hsiang-Wen, Jürgen Schmidt, Sascha Kempf, Frank Postberg, Georg Moragas-Klostermeyer, Martin Seiß, Holger Hoffmann, et al. 'In situ Collection of Dust Grains Falling from Saturn's Rings into its Atmosphere'. *Science* 362, no. 6410 (2018): 49.

Hubbard, Ben. 'Saudi Textbook Withdrawn over Image of Yoda with King'. *New York Times*, 21 September 2017. https://www.nytimes.com/2017/09/21/world/middleeast/saudi-yoda-king-textbooks.html.

Hürriyet Daily News. 'Antalya Film Fest Ends with Awards, Controversy'. *Hürriyet Daily News*, 8 December 2015. http://www.hurriyetdailynews.com/antalya-film-fest-ends-with-awards-controversy.aspx?pageID=238&nID=92176&NewsCatID=381.

Ḥūsh, Rāmiz. 'Zuwwār min al-faḍāʾ fī wathāʾiq tārīkhīyah'. *Al-Khayāl al-ʿIlmī*, no. 47 (2013): 148–51.

Ibn-i Ṣāfī. *Faẓāʾī hangāmah*. Lāhaur: Asrār, 1968.

Ibn-i Ṣāfī. *Zīrolenḍ kī talāsh*. Lāhaur: Asrār, 1978.

Ibn-i Ṣāfī. *Shūgar benk*. Lāhaur: Asrār, 2000.

Ibn-i Ṣāfī. *Thirīsiyā kī wāpsī*. Lāhaur: Asrār, n.d.

Ikabāla, Muham'mada Jāphara [see also Iqbal, Muhammed Zafar]. *Mahākāśe mahātrāsa*. Dhaka: Gyankosh, 1977.

Ikabāla, Muham'mada Jāphara [see also Iqbal, Muhammed Zafar]. *Trāitana ekti grahēra nāma*. Dhaka: Kakoli Prokashon, 1988.

Ikabāla, Muham'mada Jāphara [see also Iqbal, Muhammed Zafar]. *Nisḥanga grahachāri*. Dhaka: Somoy Prokashon, 1994.

Imarisha, Walidah. 'Right Rhyming'. *Philadelphia City Paper*, 8–15 February 2001.

Imbrogno, Philip J. *Interdimensional Universe: The New Science of UFOs, Paranormal Phenomena and Otherdimensional Beings*. Woodbury: Llewellyn, 2008.

International UFO Reporter. 'UFO Interest in Indonesia'. *International UFO Reporter* 1, no. 2 (1976).

İnanç, Çetin. *Dünyayı Kurtaran Adam* (Anıt, 1982).

ʿInāyat, Rājī. *Sirr al-aṭbāq al-ṭāʾirah*. Al-ṭabʿah al-sābiʿah. Bayrūt: Dār al-Shurūq, 1995.

Inquiry. 'Flying Saucer Domes, Rocket Minarets'. *Inquiry* 3, no. 7 (1986): 69–71.

Iqbal, Muhammed Zafar [see also Ikabāla, Muham'mada Jāphara]. 'Search for Parity Non-Conservation in the Hydrogen Atom'. PhD thesis, University of Washington, 1983.

Iqbal, Muhammed Zafar [see also Ikabāla, Muham'mada Jāphara]. 'Doing Science in Bangla'. *Daily Star*, 21 February 2004. http://www.thedailystar.net/suppliments/ekush04/ekush03.html#08.

Iran Computer and Video Games Foundation. 'Devil in Capital'. *Iran Computer and Video Games Foundation*, 2017. http://en.ircg.ir/game/26/Devil-in-Capital.

Iran Computer and Video Games Foundation. 'Footcardia'. *Iran Computer and Video Games Foundation*, 2017. http://en.ircg.ir/game/7/Footcardia.

Iran Computer and Video Games Foundation. 'The Look of Evil'. *Iran Computer and Video Games Foundation*, 2017. http://en.ircg.ir/game/17/The-Look-of-Evil.

Iranian Students' News Agency. 'Anjuman-i Fīzīk-i Īrān bah bihtarīn dāstān-i ʿilmī takhayyulī sāl jāyizah mī dahad'. *Iranian Students' News Agency*, 29 September 2004. https://www.isna.ir/news/8307-03280/.

Iranian Students' News Agency. 'Musābaqah-i naqqāshī va dāstān-i ʿilmī takhayyulī bā mawẕūʿ-i nujūm va faẓā bargozār mī shavad'. *Iranian Students' News Agency*, 19 July 2017. https://www.isna.ir/news/96042816645/.

Īrfinj, Wāshinjtūn. *Usṭūrat Slībī Hūlū*. Translated by Aḥmad Khālid Tawfīq. Al-Qāhirah: al-Muʾassasah al-ʿArabīyah al-Ḥadīthah, n.d.

Islam Online. 'Book Review: Islamic Science Fiction'. *Islam Online* [c. 2000]. https://archive.islamonline.net/?p=1156.

Ismāʿīl, Yaḥyá. 'Al-aṭbāq al-ṭāʾirah'. *Al-Thaqāfah*, no. 70 (17 November 1964): 38–39.

Istrībir, Vāyitlī. *Asrār-i busqāb'hā-yi parandah yū. if. aw*. Translated by Dāriyūsh Adīb. Yādvārah-'i Kitāb, 1991.

Jaini, Azrul. *Galaksi Muhsinin*. Selangor: PTS, 2008.

Jaini, Azrul. 'Saifaiislami: Mukadimah'. *Saifai Islami*, 3 September 2008. http://saifaiislami.blogspot.com/2008/09/saifaiislami-mukadimah.html.

Jaini, Azrul. 'Siapakah Liga Lanun?' *Saifai Islami*, 7 September 2008. http://saifaiislami.blogspot.com/2008/09/siapakah-liga-lanun.html.

Jaini, Azrul. 'Pejuang Angkasa Galaksi Muhsinin: Ababil'. *Saifai Islami*, 13 September 2008. http://saifaiislami.blogspot.com/2008/09/pejuang-angkasa-galaksi-muhsinin-ababil.html.

Jaini, Azrul. '[GM] Mujahidin Galaksi Muhsinin'. *Saifai Islami*, 23 September 2008. http://saifaiislami.blogspot.com/2008/09/infantri-galaksi-muhsinin.html.

Jaini, Azrul. '[GM] Hologram Hijrah'. *Saifai Islami*, 28 October 2008. http://saifaiislami.blogspot.com/2008/10/gm-hologram-hijrah.html.

Jaini, Azrul. '[ESC] Algoritma TAQWA (3) – Penghabisan'. *Saifai Islami*, 26 November 2008. http://saifaiislami.blogspot.com/2008/11/baik-engkau-menyerah-cyborg-tentu-litar.html.

Jaini, Azrul. '[GM] Aadiyat Ad-100'. *Saifai Islami*, 15 December 2008. http://saifaiislami.blogspot.com/2008/12/gm-aadiyat.html.

Jaini, Azrul. 'Cerpen Latar GM: Kembalinya Militia Zion (1)'. *Saifai Islami*, 26 June 2010. http://saifaiislami.blogspot.com/2010/06/cerpen-latar-gm-kembalinya-militia-zion.html.

Jalal, Maán. 'These Guys Know Their Aliens'. *Khaleej Times*, 26 June 2016. http://www.khaleejtimes.com/these-guys-know-their-aliens.

Jamaludin, Ahmad. 'Humanoid Encounters in Malaysia'. *MUFON UFO Journal*, no. 141 (1979): 7–9.

Jamaludin, Ahmad. 'Tales from Malaysia'. *Fortean Times* 35 (1981): 30–32.

Jamaludin, Ahmad. 'The Malaysian UFO Scene: A Further Report'. *Flying Saucer Review* 30, no. 5 (1985): 10–12.

Janmohamed, Shelina. 'From Mosques on Mars to Meeting Martians: The Dilemmas Awaiting Muslims in Space'. *The National*, 16 August 2018. https://www.thenational.ae/opinion/comment/from-mosques-on-mars-to-meeting-martians-the-dilemmas-awaiting-muslims-in-space-1.760585.

Jawharī, Ṭanṭāwī. *Al-jawāhir fī tafsīr al-Qur'ān al-karīm*. Al-Ṭab'ah al-Thāniyah. Vol. 1. Miṣr: Maṭba'at Muṣṭafá al-Bābī al-Ḥalabī wa-Awlādihī, 1932.

Jawharī, Ṭanṭāwī. *Al-aḥlām fī al-siyāsah wa-kayfa yataḥaqqaq al-salām al-'āmm*. Miṣr: Maṭba'at Muṣṭafá al-Bābī al-Ḥalabī wa-Awlādihī, 1935.

Johnson, Michelle. '*World Literature Today*'s 75 Notable Translations of 2016'. *World Literature Today*, 12 December 2016. https://www.worldliteraturetoday.org/blog/lit-lists/world-literature-todays-75-notable-translations-2016.

Jovanovic, Dragana. '"This is a Historic Moment": "Black Panther" Breaks Saudi's 35-year Cinema Ban with Men, Women Seated Together'. *ABC News*, 19 April 2018. https://abcnews.go.com/International/black-panther-break-saudi-arabias-35-year-cinema/story?id=54333816.

Jum'ah, al-Sayyid Ḥasan. 'Al-sīnimā al-nāṭiqah: māḍīhā wa-ḥāḍiruhā wa-mustaqbaluhā'. *Al-Hilāl* 38, no. 2 (1929): 219–22.

Jum'ah, al-Sayyid Ḥasan. 'Al-sīnimā fī khidmat al-adyān: tamthīl qiṣaṣ al-kutub al-muqaddasah 'alá al-lawḥah al-fiḍḍīyah'. *Al-Hilāl* 38, no. 6 (1930): 682–88.

Jum'ah, al-Sayyid Ḥasan. 'Al-thaqāfah al-sīnimā'īyah wa-atharuhā fī al-'ālam'. *Al-Hilāl* 39, no. 4 (1931): 577–84.

Jum'ah, al-Sayyid Ḥasan. ''Arūs min al-Mirrīkh'. *Al-Hilāl* 58, no. 1 (1950): 137–46.

Jum'ah, al-Sayyid Ḥasan. 'Alf laylah wa-laylah 'alá al-shāshah al-bayḍā''. *Al-Hilāl* 60, no. 10 (1952): 95–100.

Junaidi, A. 'Dewi "Dee" Lestari: Love, Spirituality and Ecology'. *Jakarta Post*, 2 April 2006. http://www.thejakartapost.com/news/2006/04/02/dewi-039dee039-lestari-love-spirituality-and-ecology.html.

Jurado, Cristina. 'An Interview with Noura Al Noman'. *The World SF Blog*, 25 March 2013. https://worldsf.wordpress.com/2013/03/25/monday-original-content-an-interview-with-noura-al-noman/.

Jurdāq, Manṣūr Ḥannā. 'Tura' al-Mirrīkh wa-al-ḥayāt fīhi'. *Al-Muqtaṭaf* 33, no. 2 (1908): 107–13.

Kains, N., R. A. Street, J.-Y. Choi, C. Han, A. Udalski, L. A. Almeida, F. Jablonski, et al. 'A Giant Planet beyond the Snow Line in Microlensing Event OGLE-2011-BLG-0251'. *Astronomy & Astrophysics* 552 (2013): A70.

Kaplan, Ilana. 'Man Booker Prize International 2018 Shortlist Announced'. *The Independent*, 12 April 2018. https://www.independent.co.uk/arts-entertainment/books/news/man-booker-prize-international-shortlist-2018-nominees-white-book-world-goes-on-a8302126.html.

Karaçelik, Tolga. *Sarmaşık* (M3 Film, 2015).

Kay, Jeremy. 'Comic-Con: Qatari Showrunner Ahmed Al Baker Talks 'Medinah''. *Screen Daily*, 24 July 2017. https://www.screendaily.com/features/-comic-con-qatari-showrunner-ahmed-al-baker-talks-medinah/5120238.article.

Kaya, Cem. *Remake, Remix, Rip-Off: About Copy Culture & Turkish Pop Cinema* (2014).

Kazantsev, Alexander. 'A Visitor from Outer Space'. In *A Visitor from Outer Space: Science-Fiction Stories by Soviet Writers*, 110–48. Moscow: Foreign Languages Publishing House [1960s?].

Kazantsev, Alexander. 'Explosion: The Story of a Hypothesis'. In *Red Star Tales: A Century of Russian and Soviet Science Fiction*, edited by Yvonne Howell, translated by Nora Seligman Favorov, 224–52. Montpelier: Russian Life, 2015.

Khan, Saadeqa. 'Pakistan's Man on the Mission to Enceladus'. *Dawn*, 1 July 2018. https://www.dawn.com/news/1417071.

Khawaja, Nozair A. 'Organic Compounds in Saturn's E-ring and its Compositional Profile in the Vicinity of Rhea'. Dissertation, Ruprecht-Karls-Universität Heidelberg, 2016.

Khiḍr, ʿAbbās. 'Al-adab wa-al-fann fī usbūʿ'. *Al-Risālah*, no. 945 (1951): 926–29.

Khurram, Humāyūn, and Riẓā Rāmiz. *Yawgā darmānī*. Tihrān: Muḥsinī, 1997.

Khurram, Humāyūn, and Riẓā Rāmiz. *Āmūzish-i inirzhī darmānī: āshnāyī nīrūhā-yi shafābakhsh-i insān*. Tihrān: Muḥsinī, 1999.

Kibria, Asjadul. 'Masud Rana's Qazi Anwar Husain'. *The Financial Express*, 21 July 2018. https://thefinancialexpress.com.bd/views/masud-ranas-qazi-anwar-husain-1532167407.

Kīnj, Stīfin. *Al-shayṭānah*. Translated by Aḥmad Khālid Tawfīq. Al-Qāhirah: al-Muʾassasah al-ʿArabīyah al-Ḥadīthah, n.d.

Klārk, Arthar. 'Sa-nusāfir ilá al-Qamar'. *Al-Hilāl* 58, no. 1 (1950): 97–100.

Klārk, Arthar. *Ūdīsā al-faḍāʾ*. Translated by Aḥmad Khālid Tawfīq. Al-Qāhirah: al-Muʾassasah al-ʿArabīyah al-Ḥadīthah, n.d.

Köhler, Fabian. '"No One Bombs for Peace": Syrian Artist Describes Life at War'. *Televisión del Sur*, 21 October 2016. http://www.telesurtv.net/english/opinion/No-One-Bombs-for-Peace-Syrian-Artist-Describes-Life-at-War-20161020-0021.html.

Kosemen, C. M. *All Tomorrows*, 2004.

Kosemen, C. M. 'Frequently Asked Questions.' *Snaiad*, 2014. https://canopy.uc.edu/bbcswebdav/users/gibsonic/Snaiad/sndfaq.html.

Kosemen, C. M. 'Life on Snaiad'. *Snaiad*, 2014. https://canopy.uc.edu/bbcswebdav/users/gibsonic/Snaiad/sndallclades.html.

Kosemen, C. M. 'Links'. *Snaiad*, 2014. https://canopy.uc.edu/bbcswebdav/users/gibsonic/Snaiad/sndlinks.html.

Kosemen, C. M. 'Snaiad: Life on Another World'. *Snaiad*, July 2014. https://canopy.uc.edu/bbcswebdav/users/gibsonic/Snaiad/snduterus.html.

Kosemen, C. M. *Osman Hasan and the Tombstone Photographs of the Dönmes*. Second edition. İstanbul: Libra, 2015.

Kosemen, C. M. *Tangent Worlds*. Second edition. 2016.

Kosemen, C. M. 'CV'. C. *M. Kosemen*. Accessed 17 March 2018.

Kreis, Alex. 'Calligraphy'. In *Islamicates Volume I: Anthology of Science Fiction Short Stories Inspired from Muslim Cultures*, edited by Muhammad Aurangzeb Ahmad, 1–10. Lahore: Mirza Book Agency, 2016.

Krich, John. '"Star Wars" as a Shadow Play'. *Wall Street Journal*, 3 July 2014. https://www.wsj.com/articles/star-wars-as-a-shadow-play-1404383321.

Krishtūn, Māykil. *Sulālat Andrūmīdā*. Translated by Aḥmad Khālid Tawfīq. Al-Qāhirah: al-Muʾassasah al-ʿArabīyah al-Ḥadīthah [c. 1995].

Kronk, Gary W., and Maik Meyer. *Cometography: A Catalog of Comets*. Vol. 5. Cambridge: Cambridge University Press, 2010.

Kunak, Göksu. 'An Interview with Monira Al Qadiri'. *Berlin Art Link*, 14 June 2015. http://www.berlinartlink.com/2015/06/14/artfeminism-an-interview-with-monira-al-qadiri/.

Kutyreva, A. P., B. B. Intykbayeva, and Zh. Kuatova. 'Characteristics of the Optical Properties of Alpine Plants of Eastern Pamir'. In *Observations of the Moon, Mars, Uranus, and the Stars: Optical Properties of Plants*, edited by G. A. Tikhov, 74–121. Washington: National Aeronautics and Space Administration, 1966.

Laswd, Amar Abdusalam. 'Studies in Relation to the Possible Extraterrestrial Origin of Bacteria'. PhD thesis, University of Sheffield, 2008.

Lawrence, T. E. *Lawrence of Arabia: Seven Pillars of Wisdom*. Norwalk: Easton, 1992.

Lestari, Dee. *Supernova Episode: Partikel*. Yogyakarta: Bentang, 2012.

Lestari, Dee. 'Partikel (Supernova #4)'. *Goodreads*. Accessed 31 July 2019. https://www.goodreads.com/book/show/13582635-partikel.

Lestari, Dewi. *Supernova: The Knight, The Princess and the Falling Star*. Translated by Harry Aveling. Jakarta: Lontar Foundation, 2011.

Nawfal, ʿAbd al-Razzāq. *Al-samāʾ wa-ahl al-samāʾ*. Al-Qāhirah: al-Shaʿb, 1969.

Nawfal, ʿAbd al-Razzāq. *Allāh wa-al-ʿilm al-ḥadīth*. Ṭabʿah jadīdah. Al-Qāhirah: Dār al-Shurūq, 1998.

Lūkās, Jūrj. *Ḥarb al-nujūm*. Edited by Nabīl Fārūq. Translated by Īnās al-Najjār. Al-Qāhirah: al-Muʾassasah al-ʿArabīyah al-Ḥadīthah, n.d.

Maack, Benjamin. 'Türkische B-Movies: Süpertrash aus Hüllywood'. *Spiegel Online*, 27 April 2012. http://www.spiegel.de/einestages/tuerkische-b-movies-a-947563.html.

Maʿāṭī, Ṣalāḥ. 'Nihād Sharīf qāhir al-zaman'. *Al-Khayāl al-ʿIlmī*, no. 34 (2011): 12–25.

Maʿāṭī, Ṣalāḥ. 'Rajul zādahu al-khayāl /1-2/'. *Al-Khayāl al-ʿIlmī*, no. 46 (2013): 78–89.

Maestrone, Frank E. '"UFO" Sightings Cause Security Concern in Kuwait'. *WikiLeaks*, 29 January 1979. https://wikileaks.org/plusd/cables/1979KUWAIT00486_e.html.

Mahmud, Faisal. 'Bangladesh: Why was Science Fiction Writer Zafar Iqbal Attacked?' *Al Jazeera*, 13 March 2018. https://www.aljazeera.com/indepth/features/bangladesh-science-fiction-writer-zafar-iqbal-attacked-180313093958357.html.

Mahmud, Faisal. 'Explaining the Attack on Zafar Iqbal, One of Bangladesh's Top Academics'. *The Wire*, 15 March 2018. https://thewire.in/south-asia/explaining-the-attack-on-zafar-iqbal-one-of-bangladeshs-top-academics.

Maillet, Benoît de. *Telliamed ou Entretiens d'un Philosophe Indien avec un Missionnaire François sur la Diminution de la Mer, la Formation de la Terre, l'Origine de l'Homme, & c.* Vol. 1. Amsterdam: L'honoré & Fils, 1748.

Maillet, Benoît de. *Telliamed; Or, the World Explain'd; Containing Discourses between an Indian Philosopher and a Missionary, on the Diminution of the Sea, the Formation of the Earth, the Origin of Men & Animals: And Other Singular Subjects, Relating to Natural History & Philosophy*. Baltimore: D. Porter, 1797.

Malik, Candra. 'Dewi "Dee" Lestari Finds Her Freedom'. *Jakarta Globe*, 25 July 2011. http://www.thejakartaglobe.com/lifeandtimes/dewi-dee-lestari-finds-her-freedom/455142.

Malik, Sarah. 'Navigating Sex, Politics and #metoo in Indonesian Literature'. *Topics*, 23 January 2018. https://www.sbs.com.au/topics/life/culture/article/2018/01/11/navigating-sex-politics-and-metoo-indonesian-literature.

Mansouri, Reza. 'Impact of Sanctions Regime on Science and Scientists'. Presentation at the research round-table on Science and Scientific Production in the Middle East, Georgetown University Qatar, 22 February 2018.

Manṣūr, Anīs. *Alladhīna habaṭū min al-samā'*. Al-Qāhirah; Bayrūt: Dār al-Shurūq, 1971.

Manṣūr, Anīs. *Alladhīna ʿādū ilá al-samā'*. Al-Qāhirah: Dār al-Shurūq, 1977.

Manṣūr, Anīs. *Alladhīna habaṭū min al-samā'*. Al-ṭabʿah al-thāminah ʿasharah. Al-Qāhirah: Dār al-Shurūq, 2001.

Manṣūr, Anīs. *Alladhīna ʿādū ilá al-samā'*. Al-ṭabʿah al-khāmisah ʿasharah. Al-Qāhirah: Dār al-Shurūq, 2003.

Maqsood, Maham. 'A Talk with Dr. Fariha Hasan about Astrobiology and Career'. *Scientia*, 26 January 2019. https://scientiamag.org/a-talk-with-dr-fariha-hasan-about-astrobiology-and-career/.

Marrāsh, Fransīs Fatḥ Allāh. *Shahādat al-ṭabīʿah fī wujūd Allāh wa-al-sharīʿah*. Bayrūt: Maṭbaʿat al-Amrīkān, 1892.

Maududi, Sayyid Abul Ala. '65. Surah At Talaq (Divorce)'. *Tafhim al-Qur'an – The Meaning of the Qur'an*, 2009. http://www.englishtafsir.com/quran/65/index.html.

Mazhar, Parvaiz, and Saadia Qamar. 'Saeed Rizvi Steps up his Game in Film-making'. *Express Tribune*, 11 March 2014. https://tribune.com.pk/story/681489/saeed-rizvi-steps-up-his-game-in-film-making/.

McLellan, Dennis. 'Reza Badiyi Dies at 81; Prolific TV Director'. *Los Angeles Times*, 22 August 2011. http://articles.latimes.com/2011/aug/22/local/la-me-reza-badiyi-20110822.

Medinah Show Uncut. 'About'. *Medinah Show Uncut*, 4 March 2016. https://arabtelemediauncut.net/about-this-blog/.

Merchant, Brian. 'Dubai's First Sci-Fi Film Is a Reminder That Dubai Itself Is Not Actually Science Fiction'. *Motherboard*, 30 April 2013. https://motherboard.vice.com/en_us/article/jpp3zk/dubais-first-sci-fi-film-a-reminder-that-dubai-is-real.

Mimouni, Jamal, and Nidhal Guessoum. 'Islam and Extraterrestrial Life'. *Islam & Science*, 16 January 2015. http://islam-science.net/islam-and-extraterrestrial-life-2908/.

Miyake, N., T. Sumi, Subo Dong, R. Street, L. Mancini, A. Gould, D. P. Bennett, et al. 'A Sub-Saturn Mass Planet, MOA-2009-BLG-319Lb'. *Astrophysical Journal* 728, no. 2 (2011): 120.

Mizrāḥī, Tūjū. *Alf laylah wa-laylah*. Al-Qawmīyah lil-Tawzīʿ wa-al-Tijārah, 1941.

Mizrāḥī, Tūjū. *ʿAlī Bābā wa-al-arbaʿīn ḥarāmī*. Al-Qawmīyah lil-Tawzīʿ wa-al-Tijārah, 1942.

Monir, Alexandra. 'Author's Note: The Science of The Final Six'. *Alexandra Monir*, 1 March 2018. https://www.alexandramonir.com/the-final-six/authors-note-science-of-the-final-six/.

Morayef, Soraya. 'Arab Science Fiction: Thriving Yet Underappreciated'. *Al-Fanar Media*, 1 December 2014. http://www.al-fanarmedia.org/2014/12/arab-science-fiction-thriving-yet-underappreciated/.

Morgan, Cheryl. 'A Conversation with Ahmed Khaled Towfik'. *Locus* 68, no. 3 (2012): 28.

Muftāḥ, Maḥmūd ʿAbd al-Raḥmān. *Al-samāʾ wa-al-aṭbāq al-ṭāʾirah*. Al-Dawḥah: Maṭābiʿ ʿAlī ibn ʿAlī, 1985.

Muraki, Y., C. Han, D. P. Bennett, D. Suzuki, L. A. G. Monard, R. Street, U. G. Jorgensen, et al. 'Discovery and Mass Measurements of a Cold, 10 Earth Mass Planet and Its Host Star'. *Astrophysical Journal* 741, no. 1 (2011): 22.

Muṣṭafá, Niyāzī. *Ṭāqiyat al-ikhfāʾ* (Naḥḥās Fīlm, 1944).

Muṣṭafá, Niyāzī. *Min ayna laka hādhā?* (Bahnā Fīlm, 1952).

Muṣṭafá, Niyāzī. *Sirr ṭāqiyat al-ikhfāʾ* (Al-Sharq lil-Tawzīʿ, 1959).

Naderi, Firouz. 'Estimation and Detection of Images Degraded by Film-Grain Noise'. PhD thesis, University of Southern California, 1976.

Naderi, Firouz. 'NASA's Origins Program: The Search for Our Cosmic Roots and, … … Galactic Cousins'. *Jet Propulsion Laboratory*, 1999.

Naderi, Firouz. *Facebook*, 2 March 2017. https://www.facebook.com/firouz.naderi.9/posts/10208945915150751.

Naderi, F., and A. A. Sawchuk. 'Detection of Low-Contrast Images in Film-Grain Noise'. *Applied Optics* 17, no. 18 (1978): 2883–91.

Nar, Ali. *Uzay Çiftçileri*. İstanbul: Elif Yayınları, 1988.

Naṣīr, Shādī. 'Liqāʾ maʿa al-duktūr Ṭālib ʿUmrān'. *ʿĀlam Nūḥ*, May 2012.

Neidich, Scott. 'Why the Star Trek films are the Wrong Place for the Hijab'. *Medium*, 3 August 2017. https://medium.com/@sdneidich/why-the-star-trek-films-are-the-wrong-place-for-the-hijab-1be3804b2abe.

Newbould, Chris. 'Aerial Assault: New Emirati Sci-Fi Drama Invades Cinemas'. *The National*, 19 June 2016. https://www.thenational.ae/arts-culture/aerial-assault-new-emirati-sci-fi-drama-invades-cinemas-1.202681.

Nimr, Fāris. 'Baʿda ʿahdī bi-ʿilm al-falak'. *Al-Muqtaṭaf* 92, no. 5 (1938): 483–89.

Omran, Taleb [see also ʿUmrān, Ṭālib]. 'Structures on the Tangent Bundles'. PhD thesis, Aligarh Muslim University, 1984.

Omran, Taleb [see also ʿUmrān, Ṭālib]. 'Almost Product Structures in Principal Fibre Bundles over Almost Paracontact Manifold'. *Journal of the University of Kuwait (Science)* 16, no. 2 (1989): 215–21.

Ordway, III, Frederick I., James Patrick Gardner, and Mitchell R. Sharpe. *Basic Astronautics*. Englewood Cliffs: Prentice-Hall, 1962.

Osman, Sara. 'Morocco Observatory Helps Find Worlds Not Marked in the Atlas'. *Nature Middle East*, 31 January 2018. http://www.natureasia.com/en/nmiddleeast/article/10.1038/nmiddleeast.2018.12

Othman, Mazlan. 'Supra-Earth Affairs'. *Philosophical Transactions of the Royal Society A* 369, no. 1936 (2011): 693–99.

Özonuk, Şinasi. *Baytekin: Fezada Çarpisanlar* (1967).

Pakistan Today. 'Pervez Hoodbhoy Joins FC College'. *Pakistan Today*, 9 September 2013. https://www.pakistantoday.com.pk/2013/09/09/pervez-hoodbhoy-joins-fc-college/.

Palmer, James. 'Kazakhstan Spent $5 Billion on a Death Star and It Doesn't Even Shoot Lasers'. *Foreign Policy*, 15 June 2017. https://foreignpolicy.com/2017/06/15/kazakhstan-spent-5-billion-on-a-death-star-and-it-doesnt-even-shoot-lasers/.

Pamuk, Orhan. *Snow*. Translated by Maureen Freely. London: Faber and Faber, 2005.

Par, Zafer. *Badi*. (1983).

Parin, V. V. *Cosmos – Earth*. Translated by Translation Services Branch. Wright-Patterson Air Force Base: Foreign Technology Division, 1963.

Parsonson, Corrie. 'Author Alexandra Monir Writes Sci-Fi Book with Iranian-American Female Lead'. *Kayhan Life*, 24 January 2018. https://kayhanlife.com/author-alexandra-monir-writes-sci-fi-book-iranian-american-female-lead/.

Pasaribu, Norman Erikson. 'A History-to-Come of Helmbrellas: Their Features and Fates'. *Asian American Writers' Workshop*, 13 December 2017. https://aaww.org/a-history-to-come-of-helmbrellas-their-features-and-fates/.

Pennington, Roberta. '"UFO" Spotted at Abu Dhabi School'. *The National*, 23 November 2013. http://www.thenational.ae/uae/education/ufo-spotted-at-abu-dhabi-school.

Perel', Yu. G. '"Visitor from the Cosmos," by A. Kazantsev'. *Soviet Astronomy* 3 (1959): 375–79.

Perry, Sarah. 'Frankenstein in Baghdad by Ahmed Saadawi Review – Strange, Violent and Wickedly Funny'. *The Guardian*, 16 February 2018. http://www.theguardian.com/books/2018/feb/16/frankenstein-in-baghdad-by-ahmed-saadawi-review.

Philips, Abu Ameenah Bilaal. *The Ansar Cult in America*. Second edition. Riyadh: Tawheed, 1990.

Pickthall, Marmaduke. *The Meaning of the Glorious Koran: An Explanatory Translation*. Second impression. London: George Allen & Unwin, 1948.

Plackis-Cheng, Paksy. 'Saks Afridi: Ad Man Turned Artist'. *Impactmania*, 11 July 2017. http://www.impactmania.com/5624/ad-man-saks-afridi-turned-artist/.

Platt, Jane. 'Public Lectures Explore NASA Search for "Cosmic Roots"'. *Jet Propulsion Laboratory*, 11 January 1999. https://www.jpl.nasa.gov/releases/99/vkorigins.html.

Platt, Jane. 'JPL Announces Personnel Appointments'. *Jet Propulsion Laboratory*, 20 July 2011. http://www.jpl.nasa.gov/news/news.php?feature=3073.

Postberg, Frank, Nozair Khawaja, Bernd Abel, Gael Choblet, Christopher R. Glein, Murthy S. Gudipati, Bryana L. Henderson, et al. 'Macromolecular Organic Compounds from the Depths of Enceladus'. *Nature* 558, no. 7711 (2018): 564–68.

Pourahmad, Ali. 'About HSP'. *Hundred Studio Productions*. Accessed 27 December 2017. http://hundredstudio.com/about.html.

Presidency of Islamic Researches, Ifta, Call and Guidance, ed. *The Holy Qur-ān: English Translation of the Meanings and Commentary*. Al-Madinah Al-Munawarah: King Fahd Holy Qur-ān Printing Complex [1989/90].

PressTV. 'Asteroid Named after Iranian Scientist'. *PressTV*, 29 March 2016. https://www.presstv.com/Detail/2016/03/29/458180/NASA-Firouz-Naderi-5515-1989-EL1-main-asteroid-belt.

PressTV. 'Iran Online Game Tops German Contest'. *Iran Computer and Video Games Foundation*, 16 July 2016. http://en.ircg.ir/press/16/Iran-online-game-tops-German-contest.

Quṭb, Muḥammad. 'Muqaddimat al-masraḥīyah'. In *Al-buʿd al-khāmis*, by Aḥmad Rāʾif, 7–42. Al-Qāhirah: al-Zahrāʾ lil-Iʿlām al-ʿArabī, 1987.

Rahman, Md. Mahbur. 'A Successful Seat of Knowledge'. *Star Insight* 1, no. 3 (2006). http://archive.thedailystar.net/starinsight/2006/08/01/guru.htm.

Rahvar, Sohrab. 'Exoplanets: Exploring Unknown Worlds'. Presentation at the 21st IPM Physics Spring Conference, Institute for Research in Fundamental Sciences, Tehran, May 2014. http://physics.ipm.ac.ir/conferences/21stspring/note/S.Rahvar.pdf.

Rahvar, Sohrab. 'Curriculum Vitae'. *Physics Society of Iran*, 2016. http://www.psi.ir/upload/election/files/poll35/cv_rahvar.pdf.

Rahvar, Sohrab. 'Gravitational Microlensing Events as a Target for the SETI Project'. *Astrophysical Journal* 828, no. 1 (2016): 19.

Rāʾif, Aḥmad. *Al-bawwābah al-sawdāʾ*. Al-ṭabʿah al-thālithah al-sharʿīyah. Al-Qāhirah: al-Zahrāʾ lil-Iʿlām al-ʿArabī, 1986.

Rāʾif, Aḥmad. *Al-buʿd al-khāmis*. Al-Qāhirah: al-Zahrāʾ lil-Iʿlām al-ʿArabī, 1987.

Rāʾif, Aḥmad. *Sarādīb al-Shayṭān: ṣafaḥāt min tārīkh al-ikhwān al-Muslimīn*. Al-ṭabʿah al-thāniyah. Al-Qāhirah: al-Zahrāʾ lil-Iʿlām al-ʿArabī, 1990.

Rana, Masud. 'Muhammad Zafar Iqbal'. *WeLoveBD.com*, 8 March 2013. http://welovebd.com/culture/zafar-iqbal.php.

Rasheed, Rabeea Abdul. 'Astrobiology at Middle School Level in Pakistan'. *19th EANA Astrobiology Conference*, 2019. https://eana2019.sciencesconf.org/282928/.

Rattenbury, N. J., D. P. Bennett, T. Sumi, N. Koshimoto, I. A. Bond, A. Udalski, Y. Shvartzvald, et al. 'Faint-Source-Star Planetary Microlensing: The Discovery of the Cold Gas-Giant Planet OGLE-2014-BLG-0676Lb'. *Monthly Notices of the Royal Astronomical Society* 466, no. 3 (2017): 2710–17.

Rāymūnd, Alīks. *Flāsh Jūrdun*. Edited by Nabīl Fārūq. Al-Qāhirah: al-Mu'assasah al-'Arabīyah al-Ḥadīthah, n.d.

Reyes, Mike. 'Where Dubai Was Originally Supposed to Hit in Independence Day: Resurgence'. *Cinemablend*, 4 July 2016. https://www.cinemablend.com/news/1530410/where-dubai-was-originally-supposed-to-hit-in-independence-day-resurgence.

Rībīrā, Anṭūniyū. *Al-mukhtaṭifūn ... min al-faḍā' al-khārijī*. Translated by Khālid Munīr Ḥamshū. Dimashq, 1987.

Rizvi, Saeed. *Shanee* (Eveready Pictures, 1989).

Roberts, Adam. 'The Best SF and Fantasy Books of 2016'. *The Guardian*, 30 November 2016. https://www.theguardian.com/books/2016/nov/30/best-sf-and-fantasy-books-2016-adam-roberts.

Robinsoni, Benito. *Topaz Duo: Cosmic Phoenix* (2012).

Rouhizad, Bahman. 'Correspondence'. *Center for UFO Studies Associate Newsletter* 1, no. 4 (1980): 4.

Ruhselman, Bedri. *Ruh ve Kâinat*. İstanbul: Gayret Kitabevi, 1946.

Ryu, Y.-H., J. C. Yee, A. Udalski, I. A. Bond, Y. Shvartzvald, W. Zang, R. Figuera Jaimes, et al. 'OGLE-2016-BLG-1190Lb: The First *Spitzer* Bulge Planet Lies Near the Planet/Brown-Dwarf Boundary'. *Astronomical Journal* 155, no. 1 (2018): 40.

S., Bissme. 'Writing for Change'. *The Sun Daily*, 31 July 2008. http://www.thesundaily.my/node/164367.

Sadar, Claire. 'Turkish Film Sarmasik (Ivy) Is Genre-Bending and Thought-Provoking'. *Muftah*, 18 September 2016. https://muftah.org/turkish-film-sarmasik-ivy-genre-bending-thought-provoking/.

Sajadian, Sedighe. 'Simulation of a Strategy for the Pixel Lensing of M87 by HST'. Presentation at the 15th International Conference on Gravitational Microlensing, University of Salerno, January 2011. http://smc2011.physics.unisa.it/talks/sajadian.pdf.

Sajadian, Sedighe. 'Simulation of a Strategy for the Pixel Lensing of M87 by HST'. Presentation at the 19th Spring Physics Conference, Institute for Research in Fundamental Sciences, May 2012. http://physics.ipm.ac.ir/conferences/19thspring/files/sajadian.pdf.

Ṣalāḥ, 'Alī Mutawallī. 'Ḥūrīyah min al-Mirrīkh'. *Al-Risālah*, no. 938 (1951): 733–35.

Salāmah, Ṣafāt. 'Raḥīl 'amīd al-khayāl al-'ilmī al-'Arabī'. *Al-Sharq al-Awsaṭ*, no. 11729 (8 January 2011). http://archive.aawsat.com/leader.asp?section=3&issueno=11729&article=602933.

Saleem, Mazin. 'Iraq+100: Stories from a Century after the Invasion, Edited by Hassan Blasim'. *Strange Horizons*, 24 April 2017. http://strangehorizons.com/non-fiction/iraq100-stories-from-a-century-after-the-invasion-edited-by-hassan-blasim/.

Sālim, 'Alī. 'Ḥīn fashilat "al-nās illī fī al-samā al-thāminah"'. *Al-Qāhirah*, 17 January 2012. http://www.alkaheranews.com/details.php?pId=16&aId=3384.

Samaha, Abdel Hamid. 'Notes as to Cosmological Ideas in Al Quran'. *Meddelanden fran Lunds Astronomiska Observatorium II*, no. 96 (1938): 3–5.

Samāḥah, ʿAbd al-Ḥamīd. *Fī aʿmāq al-faḍāʾ*. Al-ṭabʿah al-thālithah. Bayrūt: Dār al-Shurūq, 1980.

Saner, Hulki. *Turist Ömer Uzay Yolunda* (1973).

Sanger, David E., and William J. Broad. 'U.S. Revives Secret Program to Sabotage Iranian Missiles and Rockets'. *New York Times*, 14 February 2019. https://www.nytimes.com/2019/02/13/us/politics/iran-missile-launch-failures.html.

Sārah. 'Nihād Sharīf: rāʾid al-khayāl al-ʿilmī fī al-adab al-ʿArabī'. *Al-Dawḥah*, no. 2 (February 1985): 78–82.

Sarıkaya, Halûk Egemen. *Uzaylılar ve Uçandaireler*. İstanbul: Milliyet Yayınları, 1975.

Sarıkaya, Halûk Egemen. 'UFO Flap in Turkey'. *Flying Saucer Review* 27, no. 5 (1982): 26–27.

Sarıkaya, Halûk Egemen. *Türkiye UFO Raporu*. Istanbul: Bilim Araştırma Merkezi, 1985.

Sarıkaya, Halûk Egemen, and Suat Bergil. *Ufoloji: Dünya-Dışı Zeki Varlıklar Bilimi*. İstanbul: Bilim Araştırma Grubu, 1977.

Sarıkaya, Halûk Egemen, and Suat Bergil. *Ekminezi: Geçmiş Yaşamlara Transla Geri Dönüşler*. İstanbul: Bilim Araştırma Merkezi, 1978.

Sarıkaya, Halûk Egemen, and Suat Bergil. *UFO & Apollo: Ortak Uzay Uçuşlari*. İstanbul: Bilim Araştırma Merkezi, 1978.

Sarkīs, Yūsuf Ilyān. *Muʿjam al-maṭbūʿāt al-ʿArabīyah wa-al-Muʿarrabah*. Vol. 1. Al-Qāhirah: Maktabat al-Thaqāfah al-Dīnīyah, n.d.

Sbīlbirj, Stīvin. *Liqāʾāt min al-nawʿ al-thālith*. Translated by Aḥmad Khālid Tawfīq. Al-Qāhirah: al-Muʾassasah al-ʿArabīyah al-Ḥadīthah, 1994.

Schenectady Gazette. 'Arabs Report First UFO in Kuwait'. *Schenectady Gazette* 85, no. 38 (14 November 1978): 3.

Sears, Derek W. G. 'Oral Histories in Meteoritics and Planetary Science – XXI: Donald Burnett'. *Meteoritics & Planetary Science* 48, no. 9 (2013): 1715–32.

Serajul Islam, Mohammed. 'Prof Zafar Iqbal, Wife Dr Yasmeen Haque Get Death Threat'. *Dhaka Tribune*, 15 October 2016. https://www.dhakatribune.com/bangladesh/2016/10/15/prof-zafar-iqbal-his-wife-get-death-threat.

Shahrābī, Ḥusayn. 'Chirā bāyad ʿilmī takhayyulī khvānad?' *Nujūm*, no. 267 (2018): 49.

Sharīf, Nihād. *Qāhir al-zaman*. Al-Qāhirah: Dār al-Hilāl, 1972.

Sharīf, Nihād. *Raqm 4 yaʾmurukum*. Al-Qāhirah: Muʾassasat Akhbār al-Yawm, 1974.

Sharīf, Nihād. 'Al-hijrah ilá al-mustaqbal'. *Al-Dawḥah*, no. 3 (March 1977): 110–13.

Sharīf, Nihād. *Anā ... wa-kāʾināt al-faḍāʾ*. Al-Qāhirah: Kitāb al-Yawm, 1983.

Sharīf, Nihād. *Al-shayʾ*. Al-Qāhirah: al-Hayʾah al-Miṣrīyah al-ʿĀmmah lil-Kitāb, 1989.

Sharīf, Nihād. 'Muqaddimah'. In *Thuqb fī jidār al-zaman: qiṣaṣ min al-khayāl al-ʿilmī*, by Ṭālib ʿUmrān, 3–11. Al-Hayʾah al-Miṣrīyah al-ʿĀmmah lil-Kitāb, 1992.

Sharīf, Nihād. *Alladhī taḥaddá al-iʿṣār*. Cairo: Kotobarabia, 2005.

Sharīf, Nihād. *Al-shayʾ*. Cairo: Kotobarabia, 2005.

Sharīf, Nihād. *Ibn al-nujūm*. Al-Jīzah: Nahḍat Miṣr, 2008.

Shaykhū, Luwīs. 'Ḍarar al-mā' al-muqaddas'. *Al-Mashriq* 1, no. 18 (1898): 860–61.
Shaykhū, Luwīs. 'Sukkān al-Mirrīkh'. *Al-Mashriq* 4, no. 4 (1901): 173–79.
Shklovski, I. S., and Carl Sagan. *Intelligent Life in the Universe*. San Francisco: Holden-Day, 1966.
Siddiqi, Mohamad Abul Hasan. 'The Quran and the Science of Astronomy'. *Muslim India and Islamic Review* 1, no. 5 (1913): 170–71.
Ṣidqī, Muḥammad Tawfīq. 'Al-Qur'ān wa-al-'ilm 4: tafsīr min al-lughah wa-al-tārīkh wa-al-jughrāfiyā wa-al-ṭibb'. *Al-Manār* 11, no. 6 (1908): 441–54.
Ṣidqī, Muḥammad Tawfīq. ''Ilm al-falak wa-al-Qur'ān: naẓrah fī al-samawāt wa-al-arḍ'. *Al-Manār* 14, no. 8 (1911): 577–600.
Skowron, J., I.-G. Shin, A. Udalski, C. Han, T. Sumi, Y. Shvartzvald, A. Gould, et al. 'OGLE-2011-BLG-0265Lb: A Jovian Microlensing Planet Orbiting an M Dwarf'. *Astrophysical Journal* 804, no. 1 (2015): 33.
Sorak, Ömer Faruk. *G.O.R.A.: A Space Movie* (BKM Film, 2004).
Speigel, Lee. 'WikiLeaks Documents Reveal United Nations Interest in UFOs'. *Huffington Post*, 29 October 2016. https://www.huffingtonpost.com/entry/wikileaks-ufos-united-nations_us_5813aa17e4b0390e69d0322e.
StarTrek.com. 'Beyond's Commodore Paris, Shohreh Aghdashloo'. *StarTrek.com*, 6 August 2016. http://www.startrek.com/article/beyonds-commodore-paris-shohreh-aghdashloo.
Stephen, N. 'Nature's Problems, No. 1: The Problem of Life'. *Islamic Review & Muslim India* 4, no. 1 (1916): 31–38.
Straits Times. 'Top Bangladesh Sci-Fi Writer Zafar Iqbal Stabbed in Head at Seminar'. *Straits Times*, 4 March 2018. http://www.straitstimes.com/asia/south-asia/top-bangladesh-sci-fi-writer-zafar-iqbal-stabbed-in-head-at-seminar.
Ṣumaydah, Muḥammad al-Māṭirī. 'Min qiṣaṣ al-'ushshāq … al-yawm dhikrá raḥīlihi. Ismā'īl Yāsīn : al-ḥubb wa-al-fann wa-al-mu'ānāh'. *Al-Shurūq*, 24 May 2017.
Sundaram, T. P. *Trip to Moon* (Friends Video, 1967).
Suslov, A. K. 'C. Flammarion – Forefather of Astrobiology'. In *Observations of the Moon, Mars, Uranus, and the Stars: Optical Properties of Plants*, edited by G. A. Tikhov, 288–95. Washington: National Aeronautics and Space Administration, 1966.
Tanveer, Asim, and Maria Golovnina. 'Al Qaeda's Shadowy New "Emir" in South Asia Handed Tough Job'. *Reuters*, 10 September 2014. https://www.reuters.com/article/us-southasia-alqaeda-insight/al-qaedas-shadowy-new-emir-in-south-asia-handed-tough-job-idUSKBN0H42DN20140909.
Tawfīq, Aḥmad Khālid [see also Towfik, Ahmed Khaled]. *Imbarāṭūrīyat al-nujūm*. Al-Qāhirah: al-Mu'assasah al-'Arabīyah al-Ḥadīthah, 1995.
Tawfīq, Aḥmad Khālid [see also Towfik, Ahmed Khaled]. *Fī jānib al-nujūm*. Al-Qāhirah: al-Mu'assasah al-'Arabīyah al-Ḥadīthah, 2004.
Tawfīq, Aḥmad Khālid [see also Towfik, Ahmed Khaled]. *Arḍ. Qamar. Arḍ*. Al-Qāhirah: al-Mu'assasah al-'Arabīyah al-Ḥadīthah, 2005.

Tawfīq, Aḥmad Khālid [see also Towfik, Ahmed Khaled]. *Yūtūbiyā*. Al-Qāhirah: Dār Mayrīt, 2008.

Tehrani, Faisal [see also Musa, Mohd Faizal]. *1511H [Kombat]*. Kuala Lumpur: Utusan, 2004.

Tibet, Kartal. *Dünyayı Kurtaran Adam'ın Oğlu* (Tiglon, 2006).

Tikhoff, G. A. 'Note préliminaire sur la photographie de la planète Mars au moyen du 30 pouces de Poulkovo'. *Bulletin de l'Académie Impériale des Sciences de St.-Pétersbourg*, 3, no. 15 (1909): 1039–1042.

Tikhoff, G. A. 'L'application des filtres sélecteurs à l'étude des surfaces de Mars et de Saturne'. *Mitteilungen der Nikolai-Hauptsternwarte zu Pulkowo* 4 (1911): 73–84.

Tikhov, G. A. 'Is Life Possible on Other Planets?' *Journal of the British Astronomical Association* 65, no. 3 (1955): 193–204.

Tikhov, G. A. 'What Is Astrobotany?' *Spaceflight* 2, no. 3 (1959): 74–77.

Tikhov, G. A. *Reaching for the Stars*. Translated by A. Shkarovsky. Moscow: Foreign Languages Publishing House, 1960.

Tikhov, G. A., ed. *Observations of the Moon, Mars, Uranus, and the Stars: Optical Properties of Plants*. Washington: National Aeronautics and Space Administration, 1966.

Time. 'An Interview with Hafez Assad'. *Time* 128, no. 16 (1986): 32–33.

Towfik, Ahmed Khaled [see also Tawfīq, Aḥmad Khālid]. *Utopia*. Translated by Chip Rosetti. Bloomsbury Qatar Foundation Publishing, 2011.

Udalski, A., Y.-H. Ryu, S. Sajadian, A. Gould, P. Mroz, R. Poleski, M. K. Szymanski, et al. 'OGLE-2017-BLG-1434Lb: Eighth $q < 1 \times 10^{-4}$ Mass-Ratio Microlens Planet Confirms Turnover in Planet Mass-Ratio Function'. *Acta Astronomica* 68, no. 1 (2018): 1–48.

ʿUmar, Maulanā ʿĀṣim. *Tīsrī jang-i ʿaẓīm aur dajjāl*. Karāchī: al-Hijrah Pablīkaishan, 2007.

ʿUmar, Maulanā ʿĀṣim. *Barmūdā tikon aur Dajjāl*. Karāchī: Alhijrah Publication, 2009.

ʿUmar, Maulanā ʿĀṣim. *Dajjāl kā lashkar Blaik Wāṭir*. Jamia Hafsa Urdu Forum, 2009.

ʿUmrān, Ṭālib [see also Omran, Taleb]. *Al-ʿālam min ḥawlinā*. Dimashq: Wizārat al-Thaqāfah wa-al-Irshād al-Qawmī, 1976.

ʿUmrān, Ṭālib [see also Omran, Taleb]. *Al-azmān al-muẓlimah*. Dimashq: Dār al-Fikr, 2003.

ʿUmrān, Ṭālib [see also Omran, Taleb]. *Al-baḥth ʿan ʿawālim ukhrá*. Dimashq: Dār al-Fikr, 2004.

ʿUmrān, Ṭālib [see also Omran, Taleb]. *Fī kawkab shabīh bi-al-Arḍ*. Dimashq: Dār al-Fikr, 2004.

ʿUmrān, Ṭālib [see also Omran, Taleb]. *Dawwāmāt al-khawf*. Dimashq: Dār al-Fikr, 2009.

ʿUmrān, Ṭālib [see also Omran, Taleb]. 'Maʿa Najīb Maḥfūẓ'. *Dawāʾir al-Ibdāʿ* 8 (2016): 4–7.

United Nations Development Programme. *Arab Human Development Report 2003: Building a Knowledge Society*. New York: United Nations Development Programme, 2003.

United Nations Office for Outer Space Affairs. 'Programme of Activities: United Nations/Islamic Republic of Iran Workshop on the Use of Space Technology for Dust Storm and Drought Monitoring in the Middle East Region'. *UNOOSA*, 11 November 2016. http://www.unoosa.org/documents/pdf/psa/activities/2016/Iran/UN-Iran-Workshop_2016-draftagenda.pdf.

UN News Centre. 'Interview with Mazlan Othman, Director of the Office for Outer Space Affairs'. *United Nations*, 4 October 2011. http://www.un.org/apps/news/newsmakers.asp?NewsID=43.

Ūrwīl, Jūrj. *1984*. Translated by Aḥmad Khālid Tawfīq. Vol. 1. Al-Qāhirah: al-Muʾassasah al-ʿArabīyah al-Ḥadīthah, n.d.

Varma, Anuradha. 'The Son of Ibne Safi!' *Times of India*, 23 May 2011. http://timesofindia.indiatimes.com/life-style/spotlight/The-son-of-Ibne-Safi/articleshow/8270314.cms.

Victory, Ebrahim. *The Wonders of the Universe*. Los Angeles: Magbit Foundation, 1997.

Wainwright, Milton, and Fawaz Alshammari. 'The Forgotten History of Panspermia and Theories of Life from Space'. *Journal of Cosmology* 7 (2010): 1771–76.

Warn, Yūliyūs [See also Fīrn, Jūl]. *Al-riḥlah al-jawwīyah fī al-markabah al-hawāʾīyah*. Translated by Yūsuf Ilyān Sarkīs. Ṭabʿah thāniyah muṣaḥḥaḥah. Bayrūt: Maṭbaʿat al-Abāʾ al-Mursalīn al-Yasūʿīyīn, 1884.

Waṣfī, Raʾūf. *Al-kawn wa-al-thuqūb al-sawdāʾ*. Al-Kuwayt: al-Majlis al-Waṭanī lil-Thaqāfah wa-al-Funūn wa-al-Ādāb, 1979.

Waṣfī, Raʾūf, trans. *Al-ḥāsib al-ālī*. Al-ṭabʿah al-thālithah. Al-Kuwayt: Muʾassasat al-Kuwayt lil-Taqaddum al-ʿIlmī, 1989.

Waṣfī, Raʾūf. *Al-ḥubb al-mustaḥīl*. Al-Qāhirah: al-Muʾassasah al-ʿArabīyah al-Ḥadīthah, n.d.

Waṣfī, Raʾūf. *Al-insān al-ālī al-qātil*. Al-Qāhirah: al-Muʾassasah al-ʿArabīyah al-Ḥadīthah, n.d.

Waṣfī, Raʾūf. *Al-vayrūsāt al-dhakīyah*. Al-Qāhirah: al-Muʾassasah al-ʿArabīyah al-Ḥadīthah, n.d.

Waṣfī, Raʾūf. *Amīrat al-faḍāʾ*. Al-Qāhirah: al-Muʾassasah al-ʿArabīyah al-Ḥadīthah, n.d.

Waṣfī, Raʾūf. *Ashbāḥ fī al-faḍāʾ*. Al-Qāhirah: al-Muʾassasah al-ʿArabīyah al-Ḥadīthah, n.d.

Waṣfī, Raʾūf. *Ghazw min ʿālam ākhar*. Al-Qāhirah: al-Muʾassasah al-ʿArabīyah al-Ḥadīthah, n.d.

Waṣfī, Raʾūf. *Ightiyāl kumbiyūtir*. Al-Qāhirah: al-Muʾassasah al-ʿArabīyah al-Ḥadīthah, n.d.

Waṣfī, Raʾūf. *Mudhannab al-dimār*. Al-Qāhirah: al-Muʾassasah al-ʿArabīyah al-Ḥadīthah, n.d.

Waṣfī, Raʾūf. *Qīthārat al-mawt*. Al-Qāhirah: al-Muʾassasah al-ʿArabīyah al-Ḥadīthah, n.d.

Waṣfī, Raʾūf. *Ruʿb taḥt al-mijhar*. Al-Qāhirah: al-Muʾassasah al-ʿArabīyah al-Ḥadīthah, n.d.

Waṣfī, Ra᾽ūf. *Shawāṭi᾽ al-abadīyah*. Al-Qāhirah: al-Mu᾽assasah al-ʿArabīyah al-Ḥadīthah, n.d.
Waṣfī, Ra᾽ūf. *Sirr kitāb al-mawtá*. Al-Qāhirah: al-Mu᾽assasah al-ʿArabīyah al-Ḥadīthah, n.d.
Waṣfī, Ra᾽ūf. *Thawrat al-rūbūt*. Al-Qāhirah: al-Mu᾽assasah al-ʿArabīyah al-Ḥadīthah, n.d.
Waṣfī, Ra᾽ūf. 'Al-ḥubb ya᾽tī min aʿmāq al-kawn'. *Al-Adab al-ʿIlmī*, no. 25 (2015): 96–101.
Waylz, H. J. [see also Wells, H. G]. *Al-rajul al-khafī*. Translated by Ra᾽ūf Waṣfī. Al-Qāhirah: al-Markaz al-Qawmī lil-Tarjamah, 2009.
Waylz, H. J. [see also Wells, H. G]. *Bashar ka-al-arbāb*. Translated by Ra᾽ūf Waṣfī. Al-Qāhirah: al-Markaz al-Qawmī lil-Tarjamah, 2010.
Weaver, Matthew. 'UN Plan for "Alien Ambassador" a Case of Science Fiction?' *The Guardian*, 27 September 2010. http://www.theguardian.com/news/blog/2010/sep/27/un-alien-ambassador-mazlan-othman.
Webster, Guy. 'JPL's New Associate Director Led Successful Mars Exploration'. *Jet Propulsion Laboratory*, 23 February 2005. http://www.jpl.nasa.gov/news/news.php?feature=740.
Wells, H. G. [see also Waylz, H. J.]. *A Short History of the World*. New York: Macmillan, 1922.
Wren, Christopher S. 'Egypt Requests Right to Punish Killers of Editor'. *New York Times*, 19 February 1978.
Yahya, Harun. 'Dawkins is No More Darwinist! He Converted to Space Religion!' *Harun Yahya*, 9 November 2009. http://harunyahya.com/en/Articles/18787/dawkins-is-no-more-darwinist.
Yamānī, Muḥammad ʿAbduh. *Naẓarāt ʿilmīyah ḥawl ghazw al-faḍā᾽*. Jiddah [c. 1978].
Yamānī, Muḥammad ʿAbduh. *Al-aṭbāq al-ṭā᾽irah: ḥaqīqah am khayāl?* Al-Riyāḍ: al-Maṭābiʿ al-Ahlīyah lil-Ūfsit, 1980.
Yamānī, Muḥammad ʿAbduh. *Hal naḥnu waḥdanā fī hādhā al-kawn?* Al-Manāmah: Bayt al-Qur᾽ān, 1992.
Yaqoob, Tahira. 'Ahmed Khaled Towfik, Egypt's Doctor of Escapism'. *The National*, 16 March 2012. https://www.thenational.ae/arts-culture/books/ahmed-khaled-towfik-egypt-s-doctor-of-escapism-1.391594.
Yates, Athol. *Catastrophes, Crashes and Crimes in the UAE: Newspaper Articles of the 1970s*. Surbiton: Medina, 2016.
Yılmaz, Cem, and Ali Taner Baltacı. *A.R.O.G: Bir Yontma Taş Film* (UIP Filmcilik, 2008).
York, Malachi Z. *Man from Planet Rizq*. Eatonton: Holy Tabernacle Ministries [c. 1993].
York, Malachi Z. *Rizq and Illyuwn: Fact or Fiction?* Scroll 151. Eatonton: Holy Tabernacle Ministries, n.d.
York, Malachi Z. *360 Questions to Ask Orthodox Sunni Muslims*. Vol. 2. Eatonton: Holy Tabernacle Ministries, n.d.

Yurdozu, Farah. 'A Paranormal Family Tradition'. *Farah Yurdozu*, 1 October 2006. http://farahsufos.blogspot.qa/2006/10/paranormal-family-tradition.html.

Yurdozu, Farah. 'Visitors from the Stars in Ancient Shamanic Turkish Tribes'. *Farah Yurdozu*, 1 October 2006. http://farahsufos.blogspot.qa/2006/10/visitors-from-stars-in-ancient.html.

Yurdozu, Farah. 'The UMMO Letters'. *Farah Yurdozu*, 23 January 2008. http://farahsufos.blogspot.qa/2008/01/ummo-letters.html.

Yurdozu, Farah. 'Mysterious Beings at Turkish Movie Set'. *Farah Yurdozu*, 2 March 2008. http://farahsufos.blogspot.qa/2008/03/mysterious-beings-at-turkish-movie-set.html.

Yurdozu, Farah. 'Hittites; The First ET-Hybrid Civilization on Turkey'. *Farah Yurdozu*, 8 September 2008. http://farahsufos.blogspot.qa/2008/09/hittites-first-et-hybrid-civilization.html.

Yurdözü, Farah. 'Farah Yurdozu'. *The Jerry Pippin Show*. Accessed 12 January 2018. http://www.jerrypippin.com/Paranormal_Farah_Yurdozu.htm.

Yurdozu, Farah, and Richard Day Gore. *Confessions of a Turkish Ufologist*. Seven Houses, 2009.

Yūsuf, Fatḥ al-Raḥmān. 'Nūrah al-Nūmān: riwāyāt "al-khayāl al-ʿilmī" ṭarīqunā li-ithrāʾ maktabat al-ṭifl'. *Al-Sharq al-Awsaṭ*, 31 January 2014. https://aawsat.com/home/article/28531.

Zahr, ʿAbd al-Masīḥ. 'Al-ḥayāt fī al-ajrām al-samāwīyah'. *Al-Mashriq* 28, no. 4 (1930): 241–49.

Zahr, ʿAbd al-Masīḥ. 'Al-ʿilm al-ḥaqīqī yuthbit wujūd Allāh 1'. *Al-Mashriq* 29, no. 3 (1931): 205–10.

Zahr, ʿAbd al-Masīḥ. 'Al-ʿilm al-ḥaqīqī yuthbit wujūd Allāh 2'. *Al-Mashriq* 29, no. 4 (1931): 250–57.

Zirkle, Conway. 'An Appraisal of Science in the USSR'. In *Soviet Science*, edited by Ruth C. Christman, 100–108. Washington: American Association for the Advancement of Science, 1952.

Zirkle, Conway. 'The Involuntary Destruction of Science in the USSR'. *Scientific Monthly* 76, no. 5 (1953): 277–83.

Zriqat, Thaer. 'Portrait of a Nation: The Author on an Intergalactic Mission to Expand Arab Readers' Minds'. *The National*, 22 September 2016. https://www.thenational.ae/uae/portrait-of-a-nation-the-author-on-an-intergalactic-mission-to-expand-arab-readers-minds-1.201244.

Secondary sources

Ahmad, Ali Nobil. 'Film and Cinephilia in Pakistan: Beyond Life and Death'. *BioScope: South Asian Screen Studies* 5, no. 2 (2014): 81–98.

Ahmadi, Ahmad. 'Iran'. In *Video Games around the World*, edited by Mark J. P. Wolf, 271–91. Cambridge: MIT Press, 2015.

Aksoy, Nüzhet Berrin. 'The Adventures of the Graphic Novel in Turkey'. In *Sequential Art: Interdisciplinary Approaches to the Graphic Novel*, edited by Kathrin Muschalik and Florian Fiddrich, 3–10. Oxford: Inter-Disciplinary Press, 2016.

Alessio, Dominic, and Jessica Langer. 'Science Fiction, Hindu Nationalism and Modernity: Bollywood's *Koi ... Mil Gaya*'. In *Science Fiction, Imperialism and the Third World Essays on Postcolonial Literature and Film*, edited by Ericka Hoagland and Reema Sarwal, 156–70. Jefferson: McFarland, 2010.

Al-Ghazzi, Omar. 'Grendizer Leaves for Sweden: Japanese Anime Nostalgia on Syrian Social Media'. *Middle East Journal of Culture and Communication* 11, no. 1 (2018): 52–71.

ʿAlī, Aḥmad Yusrī Fuhayd. 'Abʿād al-zamān wa-al-makān fī riwāyat al-khayāl al-ʿilmī'. Risālat duktūrāh, Jāmiʿat al-Iskandarīyah, 2010.

Al-Sayyid, Muḥammad Ṣabrī. 'Nihād Sharīf'. *Al-Qiṣṣah* 52 (1987): 137–42.

Al-Shammās, ʿĪsá. 'Al-nadwah al-ūlá li-kuttāb al-khayāl al-ʿilmī fī al-waṭan al-ʿArabī''. *Majallat Jāmiʿat Dimashq* 24, no. 1 (2008): 423–37.

Al-Shārūnī, Yūsuf. '"Nihād Sharīf": rāʾidan lil-khayāl al-ʿilmī fī al-adab al-ʿArabī'. *Ibdāʿ* 15, no. 8 (1997): 52–58.

Amir Shahkarami, Sayed Najmedin. 'The Pre-Production Phase in the Making of Iranian Full-Length Animated Films 1979–2012'. PhD thesis, University of West London, 2013.

Anderson, Benedict. *Imagined Communities: Reflections on the Origin and Spread of Nationalism*. Revised and extended edition. London: Verso, 1991.

Ansari, S. M. Razaullah. 'Introduction of Modern Western Astronomy in India during 18–19 Centuries'. *Indian Journal of History of Science* 20 (1985): 363–402.

Ansari, S. M. Razaullah. 'European Astronomy in Indo-Persian Writings'. In *History of Oriental Astronomy*, edited by S. M. Razaullah Ansari, 133–44. Dordrecht: Springer, 2002.

Asghar, Anila, Salman Hameed and Najme Kishani Farahani. 'Evolution in Biology Textbooks: A Comparative Analysis of 5 Muslim Countries'. *Religion & Education* 41, no. 1 (2014): 1–15.

Ashcroft, Bill, Gareth Griffiths, and Helen Tiffin. *The Empire Writes Back: Theory and Practice In Post-Colonial Literatures*. Second edition. London: Routledge, 2002.

Atallah, Nadine. 'Modernism, Feminism and Science Fiction: *Words as Silence, Language as Rhymes* by Marwa Arsanios'. *Asiatische Studien* 70, no. 4 (2017): 1219–47.

Atılgan, İnanç. *Einführung in die türkische Science-Fiction-Literatur: Von der osmanischen Zeit bis 2000*. Klagenfurt: Wieser, 2008.

Auji, Hala. *Printing Arab Modernity: Book Culture and the American Press in Nineteenth-Century Beirut*. Leiden: Brill, 2016.

Auji, Hala. 'Printed Images in Flux: Examining Scientific Engravings in Nineteenth-Century Arabic Periodicals'. In *Visual Design: The Periodical Page as a Designed Surface*, edited by Andreas Beck, Nicola Kaminski, Volker Mergenthaler and Jens Ruchatz, 119–36. Hannover: Wehrhahn, 2019.

Aydin, Cemil. *The Idea of the Muslim World: A Global Intellectual History*. Cambridge: Harvard University Press, 2017.

Ayed, Kawthar [see also ʿAyyād, Kawthar]. 'La fiction d'anticipation arabe sous les auspices du cauchemars'. *Eidôlon*, no. 73 (2006): 49–58.

Ayed, Kawthar [see also ʿAyyād, Kawthar]. 'L'Image de soi et de l'autre dans deux romans d'anticipation dystopique'. *Nouvelles Études Francophones* 22, no. 2 (2007): 102–11.

Ayed, Kawthar [see also ʿAyyād, Kawthar]. 'Lucien de Samosate le Syrien: The First (Unofficial) Arab Science Fiction Conference'. *Science Fact & Science Fiction Concatenation*, 15 September 2007. http://www.concatenation.org/conrev/lucien.html.

Ayed, Kawthar [see also ʿAyyād, Kawthar]. 'La science-fiction arabe: Une transgression littéraire pour une transgression politique'. *LiCArC: Littérature et culture arabes contemporaines*, no. 1 (2013): 27–39.

Aysha, Emad El-Din. 'Better Late than Never: The Transmutations of Egyptian SF in the Work of Hosam El-Zembely'. *Foundation: The International Review of Science Fiction* 47, no. 131 (2018): 6–14.

Aysha, Emad El-Din. 'SF in Iran: Interview'. *Samovar*, 9 February 2019. http://samovar.strangehorizons.com/2019/02/09/sf-in-iran-interview/.

Aysha, Emad El-Din. 'In Protest: The Sci-Fi Contribution to Arabic Resistance Literature'. *Monthly Review*, 26 June 2019. https://mronline.org/2019/06/26/in-protest-the-sci-fi-contribution-to-arabic-resistance-literature/.

ʿAyyād, Kawthar [see also Ayed, Kawthar]. 'Al-khayāl al-istishrāfī al-siyāsī al-ʿArabī'. *Al-Khayāl al-ʿIlmī*, nos. 5/6 (2008): 38–49.

ʿAyyād, Kawthar [see also Ayed, Kawthar]. 'Adab al-khayāl al-ʿilmī fī al-Maghrib al-ʿArabī'. *Al-Khayāl al-ʿIlmī*, no. 12 (2009): 12–25.

ʿAyyād, Kawthar [see also Ayed, Kawthar]. 'Adab al-khayāl al-ʿilmī fī al-ʿālam al-ʿArabī'. *Al-Mawqif al-Adabī* 44, no. 530 (2015): 64–76.

Badawi, M. M. *Modern Arabic Drama in Egypt*. Cambridge: Cambridge University Press, 1987.

Bahler, Kristen. 'The Alien Race: "All Eyes on Egipt" and the Cult of Nuwaubianism'. *Vice*, 28 February 2015. https://www.vice.com/en_us/article/dpwbex/the-alien-race-all-eyes-on-egipt-and-the-nuwaubian-cult.

Bailey, Julius H. 'The Final Frontier: Secrecy, Identity, and the Media in the Rise and Fall of the United Nuwaubian Nation of Moors'. *Journal of the American Academy of Religion* 74, no. 2 (2006): 302–23.

Barbaro, Ada. *La fantascienza nella letteratura araba*. Roma: Carocci, 2013.

Barbaro, Ada. 'Marginality as a Genre: Science Fiction in Arabic Literature and the Case of the Egyptian Writer Nihād Šarīf'. In *Aux marges de la littérature arabe contemporaine*, edited by Laurence Denooz and Xavier Luffin, 39–49. Helsinki: Academia Scientiarum Fennica, 2013.

Barbaro, Ada. 'Where Science Fiction and *al-Khayal al-'Ilmī* Meet'. In *Other Worlds and the Narrative Construction of Otherness*, edited by Esterino Adami, Francesca Bellino and Alessandro Mengozzi. Mimesis International, 2017.

Battaglia, Debbora. 'Insiders' Voices in Outerspaces'. In *E. T. Culture: Anthropology in Outerspaces*, edited by Debbora Battaglia, 1–37. Durham: Duke University Press, 2005.

Bausani, Alessandro. 'Niẓāmī di Gangia e la "Pluralità dei mondi"'. *Rivista degli studi orientali* 46, nos. 3/4 (1971): 197–215.

Bearman, Joshuah. 'How the CIA Used a Fake Sci-Fi Flick to Rescue Americans from Tehran'. *Wired*, 24 April 2007. https://www.wired.com/2007/04/feat_cia/.

Ben-Zaken, Avner. 'The Heavens of the Sky and the Heavens of the Heart: The Ottoman Cultural Context for the Introduction of Post-Copernican Astronomy'. *British Journal for the History of Science* 37, no. 1 (2004): 1–28.

Biçer, Ramazan. 'Heretik Bir New Age Tarikati Dünya Kardeşlik Birligi Mevlana Yüce Vakfi'. *Ekev Akademi Dergisi* 10, no. 29 (2006): 27–50.

Biçer, Ramazan. 'Kutsal Kitaplar Üstü Apokrif Kutsal: "Bilgi Kitabı"'. *Kelam Araştırmaları Dergisi* 5, no. 2 (2007): 15–40.

Bigliardi, Stefano. 'What Would Ron Choose from the Islamic Basket? Notes on Scientology's Construction of Islam'. *Temenos* 51, no. 1 (2015): 95–121.

Bigliardi, Stefano. *La mezzaluna e la Luna dimezzata: Islam, pseudoscienza e paranormale*. Padova: CICAP, 2018.

Bigliardi, Stefano. 'La paleoastronautica di Erich von Däniken'. *Query* 9, no. 36 (2018): 32–40.

Billingsley, Anthony. *Political Succession in the Arab World: Constitutions, Family Loyalties and Islam*. Abingdon: Routledge, 2010.

Bluhm, Jutta E. 'A Preliminary Statement on the Dialogue Established between the Reform Magazine *al-Manār* and the Malayo-Indonesian World'. *Indonesia Circle* 32 (1983): 35–42.

Botz-Bornstein, Thorsten. 'The "Futurist" Aesthetics of ISIS'. *Journal of Aesthetics & Culture* 9, no. 1 (2017): 1–13.

Boutz, Gary Monroe. 'Generic Cues and Generic Features in Arabic Science Fiction: The Novels of Kassem Kassem'. PhD thesis, Georgetown University, 2011.

Brady, Amy. 'What Palestine Might Be Like in 2048'. *Chicago Review of Books*, 29 July 2019. https://chireviewofbooks.com/2019/07/29/what-palestine-might-be-like-in-2048/.

Briot, Danielle. 'The Creator of Astrobotany, Gavriil Adrianovich Tikhov'. In *Astrobiology, History, and Society*, edited by Douglas A. Vakoch, 175–85. Heidelberg: Springer, 2013.

Burton, Elise K. 'Teaching Evolution in Muslim States: Iran and Saudi Arabia Compared'. *Reports of the National Center for Science Education* 30, no. 3 (2010): 25–29.

Calderini, Simonetta. '*Tafsīr* of *ʿālamīn* in *rabb al-ʿālamīn*, Qurʾān 1:2'. *Bulletin of the School of Oriental and African Studies, University of London* 57, no. 1 (1994): 52–58.

Campbell, Ian. 'Some Developments in Indonesian Literature since 1998'. *Review of Indonesian and Malaysian Affairs* 36, no. 2 (2002): 35–80.

Campbell, Ian. '"Still a Better Love Story than *Twilight*": Abbas and Bahjatt's *HWJN*, the Saudi State, and Sexual Politics'. *New York Review of Science Fiction* 305 (2014). http://www.nyrsf.com/2014/02/ian-campbell-still-a-better-love-story-than-twilight-abbas-and-bahjatts-hwjn-the-saudi-state-and-sex.html.

Campbell, Ian. 'Prefiguring Egypt's Arab Spring: Allegory and Allusion in Aḥmad Khālid Tawfīq's *Utopia*'. *Science Fiction Studies* 42, no. 3 (2015): 541–56.

Campbell, Ian. 'False Gods and Libertarians: Artificial Intelligence and Community in Aḥmad 'Abd al-Salām al-Baqqāli's *The Blue Flood* and Heinlein's *The Moon Is a Harsh Mistress*'. *Science Fiction Studies* 44, no. 1 (2017): 43–64.

Campbell, Ian. *Arabic Science Fiction*. Cham: PalgraveMacmillan, 2018.

Campbell, Robert Bell. 'The Arabic Journal, *al-Mashriq*: Its Beginnings and First Twenty-Five Years under the Editorship of Père Louis Cheikho, S.J.' PhD thesis, University of Michigan, 1972.

Charbel, Paul. 'Deconstructing the Desert: The Bedouin Ideal and the True Children of Tatooine'. In *A Galaxy Here and Now: Historical and Cultural Readings of Star Wars*, edited by Peter W. Lee, 138–61. Jefferson: McFarland, 2016.

Choi, Charles Q. 'Artistic Astrobiology: Bridging Biology and Space'. *Astrobiology Magazine*, 19 July 2012. https://www.astrobio.net/retrospections/artistic-astrobiology-bridging-biology-and-space/.

Cohen, Barry M. 'The Descent of Lysenko'. *Journal of Heredity* 56, no. 5 (1965): 229–33.

Cohen, Claudine. 'L' « Anthropologie » de Telliamed'. *Bulletins et Mémoires de la Société d'anthropologie de Paris* 1, no. 3 (1989): 45–55.

Cohen, Claudine. *Science, libertinage et clandestinité à l'aube des Lumières: Le transformisme de Telliamed*. Paris: Presses Universitaires de France, 2011.

Cole, Juan Ricardo. 'Rashid Rida on the Baha'i Faith: A Utilitarian Theory of the Spread of Religions'. *Arab Studies Quarterly* 5, no. 3 (1983): 276–91.

cooke, miriam. *Dissident Syria: Making Oppositional Art Official*. Durham: Duke University Press, 2007.

cooke, miriam. *Dancing in Damascus: Creativity, Resilience, and the Syrian Revolution*. New York: Routledge, 2017.

Cooperson, Michael. 'Remembering the Future: Arabic Time-Travel Literature'. *Edebiyât* 8, no. 2 (1998): 171–89.

Crossley, Robert. 'Percival Lowell and the History of Mars'. *Massachusetts Review* 41, no. 3 (2000): 297–318.

Crowe, Michael J. *The Extraterrestrial Life Debate, 1750–1900*. Mineola: Dover, 1999.

Cubitt, Sean. 'Phalke, Méliès, and Special Effects Today'. *Wide Angle* 21, no. 1 (1999): 115–30.

Curtis, Edward E. 'Science and Technology in Elijah Muhammad's Nation of Islam: Astrophysical Disaster, Genetic Engineering, UFOs, White Apocalypse, and Black Resurrection'. *Nova Religio* 20, no. 1 (2016): 5–31.

Dance, Amber. 'Terraforming a Volcano, Artfully'. *Proceedings of the National Academy of Sciences* 113, no. 16 (2016): 4234–35.

Daneshgar, Majid. *Ṭantāwī Jawharī and the Qur'ān: Tafsir and Social Concerns in the Twentieth Century*. Abingdon: Routledge, 2018.

Demidov, Sergei S. 'Russia and the U.S.S.R.' In *Writing the History of Mathematics: Its Historical Development*, edited by Joseph W. Dauben and Christoph J. Scriba, 179–98. Basel: Birkhäuser, 2002.

Dick, Steven J. *Plurality of Worlds: The Origins of the Extraterrestrial Life Debate from Democritus to Kant*. Cambridge: Cambridge University Press, 1982.

Dick, Steven J. *Life on Other Worlds: The 20th-Century Extraterrestrial Life Debate*. Cambridge: Cambridge University Press, 1998.

Dönmez-Colin, Gönül. *The Routledge Dictionary of Turkish Cinema*. Abingdon: Routledge, 2014.

Doostdar, Alireza. 'Empirical Spirits: Islam, Spiritism, and the Virtues of Science in Iran'. *Comparative Studies in Society and History* 58, no. 2 (2016): 322–49.

Doostdar, Alireza. *The Iranian Metaphysicals: Explorations in Science, Islam, and the Uncanny*. Princeton: Princeton University Press, 2018.

Ducène, Jean-Charles. 'Les sources arabes du Telliamed de Benoît de Maillet (1656–1738) et la fiction du Omar al-Aleem'. *Rocznik Orientalistyczny* 56, no. 2 (2003): 29–42.

Dunning, Brian. 'The Tehran 1976 UFO'. *Skeptoid*, 12 June 2012. https://skeptoid.com/episodes/4315.

Eberhart, George M. *UFOs and the Extraterrestrial Contact Movement: A Bibliography*. Vol. 1. Metuchen: Scarecrow, 1986.

Eghigian, Greg. '"A Transatlantic Buzz": Flying Saucers, Extraterrestrials and America in Postwar Germany'. *Journal of Transatlantic Studies* 12, no. 3 (2014): 282–303.

El-Mazzaoui, Farid. 'Film in Egypt'. *Hollywood Quarterly* 4, no. 3 (1950): 245–50.

Elmjouie, Yara. 'The Game Industry of Iran'. *Polygon*, 14 January 2016. https://www.polygon.com/features/2016/1/14/10757460/the-game-industry-of-iran.

Elshakry, Marwa. 'Darwin's Legacy in the Arab East: Science, Religion and Politics, 1870–1914'. PhD thesis, Princeton University, 2003.

Elshakry, Marwa. 'The Gospel of Science and American Evangelism in Late Ottoman Beirut'. *Past and Present* 196, no. 1 (2007): 173–214.

Elshakry, Marwa. *Reading Darwin in Arabic, 1860–1950*. Chicago: University of Chicago Press, 2013.

El-Zein, Amira. *Islam, Arabs, and Intelligent World of the Jinn*. Syracuse: Syracuse University Press, 2009.

Eqbal, Khurshid. 'Urdu Mein Science Fiction Ki Riwayat (The Tradition of Urdu Science Fiction)'. PhD thesis, University of Burdwan, 2012.

Erdoğan, Nezih, and Deniz Göktürk. 'Turkish Cinema'. In *Companion Encyclopedia of Middle Eastern and North African Film*, edited by Oliver Leaman, 533–73. London: Routledge, 2001.

Erdoğan, Nezih, and Dilek Kaya. 'Institutional Intervention in the Distribution and Exhibition of Hollywood Films in Turkey'. *Historical Journal of Film, Radio and Television* 22, no. 1 (2002): 47–59.

Fawcett, Lawrence, and Barry J. Greenwood. *UFO Cover-Up: What the Government Won't Say*. New York: Simon & Schuster, 1992.

Finley, Stephen C. 'The Meaning of *Mother* in Louis Farrakhan's "Mother Wheel": Race, Gender, and Sexuality in the Cosmology of the Nation of Islam's UFO'. *Journal of the American Academy of Religion* 80, no. 2 (2012): 434–65.

Foss, Clive. 'Kemal Atatürk: Giving a New Nation a New History'. *Middle Eastern Studies* 50, no. 5 (2014): 826–47.

Fossett, Katelyn. 'Can Science Fiction Survive in Saudi Arabia?' *Foreign Policy*, 10 December 2013. https://foreignpolicy.com/2013/12/10/can-science-fiction-survive-in-saudi-arabia/.

Frisk, Liselotte, and Peter Åkerbäck. *New Religiosity in Contemporary Sweden: The Dalarna Study in National and International Context*. Sheffield: Equinox, 2015.

Gaffney, Jane. 'The Egyptian Cinema: Industry and Art in a Changing Society'. *Arab Studies Quarterly* 9, no. 1 (1987): 53–75.

García, Michael Nieto. 'The Indonesian Free Book Press'. *Indonesia* 78 (2004): 121–45.

Gargaud, Muriel, and Stéphane Tirard. 'Exobiology: An Example of Interdisciplinarity at Work'. In *Astronomy at the Frontiers of Science*, edited by Jean-Pierre Lasota, 337–50. Dordrecht: Springer, 2011.

Geppert, Alexander C. T. 'Extraterrestrial Encounters: UFOs, Science and the Quest for Transcendence, 1947–1972'. *History and Technology* 28, no. 3 (2012): 335–62.

Geppert, Alexander C. T. 'European Astrofuturism, Cosmic Provincialism: Historicizing the Space Age'. In *Imagining Outer Space: European Astroculture in the Twentieth Century*, edited by Alexander C.T. Geppert, 3–24. Basingstoke: Palgrave Macmillan, 2012.

Ghaeni, Zohreh. 'The History of Children's Literature (1900–1940)'. In *Literature of the Early Twentieth Century: From the Constitutional Period to Reza Shah*, edited by Ali-Asghar Seyed-Gohrab, 448–69. London: I.B.Tauris, 2015.

Gilham, Jamie. *Loyal Enemies: British Converts to Islam 1850–1950*. New York: Oxford University Press, 2014.

Gilham, Jamie. 'Marmaduke Pickthall and the British Muslim Convert Community'. In *Marmaduke Pickthall: Islam and the Modern World*, edited by Geoffrey P. Nash, 47–71. Leiden: Brill, 2017.

Gittinger, Mattiebelle. 'Extraterrestrial Inspiration – a Remarkable Batik from the Textile Museum Collection'. In *Building on Batik: The Globalization of a Craft*

Community, edited by Michael Hitchcock and Wiendu Nuryanti, 227–35. Aldershot: Ashgate, 2000.

Glaser, Ed. 'Turkish Flash Gordon'. *Neon Harbor*, 28 January 2015. http://neonharbor.com/turkish-flash-gordon/.

Glaser, Ed. 'Long-Lost 35mm Print of Cult Film "Turkish Star Wars" Rediscovered'. *Neon Harbor*, 7 July 2016. http://neonharbor.com/long-lost-35mm-print-of-cult-film-turkish-star-wars-rediscovered/.

Goldschmidt, Arthur. *Biographical Dictionary of Modern Egypt*. Boulder: Lynne Rienner, 2000.

Gordin, Michael D. *The Pseudoscience Wars: Immanuel Velikovsky and the Birth of the Modern Fringe*. Chicago: University of Chicago Press, 2012.

Gosling, David L. *Science and the Indian Tradition: When Einstein Met Tagore*. Abingdon: Routledge, 2007.

Grandjean, Joan. 'Les collages surréalistes d'Ayham Jabr'. *On Orient*, 22 March 2018. http://onorient.com/collages-numeriques-surrealistes-ayham-jabr-24246-20180322.

Grant, Edward. 'Scientific Imagination in the Middle Ages'. *Perspectives on Science* 12, no. 4 (2004): 394–423.

Gratien, Christopher. '"Man of the Impossible": Nationalism and Creating New Heroes in Post-Nasser Egypt'. MA thesis, Georgetown University, 2008.

Gray, Eliza. 'The Mothership of All Alliances: Scientology and the Nation of Islam'. *New Republic*, 5 October 2012. https://newrepublic.com/article/108205/scientology-joins-forces-with-nation-of-islam.

Green, Nile. 'Spacetime and the Muslim Journey West: Industrial Communications in the Making of the "Muslim World"'. *American Historical Review* 118, no. 2 (2013): 401–29.

Green, Nile. *Terrains of Exchange: Religious Economies of Global Islam*. Oxford: Oxford University Press, 2015.

Günel, Gökçe. *Spaceship in the Desert: Energy, Climate Change, and Urban Design in Abu Dhabi*. Durham: Duke University Press, 2019.

Gürata, Ahmet. 'Tears of Love: Egyptian Cinema in Turkey (1938–1950)'. *New Perspectives on Turkey* 30 (2004): 55–82.

Guthke, Karl S. *The Last Frontier: Imagining Other Worlds from the Copernican Revolution to Modern Science Fiction*. Translated by Helen Atkins. Ithaca: Cornell University Press, 1990.

Güvenç, Serhat, and Lerna K. Yanik. 'Turkey's Involvement in the F-35 Program: One Step Forward, Two Steps Backward?' *International Journal* 68, no. 1 (2013): 111–29.

Habib, S. Irfan. 'Reconciling Science with Islam in 19th Century India'. *Contributions to Indian Sociology* 34, no. 1 (2000): 63–92.

Habib, S. Irfan. 'Viability of Islamic Science: Some Insights from 19th Century India'. *Economic and Political Weekly* 39, no. 23 (2004): 2351–55.

Hanif, Mohsen, and Tahereh Rezaei. 'Ins and Outs of Power in *No Heaven for Gunga Din*'. *Forum for World Literature Studies* 8, no. 3 (2016): 481–90.

Hanson, Carl A. 'Portuguese Cosmology in the Late Seventeenth Century'. *Mediterranean Studies* 1 (1989): 75–85.

Haridi, Alexander. *Das Paradigma der „islamischen Zivilisation" – oder die Begründung der deutschen Islamwissenschaft durch Carl Heinrich Becker (1876–1933): Eine wissenschaftsgeschichtliche Untersuchung*. Würzburg: Ergon, 2005.

Harley, Gail M., and J. Gordon Melton. 'World Brotherhood Union Mevlana Supreme Foundation'. In *Religions of the World: A Comprehensive Encyclopedia of Beliefs and Practices*, edited by J. Gordon Melton and Martin Baumann, 1:3124–25. Second edition. Santa Barbara: ABC-CLIO, 2010.

Hecht, Gabrielle. *Being Nuclear: Africans and the Global Uranium Trade*. Cambridge: MIT Press, 2012.

Hegghammer, Thomas. 'Introduction: What Is Jihadi Culture and Why Should We Study It?' In *Jihadi Culture: The Art and Social Practices of Militant Islamists*, edited by Thomas Hegghammer, 1–21. Cambridge: Cambridge University Press, 2017.

Hellyer, Peter. 'Book Review: UFOs, Hijackings and Threats from the 1970s Surface in Catastrophes, Crashes and Crimes in the UAE'. *The National*, 16 March 2017. http://www.thenational.ae/arts-life/the-review/book-review-ufos-hijackings-and-threats-from-the-1970s-surface-in-catastrophes-crashes-and-crimes-in-the-uae.

Hill, Peter. 'Early Translations of English Fiction into Arabic: *The Pilgrim's Progress* and *Robinson Crusoe*'. *Journal of Semitic Studies* 60, no. 1 (2015): 177–212.

Hill, Peter. 'The First Arabic Translations of Enlightenment Literature: The Damietta Circle of the 1800s and 1810s'. *Intellectual History Review* 25, no. 2 (2015): 209–33.

Hill, Peter. 'Utopia and Civilisation in the Arab Nahda'. PhD thesis, University of Oxford, 2015.

Hill, Peter. 'The Arabic Adventures of *Télémaque*: Trajectory of a Global Enlightenment Text in the *Nahḍah*'. *Journal of Arabic Literature* 49, no. 3 (2018): 171–203.

Hirschler, Konrad. 'The "Pharao" Anecdote in Pre-Modern Arabic Historiography'. *Journal of Arabic and Islamic Studies* 10 (2010): 45–74.

Hochberg, Gil. '"Jerusalem, We Have a Problem": Larissa Sansour's Sci-Fi Trilogy and the Impetus of Dystopic Imagination'. *Arab Studies Journal* 26, no. 1 (2018): 34–57.

Hodgson, Marshall G. S. *The Venture of Islam: Conscience and History in a World Civilization*. Vol. 1. Chicago: University of Chicago Press, 1974.

Holt, Elizabeth M. 'Narrative and the Reading Public in 1870s Beirut'. *Journal of Arabic Literature* 40, no. 1 (2009): 37–70.

Holt, Elizabeth M. 'Narrating the *Nahda*: The Syrian Protestant College, *al-Muqtataf*, and the Rise of Jurji Zaydan'. In *One Hundred and Fifty*, edited by Nadia Maria El-Cheikh, Lina Choueiri and Bilal Orfali, 273–79. Beirut: AUB Press, 2016.

Holton, Gerald. *The Scientific Imagination*. Cambridge: Harvard University Press, 1998.

Hullmeine, Paul. 'Al-Bīrūnī and Avicenna on the Existence of Void and the Plurality of Worlds'. *Oriens* 47, nos. 1/2 (2019): 114–44.

Hutchins, William Maynard. *Tawfiq al-Hakim: A Reader's Guide*. Boulder: Lynne Rienner, 2003.

Ibrāhīm, Ḥāmid. 'Nihād Sharīf fī (Anā wa-kāʾināt al-faḍāʾ): irhāṣāt adab al-khayāl al-ʿilmī'. *Al-Khayāl al-ʿIlmī*, no. 1 (2008): 120–26.

Iqbal, Muzaffar. 'Islamic Theology Meets ETI'. In *Astrotheology: Science and Theology Meet Extraterrestrial Life*, edited by Ted Peters, 216–27. Eugene: Cascade, 2018.

Işiklar Koçak, Müge, and Elif Aydın. 'Science Fiction in Turkey: Survival of a Genre through Retranslations and Reprints'. *Dokuz Eylül Üniversitesi Edebiyat Fakültesi* 4, no. 1 (2017): 31–42.

Jones, Toby C. 'Toxic War and the Politics of Uncertainty in Iraq'. *International Journal of Middle East Studies* 46, no. 4 (2014): 797–799.

Karademir, Burcu Sarı. 'Turkey as a "Willing Receiver" of American Soft Power: Hollywood Movies in Turkey during the Cold War'. *Turkish Studies* 13, no. 4 (2012): 633–45.

Kaur, Raminder. 'The Fictions of Science and Cinema in India'. In *Routledge Handbook of Indian Cinemas*, edited by K. Moti Gokulsing and Wimal Dissanayake, 282–96. Abingdon: Routledge, 2013.

Kazi, Ushah. 'Pakistani Sci-Fi from Shanee to Project Ghazi'. *The Kollective*, 4 July 2017. https://www.thekollective.pk/2017/07/04/pakistani-sci-fi-shanee-project-ghazi/.

Kennedy, Kara. 'Epic World-Building: Names and Cultures in *Dune*'. *Names* 64, no. 2 (2016): 99–108.

Khammas, Achmed A. W. 'The Almost Complete Lack of the Element of "Futureness"'. Translated by Don Mac Coitir. *Telepolis*, 10 October 2006. https://www.heise.de/tp/features/The-Almost-Complete-Lack-of-the-Element-of-Futureness-3408243.html.

Khan, Ali, and Ali Nobil Ahmad. 'From *Zinda Laash to Zibahkhana*: Violence and Horror in Pakistani Cinema'. *Third Text* 24, no. 1 (2010): 149–61.

Khānlarī, Javād. 'Pazhūhishī pīrāmūn-i utūpiyā-yi mudirn va rūykard-i ān dar āsār-i Ṭālib ʿUmrān navīsandah-'i Sūrī'. *Adab-i ʿArabī* 8, no. 1 (2016): 77–94.

Kharitonov, A. V., and E. Y. Vilkoviskij. 'Life and Activities of Academician V.G. Fesenkov'. *Astronomical and Astrophysical Transactions* 24, no. 4 (2005): 261–64.

King, Jacob Michael. 'Clearing the Planet: The Adoption of the Teachings of L. Ron Hubbard by Louis Farrakhan, and Its Significance for the Eschatology of the Nation of Islam'. MA thesis, Claremont Graduate University, 2014.

Kleinman, Adam. 'On Sophia Al-Maria's The Girl Who Fell to Earth'. *E-flux*, February 2013. https://www.e-flux.com/journal/42/60258/on-sophia-al-maria-s-the-girl-who-fell-to-earth/.

Korol, Alexander G. *Academy of Sciences of the Kazakh SSR*. Cambridge: Massachusetts Institute of Technology, 1964.

Kretowicz, Steph. 'Positive Realism with Kuwaiti Artist Monira Al Qadiri'. *I-D*, 28 November 2014. https://i-d.vice.com/en_uk/article/j58pnp/positive-realism-with-kuwaiti-artist-monira-al-qadiri.

Lakkad, Abhishek Vikas. 'Cultural Imaginaries of Science: A Brief History of Indian Science-fiction Cinema'. *Studies in South Asian Film & Media* 6, no. 2 (2015): 105–20.

Lelyveld, David. 'Disenchantment at Aligarh: Islam and the Realm of the Secular in Late Nineteenth Century India'. *Die Welt des Islams* 22, no. 1 (1982): 85–102.

Lent, John A. *Asian Comics*. Jackson: University Press of Mississippi, 2015.

Lieb, Michael. *Children of Ezekiel: Aliens, UFOs, the Crisis of Race, and the Advent of End Time*. Durham: Duke University Press, 1998.

Livingston, John W. *In the Shadows of Glories Past: Jihad for Modern Science in Muslim Societies, 1850 to the Arab Spring*. Abingdon: Routledge, 2018.

Long, C. W. R. 'Taufīq al-Ḥakīm and the Arabic Theatre'. *Middle Eastern Studies* 5, no. 1 (1969): 69–74.

Madoeuf, Anna, and Delphine Pagès-El Karoui. 'Le Caire en 2015 et en 2023 : deux dystopies anticipatrices? Les avenirs funestes de la capitale égyptienne dans Tower of Dreams et Utopia'. *Annales de géographie*, no. 709–710 (2016): 360–77.

Makdisi, Ussama. *Artillery of Heaven: American Missionaries and the Failed Conversion of the Middle East*. Ithaca: Cornell University Press, 2008.

Marten, Michael. *Attempting to Bring the Gospel Home: Scottish Missions to Palestine, 1839–1917*. London: I.B. Tauris, 2006.

Martinez, Alberto A. 'Giordano Bruno and the Heresy of Many Worlds'. *Annals of Science* 73, no. 4 (2016): 345–74.

Maziad, Marwa. 'Qatar: Cultivating "the Citizen" of the Futuristic State'. In *Representing the Nation: Heritage, Museums, National Narratives and Identity in the Arab Gulf States*, edited by Pamela Erskine-Loftus, Victoria Penziner Hightower and Mariam Ibrahim Al-Mulla, 123–40. Abingdon: Routledge, 2016.

McKim, Richard. 'The Life and Times of E.M. Antoniadi, 1870–1944. Part 1: An Astronomer in the Making'. *Journal of the British Astronomical Association* 103, no. 4 (1993): 164–70.

McKim, Richard. 'The Life and Times of E. M. Antoniadi, 1870–1944. Part 2: The Meudon Years'. *Journal of the British Astronomical Association* 103, no. 5 (1993): 219–27.

Merawati, Fitri. 'Perkembangan Fiksi Ilmiah Karya Pengarang Indonesia Tahun 1980-an dan 2000-an Pendidikan Bahasa dan Sastra Indonesia'. *Gramatika* 3, no. 2 (2015): 141–51.

Mignon, Laurent. 'Entre quête scientifique et quête identitaire : la littérature d'anticipation turco-ottomane'. *Cycnos* 22, no. 2 (2006). http://revel.unice.fr/cycnos/index.html?id=591.

Mneimneh, Hassan. '"Futurism" is Shaping up as an Alternative to Islamism, and It May Need to Be Protected from Its Champions'. *Washington Institute for Near East Policy*, 4 September 2018. https://www.washingtoninstitute.org/policy-analysis/view/futurism-is-shaping-up-as-an-alternative-to-islamism-but-it-may-need-protec.

Moore, Lindsey. '"What Happens After Saying No?" Egyptian Uprisings and Afterwords in Basma Abdel Aziz's *The Queue* and Omar Robert Hamilton's *The City Always Wins*'. *CounterText* 4, no. 2 (2018): 192–211.

Mukharji, Projit Bihari. 'Technospatial Imaginaries: Masud Rana and the Vernacularization of Popular Cold War Geopolitics in East Pakistan, 1966–1971'. *History and Technology* 31, no. 3 (2015): 324–40.

Muller, Nat. 'Tomorrow Girls: Sci-Fi, Other Worlds and Geo-Politics in Media Art from the Middle East'. *Di'van: A Journal of Accounts* 3 (2017): 114–21.

Murphy, Sinéad. 'Science Fiction and the Arab Spring: The Critical Dystopia in Contemporary Egyptian Fiction'. *Strange Horizons*, 30 October 2017. http://strangehorizons.com/non-fiction/science-fiction-and-the-arab-spring-the-critical-dystopia-in-contemporary-egyptian-fiction/.

Musa, Mohd Faizal [see also Tehrani, Faisal]. 'Exploration on Islamic Literature Policy in Malaysia'. *World Journal of Islamic History and Civilization* 1, no. 4 (2011): 226–33.

Naficy, Hamid. 'Islamizing Film Culture in Iran'. In *Iran: Political Culture in the Islamic Republic*, edited by Samih K. Farsoun and Mehrdad Mashayekhi, 123–48. London: Routledge, 1992.

Naficy, Hamid. *The Making of Exile Cultures: Iranian Television in Los Angeles*. Minneapolis: University of Minnesota Press, 1993.

Naficy, Hamid. 'Iranian Cinema under the Islamic Republic'. *American Anthropologist* 97, no. 3 (1995): 548–58.

Naylor, Simon, and James R. Ryan. 'The Mosque in the Suburbs: Negotiating Religion and Ethnicity in South London'. *Social & Cultural Geography* 3, no. 1 (2002): 39–59.

Nisar, Muhammad Azfar, and Ayesha Masood. 'The Nostalgic Detective: Identity Formation in Detective Fiction of Pakistan'. *Pakistaniaat* 4, no. 3 (2012): 33–60.

Nuruddin, Yusuf. 'Ancient Black Astronauts and Extraterrestrial Jihads: Islamic Science Fiction as Urban Mythology'. *Socialism and Democracy* 20, no. 3 (2006): 127–65.

Olsa Jr, Jaroslav, and Nada Obadalová. 'SF in the Arab Gulf States and Iran'. *Locus* 47, no. 1 (2001): 46–47.

Omarov, Tuken B., and Bulat T. Tashenov. 'Tikhov's Astrobotany as a Prelude to Modern Astrobiology'. In *Perspectives in Astrobiology*, edited by R.B. Hoover, A. Yu. Rozanov and R.R. Paepe, 86–87. Amsterdam: IOS, 2005.

Ouasti, Boussif. 'La description de l'Égypte'. *Dix-huitième siècle* 22, no. 1 (1990): 73–82.

Özçınar, Meral. 'A Cornerstone of Turkish Fantastic Films: From Flash Gordon to Baytekin'. In *Comics as a Nexus of Cultures: Essays on the Interplay of Media,*

Disciplines and International Perspectives, edited by Mark Berninger, Jochen Ecke and Gideon Haberkorn, 164–74. Jefferson: McFarland, 2010.

Palmer, Susan. *The Nuwaubian Nation: Black Spirituality and State Control*. Farnham: Ashgate, 2010.

Parikka, Jussi. 'Middle East and Other Futurisms: Imaginary Temporalities in Contemporary Art and Visual Culture'. *Culture, Theory and Critique* 59, no. 1 (2018): 40–58.

Peker, Deniz, Gulsum Gul Comert and Aykut Kence. 'Three Decades of Anti-evolution Campaign and Its Results: Turkish Undergraduates' Acceptance and Understanding of the Biological Evolution Theory'. *Science & Education* 19, nos. 6–8 (2010): 739–55.

Pipes, Daniel. '"How Dare You Defame Islam"'. *Commentary* 108, no. 4 (1999): 41–45.

Piscatori, James. 'The Rushdie Affair and the Politics of Ambiguity'. *International Affairs* 66, no. 4 (1990): 767–89.

Qāsim, Maḥmūd. 'Al-taqārub al-fikrī bayna Nihād Sharīf wa-Jūl Fīrn'. *Ibdāʿ*, no. 4 (1984): 116–19.

Qāsim, Maḥmūd, and Yaʿqūb Wahbī. *Dalīl al-mumaththil al-ʿArabī fī sīnimā al-qarn al-ʿishrīn*. Majmūʿat al-Nīl al-ʿArabīyah, 1999.

Qualey, M. Lynx. 'Sci-Fi Iraq: Authors Envision Their Country in 2103, a Century After the U.S. Invasion'. *In These Times*, 12 December 2016. http://inthesetimes.com/article/19688/sci-fi-iraq-plus-100-baghdad-us-invasion.

Qualey, M. Lynx. 'The Director of the Egyptian Society for Science Fiction on Arabic SF's Past, Present, and Future'. *Arabic Literature (in English)*, 28 March 2018. https://arablit.org/2018/03/28/the-director-of-the-egyptian-society-for-science-fiction-on-arabic-sfs-past-present-and-future/.

Qualey, M. Lynx. 'Future-focused "Palestine +100" Wins PEN Translates Award'. *ArabLit: Arabic Literature and Translation*, 18 December 2018. https://arablit.org/2018/12/18/future-focused-palestine-100-wins-pen-translates-award/.

Raina, Dhruv. 'The French Jesuit Manuscripts on Indian Astronomy: The Narratology and Mystery Surrounding a Late Seventeenth – Early Eighteenth Century Project'. In *Looking at It from Asia: The Processes That Shaped the Sources of History of Science*, 115–40. Dordrecht: Springer, 2010.

Rani, Bhargav. 'Science Fiction in the Arab World: Tawfiq Al-Hakim's Voyage to Tomorrow'. *Arab Stages* 1, no. 2 (2015). http://arabstages.org/2015/04/science-fiction-in-the-arab-world-tawfiq-al-hakims-voyage-to-tomorrow/.

Read, Carveth. 'De Maillet'. *Fortnightly Review* 14, no. 79 (1873): 54–63.

Rekabtalaei, Golbarg. 'Cinematic Revolution: Cosmopolitan Alter-cinema of Pre-revolutionary Iran'. *Iranian Studies* 48, no. 4 (2015): 567–89.

Rieder, John. *Science Fiction and the Mass Cultural Genre System*. Middletown: Wesleyan University Press, 2017.

Rodgers, Terence. 'Restless Desire: Rider Haggard, Orientalism and the New Woman'. *Women: A Cultural Review* 10, no. 1 (1999): 35–46.

Rubtsov, Vladimir. *The Tunguska Mystery*. Dordrecht: Springer, 2009.

Saif, Salem. 'Blade Runner in the Gulf'. *Jacobin*, 2 November 2017. http://jacobinmag.com/2017/11/gulf-states-oil-capital-ecological-disaster.

Sakr, Naomi. 'Placing Political Economy in Relation to Cultural Studies: Reflections on the Case of Cinema in Saudi Arabia'. In *Arab Cultural Studies: Mapping the Field*, edited by Tarik Sabry, 214–33. London: I.B. Tauris, 2011.

Sandner, David. 'Shooting for the Moon: Méliès, Verne, Wells, and the Imperial Satire'. *Extrapolation* 39, no. 1 (1998): 5–25.

Sardar, Ziauddin. 'Ibn-e-Safi, BA'. *Critical Muslim* 4 (2012): 133–42.

Schwartz, Matthias. *Die Erfindung des Kosmos: Zur sowjetischen Science Fiction und populärwissenschaftlichen Publizistik vom Sputnikflug bis zum Ende der Tauwetterzeit*. Frankfurt am Main: Peter Lang, 2003.

Schwartz, Matthias. 'Wunder mit wissenschaftlicher Begründung. Verzauberter Alltag und entzauberte Ideologie in der sowjetischer Science Fiction der Nachkriegszeit'. *Berliner Osteuropa Info* 23 (2005): 100–109.

Schwartz, Matthias. 'Guests from Outer Space: Occult Aspects of Soviet Science Fiction'. In *The New Age of Russia: Occult and Esoteric Dimensions*, edited by Birgit Menzel, Michael Hagemeister, and Bernice Glatzer Rosenthal, 211–37. München: Otto Sagner, 2011.

Sharma, Virendra Nath. 'Jai Singh, His European Astronomers and the Copernican Revolution'. *Indian Journal of History of Science* 18, no. 1 (1982): 333–44.

Sheehi, Stephen. 'Arabic Literary-Scientific Journals: Precedence for Globalization and the Creation of Modernity'. *Comparative Studies of South Asia, Africa and the Middle East* 25, no. 2 (2005): 438–48.

Sibireva, Olga. 'Freedom of Conscience in Russia: Restrictions and Challenges in 2017'. In *Xenophobia, Freedom of Conscience and Anti-Extremism in Russia in 2017*, edited by Verkhovsky Alexander, 93–125. Moscow: SOVA Center for Information and Analysis, 2018.

Sievers, Eric W. 'Academy Science in Central Asia 1922–1998'. *Central Asian Survey* 22, nos. 2/3 (2003): 253–79.

Smith, Iain Robert. '"Beam Me up, Ömer": Transnational Media Flow and the Cultural Politics of the Turkish Star Trek Remake'. *Velvet Light Trap* 61, no. 1 (2008): 3–13.

Snir, Reuven. 'The Emergence of Science Fiction in Arabic Literature'. *Der Islam* 77, no. 2 (2000): 263–85.

Solomon, Matthew. 'Introduction'. In *Fantastic Voyages of the Cinematic Imagination: Georges Méliès's* Trip to the Moon, edited by Matthew Solomon, 1–24. Albany: State University of New York Press, 2011.

Somekh, Sasson. 'Biblical Echoes in Modern Arabic Literature'. *Journal of Arabic Literature* 26 (1995): 186–200.

Stolz, Daniel A. *The Lighthouse and the Observatory: Islam, Science, and Empire in Late Ottoman Egypt*. Cambridge: Cambridge University Press, 2018.

Stuster, J. Dana. 'WikiLeaked: The Soviet Space Junk That Became a Moroccan UFO'. *Foreign Policy*, 11 April 2013. http://foreignpolicy.com/2013/04/11/wikileaked-the-soviet-space-junk-that-became-a-moroccan-ufo/.

Szyska, Christian [see also Tsīskā, Krīstiyān]. 'On Utopian Writing in Nasserist Prison and Laicist Turkey'. *Die Welt des Islams* 35, no. 1 (1995): 95–125.

Tahir, Ungku Maimunah Mohd. *Modern Malay Literary Culture: A Historical Perspective*. Singapore: Institute of Southeast Asian Studies, 1987.

Tarikhi, Parviz. *The Iranian Space Endeavor: Ambitions and Reality*. Cham: Springer, 2015.

Tartoussieh, Karim. 'Pious Stardom: Cinema and the Islamic Revival in Egypt'. *Arab Studies Journal* 15, no. 1 (2007): 30–43.

Tasar, Eren. *Soviet and Muslim: The Institutionalization of Islam in Central Asia, 1943–1991*. New York: Oxford University Press, 2017.

Tejfel, Victor. 'Gavriil Adrianovich Tikhov (1875-1960): A Pioneer in Astrobiology'. In *Highlights of Astronomy as Presented at the XVII General Assembly, 2009*, edited by Ian F. Corbett, 720–21. Cambridge: Cambridge University Press, 2010.

Tiwari, Rajive. 'A Transnarrative for the Colony: Astronomy Education and Religion in 19th Century India'. *Economic and Political Weekly* 41, no. 13 (2006): 1269–77.

Toprak, Zafer. *Darwin'den Dersim'e Cumhuriyet ve Antropoloji*. İstanbul: Doğan, 2012.

Tsīskā, Krīstiyān [see also Szyska, Christian]. 'Ḥawla al-kitābah al-ṭūbāwīyah fī sujūn Jamāl ʿAbd al-Nāṣir'. *Al-Karmil*, no. 18–19 (1998): 115–42.

Udías, Agustín. *Searching the Heavens and the Earth: The History of Jesuit Observatories*. Dordrecht: Kluwer, 2003.

Villain, Jacques. 'A Brief History of Baikonur'. *Space Policy* 12, no. 2 (1996): 129–34.

Wagar, W. Warren. 'H. G. Wells and the Scientific Imagination'. *Virginia Quarterly Review* 65, no. 3 (1989): 390–400.

Wainwright, Milton, Amar Laswd, and Fawaz Alshammari. 'Bacteria in Amber Coal and Clay in Relation to Lithopanspermia'. *International Journal of Astrobiology* 8, no. 2 (2009): 141–43.

Wainwright, Milton, Fawaz Alshammari, and Khalid Alabri. 'Are Microbes Currently Arriving to Earth from Space?' *Journal of Cosmology* 7 (2010): 1692–1702.

Wakeford, Iain. 'Wells, Woking and *The War of the Worlds*'. *The Wellsian*, no. 14 (1991): 18–29.

Walker, Jim. 'Urdu Science Fiction – Where Is It?' *The Science Fiction Foundation*, 31 December 2010. http://www.sf-foundation.org/publications/essays/walker.html.

Wass, Janne. 'Where Did You Get This?' *Scifist*, 9 December 2015. https://scifist.wordpress.com/2015/12/09/where-did-you-get-this/.

Wass, Janne. 'Ucan daireler Istanbul'da'. *Scifist*, 14 February 2017. https://scifist.wordpress.com/2017/02/14/ucan-daireler-istanbulda/.

Weintraub, David A. *Religions and Extraterrestrial Life: How Will We Deal With It?* Cham: Springer, 2014.

Weitbrecht, H. U. 'A Moslem Mission to England'. *Muslim World* 4, no. 2 (1914): 195–202.

Westfahl, Gary. *The Spacesuit Film: A History, 1918–1969*. Jefferson: McFarland, 2012.

Whitaker, Brian. *What's Really Wrong with the Middle East*. London: Saqi, 2009.

Whitaker, Brian. 'Star Trekking through the Middle East'. *Al-bab.com*, 3 October 2013. http://al-bab.com/blog/2013/10/star-trekking-through-middle-east.

Wieringa, E. P. 'A *Ta'ziya* from Twenty-first-century Malaysia: Faisal Tehrani's Passion Play *Karbala*'. In *Shi'ism in South East Asia: 'Alid Piety and Sectarian Constructions*, edited by Chiara Formichi and R. Michael Feener, 223–46. New York: Oxford University Press, 2015.

Womack, Ytasha. *Afrofuturism: The World of Black Sci-Fi and Fantasy Culture*. Chicago: Lawrence Hill, 2013.

Yaapar, Md. Salleh. 'The Empire Strikes Back: Re-Writing Malay History and Identity in Faisal Tehrani's Novel *1515*'. *Kunapipi* 32, no. 1 (2010): 80–88.

Yorulmaz, Bilal, and William L. Blizek. 'Islam in Turkish Cinema'. *Journal of Religion & Film* 18, no. 2 (2014).

Zaki, Hoda M. 'Orientalism in Science Fiction'. In *Food for Our Grandmothers: Writings by Arab-American and Arab-Canadian Feminists*, edited by Joanna Kadi. Boston: South End, 1994.

Zakī, Muṣṭafá. *Wurūd lā tubdhal: shakhṣīyāt wa-ḥikāyāt min zaman fāt*. Al-Qāhirah: Shams, 2010.

Zenkovsky, Serge A. 'Ideological Deviation in Soviet Central Asia'. *Slavonic and East European Review* 32, no. 79 (1954): 424–37.

Zook, Darren C. 'Making Space for Islam: Religion, Science, and Politics in Contemporary Malaysia'. *Journal of Asian Studies* 69, no. 4 (2010): 1143–66.

Index

References to illustrations are in *italics*.

Abaza, Roushdy 86–7
Abbas, Ibraheem 8
Abbasid Empire 32
Abdel Aziz, Basma 141–2
Abdel Wahab, Hamada 86–7, 90
Abdul Hakim, Mansoor 130–2
Abdulrazzak, Hassan 192–3
Abu Dhabi 14, 38, 137, 168, 194, 201
Abu Taleb, Mirza 44, 46
Academy Awards 180–1
Achaemenid Empire 34
Adib, Dariyush 126
The Adventures of Telemachus (Fénelon) 39
advertising 37
Aerials (film) 201–2
Afghanistan 77
Afridi, Saks 205–6, *206*
Afrofuturism 111, 177, 206, 207
age ratings 190
Agha, Riad 4–5, 16
Aghdashloo, Shohreh 99
Agra College 44–5, 46
Agrest, Matest 118
Agus, Arfian 171
Ahmad, Asrar *see* Ibne Safi
Ahmadiyya 9, 12, 46, 48
Ahmad, Mirza Tahir 12–13
Ahmad, Muhammad Aurangzeb 32, 208–9, *209*
Ahmad, Shahnon 22
Ahmed, Anwar 82, 84
Ahmed, Gazi Shahabuddin 145
Ahmed, Humayun 146
Ahmed, Mansoor 28
Ahmed, Sultan 74
Ajwan (Al Noman) 138–9
Akher Saa (magazine) 149, 152
Akhtar, Jamshed 15–16, 18
Aladdin (Disney) x, 136
al-Ashqar, Umar 129–32, 136
al-Assad, Bashar 1, 6
al-Assad, Hafez 7, 13
Al-Azzawi, Fadhil 37
Al Baker, Ahmed 204
al-Baqqālī, ʿAbd al-Salām *see* Bakkali, Abdessalam
al-Biruni 10–11, 167
al-Buraq 19, 124
al-Bustani, Butrus 50
Aldoha (magazine) 120, 153, 154
Alexander the Great 25
al-Farabi 16
Algeria 107
al-Hakim, Tawfiq 84–5, 88, 90, 149, 153
al-Haqqani, Sheikh Nazim 110
Al-Hilal (magazine) 60–1, 80, 82, 84, 87, 142
Ali, Abdullah Yusuf 11
Ali Baba and the Forty Thieves (film) 80, 81
Al-Ibrahim, Taibah 4
Alice in Wonderland (Carroll) 171, 184
The Alien (film script) 74
aliens *see* extraterrestrial life
Aliens and Flying Saucers (Sarıkaya) 122
Alien Technology (Al Qadiri) 203
Aligarh Muslim University 7, 46, 143
Ali, Syed Muneeb xii, 42
Al-Jahdhami, Abdullah *see* Shaweesh
al-Jisr, Husayn 52
Allah, Ahmad ʿAbd 155
Allah as life force 29, 48, 63
All Eyes on Egipt Bookstore 116, 117
All Tomorrows (Kösemen) 197–9
al-Maʿarri 16, 149
Al-Machriq (periodical) 50, 55, 61
al-Manār (periodical) 52, 56, 57–8
al-Maqrizi 40
Al-Maria, Sophia 202–3

al-Mas'udi 40
al-Mu'assasah al-'Arabīyah al-Ḥadīthah *see* Modern Arab Establishment
Al-Muktataf (periodical) 50, 51–3, 56, 57, 60
al-Munajjid, Muhammad 7–8, 205
Al Mushrif School, Abu Dhabi 137
Al-Nahhas, Adil 110
Al Noman, Noura 137–9, 141, 174
Al Qadiri, Monira 203
al-Qadisiyah 19
Al-Qaeda 15, 111, 132, 176
al-Qaradawi, Yusuf 15
al-Qazwini, Zakariya 40
Alshammari, Fawaz 29, 41
al-Sibā'ī, Yūsuf *see* El-Sebai, Youssef
Alsubai, Khalid 181–2, 184
al-Suyuti 133
al-Tabari 18
al-Tabīb (periodical) 54–5
al-Yaziji, Ibrahim 54
al-Zambīlī, Ḥusām *see* Elzembely, Hosam
al-Zawahiri, Ayman 132
America 2030 (Elzembely) 19–20
American Association for the Advancement of Science 28, 66
American Astronomical Society 183, 184
American Mission Press, Beirut 50, 51
Ammoun, Iskender 51
Ancient Aliens (TV series) 187
The Andromeda Strain (Crichton) 163
The Angel of Peace (Sanatizadeh) 191
angels 10
animation 189
anime 2
Ansaar Pure Sufi 114
Ansaaru Allah 114–15
Ansar al Islam 175, 176
Ansari, Anousheh 27, 180
Ansari, Nisar Ahmad 74
Ansarullah Bangla Team 175
antichrist 131
Antoniadi, Eugène 58–60, 65, 70
apocalypse 110
apps 189
Arab Human Development Report 2003 (United Nations) 5–6
Arabian Nights 35, 80
Arabic Encyclopedia (al-Bustani) 50
Arab Spring 142, 165
Arab Telemedia Group 204
architecture, futuristic 38
Area X (Handayani) 172–3, 174
Are We Alone in this Universe? (Yamani) 128
Argo (film) 78
Aristotle 10
The Army of the Antichrist: Blackwater (Umar) 132
Around the World in Eighty Days (Verne) 79
Arrissalah (magazine) 12
art
    evolution 196–8
    extraterrestrials 203–4
    Martians 1
    Moon 177
    'My Galactic Dream' contest 187
    Star Trek 209
    surrealism 1
    terraforming 30–1
    UFOs 205
Asharq Al-Aswat (newspaper) 157
Asia-Pacific Science Fiction Convention, Beijing 21
Asia Science Fiction Association 21
Asimov, Isaac 5, 165, 187
Asmandez (game series) 190–1
Assassins 134, 196
Association of Arab Science Fiction Writers 4
Astana, Kazakhstan 38
asteroids 179–80
astrobiology
    criticism 129
    definition x
    development 26
    missionaries 41–2
    Soviet developments 65, 66, 67
    supernatural force 29
Astrobiology Network of Pakistan 28, 29, 30, 42, 180, 194
astrobotany 26, 65, 66, 67, 69
astronauts
    ancient civilizations 117–19, 121, 135
    Baikonur Cosmodrome 27
    Islamic guidelines 13–14
The Astronauts (Lem) 69

astronomy
heliocentrism 43, 44, 46, 48, 49, 69
Qur'an 48, 56–7
in science fiction 150
Astrophysical Journal 184
Atatürk, Kemal 16, 91, 123, 135–6
Aubakirov, Toktar 27
auditing 113
authoritarianism x, 35, 210
Avci Baytekin (comic strip) 94
Avicenna *see* Ibn Sina
Ayaz Astronomical Society 187
Ayed, Kawthar 4
Aysha, Emad El-Din xii, 32
Azad, Reza Roosta 185
Azmi, Bahram 189

Baalbek temple complex, Lebanon 118
bacteria 29, 41, 61
Badayuni, Shakeel 74
Badiyi, Reza 99
Bahjatt, Yasser 8
Baikonur Cosmodrome 26–7, 64
Bakhsheshi, Iraj Fazel 34, 194–5, 201
Bakkali, Abdessalam 31
Balkan Wars 16
Bangladesh 145–8, 175–6
Barkaoui, Khalid 182
batik cloth 37
Battle between the Stars (Wasfi) 167
Battle of the Planets (Farouk) 160
Battlestar Galactica 164, 204
Baweja, Tehseen 8–9
Baytekin: Battle in Space (film) 94–5, 100
Baytekin (comic) 94
The Begum's Fortune (Verne) 79
Behna Films 81, 86
Belkhodja, Abdelaziz 31–2, 33
belly dancing 93, 98
Ben-Hur (film) 80, 91
Benkhaldoun, Zouhair 182
Bermuda 130, 131
The Bermuda Triangle and the Antichrist (Umar) 132
Besson, Luc 103
Beware of the Antichrist Who Invades the World from the Bermuda Triangle (Dawud) 130, 131, 132
The Bible, the Quran, and Science (Bucaille) 133
Biçer, Ramazan 196
Bihari, Shamsul Huda 75
binary stars 182
Black Panther (film) 205
Blasim, Hassan 192
The Blue Flood (Bakkali) 31
Bode, Johann Elert 151
Bollywood 73–5
Bond, Alistair 137
Bozorgmehr 190
Bradbury, Ray 164, 187
Bridenstine, Jim 28
British Astronomical Association 59, 66
British Muslim Society 48
Bruno, Giordano 43, 45
Bucaille, Maurice 133
Büchner, Ludwig 55–6
Buddy (film) 122
Bunyan, John 50
Burj Khalifa, Dubai 201, 202
Burnett, Donald 179
Burton, LeVar 210

Campbell, John W. 155
Carter, Jimmy 129
Carthage 31–2, 33
Cassini orbiter 27, 179, 180
Catholicism 39–40, 43, 49–50
censorship *see also* repression
of authors 173, 193–4
criticism 35
effect on creative expression x, 35, 210
film 72–3, 98
Saudi Arabia 8
as source of fiction 138
Turkey 91, 195, 200
Central Intelligence Agency (CIA) 77–8, 107, 183
Chambers, John 78
Chariots of the Gods? (von Däniken) 121, 127, 132
Charroux, Robert 117
Cheikho, Louis 50, 51–2, 55
Childhood's End (Clarke) 206
children 5, 9, 137
CHNOPS 29
Christianity
doctrine of divinity 52
missionaries 41–3, 45, 49–50, 52
Church of Scientology 112–13

Churchward, James 16
cinemas 75–6, 77 *see also* film
Circles of Creativity (journal) 4
city skylines x
civilizations, religious framing 35
Clarke, Arthur C. 82, 163, 187, 191, 206
climate and world building 33
Close Encounters of the Third Kind (film) 71, 98, 129
Close Encounters of the Third Kind (novel) 125, 163
Cocktail 2000 (Farouk) 159
Cohen, Claudine 41
Cold War 36, 86, 90, 161
colonialism, Western 23, 44, 58
colonization, science fiction 25, 31–2
comets 27
Comic-Con 209–10
comics 94
Committee for the Promotion of Virtue and the Prevention of Vice, Saudi Arabia 8
Communion: A True Story (Strieber) 126
computers 174
conferences and symposiums
  Asia-Pacific Science Fiction Convention 21
  Comic-Con 209–10
  Institute for Research in Fundamental Sciences, Iran 185
  'Islam as a Source of Arts' 22
  Lucian the Syrian Symposium 4, 157
  'Robofight' 175–6
Confessions of a Turkish Ufologist (Yurdözü) 135–6
conservatism x, 8, 9, 210
conspiracism 113, 131–2, 133–4, 136
Contact (Sagan) 156
Copernicanism 43, 44, 49
copyright 189
Çorak, Vedia Bülent Önsü 124–5, 195, 196, 199
COSIMA (Cometary Secondary Ion Mass Analyser) 27
The Craft (Al Qadiri) 204
crafts, traditional 37
creationism 194
creativity 9, 26, 137
Creighton, Gordon 109–10, 126
Crichton, Michael 163
criticism
  censorship 35
  criticism 200–1
  education 5
  under repression 6, 142
  of Western intervention 1, 6–7, 23–4, 26, 191, 192–3
  of world superpowers 143
crossword puzzles 37
cryogenics 150, 154
Cyrano de Bergerac 40
Cyrus the Great 34

dābbah 12–13
Damascus Under Siege (Jabr) 1, 2, 3
Dar Al-Hilal 152
Dark Times (Omran) 6–7
Darwin, Charles 53, 56
Davoodi, Abolhassan 77, 98
da'wah 15–16
Dawud, Muhammad 'Isa 130–2
death threats 148
Defoe, Daniel 50
de Fontanelle, Bernard 40
de Lalande, Jérôme 49
de Maillet, Benoît 39–41
DeMille, Cecil 80
In the Depths of Space (Samaha) 63
Description of Egypt (de Maillet) 39
deserts 33, 86, 96
Desi Star Trek 209, *209*
Deutsche Forschungsgemeinschaft 28
digital technology 174
Disney x, 136
diversity 9
The Djinn Connection (Guiley) 136–7
Djokolelono 169
Doha, Qatar x, 202–3
Dominik, Martin 186
Dönmeh 196
Douglass, Andrew Ellicott 55
Dracula in Istanbul (film) 92
Dracula in Pakistan (film) 72
Dreams of Politics and How Universal Peace Can Be Realized (Jawhari) 62
Dune (Herbert) 96–7, 138
Duret, Noël 49
Duru, Orhan 121–2
dystopias 141–2, 164–5

East India Company 44
eclipses 44
education
  authoritarianism 5–6, 35
  economic vs creative 9
  evolution vs creationism 194, 195, 200
  imagination 137
  science in native language 147
Egypt
  de Maillet's book 39, 40
  film 78, 81–2, 86–7
  science fiction 18, 21, 141, 149–57, 159–68
  theatre and plays 83–5, 87–90
Egyptian Pocket Novels 158, 159, 165
Egyptian Society for Science Fiction 21, 32
Egyptian Story Club 152
Einstein, Albert 61
Elachi, Charles 179
El-Baz, Farouk 119
El-Ola, Zahrat 83
El-Sadat, Anwar 76, 119
El-Sebai, Youssef 152–3, 155
El-Sheikh, Kamal 155
Elyta, Riawani 33
Elzembely, Hosam xii, 18–20, 21, 32
Empire of the Stars (Towfik) 164
Enayat, Ragy 120, 121
Enceladus 180
England 46–7
Envisioning Progress and Islamic Civilization in a Dream (Nazım) 16
Ephesus, as film location 95
Epistle of Forgiveness (al-Maʿarri) 16
Erçin, Orhan 92
Esfandiary, Fereidoun M. 98 *see also* FM-2030
E.T. Armies (game) 190, 191
E.T. the Extra-Terrestrial (film) 74, 101, 122
eugenics 112
Europa 180, 181
European Astrobiology Network Association 28
European Research Council 28
evolution 7, 49–50, 56, 194–5, 196–9
exoplanets 181–3, 184–6
extraterrestrial life
  ancient civilizations 117–19, 121, 135, 168
  appearance 14–15
  film 79, 92, 100, 101, 188, 200, 203
  meteorites 60–1
  microorganisms 28, 185
  Moon 52
  Qur'an x, 11, 12–13, 35, 57, 62, 69, 110, 120
  religion 13, 156
  in science fiction 20, 82–4, 151–3, 159–60, 166–8, 192–3, 195, 197–9
  search for x, 129, 179, 184–5, 210
  sightings on Earth 109
  solar planets 53, 54–5, 56, 63, 180
extremism 23–4, 26, 176
extremophiles 185

Fahrenheit 451 (Bradbury) 164
Faisal, Daoud 114
Faisal (Saudi king) 76
Falling into the Sun (Djokolelono) 169
Fantasy (Towfik) 162–3
Fares, Mohammed 27
Farhadi, Asghar 180
Farouk, Nabil 157–62, 163, 168, 174
Farrakhan, Louis 112, 113
Fatar, Syila 33
fatwas on reading science fiction 7–8
Federation of Malaysian Islamic Writers 22
Fénelon, François 39, 41
Fermi paradox 185
Fesenkov, Vasiliy 63–4, 68
fiction *see also* science fiction
  alternate history 23
  children's 138
  religious 9, 10
1511 Hijri (Combat) (Tehrani) 23–4
1515 (Tehrani) 23
The Fifth Dimension (play) 89–90
The Fifth Element (film) 103
film *see also* cinemas
  Academy Awards 180–1
  censorship 72–3, 98
  copyright 99–100, 102
  Egypt 78, 81–2, 86–7
  extraterrestrials on Earth 71, 74, 77
  flying saucers 71–2, 74
  India 73–5, 80
  Iran 77, 97–8, 188–9
  Islam 72

locations 33, 86, 95, 97, 99–100, 201, 209
overview 36
Pakistan 71–3
Qatar 203
religion 80
scientific use 81
secularism compared to Islamism 75
solar planets life 70
space travel 69, 74, 78–9
Turkey 78, 91–6, 99–103, 122, 200–1
United Arab Emirates 201–2
First Spaceship on Venus (film) 69, 75
Five Weeks in a Balloon (Verne) 51
Flammarion, Camille 53–4, 59, 61, 65, 122, 127
Flash Gordon 37, 94, 100, 163
flying carpets 35
The Flying Saucer (film) 92
Flying Saucer Review (FSR) 108, 109–10, 124, 126
flying saucers *see* UFOs
Flying Saucers over Istanbul (film) 92–3
Flying Saucers: Truth or Fiction (Yamani) 119
FM-2030 98, 190–1
The Forest of Justice (Marrash) 50
Forman, Charles 42
Forman Christian College, Lahore 42, 46
Fortean Times 108
fossils 33
Foster and Partners 38
Frankenstein in Baghdad (Saadawi) 194
Freemasons 132, 134
free speech as propaganda facade 6
FSR see Flying Saucer Review
Future File (Farouk) 159–61
futurisms/futurists 111, 176, 177, 202, 204–7, 210

Gaddafi, Muammar 112
Gagarin, Yuri 65
Galatasaray football club 102
Galaxy of the Virtuous (Jaini) 25–6
Galileo Galilei 43
games/gaming 20, 24, 37, 174, 189–91
Gaza 168
Geller, Uri 124
Genesis 47
geocentricism 49, 66
Gezen, Müjdat 101
Ghaffari, Mujtaba 187
Ghalayini, Basma 193–4
Ghamrawy, Muhammad 11–12, 120
Ghanem, Zuhair 6
Ghotbzadeh, Sadegh 178
Ghubash, Ghanem 201
Gilgamesh 118, 190
Gill, Gordon 38
The Girl Who Fell to Earth (Al-Maria) 203
Global Construction of Flying Saucers (Science Research Center) 127
Global Pocket Novels 163, 164
God and Modern Science (Naufal) 69
gods, extraterrestrial life 118, 121, 126, 173–4
Göktürks 135
Golkarian, Ghadir 127
Gomaa, El-Sayyed Hassan 80–1, 82–3
Gomorrah 118
Google Doodles 165
G.O.R.A.: A Space Movie (film) 103, 200
Gordin, Michael 29
Grant, Charles 44
Grenada 108
Guardian Angel (Bakhsheshi) 34
Guiley, Rosemary Ellen 136–7
Gulf Weekly Mirror 106
Gulls of Lake Siljan 196

Habitat-OASIS (Habitability of Oceans and Aqueous Systems on Icy Satellites) 27
Hachtroudi, Mohsen 127
Haggard, Henry Rider 143
Haghighipour, Nader 182–3, 185
Hagia Sophia, Istanbul 59, 124
Hahn, Otto 60
The Half-Humans (Elzembely) 19
Hall, Hal 32
Hamas 111, 130
Hameed, Salman 8
Hamsho, Khaled 108, 110
Handayani, Eliza Vitri 37, 171–4
Haque, Yasmeen 146, 148
Harb, Talaat 81
Hasan, Fariha 29
Hasina, Sheikh 175–6
Hassan II, King of Morocco 107

Heaven and the People of Heaven (Naufal) 118
Heinlein, Robert 84, 96, 157, 163
heliocentrism 43, 44, 46, 48, 49, 69
Herbert, Frank 96–7, 138
herpes virus 20
Herschel, John 45
Herschel, William 61
The Hidden Threads (Dawud) 132
Hikmet, Nâzım 123
Hindu mythology 44
Hirst, Damien 207
Hittites 135
HIV 132, 134
Hodgson, Marshall 1
Homoti (film) 101–2
Hoodbhoy, Pervez 8, 9, 42
Hope Mars Mission 14
hostage rescues 77–8
Hubbard, L. Ron 113
Hundred Studio Productions 77
Husayn, Mir Muhammad 43–4
Hussain, Anwar 75
Hussain, Qazi Anwar 145–6
Hussein, Abdul Razak 22
Huygens, Christiaan 40
HWJN (Abbas & Bahjatt) 8, 10
Hynek, J. Allen 108, 125

I and the Space Beings (Sherif) 153–4, 155
ibn ʿAbbas, ʿAbd Allah 13
Ibne Safi 37, 143–5, 159
Ibn Sina 10–11, 127, 167
Ibn Taymiyah 133
Ibn Tufayl 16, 149
Ibrahim, Anwar 23
Ibrahim of Szigetvár 49
I Dream of Jeannie (TV series) 136
I Love Earth (film) 77, 98
imagination
  censorship 8
  creativity 26, 137
  education 5, 9
  scientific 29–30, 187–8, 210
Imani, Blair 209–10
Imbrogno, Philip 136
Imran (Ibne Safi) 143–4
İnanç, Çetin 99–100, 102
ʿInāyat, Rājī *see* Enayat, Ragy
independence 32
Independence Day: Resurgence (film) 201, 202
India
  Aligarh Muslim University 7
  film 73–5, 80
  missionaries 42–3
Indonesia 30–1, 33, 108, 168–73
innovation 9
'Insider Outsider' (Afridi) 205
Institute of Astronomy and Physics, Almaty 64
Institute of Language and Literature, Kuala Lumpur 22
intelligence 199
Interdimensional Universe (Imbrogno) 136
International Journal of Astrobiology 29
International Space Station 13
International UFO Reporter 108, 124
Intykbayeva, B. B. 68
The Invincible (Lem) 191
The Invisible Man (film) 81
The Invisible Man in Istanbul (film) 92
Iqbal, Muhammed Zafar 146–9, 175–6
Iran
  diaspora 98–9, 177–8, 180–1, 183
  exoplanet research 184–6
  film 77, 97–8, 188–9
  games industry 189–91
  Joint Comprehensive Plan of Action 183
  sanctions 77, 125, 183–4, 185, 186–8, 189
  science fiction 187–8, 191–2, 194–5
  space programmes 210
  UFOs 107, 125–7
  World War II 191
Iranian National Observatory 183
Iraq 126, 192–3, 194
Iraq+ 100 (Blasim) 192–3
Irving, Washington 164
ISIS 176
Islam, practicalities on International Space Station 13–14
'Islam and I' (Handayani) 173–4
Islam and Science Fiction (website) 32, 208
Islamicates Volume I (ed. Ahmad) 208
'Islamic civilization,' use of term 34–5

Islamic Mission of America 114
Islamic 'nation,' use of term 34
Islamic Review & Muslim India (journal) 48
Islamic science fiction 15–16, 17–19, 23–6, 89, 101, 208
Islamic Sci-fi (blog) 25
Islam in the Age of Science (Ghamrawy) 12
Islam Online (website) 15–16
Islam Question and Answer (website) 7–8
Ismail, Taufiq 172–3
Ivy (film) 200

Jabr, Ayham 1–2, 6, 10, 36
Jaini, Azrul xii, 24–6, 37
Jai Singh II 43
Jama, Riya 207–8
Jamaludin, Ahmad 108, 109
James Bond (Fleming) 100, 143–5, 157, 159
Janmohamed, Shelina 14
Java 30–1, 37
Javan, Rambod 188–9
Jawhari, Tantawi 62
Jeans, James Hopwood 62
Jessup, Morris 131
Jesuits 42–3, 50, 51
The Jewels (Jawhari) 62
jihadists 26
jinn 10, 109–10, 126, 129–30, 133, 135, 136–7
Journal of Cosmology 29
Journal of Islamic Science 15
Journal of the British Astronomical Association 66
journals 36
Journey to the Centre of the Earth (Verne) 51
Journey to the Moon (film) 86–7, 88
Jum'ah, al-Sayyid Ḥasan *see* Gomaa, El-Sayyed Hassan
jumlakah 7
Jungle Fire (Ibne Safi) 144–5
Jupiter 43, 53, 180
Jurdak, Mansur 56

Kaaba, Mecca 13, 23, 124, 134
Kamal-ud-Din, Khwaja 46–7, 48
Karaçelik, Tolga 200
Karbala (Tehrani) 24
Kardashev scale 185
Kary-Niyazov, Tashmukhamed 63
Kazakhstan 26–7, 38, 63–6
Kazakhstan Academy of Sciences 65, 66
Kazantsev, Alexander 68–9, 75, 118
Keilany, Kamel 149
Kemalism 135–6
Keyhoe, Donald 119
Khalifa, Rashad 15
Khan, Abdul Aziz 132–4
Khatami, Mohammad 20
Khawaja, Nozair xii, 27–8, 180
Khorram, Homayoun 127
Khwarizmi Science Society 28
Kilani, Mustapha 31
King, Stephen 164
Kissinger, Henry 107
Klenner, Fabian 180
Knight Templar 134
The Knowledge Book (Çorak) 125, 195, 196
Koi ... Mil Gaya (film) 74, 75
Kolosimo, Peter 117
Konrad, Mikel 92
Kösemen, Cevdet Mehmet xii, 196–200
Kreis, Alex 208–9
kris 26, 96, 196
Kubrick, Stanley 75
Kuwait
  art 203–4
  UFOs 105–6, 110

Laplace, Pierre-Simon 61
The Last Jedi (Shaweesh) 76
L'Astronomie (periodical) 59
Laswd, Amar Abdusalam 41
Lawrence of Arabia (film) 96
Lawrence, T. E. 58, 96
League of Arabic SciFiers 8
Leitner, Gottlieb 46–7
Le Mascrier, Jean-Baptiste 39
Lem, Stansiław 69, 191
Lestari, Dee 170–1, 174
Le Verrier, Urbain 62
Liapunov, Boris 68, 69
Libya 112
life *see also* extraterrestrial life
  evolution 7, 49–50, 56, 194–5, 196–9
  interpretation of *dābbah* 12–13

materialism 65, 66, 69
panspermia 40, 41, 61
supernatural force 29, 48, 63
literature, religious 9
The Living Corpse (film) 72
The Lonely Planetary Traveler (Iqbal) 148
Lord of Light (Zelazny) 78
Lord of the Rings (Tolkien) 138
'lord of the worlds' x, 10–11, 12, 45, 57
Lost Children of Babylon 116
Lowell, Percival 54, 56, 59
Lucas, George 97, 164
Lucian of Samosata 4
Lucian the Syrian Symposium 4, 157
Lysenko, Trofim 67

Madan, J. J. 80
Maestrone, Frank 105–6
magazines 36
Mahfouz, Naguib 18, 32
Mahmoud, Abd-el-Halim 12
Mahmoud, Mustafa 20
Malaysia 13, 21–4, 37, 109
Malaysian UFO Bulletin 108
Malcolm X 111, 112
Malik, Adam 108
Manarov, Musa 27
Man From Atlantis (TV series) 138
Man of the Impossible (Farouk) 159
Mansour, Anis 118–19, 121, 128
Mansouri, Reza 183–4, 187
The Man Who Saved the World (film) 99–101
Mao Zedong 129
Marrash, Francis 50–1, 62
Mars
1949 explosion 69
'canals' 36, 53, 56, 60, 64–5, 70
exploration 179
Hope Mars Mission 14
life 54, 55, 63, 67
migration 177, 210
in science fiction 82–4, 89–90, 151–2
travel to 15
Martians 1
The Martian (Weir) 187
Marvels of Creatures and Strange Things Existing (al-Qazwini) 40
Marvel Studios 205
Mashhoon, Bahram 182
Massively Multiplayer Online (MMO) game award 190
Masud Rana (Hussain) 145
materialism 65, 66, 69
The Matrix (film) 103, 176
Maududi, Abul A'la 13
Max Payne (game series) 176
Mayatepek, Hasan Tahsin 16
McDonald, James 131
The Meaning of the Glorious Koran (Pickthall) 11
Mecca 13, 17, 23, 103, 111–12, 116, 119, 124, 134, 167
MechCommander (game) 24
medieval texts 16, 29
Medinah (TV series) 204
Méliès, Georges 78–80
Menzel, Donald 119
Mercury 54, 61
Metapsychic Investigations and Scientific Research Society, Turkey 122
meteorites 60–1
Mexico 16
Michurinism 66
microlensing 184–5
microorganisms 28, 29, 61
Middle East influence on Western culture 78–80, 96–7
MiNDSTEp (Microlensing Network for the Detection of Small Terrestrial Exoplanets) 184
miracles 10
Mirdrekvandi, Ali 191
Mirrors of Dead Hours (Kilani) 31
Miscavige, David 113
missionaries
Christian 41–3, 45, 49–50, 52
Muslim 46, 48
Mizrahi, Togo 81
moderation 18–19
Modern Arab Establishment 157, 159, 162, 165
Modern Egyptian Theater 83–4
Mohammed bin Rashid Space Centre (MBRSC) 14
Mohmand, Abdul Ahad 27
monarchic republics 7
Monir, Alexandra 181

Montesquieu 40
Moon
art 177
extraterrestrial life 52
film 78–9, 86–7
science fiction 4, 90, 161, 163
moons 180
Morocco
observatories 182
satellites 210
UFOs 107
Mosaferan (TV series) 188–9
A Mosque Among the Stars (ed. Ahmad) 208
mosques
England 47
futuristic architecture 38
Hagia Sophia, Istanbul 59, 124
in space 14
SpaceMosque *206, 207*
Mostafa, Niazi 81
Mount Merapi, Java 30–1
Mubarak, Hosni 21, 88
Muftah, Mahmud 120–1
Muhammad al-Bukhari 131
Muhammad, Elijah 111–12
Muhammad, Wallace Fard 111, 114
mujahidin 25–6
Mu (legendary lost continent) 16, 135
Musabayev, Talgat 27
Musa, Mohd Faizal *see* Tehrani, Faisal
Museum of Islamic Art, Qatar 34–5
Muslim Brotherhood 88–9, 176
Muslim ibn al-Hajjaj 131, 133
Muslim India and Islamic Review (journal) 46, 47, 48
'Muslim world,' use of term 34
Mustafa, Hamdi 157, 159
Mutual UFO Network (MUFON) 108, 132
Mysterious Visitors (Trench) 131

Naderi, Firouz 178–81
Naduga (film) 81
Nahas Film 81
Nar, Ali 17–18
NASA (National Aeronautics and Space Administration) 28, 67, 178–80, 185
Nasir, Jamil 141
Nasser, Gamal Abdel 85, 88, 152
The National (Abu Dhabi newspaper) 14
National Iranian Radio and Television (NIRT) 178
nationalism 102, 148, 158, 177
nation-building 37, 143, 147
Nation of Islam 111–13, 115
Nature's Testimony to the Existence of God and Divine Law (Marrash) 51
Naufal, Abdul Razzak 69, 118, 120
Nazım, Mustafa 16, 17
Neidich, Scott 209
Neptune 54
New Richelian Ephemerides of the Celestial Movement (Duret) 49
Niblo, Fred 80
Nimr, Faris 50, 53–4, 58, 60
9/11 20, 23
Nineteen Eighty-Four (Orwell) 164
Nizami Ganjavi 10–11
No Heaven for Gunga Din (Mirdrekvandi) 191–2
Nojum (magazine) 187
Noor Iranian Film Festival, Los Angeles 99
Nova (Wasfi) 165–7
From Now On Everything Will Be Different (Handayani) 173
Nubian Islaamic Hebrews 114
'Number 4 Commands You' (Sherif) 151
numerology 15
Nuwaubian Nation 115–16, 117
A Nymph from Mars (play) 83–4, 88

observatories
Egypt 87, 88, 149–50
France 60
India 42, 43
Iran 183
Kepler 183
Morocco 182
Syria 50, 53
Ögelman, Hakkı 124
Ogoniok (magazine) 65
Okar, Zeki 121
Oktar, Adnan 195–6
Omran, Taleb 3–7, 11, 14, 21, 31–2, 75, 141, 153, 210
One Thousand and One Nights x, 16, 80, 134, 136, 149

One Thousand and One Nights (film) 81
oppression 22–3, 24
orientalism, influence on Western culture 78–80, 81, 96–7, 143
orreries 44
Orwell, George 142, 164
Oscars ceremony 180–1
Otared (Rabie) 141
Othman, Mazlan 14–15, 186
Ottoman Empire 16, 32, 48–9, 102
Özonuk, Şinasi 94

pacifism 1
Pakistan 8–9, 27–8, 71–3, 143–4
The Palace of the Arabian Nights (film) 80
Palestine 32, 193–4
Palestine+ 100 (Ghalayini) 193–4
Paley, William 45, 51
Pamuk, Orhan 18
pandemics 61
panspermia 39–40, 41, 61
Parin, Vasily 65
The Particle (Lestari) 171
Par, Zafer 122
Pasaribu, Norman Erikson 33
Pasha, Mohamed Sherif 149
The People of the Cave (play) 84–5
The People of the Eighth Heaven (play) 87–8
Peril in Space (Iqbal) 147
persecution 9
Persian Letters (Montesquieu) 40
Philips, Bilal 114
Pickering, William 55
Pickthall, Marmaduke 11
pilgrimage 13
The Pilgrim's Progress (Bunyan) 50
piracy 168
Piri Reis 17, 121, 122
PK (film) 74
The Planet Mars (Antoniadi) 60
Planet of Storms (film) 75
Planet of the Apes (film) 75
planets
  exoplanets 181–3, 184–6
  Qur'an 12, 13
  solar 53, 54–5, 56, 63, 180
plurality 10–11, 12, 29, 40, 43, 45
poetry 26, 33, 37
police, religious 8
politics
  censorship and criticism x, 200–1
  nationalist 148
  religion 35
Post, George 54
Pourahmad, Ali 77, 188
prayers
  direction of Mecca from space 13, 14
  'lord of the worlds' 11
prison 88–9
Prison of the Moon (Farouk) 161
propaganda
  facade of free speech 6
  terrorism 176
proselytization 15–16
Protestantism 49–50
Psalms 55, 62
pseudoscience 29, 51–2, 117, 122
Ptolemy 10
PTS (publisher) 24–5
puppets 37

Qatar x, 8, 15, 34, 120–1, 177, 202–3, 204
Qatar Exoplanet Survey 181–2
The Queue (Abdel Aziz) 141–2
Qur'an
  astronomy 48, 56–7
  extraterrestrial life x, 11, 12–13, 35, 57, 62, 69, 110, 120
  'lord of the worlds' x, 10–11, 12, 45, 57
  miracles 10
  numerology 15
  translations 11
  UFOs 110, 133–4
Qureshi, S. M. 74
Qutb, Muhammad 89
Qutb, Sayyid 89–90

Rabie, Mohamed 141
Raef, Ahmed 88–90, 176
Rah-E Zendegi (magazine) 178
Rahman, Faizur 175
Rahvar, Sohrab xii, 184–6, 194
Raiders of the Lost Ark (film) 100
Ramez, Reza 127
Ramzan, Sidra 29
Rasheed, Rabeea 30
Raspina Studio 190, 191

Raymond, Alex 94
Ray, Satyajit 74
Reaching for the Stars (Tikhov) 66
Red Planet (magazine) 14
regimes, criticism 7
religion
of extraterrestrial life 13
film 80, 101
and modern science 41–2, 150–1, 154–5
politics 35
sensitivities 7
as source of fiction 10, 156, 166–7
UFOs xi, 37, 110–11, 112, 113, 115, 123, 124, 128–9
religious literature 9
religious police 8
repression 6, 196, 200 *see also* censorship
resistance 7, 32, 142, 192
The Return of the Elephant (Belkhodja) 31–2
Return to the Stars (von Däniken) 119, 121
Revelation, Rationality, Knowledge and Truth (Ahmad) 12
Ribera, Antonio 108
Rida, Rashid 52
Riyadii Farxiyo (Jama) 208
Rizvi, Saeed 72, 73, 74
Robinson Crusoe (Defoe) 50
'Robofight' 175
robot citizenship 204
Roddenberry, Gene 95, 96
Rodet, Augustin 54
A.R.O.G: A Prehistoric Film (film) 103
Rokeya, Begum 139
Rome, ancient 32
Rosetta spacecraft 27
Rostam in the Twenty-second Century (Sanatizadeh) 34
Rouhizad, Bahman 125
Royal Society of London 186
Ruhselman, Bedri 122, 123
Rumi 123, 124
Rushdie, Salman 15
Russia 49, 63, 196

Saadawi, Ahmed 194
Saadeh, Khalil 54
Saberhagen, Fred 191
Sagan, Carl 67, 156
Saheki, Tsuneo 69
Said, A. Samad 22
Sajadian, Sedighe 186
Saladin 19, 25
Salam, Abdus 8, 9
Salama, Fathi 152
Salam Award for Imaginative Fiction 42
Salem, Ali 87–8
Samaha, Abdel Hamid 62–3
Sanatizadeh, Abdolhosain 34, 191
Saner, Hulki 95
Sansour, Larissa 177
Saqafi, Mirza Khalil Khan 126–7
Sarıbacak, Nadir 200–1
Sarıkaya, Halûk Egemen 122–4, 136, 195
Sarkis, Joseph 51
Sarruf, Yakub 50, 55, 60
The Satanic Verses (Rushdie) 15
satellites 84, 169, 178, 210
Satbayev, Kanysh 63, 65, 66, 68
Saturn 27, 43
Saudi Arabia
art photography 76
censorship 8
cinemas 75–6, 205
film 204
robots 204–5
Scalzi, John 187
Schaffner, Franklin 75
Schiaparelli, Giovanni 53–4, 59
science
and religion 41–2, 150–1, 154–5
sanctions 183–4
use of film 81
science fiction literature
Arabic term 30
Bangladesh 147–8
for children 138
Egypt 18, 21, 82–5, 149–57, 159–68
fatwas 7–8
Indonesia 168–73
Iran 187–8, 191–2, 194–5
Islamic 15–16, 17–19, 23–6, 89, 101, 208
Pakistan 143–4
Polish 69
publication volumes 32

reasons for underdevelopment 6
scope of genre 9
Soviet 68
United Arab Emirates 138, 139, 141
Science Fiction (Ministry of Culture, Syria) 3–4, 5, 6
Science (journal) 28
Science Research Center 122–4, 127, 136
Science Research Foundation 195–6
scientific imagination 29–30, 33, 36, 176–7, 187–8, 210
Scientific Literature (Damascus University) 4
Scientific Malaysian (magazine) 15
Scientific Views on the Conquest of Space (Yamani) 119
Scientology 112–13
The Search for Other Worlds (Omran) 6, 11, 210
In Search of Ancient Gods (von Däniken) 127
In Search of Our Origins: How the Quran Can Help in Scientific Research (Akhtar) 18
Secchi, Angelo 53
The Secret of the Flying Saucers (Enayat) 120
secularism 36, 75, 78, 91, 134, 147
Semum (film) 135
Senderens, Jean-Baptiste 61
Sen, Hiralal 80
September 11 attacks 20, 23
SETI project 184–5, 210
Sevastupulo, Katherine 59
Seven Pillars of Wisdom (Lawrence) 58, 96
shadow plays 37
Shahin, Elham 88
Shahnameh (Book of Kings) 34
Shahrabi, Hossein 187–8
Shanee (film) 71–2, 73
Sharīf, Nihād *see* Sherif, Nehad
Shaweesh 76
She (Haggard) 143
Sherif, Nehad 4, 20, 149–52, 153–7
Shia Islam 24, 77, 115
A Short History of the World (Wells) 47
Shumayyil, Shibli 55–6
Siddiqi, Mohamad Abul Hasan 47–8
Sidqi, Muhammad Tawfiq 52, 56–7, 60
simulations 173–4
Simulator Developer 190, 191
Sirius 122, 125, 136, 166
Sitchin, Zecharia 117, 136
The Sky and Flying Saucers (Muftah) 120–1
Smith, Adrian 38
Snaiad (Kösemen) 199
Snow (Pamuk) 18
socialism 123
Society of Experimental Spirit Science, Tehran 127
Sodom 118
Solar system 12, 44, 179–80
The Son of the Man Who Saved the World (film) 102–3
The Son of the Stars (Sherif) 156–7
The Sons of the Sun (Bakhsheshi) 194–5
The Sons of Two Suns (film) 201
Soviet Academy of Sciences 63
Soviet Astronomy (periodical) 63–4, 69
Space Battle (Ibne Safi) 144–5
A Space Exodus (film) 177
Space Explorer (Djokolelono) 169
Space Farmers (Nar) 17–18
Space Invaders (game) 20
SpaceMosque (Afridi) *206*, *207*
Space Princess (Wasfi) 167
space programmes 13–14, 26–7, 177, 179, 210
Spanish Flu 61
Spencer Jones, Harold 12
Spielberg, Steven 72, 74, 98, 101, 125, 129, 163
Spiritism 122, 126–7
Spy World (Ibne Safi) 143
StarCraft (game) xiii, 3, 24
Star Trek
adaptations 95–6
influence 3, 185, 203, 209–10
Iranian diaspora 99
locations 201
Romulans 32
Star Wars
adaptations xi, 36, 37, 143, 164
characters in photographic art 76
influence 3, 20, 23, 24, 99–100, 102, 103, 137, 189
locations 33, 97, 201, 209
Middle East influence 97–8
scene stealing 99–100

state institutions 35
Stephen, Nur-ud-Din 48
Stranger than Fiction (Enayat) 120
Strieber, Whitley 126
Sufism 123, 206
Sugimoto, Hiroshi 206
Sultana's Dream (Rokeya) 139
sunlight as germ carrier 61
Sun of Tomorrow (anthologies) 21
sunspots 43
supernatural force 29, 48
The Supernatural (Towfik) 162, 164
Supernova (Lestari) 170
surrealism 1
Suslov, A. K. 65
Syed Ahmad Khan 45–6, 48
Syria
    Ministry of Culture 2–4, 6
    science fiction 141
Syrian Arab News Agency 4
Syrian Civil War 1–2
Syrian Protestant College (SPC) 50, 53, 54

Takwin (magazine) 208
Taliban 77
Tangent Worlds (Kösemen) 199–200
Tawfīq, Aḥmad Khālid *see* Towfik, Ahmed Khaled
Tehran 2121 (film) 189
Tehrani, Faisal 22–4
Tekgül, Özcan 92–3, 98
telescopes 42, 43
Telliamed (de Maillet) 39–40
The Ten Commandments (film) 80, 91
terraforming 30–1
terrorism 175–6
textiles 37
theatre and plays 83–5, 87–90
Thief of Bagdad (film) 80
The Thing (Sherif) 155–6
Thomason, James 44–5
Thomson, William, Lord Kelvin 61
Those Who Descended from the Sky (Mansour) 118, 119
Those Who Returned to the Sky (Mansour) 118–19
The Throne of the Devil, the Bermuda Triangle, and the Flying Saucers (Abdul Hakim) 131
Tikhov, Gavriil 26–7, 63–6, 67, 68, 69, 70
Time Conqueror (film) 155
Time Conqueror (Sherif) 149–50, 152, 153, 154
time travel 34, 103
Tolkien, J.R.R. 138
Topaz Duo: Cosmic Phoenix (film) 203
Tourist Ömer in Star Trek 95–6
Towards the Future (film) 188
Tower of Dreams (Nasir) 141
Towfik, Ahmed Khaled 162–5, 168
Treasures from the Wreck of the Unbelievable (Hirst) 207
Treatise of Astronomy (de Lalande) 49
Trench, Brinsley Le Poer 119, 131
Trinil Gate (Elyta & Fatar) 33
Trip to Moon (film) 74, 75
A Trip to the Moon (film) 78–80, 79
Triton is a Planet's Name (Iqbal) 147–8
A True Story (Lucian) 4
Trump, Donald 180, 181
Tsiolkovsky, Konstantin 67
Tuema, Edmond 82, 86
Tunguska event 68, 69
Tunisia
    film locations 33, 97, 100
    science fiction 31
    UFOs 107
Turkey
    advertising 37
    censorship 91, 195, 200
    comics 94
    evolution vs creationism 195, 200
    film 36, 78, 91–6, 99–103, 122, 200–1
    nationalism 16–17
    ufology 121, 122–5, 128, 134–6
Turkey UFO Report 124
Turkish Space Test (TV series) 200
2001: A Space Odyssey (film) 75, 163

Ubedi, Obaidullah 45
ufology 36–7, 104, 107, 108–10, 117–25, 128–36
UFO-Nachrichten 124
UFO Robot Grendizer (anime series) 2
UFOs
    art 205
    religion xi, 37, 110–11, 112, 113, 115, 123, 124, 128–9
    sightings 105–7, 110, 125–7, 131, 134
    terminology 106–7

UFOs in the Quran (Khan) 132
The Ultimate Revelations (Akhtar) 15–16
Ulugh Beg 63
Umar, Asim 132, 134, 176
ʿUmar ibn ʿAbd al-ʿAziz 25
ʿUmrān, Ṭālib *see* Omran, Taleb
unbelief 7–8
Understanding the Qur'an (Maududi) 13
United Arab Emirates
  education 137
  film 201–2
  Mars city 177, 210
  science fiction 139, 141
  space programme 14
United Nations
  Arab Human Development Report 2003 5–6
  Committee on the Peaceful Uses of Outer Space 108, 186
  Office for Outer Space Affairs (UNOOSA) 14, 186
Université Saint-Joseph (USJ) 50, 54
Uranus 54
utopias
  Mars 56
  medieval 16
  religious framing 35, 50, 62
  science fiction 19, 31, 85, 89–90, 139
Utopia (Towfik) 164

Van Dyck, Cornelius 53, 54
The Vanishing Cap (film) 81
The Vengeful Djinn (Imbrogno & Guiley) 136
The Venture of Islam (Hodgson) 1
Venus 43, 54–5, 61, 63, 169
Vermeulen, Angelo 30–1
Verne, Jules 34, 51, 79, 149, 153, 163, 187
Victory, Ebrahim 178
video games *see* games/gaming
Vimana: Prehistoric Spacecraft (Science Research Center) 124
viruses 20
volcanoes 30–1
Voltaire 40, 41
von Däniken, Erich 117, 118, 121–2, 127–8, 132
Voyager 1 & 2 108
Voyage to Tomorrow (play) 85

Wachowski siblings 103
Wahan Ke Log (film) 73–4
Waldheim, Kurt 108
Walsh, Raoul 80
Warcraft (game series) 24
The War of the Worlds (Wells) 47
Wasfi, Raouf 165–8
Weir, Andy 187
Wells, H. G. 29, 47, 79, 149, 163
Western colonialism 23, 44, 58
Western culture, oriental influence 78–80, 81, 96–7, 143
Western dominance, resistance 32
Western intervention, criticism 1, 6–7, 23–4, 26
Whale, James 81
What's Really Wrong with the Middle East (Whitaker) 5–6
Where Did You Get This? (film) 81–2
Whitaker, Brian 5–6, 7
Who Goes There? (Campbell) 155
Wilson, Albert George 67
Woking, England 46–7
Women Who Deserve to Go to Hell (Abdul Hakim) 131
The Wonders of the Universe (Victory) 178
The Wondrous Planet (Elzembely) 19
World Brotherhood Union 124–5, 195, 196
The World of the Jinn and Devils (al-Ashqar) 129–30, 131, 132, 136
worlds
  climatic differences 33
  plurality 10–11, 12, 29, 40, 43, 45
World Space Week 187
Worlds without End (Spencer Jones) 12
World War II 36, 191
World War III and the Antichrist (Umar) 132
Wortabet, John 51
Writers' Union of Egypt 21, 152, 157, 162
Wyler, William 91

Xavier, Francis 42
The X-Files (TV series) 105, 172

Yaapar, Salleh 23
Yahya, Harun 195
Yamani, Mohamed Abdu 119–21, 128
Yarmouk 20
Yassein, Ismaïl 81, 82, 86–7
Yatakhayaloon (They Imagine) 8
Yeşilçam 91, 92, 201
Yılmaz, Cem 103
York, Dwight 113–16
You Are Not Alone (El-Sebai) 153
Yurdözü, Farah 134–7
Zahr, ʿAbd al-Masih 61–2
Zaidan, Georgie 60
Zaidi, S. A. 201
Zelazny, Roger 78
Zinda Laash (film) 72
Zirkle, Conway 66–7
Zizigulu Tales (TV series) 98

www.ingramcontent.com/pod-product-compliance
Lightning Source LLC
Chambersburg PA
CBHW052218300426
44115CB00011B/1740
9780755650361